Business of the State

CRITICAL FRONTIERS OF THEORY, RESEARCH, AND POLICY IN INTERNATIONAL DEVELOPMENT STUDIES

Series Editors

Andrew Fischer, Naomi Hossain, Briony Jones, Alfredo Saad Filho, Benjamin Selwyn, and Fiona Tregenna

The contemporary world is characterized by massive wealth alongside widespread poverty, inequality, and environmental destruction—all bound up through class, race, and gender dynamics of inequality and oppression.

Critical Frontiers of Theory, Research, and Policy in International Development Studies, the official book series of the Development Studies Association of the UK and Ireland, was established to contribute to critical thinking about local, national, and global processes of structural transformation. The series publishes cutting-edge monographs that promote critical development studies as an interdisciplinary and applied field, and shape the theory, practice, and teaching of international development for a new generation of scholars, students, and practitioners. As the series evolves, we wish to publish a diverse and inclusive range of authors whose work engages in critical, multidisciplinary, decolonial, and methodologically plural development studies.

Recent titles in the series

Disrupted Development in the Congo
The Fragile Foundations of the African Mining Consensus
Ben Radley

Politics and the Urban Frontier
Transformation and Divergence in Late Urbanizing East Africa
Tom Goodfellow

The Many Faces of Socioeconomic Change
John Toye

The Power of Proximate Peers
Reconfiguring South–South Cooperation for Equitable Urban Development
Gabriella Y. Carolini

They Eat Our Sweat
Transport Labor, Corruption, and Everyday Survival in Urban Nigeria
Daniel Agbiboa

Business of the State

Why State Ownership Matters for Resource Governance

Jewellord T. Nem Singh

OXFORD
UNIVERSITY PRESS

Great Clarendon Street, Oxford, OX2 6DP,
United Kingdom

Oxford University Press is a department of the University of Oxford.
It furthers the University's objective of excellence in research, scholarship,
and education by publishing worldwide. Oxford is a registered trade mark of
Oxford University Press in the UK and in certain other countries

© Jewellord T. Nem Singh 2024

The moral rights of the author have been asserted

All rights reserved. No part of this publication may be reproduced, stored in
a retrieval system, or transmitted, in any form or by any means, without the
prior permission in writing of Oxford University Press, or as expressly permitted
by law, by licence or under terms agreed with the appropriate reprographics
rights organization. Enquiries concerning reproduction outside the scope of the
above should be sent to the Rights Department, Oxford University Press, at the
address above

You must not circulate this work in any other form
and you must impose this same condition on any acquirer

Published in the United States of America by Oxford University Press
198 Madison Avenue, New York, NY 10016, United States of America

British Library Cataloguing in Publication Data

Data available

Library of Congress Control Number: 2023952136

ISBN 9780198892212

DOI: 10.1093/oso/9780198892212.001.0001

Printed and bound by
CPI Group (UK) Ltd, Croydon, CR0 4YY

Links to third party websites are provided by Oxford in good faith and
for information only. Oxford disclaims any responsibility for the materials
contained in any third party website referenced in this work.

For my parents Leonardo and Remedios,
who raised me to become a prolific writer.

Preface

On 20 April 2023, Chile's President Gabriel Boric announced his plan to nationalize the country's lithium industry in order to regain state control over new investment projects by creating a new state-run company to participate in the whole production cycle through joint ventures and public–private partnerships. This, he argued, aimed to not only rebalance the relationship between profit accumulation and the mitigation of environmental costs, but also save communities at the frontiers of mineral extraction from becoming 'sacrifice zones'. This move is not the first in the developing world. As early as 2009, Indonesia banned the export of raw nickel materials and sought foreign investment for refining and processing plants within the country. And on 20 February 2023, Mexico's Andrez Lopez Obrador nationalized the lithium industry, creating a state-run company to have exclusive rights to mine lithium in Mexico, despite the country having only one mine close to starting production that was owned by the Chinese.

Going back to Chile, the country holds substantial reserves of two of the key metals—copper and lithium—that are essential for decarbonization and the global energy transition. The country's dilemma—how to proceed at generating higher value-added activities in mining while supporting global efforts to reduce carbon emissions by supplying raw materials for clean energy technologies—is commonplace across the globe, in regions including Africa, Latin America, and Central and Southeast Asia. As the response of advanced industrialized countries to climate change gravitates towards the manufacturing of more hybrid and electric vehicle (EV) cars, wind turbines, and photovoltaic panels, pressures escalate for mineral producers to extract more intensively and in greater quantities, to accelerate energy-intensive mining operations, from prospecting to extraction and production, to further the reach of extractive activities in new geographical spaces. Thus, the onus of decarbonization is gradually shifting to Latin America and the rest of the Global South. Therefore, the question of how mineral states can benefit from further extraction is a necessary and important part of the global conversation on the clean energy transition. Yet, most policy recommendations regarding how to achieve a clean energy transition often neglect the significance of domestic politics of mineral-producing states, as if taking natural resources from the ground is a process wholly determined by technological forces and available private investment.

The politics of industrialization in mineral-producing states lies at the heart of global proposals for the solution to combat climate change. This book offers a warning to those who view resource nationalism as a risk to the global efforts for a just energy transition. It is true that natural resource sovereignty was at the centre of Latin America's development strategies throughout the 20th century, and it is naïve to expect the Latin American publics to simply give away their resources to supply the developed world, once again, with the primary raw materials needed to advance their interests in the on-going race for geopolitical dominance and technological innovation. Importantly, however, this book offers a slice of optimism especially for natural resource-producing states: the cases of Brazil and Chile demonstrate the best possible outcome for countries that historically have relied on natural resources for economic growth—for example, coffee, iron ore, copper, silver, and, recently, oil and lithium. Both countries built state-owned enterprises (SOEs) with a cadre of professional engineers and managers. In so doing, SOEs in strategic sectors leveraged fiscal revenues and created sectoral linkages to avert the repetition of enclave economies reminiscent of the colonial past. The case studies of state ownership in strategic natural resource sectors chosen for this book—Petrobras in Brazil's oil and gas (O&G) sector and Chile's Codelco in the copper mining sector—are exemplars of how policymakers and national elites worked on building institutional capacity and have successfully managed to mitigate the effects of the resource curse, albeit through uneven and gradual state-building. As the chapters in this book demonstrate, SOEs had—and continue—to play a developmental role in natural resource-producing states. At times, SOE managers still make mistakes at the expense of the autonomy of the company and placing at risk the gains of the company—a reality that the *Lava Jato* scandal painfully attests to in the Brazilian case. Moving forward, we need to learn from history: natural resource production can go hand in hand with industrial development. However, decision-makers need to take a longer-term view of political decisions and make a firm commitment to promote economic development through industrialization. As the East Asian developmental success story teaches us, political leaders must continually view the world as a ruthlessly competitive system; and therefore building an industrial ecosystem that can lift millions out of poverty and provide jobs requires different types of state intervention, depending on the changing international contexts. As this book shows, in the extractive resource sectors government policies that have been successful were built around SOEs that could compete and work with foreign and domestic private companies. In the quest for decarbonization, Gabriel Boric's bet on building a new public enterprise—similar to Codelco—is not simply an ideological decision; instead, it may well be that Boric has taken a lesson from history on how Chileans lost their nitrate fortunes and then fought American multinationals to regain their rights to copper, which through the success of Codelco has been the foundation of Chile's economy ever since. The geopolitical context in the 21st century has undoubtedly changed. Yet, building competitive domestic enterprises (SOEs) embedded in the growth and development strategies of national states appears to be a blueprint for dealing with strategic competition, whether we think about Korea's POSCO, Brazil's Petrobras and Codemge, or Chile's Codelco. Crucially, the rise of China as the world's second largest economy was in large part a result of successfully managed SOEs that became globally competitive—China Minmetals Corporation in mining, the SINOPEC Group and China National Petroleum Corporation (CNPC) in O&G, and the State Grid Corporation of China (SGCC) in power grid generation, to name a few. The challenge, then, is how to make these companies continually profitable while serving the strategic interest of the country. This book is a step towards trying to answer this question.

Jewellord Nem Singh

Seoul
10 May 2023

Acknowledgements

This book spanned nearly 10 years before I finally completed it, surviving at least three professional career moves, two lost relationships, and several personal tragedies in the family. Hence, writing the Acknowledgements feels like legitimately closing a chapter of my life. The original ideas of the book started as a doctoral dissertation at the University of Sheffield, UK, which were gradually transformed as the countries under examination experienced significant political changes. It was written in an overtly optimistic tone, reflecting on oil as a blessing for Brazil and the powerful effects of the export bonanza for Chile between 2002 and 2012. As the years passed, both countries faced multiple political challenges, including a grand corruption scheme in Brazil that led to political paralysis and the downfall of the first woman president of the country. The book has sought to capture what these changes mean for natural resource politics generally and to reflect on their consequences for state ownership in highly strategic industries.

At the time of writing, Lula da Silva narrowly won the presidency against Right-wing President Jaír Bolsonaro, which has signalled a shift in development strategy towards greater state control in major sectors and the need to rewrite Brazil's partnership with the US, European Union (EU), and China. In Chile, a remarkable political process to dismantle the last vestiges of the Pinochet regime is currently under way. A Constitutional Assembly has been formed to debate, and subsequently change, the neoliberal legal framework, with recent plans towards the nationalization of lithium. Yet, in both countries, natural resources remain, and are likely to be sustained, as a core pillar of their development strategy into the 21st century. Through a historical institutionalist perspective, my contribution rests on theorizing, historizing, and nuancing state ownership as part and parcel of Latin America's development strategy as the centre of gravity for economic power moves from West to East. By drawing on lessons from Latin America through a comparative political economy approach—and then relating the changes in East Asia back to Latin America—the book also makes an important step in bridging the two regions and in contributing towards 'Latin America–Asia relations' as a distinctive field of study.

As the years unfold, I became indebted to several institutions and individuals who shaped the arguments of the book. First and foremost, Professor

xii Acknowledgements

Jean Grugel wore multiple hats over the years—an extraordinary mentor, a senior colleague during my time at Sheffield's Department of Geography, and a friend who always looked after my career choices. I distinctively remember entering her office for the first time, telling her that I want to write my PhD on Brazil and natural resources despite having no background in Latin America. Her response was a warm heart to support and advise me in undertaking such a huge project. As if this was not enough, Jean read the manuscript in full and provided her reflections on the core arguments of the book during the final stages of writing. Secondly, the project received funding at various stages: Sheffield University's Overseas Research Scholarship (ORS) financed the doctoral dissertation between 2008 and 2012; the Society for Latin American Studies (SLAS) and Leiden University's Institute of Political Science provided funding for different fieldwork visits; and the International Institute of Social Studies (ISS) contributed to hire Joanna Morley as my research assistant to steer the book towards manuscript production. Finally, at Oxford University Press, the book has benefitted enormously from the support of Adam Swallow, the commissioning editor, as well as the series editors of the *Critical Frontiers of Theory, Research, and Policy in International Development* series, who saw the novelty of my argument; and the two anonymous reviewers who offered their insights on the analytical purchase of this intellectual enterprise.

My arguments benefitted from critical reflections of colleagues in Europe, East Asia, and Latin America, which by all accounts shaped the final output: Barbara Hogenboom, Lorenzo Pellegrini, Murat Arsel, Cristobal Bonelli, Olga Lucia Castillo, Isamu Okada, Rodrigo Salles dos Santos, Antulio Rosales, Lorenza Fontana, and Tim Shaw. Parts of the book have been written as journal articles and edited collections along the way, so I would like to thank my co-authors for compelling me to think beyond Latin America and be courageous about doing comparative work across the Global South—France Bourgouin, Andrew Lawrence, Jesse Salah Ovadia, and Geoffrey Chen. At Sheffield, I belonged to a group of young, brilliant, and enthusiastic PhD colleagues. Our group was cohesive and the academic environment pleasant. It made Sheffield more than a bearable place; it was a department we all felt proud to have spent our early career years in. So, thank you for the friendship that went beyond academic networking—Gabriel Silles Brügge, Laura Macleod, Adrian Gallagher, John Quinn, João Carvalho, Holly Snaith, Defne Gunay, Joe Turner, Nuray Aridici, Hilal Gezmis, Ali Onur, and our friend who left us way too early, Mark Duncan.

In my attempt to become a global scholar of development studies, I was extremely lucky in receiving the prestigious Japan Society for the Promotion of Science (JSPS) Fellowship in 2016 through my mentor Professor Jin Sato at the Institute for Advanced Studies on Asia, University of Tokyo. The succeeding year, Bettina Engels and Kristina Dietz supported my application for the Alexander von Humboldt Fellowship at the Freie Universität Berlin. The two appointments were instrumental in expanding my ambition to write a book on resource governance in the Global South. Finally, when everything was written, I had the privilege of having a wide network of supportive colleagues who agreed to read and comment on the manuscript in full—Francisco Panizza, Guanie Lim, Paul Haslam, and Chris Wylde. The book workshop was useful in structuring the big argument and pairing down the comparative aspects of the cases.

In Brazil, my views on political economy benefitted enormously from years of writing with Eliza Massi—a colleague and friend—who unrelentingly questioned my tendency to optimistically read Brazilian politics. During several fieldworks in this beautiful country, I was received as a Visiting Research Fellow at the Department of International Relations, Pontifícia Universidade Católica do Rio de Janeiro, and the Post-Graduate Programme in Anthropology and Sociology, Universidade Federal do Rio de Janeiro—many thanks for helping a young scholar learn the ropes of Brazilian politics. My friend Cristina Madarieta Murillo offered her legal knowledge to carefully map out the *Lava Jato* scandal based on US Stock Exchange documents. Jolien Ridderbusch provided me with research assistance in the last fieldwork and secured key interviews with high-level officials—including Petrobras executives—to extend the project after the *Partido dos Trabalhadores* (PT) (Workers' Party) years. My friends in Rio de Janeiro and São Paulo—Leo Lima, Leo Bastos, Jonas Rama, Luis Marola, Anne, Regina, and the family of Priscilla and Laura—have made my annual visit to Brazil worth looking forward.

In Chile, Professor Jonathan Barton from *Pontificia Universidad Católica de Chile* (PUC) guided me through the intricacies of Chilean politics and helped me understand the challenge of institutional continuity in studying incremental changes. During my stay at PUC, Codelco Andina opened their doors to me, allowing me to interview managers and union representatives, exploring their archives, and extending their network to enable me to conduct further interviews in Calama and Antofagasta. Over the years, my network of Chile experts increased. Alvaro Róman, Silke Staab, and Marina Weinberg have engaged with my statist view on mining politics. They questioned and debated with me how to best understand and interpret the political changes in a country marked by historical ruptures and political division. My flatmate Mauro and his friends Eduardo among others were essential for me to understand the class politics of Santiago.

xiv Acknowledgements

The book was written at a very difficult moment in our recent history. The COVID-19 pandemic hit and finishing this manuscript became a mission for me. I would like to thank all my friends around the world for being present, which in one way or another helped us collectively deal with grief, sadness, and social isolation. My friends since my days at the University of the Philippines Diliman, the 'Spam Folder'—Anna, Katrina, Lesther, Gabby, Ted, and Bekah—as well as Raffy and Katrin have offered support over the years. To Neil, Sophie, Sam, and my flatmate Kris, thank you for being the Filipino anchor in the Netherlands. To my family in Crossfit Amsterdam and Crossfit Icke in Berlin—Filippo, Bruna, Erik, Sotuda, Gabriela, Sjaak, Eldina, Jenny Mauermann, K Alave, Rory O'Hara, Manuela, Ulrich, and Jola—and my academic friends in Leiden—especially Matt Longo, Simon Chauchard, Andrei Poama, Billy Tsagkroni, and Adeel Hussain—congratulations for having lived through the pandemic. Finally, to friends facing similar problems of racism, structural inequality, and hierarchy in Western academia, Julie de los Reyes, Alvin Camba, and Arnie Trinidad, this book is a testament of our strength and perseverance from the Global South in changing the intellectual landscape.

No book can be finished without personal sacrifices. And for this, my family across four continents has been extremely supportive of my career pursuit as an academic in Europe. The book was finished after our *lolas* (grandmothers) Natividad Bautista Tolentino and Maria Corazon Reyes passed away to join our *lolos* (grandfathers). Our extended family in Los Angeles was a safe space for me to come whenever I felt lonely in Europe. Whenever I would return to Manila, our family in Nueva Ecija, Las Piñas, and Bicol have always been ecstatic about my short holidays, so thank you. Most importantly, this book is dedicated to my immediate family—my parents Leonardo and Remedios, and my siblings Christian, May, and Macky—as well as our new clan members, Angelique, Khing, Lexi, Khelzy, and our new sister-in-law, Anna. While we do not live in the same country, we continually share our happiness, solitude, and small laughter over many years. As with many Filipino migrant families, we are resilient and can endure the pain of distance. *Maraming Salamat po.*

Biography

Jewellord T. Nem Singh is Assistant Professor in International Development at the International Institute of Social Studies, The Hague. He is the Principal Investigator of a European Research Council (ERC) five-year Starting Grant and is a Global Fellow at the Wilson Center, Washington, DC. Nem Singh was also a recipient of two research fellowships: the Japan Society for the Promotion of Science (JSPS) Fellowship in 2016 and Alexander von Humboldt Foundation Research Award in 2017. He has served as Expert Consultant for international development agencies and civil society organizations.

Contents

List of Figures	xxi
List of Tables	xxiii

PART I.   FRAMEWORK AND BUILDING BLOCKS

1. Governing Natural Resources in the Age of Strategic Competition	**3**
Emerging Supply Chains in Renewable Energy Capitalism	7
State Ownership as a Development Strategy	12
Key Arguments	19
The Comparative Approach	24
Presentation of the Book	26
2. Theorizing State Ownership in Natural Resource Governance	**29**
The Extractivism–Development Debate: What We Do and Do Not Know	30
Resource Curse, Economic Growth, and Rentier State Models	31
Systemic Approaches to Primary Commodity Production	37
What We Do Not Know: Institutional Change in Natural Resource-Intensive Regimes	40
Historical Institutionalism as an Analytical Approach	44
A Theory of Institutional Stability and Change	46
State Ownership as a Globalization Strategy	50
Theorizing Corporate Governance Reforms in SOEs	54
Conclusions	59

PART II.   STATE OWNERSHIP IN BRAZIL AND CHILE

3. The Rise and Fall of Public Enterprises in Latin America in the 20th Century	**63**
Natural Resources as the Building Blocks of Latin America's Development Model	64
The Latin American Developmental State	67
Venezuela: Development of a Petro-State	70
Venezuela: Industrial Policy During the Oil Boom	72
Developmental States in Latin America Versus East Asia	78
4. Developmental States in Chile and Brazil	**81**
The Chilean Developmental State, 1925–1973	81
Codelco and the Consolidation of Neoliberalism in Chile, 1973–1989	91

xviii Contents

The Brazilian Developmental State, 1930–1964	94
The Military Period (1964–1985): From Strengthening to Weakening Petrobras	101
Petrobras, Offshore Development, and Brazil's Lost Decade	106
Conclusions	108

5. Chile's Mining-Led Growth Strategy, 1990–2020 — 109

Phase I: Neoliberal Continuity with Changes (1990–1999)	111
Phase II: Incremental Changes (2000–2010)	115
The New Royalty Law of 2005	117
The Subcontracting Law of 2007	121
Phase III: The Growth Model Amidst Turbulent Times (2010–2020)	127
The World Class Supplier Programme	131
Neostructuralism and Its Discontents	134
Conclusions	136

6. The Politics of Managing Codelco and Its Labour Force — 139

The Myth of Neoliberal Chile	140
The Consequences of State Ownership for Codelco	143
The Role of Codelco in 21st-Century Chile	147
The 'Labour Question' in Chilean Mining	150
Alianza Estratégica as a Corporatist Pact	153
Rising Conflicts in Private Mining	157
From Copper Mining to Lithium	158
Conclusions	162

7. Brazil's Oil-Based Industrial Strategy, 1990–2018 — 165

Neoliberalism as a (Partial) Post-Crisis Strategy (1985–1996)	166
The 'Norwegian Model' in the Brazilian Oil Industry (1997–2002)	173
Institutional Continuity of *Desenvolvimentismo* Under Cardoso	178
The PT (Workers' Party) in Power: More Continuity Than Change?	181
The Age of Oil in Brazil	182
Institutional Change in the Age of Pre-Salt	187
Attempts at Oil-Based Industrialization Under the PT	188
Brazil's Oil Governance Model in Summary	192
Conclusions	196

8. Petrobras and Brazil's Political Crisis — 197

Petrobras and Its Performance Before *Lava Jato*	198
Petrobras's Competitiveness Strategy	203
Rousseff's Developmentalist Strategy	208
The Janus Face of Corruption	209
Greasing the Wheels of Development?	214
The Impacts of Corruption on Petrobras	219
The Political Aftermath of the *Lava Jato* Scandal	221
Conclusion: The End of Developmentalism in Brazil?	223

Contents   **xix**

PART III. COMPARATIVE AND HISTORICAL DIMENSIONS OF STATE OWNERSHIP

9. State Ownership in Comparative Perspective — **229**

Key Arguments and Case Studies Compared — 230

Petrobras and Codelco Compared — 239

State–State (SOE) Relations — 240

The Political Role of SOEs in Buffering Competing Demands — 243

Redefining the Role of SOEs in Industrial Development — 246

Restructuring Corporate Governance in SOEs — 248

Extending the Argument in Latin America — 250

Resource Nationalism in Latin America — 250

Venezuela: A Petro-State Without Corporate Autonomy — 251

Peru: Neoliberalism Without State Ownership — 255

Conclusions — 259

10. The Future of Latin America's Natural Resource States in the 21st Century — **261**

Theoretical Contributions — 263

Why State Ownership Matters in the 21st Century — 266

China: The Developmental State of the 21st Century? — 267

Implications of China's Developmental State for Latin America — 273

Conclusion: Latin America in the Era of Strategic Competition — 274

References — 277

Index — 307

List of Figures

1.1 Critical minerals for clean energy technologies. 5

1.2 Primary supplies of critical raw materials for the EU. 8

1.3 Regional shares in nine key technologies across stages of the advanced manufacturing, defence, and clean energy sector supply chains. 9

1.4 Indicative clean energy technology supply chains. 11

1.5 Distinctive conceptual models of globalization strategies. 17

1.6 Growth strategies of selected middle-income countries, 1950s–2010s. 20

2.1 Pattern of institutional stability and change in natural resource governance. 43

2.2 Explaining hybrid development models in Brazil and Chile. 48

2.3 Shares of SOEs on Fortune Global 500 list. 53

2.4 SOE output to GDP in selected emerging markets. 54

3.1 Central government expenditures in total and current values, 1970–1989. 74

3.2 Central government investment and public debt, 1970–1989. 75

4.1 International prices of key exports (nitrate and copper) in Chile, 1925–1940. 82

4.2 Public and private (foreign) mining investment under Pinochet, 1976–1990. 93

4.3 Petrobras's refining capacity, 1938–1990. 106

4.4 Petrobras's oil exploration and production capacity, 1938–1990. 107

5.1 Public and private (foreign) mining investment in Chile, 1990–2009. 115

5.2 Chilean copper production in relation to copper prices, 2001–2010. 116

5.3 Fiscal contribution of the mining sector in Chile, 2000–2019. 120

5.4 Percentage share of global copper smelter (top graph) and refined copper production (bottom graph), 2010–2019. 130

5.5 Total factor productivity of the mining sector in Chile, 1990–2016. 131

6.1 Public vs. private copper mining production in Chile, 1991–2010. 144

6.2 Share of Mining to Total Actual FDI in Percentage. 144

6.3 Contribution of public enterprises (SOEs) to total fiscal revenue, 1990–2010. 148

6.4 Public opinion on the legitimacy of trade unions. 152

7.1 Average percentage of LCRs in Brazil's domestic industries, 1998–2018. 182

7.2 Balance of trade in Brazil, 1994–2018. 183

xxii List of Figures

7.3 Pre-salt O&G exploration and production—Campos and Santos Basins.	185
8.1 Petrobras's gradual accumulation of debt, 2003–2015.	200
8.2 Petrobras's net income and losses, 2003–2015.	201
8.3 Petrobras' market value and net equity, 2003–2015.	201
8.4 Petrobras's success rate in oil exploration, 2000–2010.	202
8.5 Petrobras's R&D contribution to Brazil's O&G sector, 2001–2018.	204
8.6 Total number of employees of the Petrobras system, 2003–2018.	205
8.7 Petrobras's shareholding structure, May 2020.	207
8.8 Corruption and bribery scheme involving Petrobras, political parties, and cartels.	212
9.1 Explaining hybrid development strategies in Brazil and Chile.	234
9.2 Evolution of Peruvian manufacturing and extractive industries—sectoral contribution to GDP as a percentage.	257
10.1 Key iron ore producers in the world, 2000 and 2014.	272

List of Tables

1.1 Rare earth elements (REEs) and their major industrial applications and products.   6

2.1 Typology of SOE reforms.   56

3.1 US investments in Latin American countries' manufacturing industries (in million US$).   69

3.2 Fiscal revenues of Venezuelan governments, 1917–1978 (in million bolivares).   72

4.1 Ownership of the Chilean nitrate economy (in percentage).   83

4.2 The Chilean economy, 1938–1952 (in US$ million).   86

4.3 Petrobras's finances, 1955–1960 (in million cruzeiros).   100

5.1 Selected data on the tax contribution of copper mining in Chile, 2000–2019.   121

5.2 Permanent and subcontracted workers in Codelco, 1995–2015.   124

5.3 Global refined copper and smelter production (in kMT of copper content), 2010–2019.   129

5.4 Suppliers' IPR applications, 2011–2016.   133

6.1 Corporate governance reforms in Codelco.   141

6.2 Legitimacy of trade unions from political parties' viewpoints.   151

6.3 *Alianza Estratégica* and its corporatist framework.   155

6.4 Lithium World Production, 2022-2023 (in metric tons, lithium content).   159

6.5 First-stage lithium production in Chile (in lithium carbonate equivalent tonnes).   160

7.1 Sales from privatization of the petrochemicals industry in Brazil, 1992–1996.   168

7.2 Continuity and change in Brazilian O&G sector governance, 1996–2018.   170

7.3 Risks and rewards in E&P sector contract regimes.   174

7.4 Distribution of fiscal revenues according to Brazil's 1997 Petroleum Law.   179

7.5 Bidding rounds and LC percentages in Brazil's O&G sector, 1999–2018.   191

7.6 Exploration and development activities in Brazil's O&G sector, 1999–2018.   194

7.7 Participation share (%) in Brazilian distribution segment, 2010 and 2017.   195

8.1 Top O&G producers in Brazil, 2018.   203

8.2 BNDES loans to O&G and infrastructure companies.   217

8.3 BNDES loans under the PT government, 2004–2014.   218

PART I

FRAMEWORK AND BUILDING BLOCKS

1
Governing Natural Resources in the Age of Strategic Competition

We needed a supply chain that was reliable . . . Including in critical materials like lithium, graphite, rare earth materials, which are badly needed for so many American products—we were in so desperate need of . . . That's why I committed us to build a clean energy supply chain stamped 'Made in America'.

President Joe Biden[1]

Visions will come true only when we act on them. Developed countries should not only do more themselves, but should also provide support to help developing countries do better . . . China will continue to prioritize ecological conservation and pursue a green and low-carbon path to development . . . [It will] speed up the transition to green and low-carbon energy, vigorously develop renewable energy, and plan and build large wind and photovoltaic power stations.

President Xi Jinping[2]

As global policymakers and non-governmental organizations (NGOs) sound the alarm of a climate emergency, governments swiftly committed to embrace the rapid construction of green infrastructure as the way out of the climate crisis. The race towards achieving a net-zero economy is not just a civilizational quest to solve the climate crisis. Global decarbonization, above all, is a technological race. It sets the pace for new strategic competition among industrialized countries and determines the future configuration of global power politics. The book presents the view of resource-intensive countries. Natural resources and industrial development can go hand in hand. With

[1] 'Remarks by President Joe Biden at a Virtual Event on Securing Critical Materials for a Future Made in America', 22 February 2022, https://www.whitehouse.gov/briefing-room/speeches-remarks/2022/02/22/remarks-by-president-biden-at-a-virtual-event-on-securing-critical-minerals-for-a-future-made-in-america/ (accessed 24 April 2023).
[2] 'Key quotes from Xi Jinping on Climate Change', Embassy of the People's Republic of China in the United States of America, 5 November 2021, http://us.china-embassy.gov.cn/eng/zt_120777/ydqhbh/202111/t20211106_10445008.htm (accessed 24 April 2023).

Business of the State. Jewellord T. Nem Singh, Oxford University Press. © Jewellord T. Nem Singh (2024).
DOI: 10.1093/oso/9780198892212.003.0001

4   Business of the State

an increasing demand for raw materials, how natural-resource states manage their mineral wealth will be key in enabling some countries to break away from dependent development and limited export diversification. In this current context, the task at hand for development studies is to provide guidance in identifying opportunities for structural transformation through a historically contextualized analysis of mineral governance.

In the race towards a fossil-fuel-free world, critical minerals are becoming 'hot commodities' subject to intense strategic competition among industrialized countries. Also known as critical raw materials (CRMs), these metals—produced in low quantities per day—are vital inputs for further production of various intermediate goods, such as catalysts and alloys, among other components, to be incorporated further in highly complex supply chains to produce advanced manufacturing, digital technologies, military and defence systems, and, most importantly, clean energy technologies. The historically unprecedented increase in demand for CRMs has been demonstrated by the commitment of the European Union (EU) and the US government to the rapid expansion of electric vehicle (EV) cars and the greening of the power sector. But to deliver on this promise, the question of where to source minerals became inevitably hard to answer for EU and US policymakers.

Figure 1.1 shows that to switch to renewable energy, the world will need to extract more critical minerals from the ground than the existing supply under current market conditions. Meeting the carbon emission reduction targets in the 2015 United Nations Paris Agreement on Climate Change (UN Paris Agreement) would mean an accelerated pace and increased quantity in mineral extraction and production, while building complex green technologies also requires sourcing a wide array of metals. An EV, for instance, involves more than 200 kg of several different minerals for assembly per vehicle, while conventional cars only depend on a quarter of that quantity of metals per vehicle (mostly copper and manganese). While approximately 50% of electricity produced within the EU powers the 8 billion electric motors in use, which range from small-sized electronic products such as e-bikes to large motors for heavy transport (European Commission 2020a, 34), switching to hybrid and electric vehicles anticipates manufacturing huge numbers of high-performing synchronous motors run by neodymium–iron–boron permanent magnets. The metals needed to build such motors are known as rare earth elements (REEs) which are scarcely available and are currently produced by a handful of mining companies, mostly based in Inner Mongolia, China. At the time of writing, only one REE-producing company exists outside China—Australian company Lynas—which has some processing capabilities that are currently outsourced in Malaysia. The current state

Governing Natural Resources in the Age of Strategic Competition 5

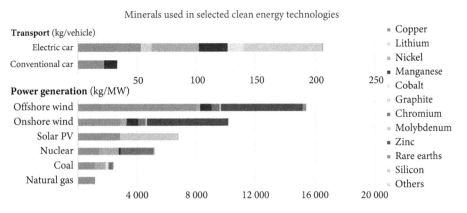

Figure 1.1 Critical minerals for clean energy technologies.
Note: PV, photovoltaic. Values are for entire vehicles including batteries, motors, and glider. Intensities for an electric car are based on a 75-kWh NMC (nickel–manganese–cobalt) 622 cathode and graphite-based anode. Values for offshore wind and onshore wind are based on the direct-drive permanent magnet synchronous generator system (including array cables) and the doubly fed induction generator system, respectively. Values for coal and natural gas are based on ultra-supercritical plants and combined-cycle gas turbines. Actual consumption can vary by project depending on technology choice, project size, and installation environment.

Source: International Energy Agency (2021, 26).

of the REE sector captures the growing anxiety portrayed in Western media and expressed by policymakers in political debates—that the world risks failing to meet its ambitious climate targets due to extreme levels of dependency on China for access to raw materials.

On the one hand, despite the complex and several stages of extraction, beneficiation, and refining of REEs, nearly 95% of these activities are currently done in China, making supply diversification strategies ineffective in the short and medium term. On the other hand, transforming REEs into high-value-added alloys and components, which then serve as intermediate inputs for multiple industrial user applications including green technologies, is by itself a lucrative but highly competitive market fought among industrialized East Asian countries. Apart from clean energy technologies, REEs are widely used across various industries, as Table 1.1 demonstrates.

Amidst the seemingly insatiable demand for critical minerals to meet the clean energy targets of the EU and US, at the cusp of recovering from the COVID-19 pandemic the world suddenly had to grapple with multiple crises. This apparent geopolitical disorder is characterized by (1) the escalation of tensions in US–China relations marked by the trade war launched by the US administration of Donald J. Trump in 2018; (2) the temporary breakdown of vital supply chains to which the COVID-19 pandemic was a major cause; and (3) a prolonged energy crisis brought about by the Russian occupation

6 Business of the State

Table 1.1 Rare earth elements (REEs) and their major industrial applications and products.

Name	Symbol	Atomic no.	Applications and products
Scandium	Sc	21	Aerospace materials, consumer electronics, lasers, magnets, **lighting**, sporting goods
Yttrium	Y	39	Ceramics, communications systems, **lighting**, frequency meters, **fuels** additive, **jet engine turbines**, televisions, microwave communications, satellites, **vehicle oxygen sensors**
Lanthanum	La	57	**Catalyst in petroleum refining**, televisions, **energy storage**, **fuel cells**, night vision instruments, **rechargeable batteries**
Cerium	Ce	58	**Catalytic converters, catalyst in petroleum refining**, glass, **diesel fuel additive**, polishing agent, pollution control systems
Praseodymium	Pr	59	**Aircraft engine alloy**, airport signal lenses, catalyst, ceramics, colouring pigment, **EVs**, fibre-optic cables, lighter flint, **magnets, wind turbines**, photographic filters, welder's glasses
Neodymium	Nd	60	Anti-lock brakes, airbags, anti-glare glass, cellphones, computers, **EVs**, lasers, magnetic resonance imaging (MRI) machines, **magnets, wind turbines**
Promethium	Pm	61	Beta source for thickness gauges, lasers for submarines, **nuclear-powered battery**
Samarium	Sm	62	Aircraft electrical systems, electronic countermeasure equipment, **EVs**, flight control surfaces, missile and radar systems, optical glass, **permanent magnets**, precision-guided munitions, stealth technology, **wind turbines**
Europium	Eu	63	**Compact fluorescent lamps (CFLs)**, lasers, televisions, tag complex for medical field
Gadolinium	Gd	64	Computer data technology, magneto-optic recording technology, microwave applications, MRI machines, power plant radiation leaks detector
Terbium	Tb	65	**CFL, EVs, fuel cells**, televisions, optic data recording, **permanent magnets, wind turbines**
Dysprosium	Dy	66	**EVs**, home electronics, lasers, **permanent magnets, wind turbines**
Holmium	Ho	67	Microwave equipment, colour glass
Erbium	Er	68	Colour glass, fibre-optic data transmission, lasers
Thulium	Tm	69	X-ray phosphors
Ytterbium	Yb	70	Improving stainless steel properties, stress gauges
Lutetium	Lu	71	Catalysts, positron emission tomography (PET) detectors

Source: Navarro and Zhao (2014, 2) in Nem Singh (2021, 4).
Bold indicates major use of the REE.

of Ukraine in 2022. Figure 1.2, published by the European Commission (2020b), underscores the continent's dependency on China beyond REEs; it also reflects the current lack of capabilities to secure other critical minerals for its future industrial competitiveness. Not only does the EU have limited supply of valuable REEs, but also the region is dependent on traditional metal commodities like nickel, phosphate, copper, and platinum groups of metals. Thus, EU policymakers understand well that mineral dependency and the changing geopolitical contexts have constrained the EU's capacity to reposition itself in the new global order in the 21st century. According to the European Commission (2020a), the absence of a regional supply chain of minerals—largely an outcome of policy choices to outsource mineral resources from overseas—puts the EU at a disadvantage over the long-term horizon. Thus, securing a stable supply of critical minerals for the EU serves both its clean energy ambitions and the promotion of its 'strategic autonomy' in an increasingly polarized world.[3]

Emerging Supply Chains in Renewable Energy Capitalism

Beyond the geopolitical perspectives, worldwide efforts to achieve clean energy transition bear significance for development studies as a discipline. As demands for minerals accelerate to meet the Green New Deal in Europe and the US, supply chains of clean energy technologies reflect the international division of labour and technological gaps between developed and developing countries. The International Energy Agency (2021, 5) conveys the costs of the global clean energy revolution: if the world meets the targets of the Paris Agreement, demand is likely to increase by 40% for copper and REEs, 60–70% for cobalt and nickel, and almost 90% for lithium in the next two decades. In this context, Latin America is home to several critical mineral deposits that would fuel the global shift to a low carbon economy. Together with other developing countries in Central and Southeast Asia as well as Africa, mineral producers are becoming sources of raw materials for the next phase of geopolitical competition and the technological race. However, as Figure 1.3 shows, the share of production of Africa and Latin America disappears as the supply chain moves up to higher value-added activities in the production of alloys and components as well as the assembly of technology-intensive exports. At best, the participation of these regions is limited at the processed materials stage. By contrast, multinational companies from East Asia, the EU, and the US remain dominant players in the downstream

---

[3] Author interview with EU Commission Official, Brussels, October 2021.

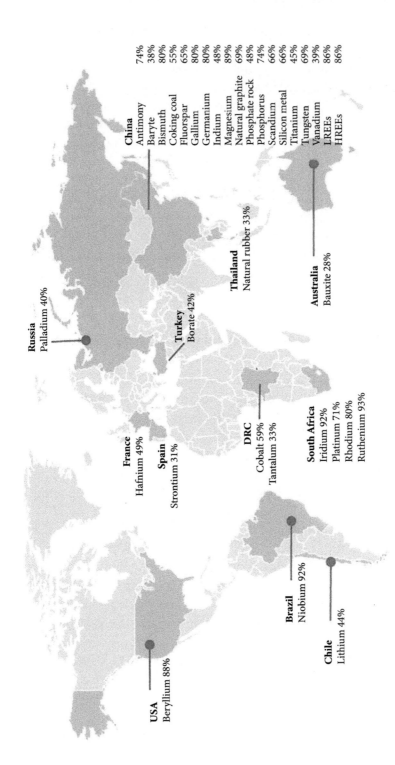

Figure 1.2 Primary supplies of critical raw materials for the EU.

Note: DRC, Democratic Republic of the Congo; HREEs, heavy rare earth elements; LREEs, light rare earth elements.

Source: European Commission (2020b, 6).

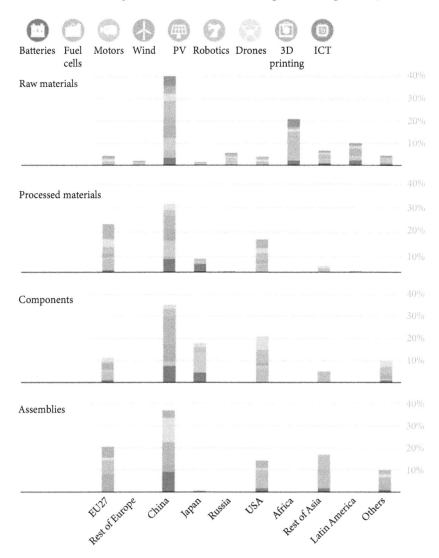

Figure 1.3 Regional shares in nine key technologies across stages of the advanced manufacturing, defence, and clean energy sector supply chains.
Note: ICT, information and communication technology.

Source: European Commission (2020a, 82).

segment of the global value chains (GVC) linking minerals and advanced manufacturing.

At face value, growth strategies for global decarbonization serve as new opportunities for mining companies to expand their operations and for

10 Business of the State

high-tech companies in various downstream activities to retain their position in the technological race. As such, structuralist scholarship might well be correct in arguing that the green energy transition is simply another epoch relegating poor, resource-rich countries as primary raw material suppliers, thereby effectively reinforcing the unequal and hierarchical world order. However, there are important differences between the current global decarbonization agenda compared to the 20th-century race for industrialization. Firstly, successful East Asian developmental states are now direct competitors of Western countries, as the biggest producers of lithium batteries and fuel cells, energy storage systems, and solar panels are not confined to European companies today. The race to produce EV cars at cost-effective prices involves Japanese, Chinese, and Korean automotive players, while other Southeast Asian countries are enmeshed within a complex assembly of car production (Doner et al. 2021). Secondly, as Figure 1.4 illustrates, China's successful export-led manufacturing strategy has been built on the back of an activist industrial policy which includes critical minerals. As early as 1991, the Chinese Communist Party (CCP) leadership had identified CRMs as a vital component of its industrial restructuring, successfully investing and eventually controlling the processing and refining of minerals before aligning its mineral sector with the wider export-led manufacturing industries. In Chapter 10, this book argues that China designed its industrial strategy as a model of state capitalism with the explicit objective of selectively restructuring major industries by enhancing the productive capabilities of its state-owned enterprises (SOEs) and promoting private national champions to participate in globalized manufacturing supply chains (see Solingen 2021).

Combined with an outward-looking policy of securing minerals and hydrocarbons in the Global South, China's industrial strategy successfully closed the loop from the raw mineral extraction and processing stage towards the production of advanced manufacturing, digital technologies, and clean energy industry (L. Chen and Chulu 2022; Kalantzakos 2018; Shih 2021), through coordinated planning, solving multiple problems at the same time. For example, by the early 2010s, the Chinese government had stepped up its support for an electric car industry to clean up pollution and reduce reliance on oil imports. In 2009 Beijing launched a pilot programme in ten cities to subsidize electric buses and public transportation. The experiment created demand for new energy vehicles (NEVs) and yielded an estimated US$60 billion in subsidies to incentivize electric car start-ups (Sanderson 2022, 39, 41; G. Yeung 2019). In this environment, domestic champions like Contemporary Amperex Technology Co. Limited (CATL) emerged to supply batteries

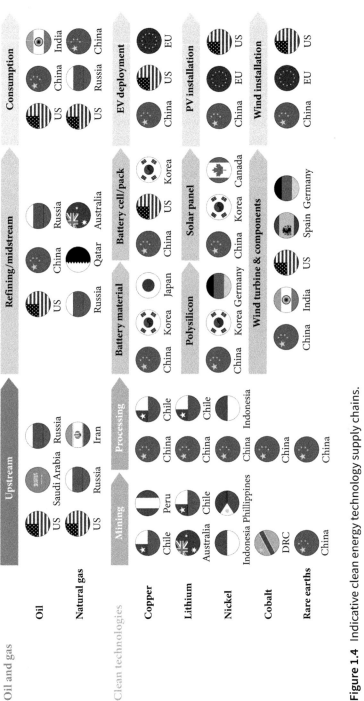

Figure 1.4 Indicative clean energy technology supply chains.

Note: China, People's Republic of China; DRC, Democratic Republic of the Congo; EU, European Union; Russia, Russian Federation; US, United States. Largest producers and consumers are noted in each case, to provide an indication rather than a complete account.

Source: International Energy Agency (2021, 29) (adapted).

12 Business of the State

to Volkswagen and BMW, thereby propelling Chinese companies as major players in global supply chains. China's strategy of securing niche markets and building new comparative advantages not only involves a gradual process of building domestic company capabilities, but also equally important was the strategic deployment of industrial policies aimed at creating market dominance through vertical integration in supply chains.

This book argues that SOEs, when subjected to corporate governance reforms aimed at harnessing competition and attuned with private sector performance, might open new pathways for technological innovation and support industrial policy. To better understand the opportunities for industrial development in Latin America in the 21st century, we need to learn from the lessons of the 20th century. In particular, the book seeks to answer this lacuna by examining an overlooked aspect of resource governance—state ownership through SOEs.

State Ownership as a Development Strategy

The extant literature on the resource curse thesis, rentier states, and neoextractivism posits that the exploitation of natural resources has anti-developmental effects for mineral-producing states, suggesting that the conditions for natural-resource-based industrialization and structural transformation of the economy are difficult to achieve. By contrast, this book presents an alternative phenomenon: *the consolidation of a growth strategy built around state-owned enterprises.* Analysing empirical evidence from Latin America, the book seeks to answer questions that are also applicable beyond the region: Why do some states continue to intervene in the affairs of SOEs, despite widely acknowledged neoliberal belief in the efficacy of markets? If SOEs are accused of being conduits of corruption and rent-seeking, why has it been so difficult to privatize these companies? And, in the absence of privatization, what alternative strategies can governments of developing countries choose to manage these politically sensitive and economically strategic industries? Put simply, the central question of the book is whether we find a developmental role specifically for SOEs—and for state ownership more broadly—in strategic natural resource sectors to promote structural transformation in the era of economic globalization.

This book offers several answers to these questions. In the first place, the book constructs an argument that emphasizes state agency within a historical institutionalist framework to analyse how states conspicuously design development strategies based on state ownership in strategic sectors of the economy. While it is acknowledged that state capacity and the political will of elites are crucial for crafting developmental states, as evidently shown in East Asia (Amsden 1992; Evans 1995), the developmental state itself has also adapted to economic globalization in regions other than East Asia. Specifically, the form of state ownership, the structure of industrial relations, and the reliance of SOEs vis-à-vis the national state have been altered to become more effective at responding to the new challenges associated with global market integration (Nem Singh and Chen 2018; H.W. Yeung 2016). While in some countries, elites have sought new comparative advantages by finding their niche in world markets through subsectors that have not been considered as a traditional source of industrialization (Massi and Nem Singh 2018; Ovadia and Wolf 2018), countries with lower levels of state capacity, so-called emerging developmental states—especially in Sub-Saharan Africa—have often constructed developmental strategies through their basic industries or commodities sector as a means for structural transformation (Behuria 2019; 2020; Clapham 2018). At question here is not only the degree of state autonomy from external and internal forces, but also the capability of elites to find new ways to industrialize amidst the constraints of the global economy.

In the political economy literature, the successful industrial experience of East Asian states has often been attributed to three key factors: (1) a high degree of state capacity, particularly a competent professional bureaucracy, which has led to highly successful development planning aimed at intensive capital accumulation; (2) a pro-business orientation among state elites, which created the 'right incentives' for policymakers to become responsive towards business demands; and (3) the presence of favourable geopolitical conditions at the international level that would provide export markets for capital-intensive goods produced in domestic sectors (Haggard 2015; Nem Singh and Ovadia 2018; Takagi et al. 2019). However, as opportunities for autonomous national development are eclipsed in a globalized world economy, middle-income countries must design new institutions and development policies effectively addressing this novel environment. Thus, it is vital to make a case for the possibilities for 'developmental states' under conditions of globalization, outside the East Asian region.

This book, using empirical evidence from Latin America, argues that SOEs, when subjected to corporate governance reforms aimed at harnessing competition and attuned with private sector performance, might open new pathways for technological innovation and support industrial policy.

14 Business of the State

The empirical chapters, based on Brazil and Chile, provide a detailed discussion about how these countries utilized their strategic oil and gas (O&G) (Brazil) and mining (Chile) industries to successfully leverage fiscal revenues, promote technological innovation, and build domestic industrial capacity. The book recognizes that countries in different regions, including from Indonesia, China, Taiwan, and Singapore, to name a few, have used state ownership in strategic industries alongside the promotion of privately owned national champions as a means of catching up in the industrialization race (Amsden 2001; 2007; H.W. Yeung 2016; 2017). More specifically, oil-exporting states like Saudi Arabia and Norway are known for their national oil companies (NOCs) whose technical expertise led to not only the vertical integration of their energy sector but also the development of cutting-edge, niche technology (Stevens 2012; Thurber and Istad 2012; Victor et al. 2012).

As Nem Singh and Chen (2018) point out, understanding the success of some SOEs would require examining not only the dynamics of corporate governance reform within the public enterprise, but also the relationship between ruling elites and SOE managers. In pursuing a state-led approach to resource extraction, the *entrepreneurial state* argument popularized by Mazzucato (2013; 2016) becomes a useful reference point, wherein the role of the state is not confined to correct market failure and to resolve coordination problems between the public and private sector. Instead, state action is guided by a 'mission-oriented process' in which states socialize both risks and rewards to ensure continuous investment in research and development (R&D) over a long period. Put simply, states through their SOEs and state-investment banks have deployed various instruments of industrial policy and finance over several decades to reduce uncertainty and risk for the private sector (Thurbon 2016).

With a focus on the O&G and mining sectors in Latin America, this book shifts the analytical lens away from extractivism as a growth model and towards the possibilities for *hybrid* development strategies formulated through SOEs in strategic industries promoting innovation and technological development. As such, it provides a much-needed correction in the political economy literature as regards the inevitability of the resource curse and the broad strokes of the political economy models visible in the burgeoning scholarship on resource politics examining the political implications of resource nationalism, neoextractivism and neodevelopmentalism in Latin America (Arsel et al. 2016; Grugel and Riggirozzi 2012; 2018; Santos and Milanez 2015).

As the empirical chapters illustrate, Brazil and Chile both defy simplistic accounts of the resource curse thesis and neoextractivism for two reasons.

Firstly, these states have designed hybrid models of development combining state intervention and market competition aimed at promoting technological innovation, rent capture maximization, and export diversification away from raw material extraction. Secondly, the book uses evidence from Chile and Brazil to place SOEs at the heart of natural resource politics and state development strategies: SOEs—understood as a state institution with a complex role as a bureaucratic arm and as a quasi-independent commercial company—have exerted influence over the strategic direction of how national states implemented purposeful intervention in the resource sector.

Thus, SOE-based growth strategies challenge the political economy and resource politics literature, which have simplistically assumed that public enterprises in natural resource sectors play very little role beyond serving as a vessel of rent-seeking, while literature that does explore renationalizations in Latin America after the 2000s typically only focus on policy instruments like retaxation and increasing local ownership in the O&G and mining sectors (Kaup 2010; Nem Singh 2018). Yet SOEs bear technical expertise to extract O&G and minerals, with technology developed in-house rather than relying on transnational capital. Technological advantage therefore becomes a powerful instrument for state managers of SOEs to assert their political autonomy from national governments. Hence, natural resources are rediscovered as a novel source of industrialization. Furthermore, as the book details, policy elites have conceived their control over the pace and scope of extractive activities as a vital strategy in successfully pursuing value addition in the mining and O&G sectors. In other words, the politics of state ownership is fundamental to the pursuit of reforms in natural resource sectors, and, consequently, through their success in achieving and exercising their autonomy from the government, to realizing the developmental potential of natural-resource-based industrialization.

In this context, external circumstances—notably commodity price boom and bust cycles in international markets—must be treated in an exogenous context upon which ruling elites design their developmental strategies, rather than a determinant and historical constraint associated with natural resource dependency. By focussing on policymaking as a process and evaluating the success of SOE-based resource growth strategies, this book explicates why state ownership in natural resource sectors has varying effects on macroeconomic performance and fiscal position of resource-producing countries (ECLAC 2013; World Investment Report 2013). While many new natural resource producers, such as Mongolia (reaching 17.2% GDP in 2011), Mozambique (with a projected compounded annual growth rate (CAGR) from 2014 to 2017 of +7.30% of GDP), Myanmar (CAGR from 2014 to 2017 of +8.30% of GDP), and the Republic of Congo (CAGR from 2014 to 2017 of +8.62% of GDP), became the world's fastest growing economies (Holodny 2015; World Bank n.d.; 2015), not every resource producer—indeed very few of them—have transformed commodity price booms into meaningful opportunities for long-term economic development (Jepson 2020).

To understand why SOEs in the O&G and mining sectors are maintained in some countries and not in others we need to examine the politics of state intervention. In this book I implore a historical institutionalist explanation that stresses the nuanced relationship between states, private companies, and SOEs which is a departure from the resource curse thesis, which views commodity price volatility, rent-seeking, and uneven sectoral development as major limitations for natural resource producers in their pursuit of export diversification and industrial expansion (Ross 1999; 2001a; 2012; Sachs and Warner 1995; 1997).[4]

The centrality of state enterprises in growth strategies appears anachronistic given the failure of socialist planning and the apparent shift towards a market economy in China during the 1990s. However, several interwoven phenomena mark the nadir of the Washington Consensus era: (1) the return of innovation-driven and sectoral development policies aimed at renewed efforts of industrialization or structural transformation (L. Chen and Chulu 2022; Kang and Jo 2021; Lewis 2013); (2) policy learning and spread of organizational structures for development planning from East Asia to Africa (Chimhowu et al. 2019; Gong et al. 2022; Hauge 2019); and (3) the changing global context in which both international financial institutions (IFIs) and Western governments adopted the language of industrial policy as a defensive globalization strategy in response to China's Belt and Road Initiative (BRI) (Bulfone 2022; Cherif and Hasanov 2019; Malkin 2022). Yet, political economy scholarship remains lacklustre at theorizing the significance of developmental states in the afterlife of neoliberal globalization. This is particularly observable in countries in the Global South, which have been subject to external pressures for market reform. Thus, in Figure 1.5, the book offers an analytical strategy for examining developmental states through the interface of two key dimensions—first, the question of how big the developmental role of the state should be; and second, the extent to which states can seek new industrial strategies away from traditional manufacturing to forge new sectorial bases for development.

---

[4] The resource curse thesis is also used to explain why natural-resource-producing states experience a persistence of weak institutions, protracted state building, and rising political conflicts between companies and communities due to intense competition for control in the O&G and mineral largesse (Arce 2014; Chaudhry 1997; Karl 1997; 1999; Sawyer and Gomez 2012; Shafer 1994).

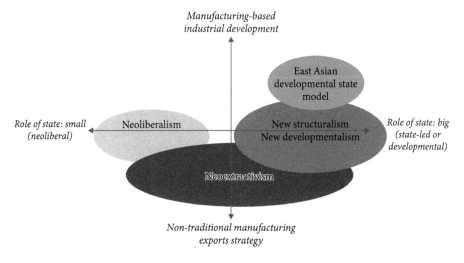

Figure 1.5 Distinctive conceptual models of globalization strategies.
Source: Author compilation based on the literature (Amsden 2001; Hamilton-Hart and H.W. Yeung 2021; H.W. Yeung 2016).

On the question of how big the developmental role of the state should be (first dimension), ruling elites are faced with the policy choice of how much (and in what form) state intervention is politically viable to pursue. The political economy literature has plenty to say on the state vs. markets debate, as well as the contested process of neoliberal reforms in Latin America and elsewhere (Haggard and Kaufman 1996; Philip and Panizza 2011; Weiss 1998; Weiss and Hobson 1995). What these insightful analyses have missed out, however, is the fact that state ownership *changed its form and scope* in the aftermath of the worldwide implementation of neoliberal reforms in the 1980s and 1990s. By the early 2000s, middle-income countries as wide ranging as Brazil, China, India, Indonesia, and Turkey had undergone significant reorganization of the management structures of their SOEs, reflecting if not mirroring some of the features of their private company counterparts (see Chapter 2; Bruton et al. 2014; Musacchio and Lazzarini 2014). Put simply, the 'logic of globalization' that presupposes a convergence towards the privatization of state companies and the deregulation of markets has in practice been applied in partial, segmented, and often contested ways, particularly in cases of SOEs in natural resource sectors with records of good economic performance (Nem Singh 2014). However, this is not simply a case of the return of state capitalism from the 2000s onwards. Rather, policy elites deliberately undertook corporate governance reforms during the neoliberal era as

18 Business of the State

a means of augmenting the capacity of both domestic enterprises and SOEs to emerge as competitive market players in the world economy.

Relatedly, the sectoral basis of the development strategy (the second dimension) is likewise significant to understanding new industrial policies in middle-income countries as arguments have emerged for using industrial policies to develop the linkages between extractive industries and the productive economy, with the mobilization of fiscal revenues to finance new initiatives in agriculture, industry, and services (Morris et al. 2012). As such, the question is not just how to design effective natural-resource-based policies to promote value-added activities and technological innovation. Equally important is recognizing the enormous challenges associated with natural resource subsectors—mining, O&G, and commodity export agriculture—to sustain the industrial strategy. On the one hand, increasing fragmentation in global supply chains has meant that regional supply chains are playing a far greater role in enabling country participation (del Prete et al. 2018; Pomfret and Sourdin 2018). Consequently, technology transfer and the development of innovation—from multinational capital or emerging Asian manufacturers towards poorer developing countries—has been difficult (Azmeh and Nadvi 2014; Gereffi 2014; Morris et al. 2012; Pananond 2013). On the other hand, the participation of developing countries in global value chains has become a common strategy for development because the gains from trade can only be realized not via traditional notions of self-sufficiency but by further integration in the world economy. However, largely due to unequal terms of trade, such development strategies have had mixed outcomes among middle- and low-income countries (del Prete et al. 2018; Pananond 2013; Tõnurist 2015). Foreign direct investment (FDI) has become increasingly central to such strategies because many global value chains based on natural resources are dominated by multinational corporations pursuing major acquisitions in the O&G and recently in mining sectors (Nem Singh 2019). In this way, Brazil and Chile offer compelling cases to consider how SOEs can develop intersectoral linkages from O&G and mining and, in the process, also find their own niche in the global economy. The fact that in both countries development strategies are not based on manufacturing but have strong resource extractive component challenges conventional wisdom on how to design blueprint industrial policies outside East Asia and a central concern of this book is therefore to understand how and why states are able to legitimize a growth strategy that combines state ownership with private capital participation. Additionally, while natural-resource-based industrialization is still the toughest case for industrial upgrading, the experience of Brazil and Chile in building forward, backward, and horizontal linkages through SOEs in the O&G and mining sectors is therefore a worthwhile analytical inquiry that adds to the growing literature examining non-traditional exports and heterodox industrial strategies found in the Global South (Massi and Nem Singh 2018; Nem Singh and Chen 2018). Figure 1.6 demonstrates the range of governance models based on political choices between manufacturing and nature resources, as well as the degree of public and private participation.

Key Arguments

This book seeks to understand why some states decide to maintain full control over their SOEs rather than privatize them, and what sort of reforms are implemented to retain the developmental functions of SOEs. Using empirical evidence from Latin America, the analysis process traces the ways in which political elites in Brazil and Chile from the 1990s onwards have crafted regulatory frameworks that guide the strategic extractive industry, alongside the attendant corporate governance reforms within SOEs, to pursue a natural-resource-based development strategy. Through a comparative analysis of two SOEs—Petrobras as Brazil's NOC and Codelco as Chile's copper mining SOE—which are situated in the broader Latin American context, the book takes a *historical institutionalist approach*, emphasizing the importance of agency and politics as contingent factors that shape the incremental institutional changes in strategic sectors.

The book makes two key interrelated arguments. First is the central importance of *historical antecedents* as a precondition for states to thwart privatization of SOEs, which is key to understanding why states maintain SOEs rather than privatize them. In countries with a tradition of industrialization, an ideological commitment against full liberalization is strongly embedded in political decision-making. Vu (2010a), for example, shows that legacies of state socialism have profoundly impacted on elites' commitment towards a developmental state strategy, thereby keeping full-scale privatization at bay even during the intense period of neoliberal reforms. Those countries with histories of industrial policymaking often develop distinctive institutional capabilities over an extended time period, which help state bureaucrats to formulate 'mission-oriented' policies to support public and private sector development (Brooks and Kurtz 2016). In the specific cases of Brazil and Chile presented in this book, I argue that political elites during the 20th century institutionalized a 'developmentalist' orientation in the O&G and mining sectors, whereby SOEs were conceived as a central pillar of a country's development strategy. By successfully embedding, and

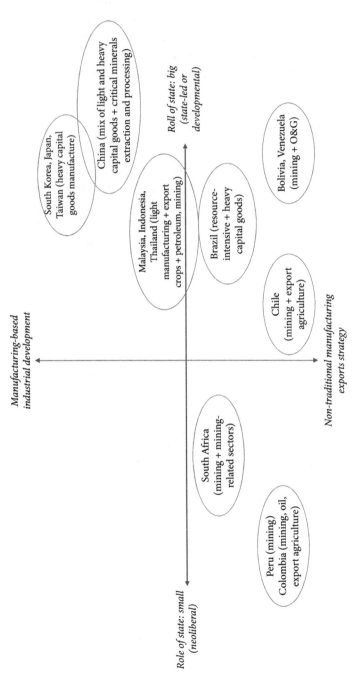

Figure 1.6 Growth strategies of selected middle-income countries, 1950s–2010s.
Source: Author compilation based on the literature (see also Nem Singh and Ovadia 2018).

thus justifying, a crucial developmental role for SOEs, state elites remained committed to protecting the public enterprise sector. While Brazilian elites implemented extensive state intervention and industrial policy via the logic of *desenvolvimentismo* (developmentalism) in the O&G sector and beyond, the reliance of Chilean elites on copper mining rents—and the mining industry more widely—meant that maintaining the profitability of Codelco was of paramount importance to the state.

Another factor might have a big influence on elite decisions to shy away from privatization: the presence of well-managed SOEs in strategic sectors that can promote state-sanctioned objectives alters the calculations of elites in determining the balance between public and private sector participation in the industry. SOEs face two conflicting roles—to promote government-sanctioned objectives and to maintain their profitability as a commercial entity. As mentioned above, to manoeuvre through these conflicting roles, the *autonomy* of state enterprises plays a vital role. State autonomy, broadly understood, refers to the relative ability of state managers of SOEs to make important decisions for the company without the direct interference of the state. This is reflected in the range of actions that SOE managers can undertake, such as hiring staff based on merit rather than because of political appointments, making commercial decisions regarding investment and business plans, as well as undertaking internal administrative reforms to adjust to external changes. All these actions constitute management decisions that can improve the overall performance of SOEs vis-à-vis the private sector. Additionally, when SOEs can compete with international O&G and mining capital, then the state can deploy SOEs as *strategic* development actors. In other words, SOEs—not just the professional civil service and state bureaucracy—can serve as a powerful weapon to build institutional capacity for economic development. And in recognizing the strategic role of SOEs in a state's development strategy, as mentioned above, the book adds to debates about the changing nature of developmental states and government intervention in the post-liberal world order beyond the East Asian context (Nem Singh and Ovadia 2018; Taylor 2020).

While Latin American governments appeared to fully embrace neoliberalism as the dominant growth strategy, the actual scope of privatization of the SOE sector has radically differed in the region. During the 1990s, states responded to pressures for liberalization and greater private sector participation. In highly lucrative sectors like O&G and mining, developing states implemented far-reaching changes in their taxation regimes, transforming subsoil rights to allow foreign ownership of mines, and altering regulatory frameworks, all designed to introduce market competition (Bebbington and

22 Business of the State

Bury 2013; Campbell 2009; Haslam and Heidrich 2016). However, the most controversial reform—the privatization of SOEs—has been the subject of political contestation. Hence, some countries successfully privatized their SOEs, whilst others decisively reoriented them towards competition while retaining state ownership.

As presented in the case studies of Brazil and Chile, both countries designed corporate governance reforms while simultaneously introducing market competition in the public enterprise sector. Put crudely, while the pressure to privatize Petrobras and Codelco was immense, political elites appeared to evade such a radical programme, implementing corporate restructuring instead, whereby the *ownership* and *management* were separated to introduce a logic of competition to the SOE. While governments in both Brazil and Chile imposed new regulations—to remove discriminatory policies between SOEs and private companies; and creating new regulatory agencies to oversee the process of competition and regulation—both cases demonstrate the uneven consequences of neoliberal reforms: policy elites were unwilling to give up control in O&G and mining sectors, and pro-market reforms were introduced only to cater to sectoral development. The protracted neoliberalism in Brazil and Chile, therefore, tells a wider story about the exercise of state agency amidst exogenous pressures linked to economic globalization.

The second key argument of this book is that the choice of states to pursue a developmental role for SOEs in the era of economic globalization necessitates closer analysis of the reforms implemented in SOE organizational structure, and a new way to assess SOE performance. If states are indeed unwilling to relinquish political control over strategic industries, how do elites seek to resolve associated problems of corruption, rent-seeking, and lack of competitiveness of their SOE sector? While there exist economic arguments about the pitfalls of state ownership and why private companies are more efficient and better at sectoral development (Krueger 1974; Shirley 1999; Shleifer 1998), some states still choose to maintain their public enterprise sector, albeit subjecting them to extensive corporate governance reforms. To address the issue of state ownership as a viable development strategy, the book constructs three major criteria upon which SOEs can be evaluated against their performance: (1) the degree to which SOEs are able to maintain corporate autonomy from states; (2) the success of SOEs in generating innovation and enhancing the productive capacity in the sector; and (3) the extent to which SOEs were able to meet the policy objectives set out by their national states.

As per above, the role of autonomy in the success of an SOE is key, and the case studies of Brazil and Chile, and later in the expanded comparison in

Chapter 9, demonstrate that SOEs with higher degrees of corporate autonomy are more likely to improve their economic performance (Priest 2016; Victor et al. 2012). SOEs with clearly delineated relationships from state agencies and government ministries are better able to follow formal corporate rules as enshrined in their governance framework; they also exhibit independent decision-making powers, especially on investment choices and business planning—both of which have significant impacts on the commercial sustainability and fiscal health of an SOE. Conversely, in SOEs where decision-making managers are frequently constrained by political interference, or where board appointments are solely based on political calculation by the state rather than by merit, the SOE is at risk of losing its autonomy. Consequently, commercial decisions that might well be politically salient for the president but damaging to the commercial competitiveness of the SOE can gradually erode the effectiveness and success of SOEs as tools for economic development. As the Brazilian experience shows, the fusion of political and economic power under the *Partido dos Trabalhadores* (PT) government exposed Petrobras to the *Lava Jato* corruption scheme, while erroneous investment decisions left the once-profitable state enterprise with huge debts and internally mismanaged. Put differently, commercial success built through corporate autonomy is a result of a delicate political balance between Petrobras, the Brazilian state, and competing rent-seeking interests, but without institutionalized checks and balances it may further entrench clientelism, rent-seeking, and political corruption. In Chapter 7 the case study explains in detail how Petrobras, under Pedro Parente, responded to regain the autonomy of the company from party politics and to salvage the NOC from bankruptcy through unpopular measures that eventually clashed with the political demands for state intervention.

A note on the argument of the book must be made before proceeding to the presentation of the book chapters. The development studies literature has expanded the conceptualization and measurement of my dependent variable—economic development. The book makes clear that the dependent variable here is *industrial development*, defined in terms of the structural transformation of national economies, moving away from primary commodities-based growth towards more complex, value-added, and manufacturing-based sectoral development (Aiginger and Rodrik 2020). Specifically, the book examines the role of SOEs in industrial development based on three key criteria: (1) the capacity of SOEs to generate sufficient rents, which can be transformed into productive assets for the rest of the economy; (2) the capacity of the domestic economy to generate higher value-added activities through sectoral linkage and spillover effects into the

24   Business of the State

non-primary sector; and (3) the power of domestic private companies to participate in the global supply chains, leading to further innovation within and outside the principal growth sector. Empirically, the study examines Brazil's Petrobras and Chile's Codelco based on these three criteria.

Overall, the book brings into conversation arguments on state ownership and economic globalization on the one hand, and debates about industrialization and natural-resource-led development strategies on the other. It offers a critique on contemporary theories of the so-called 'logic of globalization', which is frequently elevated to the central dynamic of the global political economy. As Nem Singh (2014) explains, market reforms are assumed to converge towards a pathway placing logics of free markets and privatization as the driving force of state transformation. Rather than dismissing this deterministic logic as an unimportant socializing factor in globalization, this book argues that the power of globalization is refracted in different directions through the domestic configurations within societies. Historical antecedent, political contention, and conflicts within nation states shape the institutional architecture of Latin American economic governance. By examining why Brazilian and Chilean elites have refused to privatize their SOEs despite convergent pressures towards attracting FDI and unleashing market forces, this book highlights both the contingent nature of economic reforms and the power of path dependence—especially the relative strength of SOEs as a competitive market player—in mediating and muting the power of economic neoliberalism in Latin America. Deploying a historical institutionalist analysis, the book demonstrates the need for a nuanced history of state activism to fully understand the consequences of contemporary market reforms in the construction of hybrid governance models around natural resource sectors.

The Comparative Approach

Comparison of the cases of Brazil and Chile is motivated by three intellectual rationales. Firstly, although public administrative reforms in favour of strengthening the role of the state in economic development occurred across Latin America between the 1930s and 1970s, Brazil and Chile stand out as exceptional cases of successful state-building in the region. In both countries, national elites implemented bureaucratic reforms to create a technocratic state and, in lieu of Latin America's demand for economic nationalism, created SOEs in strategic industries and instilled a developmentalist mindset among elites and society. SOEs Petrobras and Codelco were catalysts for constructing institutional capacity to negotiate foreign capital participation and to manage political conflicts in the mining and O&G industries. The survival of SOEs amidst sweeping economic reforms during the 1980s and 1990s confirms the significance of path-shaping institutional legacies as an enabling condition for the consolidation of an SOE-based development model in strategic natural resource sectors.

Secondly, in Chile and Brazil institutional transformation aimed at strengthening their economic power successfully coalesced around the idea of developmentalism more effectively than in other countries in the region. In Latin America, import substitution industrialization (ISI) failed not so much due to divergent economic logics, but rather on varying state strength among different Latin American governments. Political elites failed to implement difficult reforms to overhaul the distribution of rents, the imposition of an effective taxation regime in the extractive sector and beyond, and consistency in policy-making, especially in undertaking economic reforms.[5] In this context, Brazil and Chile have often been viewed as exceptionally strong states with effective tax capacity and possess the institutional strength to carry out consistent reforms in both political and economic realms (Limoeiro and Schneider 2019; Orihuela 2018; Soifer 2009; 2015). Beyond public goods provision, their regulatory agencies, development planning institutions, and SOEs reflect a historical accumulation of state capacity leading to impressive economic performance throughout the 20th century (Brooks and Kurtz 2016; Leão 2018; Massi 2014; Nem Singh 2014; Silva 2018). Put differently, the choice of Brazil and Chile as the case studies in this book highlights the significance of institutional continuity and change that enabled national policy elites to forge a coherent development strategy centred on the natural resource extraction–national industrialization nexus.

Finally, these two cases stand out as exemplary models of not just how to utilize natural resources for export promotion, but also how to conduct natural-resource-based development in the 21st century. As the empirical chapters show, Petrobras and Codelco are considered effective SOEs (1) in terms of their role in maximizing fiscal revenues for resource wealth accumulation and (2) in terms of their R&D contribution towards sectoral promotion, and (3), in the case of Brazil, as critical for the development of a domestic supply chain in O&G and industrial sectors. In circumstances where effective coordination mechanisms between governments and public enterprises exist, SOEs could play transformative roles for industrialization. Hence, a

---

[5] For example, the petro-state in Venezuela successfully developed certain skills such as monitoring, regulating, and promoting the mining industry, but elites failed to build extensive, penetrating, and coherent bureaucracies, as reflected in the low level of taxation in this oil country compared to its neighbours (Karl 1997, 61).

26 Business of the State

closer scrutiny of the successes and shortcomings of Petrobras and Codelco provides useful insights on contemporary natural resource governance in the developing world.

Presentation of the Book

The book is divided into three parts with nine substantive chapters. Part I outlines the main arguments of the book, which includes this introduction and the presentation of historical institutionalism as a theoretical framework (Chapter 2) premised on institutional stability and incremental change to explain the continuing role of SOEs in Latin American economic development over the 20th century. A focus on the role of agency in institutional change emphasizes state–state (SOE) relations, which is a useful conceptual lens to explain state transformation. Within this framework, corporate governance reforms within SOEs are conceived as endogenous factors shaping a diversity of state–state (SOE) relations within hybrid development strategies as a response to neoliberal economic globalization. Chapter 2 places political legacies and path dependency as organizing concepts to trace the evolution of development strategies in Latin American natural resource sectors. It also brings together the comparative political economy literature on state ownership—specifically reforms in SOEs—as a fundamental strategy to adapt to economic globalization.

Part II presents the case studies, charting the institutional transformation and political dynamics that marked the shift from state developmentalism towards a protracted neoliberal model in Brazil and Chile. Chapter 3 examines the place of state ownership in natural resource governance in Latin American states throughout the 20th century to show the significance of SOEs in developing *indigenous* industrial capacity and human capital stocks in the region, highlighting Venezuela's development as a petro-state in particular. It also presents the hard limits of this SOE-based growth that paved the way for the implementation and continuing dominance of neoliberalism in the region from the 1980s onwards. Chapter 4 considers the place of state ownership in natural resource governance in Chile and Brazil specifically, as an introduction to the case study analyses of Chile (Chapters 5 and 6) and Brazil (Chapters 7 and 8) that follow. The case study chapters themselves use the cases of SOE Codelco in Chile and NOC Petrobras in Brazil to examine the continuity and changes between natural resource developmentalism and neoliberalism in each country, tracing the regulatory reforms undertaken in Chile's mining sector (Chapter 5) and Brazil's O&G sector

(Chapter 7), as well as the internal restructuring of Codelco (Chapter 6) and Petrobras (Chapter 8) in response to the globalization strategy of their national governments. In so doing, the case studies show the rise of a hybrid development model, which combines continuity of regulatory reforms in mining (Chile) and O&G (Brazil) industries with changes to SOE governance to enhance their competitiveness and to respond to the challenge of economic globalization between 1990s and 2010s.

Chapters 5 and 6 challenge the idea of Chile as a wholly neoliberal state that rejects state intervention in its strategic copper industry as a natural-resource-based development strategy became apparent throughout the 1990s and 2000s, with Codelco playing a significant role in managing neoliberalism. This, of course, was not uncontroversial. As Chapter 6 shows, there have been periodic tensions between the state, Codelco, and labour unions in seeking the appropriate balance between the public and private mode of capital accumulation. Chapters 7 and 8 chart and explain the interaction between state developmentalism and neoliberalism in Brazil's O&G industry. Similar to Chile, the chapters demonstrate how institutional transformation prioritized maintaining state authority over the industry through several initiatives, notably local content requirements and corporate governance reforms within NOC Petrobras. This, in turn, allowed for an expansionary policy during the 2000s when the country experienced an oil bonanza following the discovery of pre-salt reserves. However, as Chapter 8 shows, Petrobras's hard-won autonomy was compromised as the company became subject of the systematic corruption exposed by the *Lava Jato* scandal. Hence, Brazil posits an example of the difficulty in insulating SOEs from rent-seeking and political intervention.

In Part III, the book examines the comparative and historical dimensions of state ownership in the natural resource sector in Latin America and beyond. Chapter 9 presents a comparative analysis of state ownership in Latin America to highlight the interactive effects of regulatory reforms and SOE activism. The final chapter (Chapter 10) presents the theoretical contributions of the book, before looking into the future of developmental states and, in particular, at the challenges for mineral producers as the climate crisis presents new opportunities for reindustrialization.

Chapter 9 presents a comparative analysis of the Brazil and Chile case studies, drawing out key similarities in the ways state–state (SOE) relations evolved in these two countries and revisiting the historical institutionalist framework and exploring the important mechanisms linking regulatory politics and SOE reforms in the mining and O&G industries. It explicitly evaluates the place of SOEs in natural resource governance in Brazil and

28 Business of the State

Chile, arguing for a recognition of the significance of state ownership and SOEs in understanding fundamental debates in the political economy that seek to address both critical real-world and normative questions: the relation between state capitalism and economic development, the role of state ownership in institutional capacity-building and industrial policy expansion in the 21st century, and the political conditions necessary for continuity in maintaining efficient, productive SOEs that can be politically autonomous, thereby reducing the possibilities of state companies being conduits of rent-seeking and corruption. The second half of the chapter looks at the other responses to economic globalization in Latin America. Specifically, it examines the difficulty of Venezuela's state ownership without corporate autonomy in pursuing industrialization and the creation of alternative export industries. At the other extreme, the chapter likewise highlights the difficulties of embracing neoliberalism without any kind of state ownership. In Peru, excessive marketization failed to generate opportunities to maximize the benefits of the mining industry and, with an extractivist model firmly in place, the possibilities for structural transformation may have been closed for the country.

Finally, Chapter 10 considers the prospects and challenges of developmental states in the 21st century—starting with China as the most recent example of efforts at building a 'developmental state'. By analysing the gradual, steady reforms leading to the 'advance of the state' and 'retreat of the market' in China, the book offers a rethinking on what lessons can be learned as regards state ownership. Beyond summarizing the theoretical contributions of the book, the chapter examines the future of mineral-producing states and why policymakers need to reexamine their assumptions about the place of state ownership in the new geopolitical context of strategic competition and climate emergency. In so doing, it proposes to rethink how resource wealth management can complement state ownership—something that the scholarship on the resource curse and neoliberalism dismissed as infeasible in the era of economic globalization.

2
Theorizing State Ownership in Natural Resource Governance

Development is essentially a record of how one thing leads to another.
Albert Hirschman[1]

This book examines how states exercise political agency in response to exogenous pressures—notably globalization—to promote a natural-resource-based development strategy. Mainstream theories on natural resources, development, and political conflicts feature the state as antithetical to economic development and state-building. This is consistent with the liberal belief that market forces, not the state, should be the motor of development, and as such these extant theories have neglected the role of states in development, first as a consequence of an intellectual bias against export-driven growth in favour of industrialization during the 1950s, and second as an outcome of prejudice against natural-resource-based development policies during the 1990s. However, all successful natural-resource-based economies in the 19th and 20th centuries required some degree of state intervention in natural resource production. In the era of contemporary globalization, the question this book considers is the scope and degree of state intervention in government policy, especially in the context of the performance of resource-rich countries seeking to overcome the limitations of their domestic economic governance models during the 20th century. This chapter focuses on the relationship between natural resources, neoliberalism, and the political economy of state intervention in the era of contemporary globalization, to build a theoretical framework that accounts for institutional change and development strategies in key strategic sectors of the national economy.

---

[1] Passage from Hirschman 1981, 75.

Business of the State. Jewellord T. Nem Singh, Oxford University Press. © Jewellord T. Nem Singh (2024).
DOI: 10.1093/oso/9780198892212.003.0002

30 Business of the State

The Extractivism–Development Debate: What We Do and Do Not Know

This book is spurred by the conviction that there are very serious lacunae in the conventional approaches to understanding the role of states in natural-resource-based growth, development strategies, and institutional development. Although there are insights to be gained from the traditional examinations of natural resource sector reforms that stress the specific properties of these sectors, as well as the interactions between host governments and multinational capital in the world economy, it is not until these factors are combined with an analysis of the underlying path-dependent processes and dynamics of state ownership that a compelling account of natural-resource-based development and globalization strategies can be constructed to confront the empirical novelty of the patterns of capacity-building in resource-rich states. In the following section, the key contributions and inadequacies of extant approaches to the understanding of natural resource development will be examined with the objective of making a case for a new theoretical framework that combines a historical institutionalist analysis and political economy scholarship of state ownership in natural resource sectors—over existing analysis premised on ecological and societal state interactions, or international-systemic factors—to highlight and better understand the foundations of natural-resource-based development strategies.

The most well-developed theoretical literature on natural-resource-based development emphasizes the specific properties of natural resources as the motor of underdevelopment, the particular state–society interactions that lead to rentierism in resource-rich countries, or the systemic factors as principal constraints of development. This literature has made a substantial contribution to understanding the role of natural resource exploitation in the developing world. However, these accounts suffer from a narrow time period of study, between the early 1960s and late 1990s, to systematically analyse the impacts of natural-resource-based development on economic growth and political development. Furthermore, analysis using the prominent rentier state model—developed to explain the persistence of authoritarianism, patronage and rent-seeking, and weak institutional capacity to manage sociopolitical contests in the O&G and mining industries—often focusses on the experience of the Middle East and African countries. These theories do not explain why Latin America has enjoyed long periods of democratic governance despite the overwhelming distributional conflicts that historically characterized its natural resource sector (Dunning 2008; Grugel and Nem

Singh 2013). And, while institutional factors are considered one of the primary drivers of economic performance in resource-rich countries (Jones and Weinthal 2010; Mehlum et al. 2006), what is often missing are direct explanations regarding the conditions upon which political elites will likely adopt path-breaking institutional reforms to mobilize political support for public interventions aimed at building strategic export sectors.

Additionally, in the literature on natural resource development, although comparative and historical evidence may provide us with clues about which development strategies worked during the nineteenth and twentieth centuries, the current second phase of economic globalization, where money, finance, and mobile capital have become centripetal forces in the international economy, posits new challenges for resource-rich countries, thereby requiring a new globalization strategy. The approach in this book is to develop a *historical institutionalist* account of natural-resource-based development that builds upon existing knowledge of resource development, but which also includes an emphasis on new developmental strategies as a response to the changing structures of the world economy.

Resource Curse, Economic Growth, and Rentier State Models

The long-standing idea that natural-resource-intensive economies face more difficulties in achieving long-run economic growth compared to resource-poor economies exists in the literature developed between the 1960s and 1990s which attributes underdevelopment to the sector-specific characteristics of commodity exports. This literature suggests that the materiality of natural resources is a key determinant of a country's economic performance. Two theories underline this argument. On the one hand, the resource curse theory focusses on the *production* aspect of mineral extraction. Resource-intensive economies are presented with particular developmental challenges that require institutional change in a country's monetary affairs and overall industrial strategy. On the other hand, rentier state models are principally concerned with *rent distribution*, whereby the curse stems from the limited extractive capacity of the state and its myopic decision-making that oftentimes led to unproductive investments of natural resource rents. In both theories, domestic-level factors play a crucial role in determining the developmental outcomes of natural resource extraction.

The resource curse, in strictly economic terms, derives economic stagnation from the direct effect of export windfalls on the real exchange rate,

32   Business of the State

also known as the *Dutch disease*. In shifting production inputs towards the booming mining, O&G, and non-tradable sectors, including services and construction, natural resource production reduces the long-run competitiveness of the non-booming export sectors such as manufacturing and agriculture by raising production costs and making non-tradable exports more expensive in the global market, thereby triggering deindustrialization and even precipitating economic collapse (Auty 1993; 2001; Humphreys et al. 2007; Ross 2001b, 305; Sachs and Warner 1995; 1999). In other words, a permanent increase in the inflows of external funds can trigger a change in the relative prices in favour of non-traded goods and against non-oil-traded (exported) goods. Not only does this lead to the crowding out of non-oil-tradables by non-tradables, it also encourages producers to shift towards non-traded investments rather than non-oil-traded goods, hence discouraging investments in manufacturing. In the context of staple exporters, an increase in commodity prices raises the relative prices of both capital inputs and manufacturing wages, thereby potentially leading to de-industrialization (Di John 2009, 38–39).

However, the idea that natural resources are antithetical for economic development was observed earlier by two economists, Raul Prebisch (1950) and Hans Singer (1950), based at the Economic Commission for Latin America and the Caribbean (ECLAC, or CEPAL in Spanish). Prebisch and Singer separately published their studies on the impacts of rising commodity export prices on long-run economic growth. Known today as the Prebisch–Singer hypothesis, both found evidence that there is a downward trend in the terms of trade between primary producers and manufacturers, using data covering up until World War II. In addition, there is an asymmetry in commodity price cycles, meaning that price slumps tend to be more enduring than price booms. Given the rapid and often unexpected transitions between boom and bust, natural resource producers must accurately estimate the duration and magnitude of commodity price cycles. Thus, the efficacy of counter-cyclical stabilization policies is contingent on the capability of governments to predict how far prices fall in a slump, and to what extent commodity exporters can cope with the longevity of price slumps (Cashin et al. 2002). For this reason, price increases in commodity exports are nothing more than temporary sources of surplus that offer short-lived opportunities for industrial investment. More recent scholarship on the Prebisch–Singer hypothesis has extended its temporal coverage and provided better measures of the estimated effects of the rate of increase in manufacturing prices in relation to primary products. Others make a distinction between unprocessed and manufactured natural resource products in their relationship with economic growth, leading to more fine-grained analysis of a country's trade diversification experience (Bloch and Sapsford 1997; Erten and Ocampo 2013; Harvey et al. 2010; Murshed and Serino 2011; Ocampo 2017). Collectively, these studies unpack the direct and indirect effects of price volatility on the growth prospects of commodity exporters.[2]

While many of these studies have deployed econometrics to demonstrate the relationship between resource abundance and economic performance, others seek to develop a political science theory to systematically test the relationship between resource abundance and institutions.[3] For political scientists, the negative link between natural resources and institutional development depends less on the presence of oil and mineral resources and more on the ways political elites manage the enormous amount of rents from the natural resource sector. This approach emphasizes the interactions between political conditions, institutional formation, and natural resource endowment—commonly referred as the 'political resource curse' (Fails and DuBuis 2015; Kurtz and Brooks 2011; Rudra and Jensen 2011; Wiens et al. 2014)—and is premised on the rentier state model. According to this theory, higher levels of mineral rents are associated with the creation of rent-seeking and corruption opportunities. The more states accrue 'unearned income' through mineral rents or foreign aid, the less state elites are compelled to earn their income through domestic taxation of the productive economy. And, with the capacity of national elites to exercise discretion and political authority over the centralized allocation of rents, the levels of state intervention tend to be higher in oil- and mineral-rich countries (Auty and Gelb 2001). For liberal economists, state intervention artificially creates rents in the form of monopoly grants (Buchanan 1980; Krueger 1974; Posner 1975), which in turn induces agents to 'waste' resources on 'unproductive activities' in an attempt to capture the rents from the sector.

---

[2] The Prebisch–Singer thesis's observation that the terms of trade for underdeveloped countries had deteriorated over time relative to developed countries was developed by the 'Cepalistas'—heterodox economists including Prebisch and Singer who were based at ECLAC (CEPAL), who articulated through the centre–periphery equation that structural heterogeneity and dualistic economies are the main sources of persistent underdevelopment in Latin America. From the 1950s, the Cepalistas promoted a series of policies aimed at achieving autonomous industrial development in Latin America, including import substitution industrialization. Premised on the logic of international competitiveness, the Cepalistas asserted that underdeveloped countries must employ some degree of trade protectionism to enter a self-sustaining development path.

[3] Using econometrics, Mehlum et al. (2006) argue that resource wealth and institutional quality are inversely correlated, wherein poor countries establishing producer-friendly as opposed to grabber-friendly institutions tend to create less opportunities for rent-seeking. Others found resource abundance to be positively correlated in fuelling civil wars, secessionism, and other resource-related conflicts (Collier and Hoeffler 2004; Ross 2001b; 2006; 2015; Uldefer 2007.

34 Business of the State

In her classic work, Terry Lynn Karl's (1997) 'paradox of plenty' describes the failure of petro-states in building insulated bureaucracies and effective economic institutions. The logic is derived from the incentive structure, which sharply influences the political behaviour of their elites. While states constructively build their relationships with society through taxation, the presence of a huge oil largesse—when financed by foreign capital—can ease the pressures to undertake costly institutional reforms, such as collecting taxes from non-oil domestic producers. This, in turn, reduces the incentives of domestic capitalists to seek improved accountability in the ways governments allocate mineral rents (Beblawi and Luciani 1987; Chaudhry 1997). During boom times, export windfall profits likewise produce indirect negative effects by encouraging excessive spending of the fiscal surplus towards consumption, thereby underinvesting in the productive economy (Gylfason 2001; Leite and Weidmann 1999).[4] Because natural resource rents come from foreign capital rather than general taxation, politicians are incentivized to generate income without needing to seek the support and cooperation of their citizens. Hence, the social contract typically emerging from political bargaining over tax between governments and producers dissipates; and resource rents weaken the link between state and society (Bräutigam et al. 2008; Levi 1988; Tilly 1992). Additionally, without an extractive bureaucracy, states lose incentives to centralize the fiscal apparatus which undermines other regulatory tasks, such as obtaining basic data about the economy, setting fiscal priorities, and establishing regulation for private companies (Bräutigam 2002). In other words, the revenue imperative which serves as stimulus for the further development of public administration and extractive institutions appears to be absent in resource-dependent economies.

This analysis on the political dynamics of O&G and mining countries has led academics and policymakers to advocate for the elimination of all forms of state-created rents, and thus makes a strong case for economic liberalization, including trade liberalization, privatization of state-owned companies, and financial deregulation. By curbing discretionary state authority over the allocation of mineral rents, it is argued that corruption and rent-seeking can be reduced and consequently can have a net positive effect on growth levels and investment. Good governance and strong political institutions, in short, are deemed as the cure to the rentier state.

The resource curse and rentier state theories have important limitations. There are at least three key critiques to raise before presenting the theoretical framework for this book. Firstly, empirical evidence in Latin America does

---

[4] However, this was challenged by a World Bank-sponsored paper (see McMahon and Moreira 2014).

not comply with the resource curse theory. In Venezuela, a key oil exporter in world trade, oil abundance coincided with *both* periods of economic growth and decline in productivity and output in the manufacturing sector (Di John 2009). Despite falling oil exports in the 1980s (which, according to the resource curse theory, should lead to economic recovery), Venezuela experienced neither any improvements in productivity growth nor political stability. Following Di John (2009), the critical factor that determines economic performance and political development is the degree of institutional consolidation and the strength of state power in managing the complex challenges of oil-based development. Technologies accompanying different development strategies require distinctive levels of selectivity and discipline in the deployment of subsidies, infant industry protection, and the coordination of investment. Therefore, while cohesive developmental states can be formed in resource-rich countries, both the resource curse and rentier state theories often dismiss this possibility.

Secondly, the predictive power of various rentier state models weakens when we consider comparative and historical evidence especially from other regions of the world. It is widely acknowledged that historical conflicts— as opposed to the character of natural resources—play a greater role in building effective states. As Kurtz (2013, 23–28) points out, there is no reason why elites will not build penetrating public bureaucracies and effective rules-based institutions during a commodity boom. Instead, the political settlements or coalitional politics mould the incentives of national elites to build extractive bureaucracies, to centralize political authority, or to create national companies to extend the institutional power of the state in enhancing the developmental impacts of natural resources (Di John 2009; Saylor 2014). Malaysia and Indonesia, for example, have successfully combined pro-poor, pro-rural spending and natural resource taxation to support their manufacturing initiatives.

Finally, despite the sophistication of rentier state theory, the link between mineral wealth and authoritarianism is tenuous outside of the Middle East and Africa (MENA) (Beblawi 1990; Beblawi and Luciani 1987).[5] In Latin America, natural-resource-based development coincided with periods of economic growth and stagnation, during which states likewise deployed multiple development strategies to manage the ensuing conflicts within the sector. Natural resource wealth was also managed under caudillos, military dictatorships, and nominal democracies across the region throughout the

---

[5] However, there is a now an established literature on state-building in resource-rich countries outside of MENA (Jones and Weinthal 2010; Saylor 2014; Weinthal and Luong 2006).

36 Business of the State

20th century (Dunning 2008; Hammond 2011).[6] And while the global oil market creates a single set of political constraints common to all oil-exporting countries, some political leaders in oil-rich states choose to invest in developing complex political institutions instead of resorting to state repression (Brownlee 2007; Saylor 2014; Smith 2007, 196). Strikingly, Herb (2014) compares the political development of democratic institutions among the five Gulf states, and while Kuwait has gradually moved towards strengthening its parliament, the United Arab Emirates (UAE) and others have remained closed to political liberalization.[7] Therefore, the presence of oil and minerals does not necessarily preclude a political trajectory, whereby national elites are incentivized to build effective political institutions to manage the oil economy. Indeed, the commodity boom has shown that 'mineral rich states can learn' from each other (Orihuela 2013), evidently shown in common policy designs to counter commodity price volatility, to construct new industrial policies, and to promote export diversification (Roll 2014; Tordo et al. 2013).

Conversely, the Petrobras corruption scandal, infamously called *Operação Lava Jato* (Operation Car Wash), in Brazil, herein *Lava Jato*, is an example of corruption and rent-seeking being embedded in the political system even prior to oil discovery. The *Lava Jato* scandal reflects how deeply entrenched patronage and clientelism were in the Brazilian political system, despite the consolidation of multiparty democracy after 1985. And during the commodity boom, oil wealth did not cause extraordinary corruption; instead, rent-seeking practices are incorporated into the PT government's strategy of maintaining the balance of forces in a governing coalition during the commodity boom. Put simply, resource wealth and corruption are not causally related in ways that the resource curse theory purports; rather, corruption needs to be unpacked as a mechanism for sustaining coalitional alliances aimed at supporting an industrial strategy. In significant ways, the complex

---

[6] In Latin America, oil was in fact associated with democratization. In Mexico and Venezuela, labour unions (who played a key role in democratization in the early 20th century) sought to nationalize oil as a means of increasing control over strategic industries. Political elites also avoided a complete breakdown of the political system by designing a mechanism for distributing oil rents among them. While Latin America was ruled by dictatorships, Venezuela remained a democracy. Oil was also the reason why the cyclical political crisis in Mexico did not lead to a total collapse of the exports-led growth model (González 2008; Karl 1990; 1997; Philip 1982). Hence, oil and democracy are not necessarily incompatible.

[7] More generally, Herb finds that rentierism does not necessarily obstruct accountability because: (1) some regimes—Saudi Arabia being the exemplary case—are able to buy off dissent and generate more rents; (2) the links between taxation and representation in European history have far less support for rentier state theory than is often supposed; (3) citizens may still want to hold their rulers accountable even without being taxed; and (4) the actual mechanism of rentier state theory may find less support outside of the Middle East simply because rent-seeking practices typically exist across polities in the Global South (Herb 1999; 2003; 2005; Hertog 2010a; 2010b; Waterbury 1994; 1997).

Systemic Approaches to Primary Commodity Production

A long-standing political economy approach to underdevelopment and the global hierarchy of states stems from an emphasis on the systemic conditions and structural expectations about the limited possibilities for peripheral nation-states in achieving technological innovation and advance in the world economy. Some suggest this structural condition is a direct result of colonialism and the sustained extraction of resources from the periphery to the capitalist centre (Lange 2003; Mahoney 2003). While resource curse theories highlight the institutional limitations of resource-rich countries as an intrinsic feature of Third World (periphery) states, world historical approaches combine spatial and temporal dimensions with natural, biogeophysical constraints on social agency.

World historical approaches view states as constituted in relational terms within a global hierarchy of nation-states. In this global hierarchy, states and markets are interwoven in a complex chain of commodity production and consumption, structured by the differential power relations between public and private actors. Stephen Bunker and his colleagues produced the most extensive analysis of extractivism and commodity production from a world historical approach, examining how some states with initial comparative advantages—through control over technology, scientific innovation, and coercive power—have retained their dominant position in world trade (Barham et al. 1994; Bunker 1984; Bunker and Ciccantell 2005). From their perspective, markets, technologies, and geographical characteristics are influential factors reshaping the chain of commodity production and consumption, in which nature-based industries appear to face both opportunities and constraints in the extraction, transport, processing, marketing, and distribution of natural resource value chains. These economic processes are structured by the uneven power relations between capitalist states in the centre who can manipulate matter and space—thanks to their advanced technological position in the world economy—and the periphery which are positioned as raw materials producer without the capacity to create value-added in their exports beyond simple processing of natural resources.

An important revision of the world historical approaches has been articulated by Paul Gellert (2010; 2012), who combined its structuralist account with commodity-based approaches to explain the success of resource-based

38 Business of the State

economies. Using Indonesia as a case study, Gellert (2010) challenges existing interpretations of Indonesia as a successful example of inclusive growth through manufacturing and agriculture that lifted millions of poor through pro-poor, pro-rural spending.[8] Indonesia is best described as an 'extractive regime', wherein *multiple* natural resources constitute the basis of production and accumulation of value, and in contrast to countries cursed with resources, its political and economic growth regime can withstand crises and last for years if not decades (Gellert 2010, 30). Importantly, extractive regimes have four distinguishing features, which deviate from traditional developmental states of East Asia. Firstly, their reliance on multiple commodities (as opposed to one or two primary raw materials) means that the state can tap fiscal revenues without necessarily building a meritocratic bureaucracy or even pockets of state effectiveness. And, given that effective state capacity is not central in collecting mineral revenues, extractive regimes experience a growth trajectory that significantly deviates from the manufacturing-led industrialization characterizing East Asian and Western European countries.

Secondly, as a consequence of this feature, natural resources become a pillar of a country's development strategy, meaning that commodities become sources of domination and legitimation as new resource-producing countries have abandoned manufacturing-based industrialization in favour of export-oriented growth, justifying government intervention in determining rent allocation as a strategy of legitimation and in managing the political conflicts within the sector. As an exemplar, multiple Latin American governments moved towards an 'extractivist strategy' by combining redistributive policies with selective recognition of the sociocultural rights of local and indigenous communities (Arsel et al. 2016; Riofrancos 2020; Svampa and Viale 2015), leading to a new type of 'compensatory state' that successfully manages resource conflicts without relinquishing commitment to extractivism (Gudynas 2020; 2016).

Thirdly, unlike heavy industries and manufacturing where footloose capital can move production based on the logic of globalization, extractive regimes are determined by their geoeconomic characteristics—enclave for minerals, extensive for fish and timber—leading to quite limited human intervention (Bebbington and Bury 2013). This, again, points to a strong role for states in the overall regulation of the industry. Finally, extractive regimes are *temporally specific* to the 20th century precisely because developing countries

---

[8] For a developmental state account of Indonesia see Henley (2012; 2015); Van Donge et al. (2012); Vu (2010a).

pursue commodity specialization due to the limited absorptive capacity of Third World states to successfully build labour-intensive manufacturing.

Interestingly, Latin American states appear to conform with such accounts. To begin with, the most important link between the region and the rest of the world was, and remains, its exportation of primary products (Bulmer-Thomas 2003, 14–15). Some countries traded products that had forward linkages, requiring further processing before export (e.g. cattle), but others exported only raw materials (e.g. bananas). Commodities that were extracted from the ground, e.g. guano, already required labour inputs, while others such as fertilizer and metal minerals required capital inputs before extraction can take place. Notwithstanding the diverse requirements of commodities exploitation, the structural distribution of state power between those with the capacity to add value and innovate in tradable goods is an important determinant within multiple routes towards export diversification and industrialization. Hence, the primary motivation in development policymaking was the need to respond to commodity price volatility and demands for export diversification, and, therefore, very few late-industrializing countries—e.g. Argentina, Brazil, Indonesia, Malaysia, and Turkey—became successful in forging a development pathway similar to industrialized countries which combined resource exploitation with manufacturing-led industrialization (Barbier 2012; Kohli 2004; Waldner 1999). For this reason, the future of extractive regimes is highly uncertain.

Unlike the resource curse literature which treats commodity-based development as an unsustainable strategy because of the intrinsic characteristics of primary commodities, world historical approaches pay attention to the limited capacity of Third World states in crafting autonomous development policies to overcome their dependency on natural resources. Peripheral states—already dealing with the socioeconomic dislocations brought forth by colonialism—are faced with structural constraints in achieving industrialization which has become more complex as globalization accelerates into the 21st century (Bunker 1984; 1988; 1996; Bunker and Ciccantell 2005). In this view the role of the state is as an intermediary between global capital and labour, acting as a conduit to attract FDI, tame disruptive labour forces, and regulate the adjustment process as countries fiercely seek to become competitive (Bunker and Cicantell 2003; 2005). As such, the durability of extractive regimes is based on a combination of regional, national, and commodity factors, which means that resource growth strategies co-exist in both periods of developmentalism and neoliberal globalization (Gellert 2010). Economic growth through natural resource extraction can thus yield towards self-directed national development with intensive commodity production.

40   Business of the State

And with economic globalization accelerating into the 21st century, states have reinforced their export strategy to seek new comparative advantages.

Nevertheless, a fundamental limitation of world historical and commodity-based literature rests on its level of analysis, namely the systemic, interdependent nature of the world economy. While these perspectives offer an important corrective to the general neglect regarding the commodification of nature and its implication for state power, it simply does not go far enough in exploring state agency under contexts of structural constraints. Perhaps strikingly, despite their focus on capitalist accumulation, there is relatively less reflection on the impacts of neoliberalism as a critical juncture that restructured the relationship between states and markets, and between states and society. It certainly does not account for multiple possibilities of state-led approaches to development. As this book suggests, there are multiple trajectories of developmental outcomes and emerging relationships between states, global capital, and state-owned companies. By neglecting this triangular relationship, scholars instead make assumptions about SOEs and their respective development strategy. It also ignores the myriad of institutional innovations in the developing world in response to the recent commodity boom (2003–2012), including the process of institutional learning around rent allocation, savings, and expenditure, as well as industrial policy through the natural resource sector (Morris et al. 2012; Mosley 2012; Orihuela 2013; Ovadia 2016). This book examines policy transformations in a more nuanced way, generating a theoretical explanation of why some resource-intensive economies use SOEs to undertake policies towards structural economic transformation, whilst others remain locked into primary commodity production. Neither the resource curse and rentier state theories nor world historical approaches to commodity production can account for the emergence of a development strategy in Brazil and Chile that is specialized on commodity production. To explain this model, it is crucial that we revisit the political agency of states and investigate the policy changes linked to natural-resource-based development.

What We Do Not Know: Institutional Change in Natural Resource-Intensive Regimes

The extant literature on natural resource extraction has focussed on either the unique political economy features of commodities or the structural embeddedness of differentiated power and economic inequality in the international economic system. However, serious lacunae exist in these conventional approaches to understanding the role of states in natural-resource-based growth, development strategies, and institutional development. Firstly, the literature on systemic and geographical determinants of natural-resource-based development prioritizes exogenous factors, which leaves little room for discussion of domestic-level explanations for why resource-intensive economies design policies to ease the effects of commodity price volatility, corruption, and rent-seeking, as well as regulating global capital and FDI in favour of domestic capital formation and economic upgrading in the global value chains.

This book takes an innovative approach to natural resource governance and institutional development by analysing the interactions between natural resources, neoliberalism, and state ownership. The point of departure is the fact that neoliberal globalization cannot be divorced from long-run processes of institution building. While international financial institutions have advocated for specific types of economic liberalization (Cook 2007; Schneider 2004b), some countries deliberately retained state control or even expanded government intervention in strategic sectors, thereby becoming a political glue to bind together political coalitions supportive of economic liberalization (Etchemendy 2011). However, the state interventions discussed in this book go well beyond the 'embedded neoliberalism'[9] of the 1990s, which emphasized supply-side measures focussed on purposive state intervention in producer-inputs markets while acceding to privatization of final-goods-producing industries. Under the embedded neoliberalism model, free market reforms have been accompanied by continuous state presence in the banking, energy, utilities, infrastructure, and corporate insurance industries to manipulate their costs directly (Kurtz and Brooks 2008, 240). This contention about state ownership goes beyond embedding cooperation and coordination between industry and government, as shown by Kurtz and Books (2008) in Costa Rica and Colombia. Instead, this book asserts that the Brazil and Chile cases analysed in the empirical chapters of the book represent instances of *state dominance* combining regulatory frameworks, placing emphasis on the balance between state control and pursuit of FDI on the one

---

[9] Kurtz and Brooks (2008, 238–244) explain embedded neoliberalism as a strategy of state-mediated international integration, emphasizing the stimulation of the production side of the economy by changing the supply and cost of capital and labour. Supply-side policies encompass support for education and technological development, as well as industrial promotion measures and public service provision, which markedly differ from industrial policy under the protectionist era. Such open economy industrial policies (Schrank and Kurtz 2005) rest heavily on a compensatory logic by seeking to offset the costs for new exporters from market imperfections imposed by the ISI or hypothetical free market alternative (Kurtz and Brooks 2008, 239). However, this interventionist strategy is not *downward* redistributive due to its uneven benefits in favour of better-off skilled workers and export-oriented business owners rather than the poorest and most vulnerable in society.

42   Business of the State

hand, while maintaining an arms-length relationship between governments and SOEs on the other hand. Hence, this book also asserts the permanent desire of national governments to control strategic sectors—notably O&G and mining—through claims of resource sovereignty, national security, or economic development.

A second lacuna in the literature stems from a generalized disconnect between natural-resource-based growth policies aimed at counteracting the effects of the resource curse and the broader developmental strategy of natural-resource-intensive states. If developing countries are heavily reliant on natural resources for capital accumulation and in raising general standards of living, we need a framework that explains institutional complementarities between natural resource extraction and industrialization, and how regulatory frameworks impact on a country's development strategy. In this instance, one cannot assume that the logic of globalization—contextualized historically and institutionally—remains without contestation in resource-intensive states, especially given the legacies of natural resource sovereignty and developmentalism in the 20th century. While states may opt for privatization of SOEs if the regulatory framework relies on private sector rents, conversely, states with high-performing SOEs may seek to refashion their regulatory institutions to make public and private capital accumulation possible (Nem Singh 2014; Pickup 2018).

This book seeks to explain the consolidation of a growth strategy built around SOEs. Figure 2.1 illustrates the two-stage argument of the book—firstly, that there has been a shift towards neoliberalism in natural resource governance in Latin America *without* the privatization of extractive SOEs; and secondly, that the retention of SOEs in the liberalization period took place amidst regulatory reforms aimed at embracing FDI and private investment in strategic O&G and mining sectors. Analysing the unique development strategies pursued in Brazil and Chile, the book offers a wider explanation as regards why states decide to maintain full control over their SOEs rather than privatize them, and what sort of reforms are implemented to retain the developmental functions of SOEs.

The argument considers the interactions between state ownership and neoliberalism in political economy scholarship focussed on traditional policy fields including macro-economic policy, monetary policy, finance, labour and employment, social protection, and industrialization (Brooks 2004; 2015; Brooks and Kurtz 2012; Cook 2007; Schrank and Kurtz 2005). In this literature, theory-building on the path-shaping influence of neoliberalism has focussed on (1) patterns of market reform negotiations and coalition building to accommodate the logic of globalization (Etchemendy 2011;

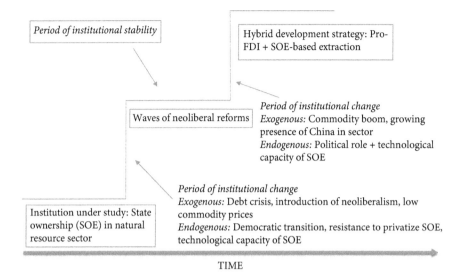

Figure 2.1 Pattern of institutional stability and change in natural resource governance.

Murillo 2001; 2009); (2) institutional creation and organizational reforms in the context of neoliberal adjustment (Amengual 2016; Brinks et al. 2020; Teichman 2003); and (3) resistance and contestation of reforms from below (Oxhorn and Ducatenzeiler 1998; Rossi 2017; E. Silva 2009). The contention behind the argument presented here rests on the lack of political economy analysis examining how commodity exports are taking a leading role in reformulating development strategies amidst the failure of reindustrialization from the 1990s onwards. Furthermore, no systematic account of the interactions between developmentalism and neoliberalism has yet been published in the context of natural resource governance. Either scholars assume a linear pathway towards privatization and market competition in the natural resource sector or that states uniformly embrace the logic of globalization to make up for the shortfall in capital and technology in natural resource extraction.[10]

The closest explanations developed from this literature on the path-shaping influence of neoliberalism are critical accounts of the resource curse and rentier state theories, which have generally dominated the natural-resources-development debate (Di John 2009; 2011; Jones and Weinthal 2010). This book builds on the neoinstitutionalist tradition in comparative

---

[10] However, there are some exceptions (e.g. Shever 2012; Toninelli 2000; Victor et al. Thurber 2012). Haslam and Heidrich (2016) also explicitly bridge neoliberalism and resource governance.

politics and political economy, which examines the role of political bargaining and institutional preconditions for a stable regime of accumulation (Bebbington et al. 2018; Saylor 2014; Thorp et al. 2012). However, the framework (analytical approach and theoretical grounding) presented in the following section departs from these perspectives because the analysis of institutional complementarities and state transformation is grounded in state–state (SOE) relations, examining not only state–foreign capital relations but also the place of SOEs in the political system. As Figure 2.1 suggests, market reforms must be conceived in two stages: firstly, as an exogenous factor implemented after the 1980s, and secondly, as an endogenous factor embedded into the political economy model which muted the tendency for outright nationalization as soon as commodity prices soared from 2003 onwards. Market reforms—in Brazil and Chile specifically—had mixed effects because of the presence of high-performing SOEs, thereby producing a hybrid model encompassing the pursuit of FDI and maintaining state authority in strategic sectors. The next section outlines the historical institutionalist framework used in this book to explain institutional stability and change in Latin American natural resource governance, specifically how twin objectives of attracting foreign capital and asserting political authority in strategic industries meld together in the attempts of state elites to craft a cohesive development strategy.

Historical Institutionalism as an Analytical Approach

The argument presented in Figure 2.1 draws explicitly from recent theories of institutional change inspired by historical institutionalism (HI). This book takes a broad definition of institutions, defined as 'humanly devised constraints that structure human interactions' (North 1990, 98–99), and, like Douglass North, it encompasses the range of regulatory laws and organizations (property rights, mining code, and contract regimes) constitutive of 'resource governance' institutions. Accordingly, institutions—as Hall (1986, 19) explicates—encompass 'formal rules, compliance procedures, and standard operating practices that structure the relationship between individuals in various units of the polity and economy'. Unlike scholars who conceive institutions as a means of reducing transaction costs, my approach places context, political conflicts, and history as key defining features of institutions. Through this approach, I highlight SOEs as *change agents* actively shaping the rules of the strategic O&G and mining sectors. For this purpose, I am interested in 'state–state (SOE)' relations, as opposed to industry and government, which are typically discussed in studies of open economy industrial policy and market liberalization (Brooks and Kurtz 2007; Cook 2007; Schamis 2002; Schneider 2004b; Schrank and Kurtz 2005).

Briefly, the HI framework fits in this project in three ways. Firstly, within the universe of new institutionalism in political science,[11] rational choice institutionalism has universalistic ambitions that place excessive emphasis on electoral rules and parliamentary politics in analysing Latin American politics (Weyland 2002), which fails to account for the role of institutional legacies and political conflicts in exploring the state–state (SOE) relationship.[12] In its attempt to offer parsimony and elegance, rational choice institutionalism neglects the autonomy of the state and the complex relationship among bureaucrats and politicians in exercising control over policymaking.[13] The emphasis on formal rules also renders the approach incapable of elucidating crisis politics (Weyland 2002, 64–65, 73).[14] While self-interest and strategic calculations are clearly important in Latin American politics, this logic of action fails to explain why SOEs were left untouched by Chilean and Brazilian elites despite simultaneous exogenous pressures and endogenous incentives towards wholesale privatization and foreign participation in natural resource industries.[15] As Figure 2.1 shows, endogenous factors—democratic transition forcing coalition building among elites, resistance by organized labour against privatizing strategic SOEs, and emergent technological capacities of SOEs—are key driving forces behind the wave of market reforms that did not necessarily lead to full sale of state assets in the 1990s. With the logic of competition deeply embedded in SOEs, their managers were interested in transforming SOEs into national champions, and by embracing profitability as a key objective again, governments actively supported resource sovereignty alongside the pursuit of FDI from 2003 onwards.

Secondly, the HI approach goes furthest in elucidating the bargaining process among contending actors as neoliberal reforms are presented to business

---

[11] For an overview see Immergut (1998); Kang (2014); Thelen (1999).

[12] Nevertheless, rational choice institutionalism has filled in important gaps in comparative politics by way of developing rigorous analysis about formal rules, electoral designs, and congressional manoeuvrings as causal factors in institutional life.

[13] However, see Pollack (1996) for an attempt to use the non-formal rational choice approach to institutional change.

[14] Some examples of rational choice institutionalism include Ames (1995); Geddes (1996); Morgenstern and Nacif (2002). Interestingly, Berrios et al. (2011) map out different policies of hydrocarbons nationalization in Latin America using a carefully formulated rational choice framework.

[15] Comparative politics scholars have recognized the need for cross-fertilization, exemplified in Wendy Hunter's work that shifted from a pure rational choice approach to explain the role of the military in policymaking towards a synthesis of rational choice and historical institutionalism to discuss the rise and consolidation of power of the Workers' Party in Brazil (Hunter 1997; 2010; see also Ames 2001).

46 Business of the State

and labour actors, and the degree to which these policies have been success-fully implemented (Etchemendy 2011; Murillo 2001; Schamis 2002). In this approach, political time constitutes a vital link to causal explanation; that is to say, *when* and *in what order* events occurred impact upon institutional life. Neoinstitutionalist literature has identified two dimensions upon which institutional change can be explained: (1) the sources of change (endogenous vs. exogenous); and (2) the time horizon by which the cause of change oper-ates (sudden vs. gradual)—which when combined can offer new insights as regards the nature of institutional change (Gerschewski 2020; Koning 2016; Mahoney and Thelen 2009; Rixen and Viola 2014). This book contributes to building theoretical insights on institutional change by examining the dis-tinctive factors that explain both the content and pace of institutional reforms constitutive of development strategies over a 30-year period.

Finally, given its emphasis on macro-processes rather than micro-level behavioural patterns, the HI approach confers political agency to the state, meaning this perspective recognizes how state actors powerfully alter polit-ical outcomes through a complex array of bureaucratic institutions (Brian 2005; Campbell 2001; Hall 1989; 1993; Hay 2001; 2011; Thelen 1999). Specifically, I make a distinction between policy elites in charge of regulatory reform processes and SOE managers who face the dual challenge of respond-ing to political pressures from state elites and promoting SOE profitability for long-run survival. As Evans (1995, 18) rightly notes, the state cannot be reduced to an aggregate of the individual interests of state actors, the vector sum of political forces, or the condensed expression of the logic of economic necessity. My emphasis on state–state (SOE) relations uncovers new relation-ships among state actors as a state-mediated globalization strategy becomes a dominant policy template for developing countries.

A Theory of Institutional Stability and Change

The advance of HI in political economy scholarship comes from the demand to incorporate history in explaining contemporary development outcomes. Specifically, process-tracing the evolution of state activism and the role of SOEs in industrial growth can explain the divergent pathways of Latin Amer-ican states away from neoliberalism towards policies to take advantage of the commodity boom. Thus, to analyse the hybrid resource governance model combining strategic state ownership and pro-FDI incentives in Brazil and Chile the book examines *continuity and change* in the pursuit of pragmatic economic reforms. The argument is as follows (see also Figure 2.2). In Phase

1, Latin American states were subject to pressures for convergence towards neoliberalism in the 1990s (as indeed were many resource-rich countries). Until this period, we can affirm a general trend in the region, whereby a shift from state-led developmentalism towards neoliberalism took place across countries and sectors. As the political economy scholarship explains, neoliberalism served as a critical juncture for the change in development paradigm.[16] Latin America was impacted by exogenous shocks—low commodity prices, debt crisis, and a general exposure to free market orthodoxy from the US and UK—as well as endogenous factors—notably a political transition to democracy, retained expertise of some high-performing SOEs, and societal rejection of privatization—leading to institutional change drifting away from old developmentalism, but not an entirely wholesale convergence towards the idealized neoliberal model. In this context, economic globalization also became a dominant force that eclipsed the possibility of returning to industrial policy or other forms of state-sponsored growth models. However, as Figure 2.2 details, idiosyncratic factors mostly derived from historical legacies and country-specific circumstances have led to *divergence* in patterns of adaptation to globalization. As countries sought institutional stability in the context of neoliberal globalization, political elites embraced distinctive SOE reforms suitable for their domestic needs. As Nem Singh (2014, 330) points out, the 'logic of globalization' often elevated as a dominant force shaping the fate of developing countries in the global political economy is in fact muted in very specific ways. While this globalizing 'logic' is an important socializing factor in globalization, its power is refracted in different directions through the domestic configurations within societies, such that the specific constellations of social and political forces are embedded historically and institutionally.

To put it differently, Brazil and Chile embraced distinctive but hybrid institutional arrangements in managing the commodity boom (2002–2012) based on the continuity of the historical relationship between national elites and their state enterprises. As noted in Figure 2.2, Chile pursued a trajectory promoting neoliberalism in its strategic mining sector—through a pro-FDI and pro-mining capital tax regime—while retaining 100% ownership of Codelco. In so doing, the state enterprise maintains economic control over Chile's

---

[16] Critical juncture is defined as 'periods of contingency in history during which constraints on actions are lifted or eased, enabling agents to exercise greater weight over institutional constraints in affecting political outcomes' (Capoccia and Kelemen 2007; Rixen and Viola 2014). However, the notion of critical juncture goes beyond the historical institutionalist school in political science and originates from economics. The literature sought to initially explain how self-reinforcing processes and feedback mechanisms have reproduced regularized patterns of economic behaviour that over time generated stable institutional equilibrium (Arthur 1989; David 1985).

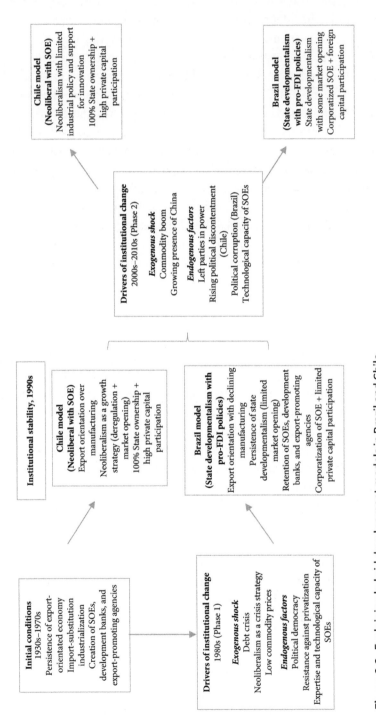

Figure 2.2 Explaining hybrid development models in Brazil and Chile.

high-quality reserves, thereby exercising autonomy over the pace and quantity of copper mineral extraction—a key competitive advantage that other copper producers do not possess. Conversely, Brazil embraced market opening reforms—notably giving international oil companies (IOCs) access to the upstream segment of the O&G value chain—while ensuring that Petrobras became an internationally competitive energy player.

In Phase 2, institutional stability and change co-vary with how actors respond to their changing exogenous and endogenous factors. With commodity prices reaching a new record high, novel forces driving institutional change shaped decision-making in resource-rich countries (Jepson 2020). With the growing presence of the Chinese state and Chinese capital in competition with US and European capital, resource-rich countries found themselves with new opportunities to reassert political authority in their natural resource industries, and with this externally induced change, some elites were motivated to pursue alternative pathways from neoliberal orthodoxy (Gallagher 2016; Gallagher and Porzekanski 2010; Nem Singh 2014; 2018, 539–544; Nem Singh and Bourgouin 2013, 4–6;). Of course, Jepson (2020) makes clear that similar opportunities do not imply convergence in development strategies; and as such, political elites responded differently to the China-induced commodity boom.

Some countries like Argentina and Brazil sought to carve spaces for national autonomous development, while others were caught with redistributive struggles and patronage inhibiting the articulation of a coherent development strategy. With these varying policy responses came quite uneven outcomes in realizing their growth potentials through natural resource exploitation. To be clear, other factors played a sizeable role in determining success—for example, the size of an economy, history of industrialization and presence of a strong domestic capitalist class, degree of autonomy of governments and planning agencies, among many others—all of which contributed to the pathways chosen by their national leaders (Brooks and Kurtz 2016; Jenkins 2018; Kurtz 2001).

Overall, the framework detailed in this chapter moves away from conventional Latin American political economy scholarship about the rise and fall of the Left. According to this perspective, the commodity boom is seen as a critical juncture that enabled Centre-Left political parties to take power, articulate programmes of social redistribution, and seek to tackle inequality as their platform for change (Levitsky and Roberts 2011; Philip and Panizza 2011; Weyland et al. 2010). This book departs from this narrative in two ways. Firstly, although the political economy scholarship recognizes the centrality of extractivism as a development strategy, the analysis has often

50   Business of the State

overlooked how the 2002 price surge demotivated elites to invest in manufacturing, instead moving towards commodity specialization as a pillar of their development policy (Andreucci 2016; Bebbington et al. 2018; Gudynas 2020). The empirical cases included in this book add a more fine-grained analysis of the political economy of development. By process-tracing how Codelco and Petrobras have adjusted both to neoliberalism *and* commodity price volatility in designing their business strategies from the 1990s to 2010s, I show that Brazil and Chile with relatively efficient SOEs still evaded investments in the manufacturing sector that could have salvaged their national economies from the inevitable price collapse that followed in 2013.

Secondly, and in relation to the point above, Brazil and Chile exhibit unique patterns of institution building aimed at crafting strong interventionist economic policies to support their domestic capitalist classes alongside the creation of a consensus over the necessity of a highly technocratic state as the answer to the industrialization question (Ferraro and Centeno 2018; Leão 2018; Silva 2008; 2018). Spurred by elite consensus towards technocracy, the political climate of the 20th century enabled the establishment of a professional bureaucracy and 'pockets of efficiency' within the state (Evans 1979; 1995). What has often been forgotten by the political economy literature, however, is that SOEs were born out of this political movement. Over time, highly autonomous and internationally competitive state companies emerged, which became extremely challenging to be privatized in Brazil and Chile. Put simply, technical expertise—achieved through decades of investment in SOEs—became a formidable obstacle to privatization and, with the rise of the Left in power, provided the ideological justification to maintain SOEs even at high costs for the state. In effect, institutional factors have influenced the consolidation of two distinctive models—neoliberalism with state ownership (Chile) and state developmentalism with foreign capital participation (Brazil). But, for this hybrid resource governance model to emerge, SOEs must survive the pressures of privatization. The final section below theorizes patterns of corporate governance reforms as an endogenous factor shaping the hybrid development model.

State Ownership as a Globalization Strategy

In stressing the role of agency in institutional change, this book emphasizes 'state–state (SOE) relations' as a conceptual leverage to explain state transformation in the context of neoliberal globalization. As Chapters 6 and 8 illustrate, managers of SOEs have actively played a role in shaping the trajectory of their relationship with national governments. With the crisis of state developmentalism leading to the rise of neoliberalism fundamentally challenging the role of the state in development, market reforms fell short of eliminating SOEs and freeing markets from the shackles of state intervention. Instead, new ideas about the role of governments in economic life shifted away from whether state intervention is legitimate, towards a question of *how far* and *in what ways* should states participate in innovation and other matters in the context of global market integration (Breznitz 2007; Limoeiro and Schneider 2019; Mazzucato 2013; 2016; Mazzucato and Penna 2015).

Historically, SOEs were created as both political and economic weapons— a means of asserting political authority over strategic industries. Since their inception, state enterprises have fallen under the jurisdiction of the state economic bureaucracy and are characterized by a 'distinctive bureaucratic governance structure, distinctive management and incentive mechanisms, and a set of provision of social services and welfare' (Brian 2005, 1). While economists have debated the merits of public enterprises for efficiency and in generating long-run economic growth (Krueger 2002; Trebat 1983), political scientists have emphasized how SOEs act as a political entity, who are part of a historical process and have become actors in their own right involved in decision-making.[17] By contrast, developmental state scholarship only recently examined SOEs as a means of reordering and restructuring the institutional environment in pursuit of new comparative advantages (Nem Singh 2022). Concurrently, the success of Chinese economic reforms has produced a swathe of scholarship explaining the similarities and differences between SOEs in the 20th and 21st centuries. SOEs were often associated with socialist planning and command economies where the state had absolute power over ownership and control of the company (Kornai 1992; Shleifer 1998). However, SOEs are equally prevalent in Western Europe as a means of political control and geo-economic assertion during the 20th century (Amatori et al. 2018; Millward 2007; Toninelli 2000).

With the advent of economic globalization, there has been widespread disagreement over SOEs, leading to at least three distinctive viewpoints, not necessarily exclusive from each other, which permeate policy and intellectual debates on state ownership. Firstly, the *social view* suggests that a massive public sector can address market imperfections that leave socially profitable investments underfinanced (Atkinson and Stiglitz 2015; Stiglitz 1993). Secondly, the *development view* emphasizes the necessity for public

---

[17] For example, Brian (2005) argues that the post-1949 state enterprise system in China reflects the institutional response of national elites to the sustained systemic crisis precipitated by the Japanese occupation of Manchuria and large-scale invasion during 1935–1945.

investments—and state interventions more widely—in circumstances where there exists scarce capital, and public distrust of private actors, and where endemic fraudulent practices persist among debtors. All these situations provide good reasons for governments to undertake comprehensive and large-scale investments in the economy (Gerscherkron 1962; Stiglitz 2002). Finally, the *political view* contends that the creation of public-owned banks and SOEs is a function of politicians' interests to appropriate rents derived from the control of financial institutions (La Porta et al. 2002). Thus, public interventions are potentially harmful because government funding may lead to wasteful use of financial resources. These three institutional logics are not always mutually exclusive, and policymakers have often used a combination of these narratives to justify their policy decisions.

Among economists, a strong case has been made about why private enterprises are better than SOEs when it comes to economic efficiency and productivity. Firstly, SOEs are only subject to 'soft budget constraints' (Kornai 1979; 1986; Kornai et al. 2003). Despite their moral and financial interest to maximize profits, SOEs are chronic loss-makers that can survive despite losses due to bail outs, financial subsidies, or other instruments. For Musacchio and Pineda Ayerbe (2019, 4–8), fiscal governance problems persist as a result of the discretionary and opportunistic nature of the financial relationship between SOEs and national governments. A mutually reinforcing rentier behaviour characterizes their fiscal pact: while SOEs enjoy wide discretion to request resources leading to soft budget constraints, governments can utilize SOEs for quasi-fiscal operations. Specifically, governments may ask SOEs to sell their goods at below-market prices, generate potential losses, or undertake high-risk projects beneficial for those in power but not necessarily for the SOE (Musacchio et al. 2015).

Secondly, from a property rights perspective, when a company has no clear residual claimant (i.e. no entity can claim the benefits or surplus), it tends to run less efficiently because there is no incentive for the stakeholders to hold the managers accountable for their performance. In other words, there are no mechanisms to discipline the agents (managers) whenever profits are not maximized (Barzel 1997; Vickers and Yarrow 1988). Conversely, the presence of public and private stakeholders in SOEs generates multiple, conflicting interests that can create a gap between the objectives and operational management of the companies.

Thirdly, public choice theories suggest that the exercise of control over the SOE by government bureaucrats and SOE state managers can further their sectoral interests but not necessarily the efficiency of the SOE (Buchanan et al. 1980). Importantly, governments have an interest to maintain non-commercial goals like employment generation and welfare distribution, which can create a tight-knit relationship between governments and SOEs. With SOEs viewed as tools for rent-seeking and unproductive investment of government revenues (Di John 2009; Krueger 1974), negatively correlating state ownership with economic performance using measures of private sector efficiency is used to gauge the commercial performance of SOEs.[18]

Prior to Chinese pursuit of state capitalism, restructuring public enterprises had been ideologically framed in terms of neoclassical economics, whereby scholars ask *how far* privatization should be pushed in public sectors rather than rethinking whether SOEs can become agents of industrial development. By the 2000s, it had become clear that state capitalism (see also Chapter 10) was returning to mainstream economic debates because Brazil, China, and Turkey—not to mention East Asian countries where strategic sectors remain under the control of states—had not fully relinquished state ownership as a development strategy (see Figures 2.3 and 2.4). To explain this empirical contradiction to theoretical prescriptions, it is worth mentioning the fact that SOEs come in different forms and sizes: for example, Petrobras

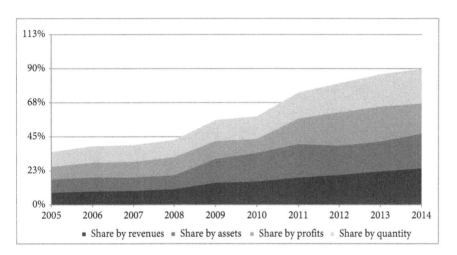

Figure 2.3 Shares of SOEs on Fortune Global 500 list.
Source: Kwiatkowski and Augustynowicz (2016, 1743) in Nem Singh and Chen (2018, 1079).

---

[18] Shirley (1999, 115) defines privatization as 'the sale of state-owned assets; a company is no longer state-owned when management control—measured as the right to appoint the managers and board of directors—passes to private shareholders'. By contrast, corporatization is defined as 'the efforts to make SOEs operate as if they were private companies facing a competitive market, or if monopolies, efficient regulation'.

54 Business of the State

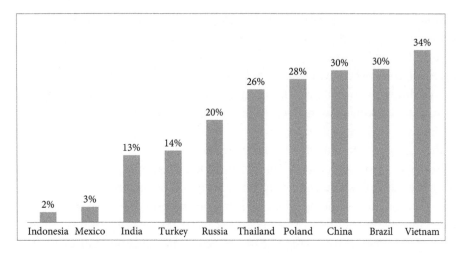

Figure 2.4 SOE output to GDP in selected emerging markets.
Source: Musacchio and Lazzarini (2014, 7) in Nem Singh and Chen (2018, 1080).

in Brazil and *Petróleos Mexicanos* (Pemex) are large SOEs in terms of operations and domestic market power, while others have substantive revenue shares as a percentage of total SOE contribution (e.g. Codelco in Chile contributes about 60% of total SOE revenues) (Musacchio and Pineda Ayerbe 2019, 10, 18). Hence, performance and leverage of SOEs can only be understood not by comparing their relative efficiency with private companies as most business studies often do[19], but by analysing their developmental roles and strategies, and how SOE managers continue to pursue them over a longer time horizon.

Theorizing Corporate Governance Reforms in SOEs

While the worldwide neoliberal trend towards privatization and market competition in the 1980s and 1990s increased the pressure to asset-strip the nation-state, efforts to privatize SOEs have been incomplete and disparate. In many cases, this pressure was widely resisted not just by trade unions but also by SOE managers, segments of national political elites, and society writ large. Although a substantial shift towards privatization took place in public utilities, telecommunications, and transportation, most strategic industries

---

[19] See Musacchio and Lazzarini (2014); Musacchio and Pineda Ayerbe (2019); Musacchio et al. (2015). These studies admit some problems when analysing SOEs: (1) comparing net incomes between SOEs and private companies is difficult; and (2) private companies competing with SOEs operate in highly regulated environments (Musacchio and Pineda Ayerbe 2019, 21–24).

were—and remain until today—in the hands of national states and regional governments. Specifically, SOEs remain dominant in key sectors, such as infrastructure including airports, electricity, ports, and telecommunications, and natural resources such as O&G (Musacchio and Pineda Ayerbe 2019). Hence, SOEs continue to thrive because they have evolved into a hybrid organization incorporating elements from the different institutional logics of private and state ownership, thereby sharply distinguishing these SOEs from their inefficient predecessors that proliferated in the 20th century (Bruton et al. 2014, 92–94; Pache and Santos 2012, 972–973).

As a result of liberalization reforms, many SOEs have been transformed through public enterprise reforms promoted by the Organisation for Economic Co-operation and Development (OECD) and other international financial institutions, leading to institutional changes over *ownership* and *control*. SOEs are hybrid organizations which thrive in complex environments. They are exposed to multiple institutional logics over an extended length of time, thereby enmeshing incompatible logics into a single institutional template while crafting a coalitional base to resolve institutional conflicts from within (Pache and Santos 2010; 2013, 973). In line with this approach, Nem Singh and Chen (2018, 1082–1084) outline the two axes of institutional reconfiguration of state–state (SOE) relations: (1) the degree of capital ownership in the SOE, or majority vs. minority shareholder ownership; and (2) whether institutional control over SOE operations is centralized or decentralized. In this way, by separating ownership from control in a post-liberal arrangement, SOEs can overcome the principal-agency dilemma.[20]

Table 2.1 maps out corporate governance reforms which capture the new SOE models found in emerging markets (Bruton et al. 2013). In the first set of reforms (axe 1), state companies have been subject to partial privatization or *corporatization*, which leads to either a majority or minority shareholder ownership structure. In a majority shareholder structure, the state holds at least 51% ownership, giving the state direct control over SOE assets and thus maintaining the influence of governments in corporate decision-making. In a minority shareholder structure, the state maintains an arms-length relationship with SOEs in which state assets—and its direct influence over decision-making—are considerably reduced. Company decisions are left to

---

[20] State ownership fails to resolve the principal agency dilemma inherent among SOEs when there are no private shareholders. With the state as the principal agent, if problems of accountability arise it is very difficult to penalize mistakes, and citizens suffer when SOEs underperform but no one is held to account— but this also reflects the diversity of state–state (SOE) relations in emerging markets capturing both the political relationship between states and SOEs and the process of mitigating institutional conflicts within the state apparatus.

56 Business of the State

Table 2.1 Typology of SOE reforms.

		Form of state control	
		Centralized	Decentralized
Degree of state ownership	Majority	Government centralizes the monitoring of SOEs under one government agency or holding company—usually requires the creation of a central SOE agency or a department of SOEs to undertake monitoring, evaluation, and sometimes privatization of state assets.[a] SOE controlled by state through 50% or more ownership of shareholder capital. *Examples*: Brazil's Petrobras, Russia's Aeroflot, China's Chery Automobil	Government leaves the monitoring, evaluation, and supervision of the SOE to managers, offering managers very wide latitude over reporting and pursuit of multiple objectives.[b] SOE controlled by state through 50% or more ownership of shareholder capital. *Examples*: New Zealand's Solid Energy, Singapore's STATS ChipPAC Ltd, US' Alaska Railroad Corporation
	Minority	Government centralizes the monitoring of SOEs under one government agency or holding company—usually requires the creation of a central SOE agency or a department of SOEs to undertake monitoring, evaluation, and sometimes privatization of state assets. SOE is a mixed enterprise with a predominant private shareholder; usually state ownership is diversified, but 'golden shares' are retained by the government to ensure control over the SOE. This is oftentimes synonymous to *corporatization* or *partial privatization* of state assets. *Examples*: Brazil's Vale and Embraer, China's Dazhong Transport, Russia's Rosgosstrakh	Government leaves the monitoring, evaluation, and supervision of the SOE to managers, offering managers very wide latitude over reporting and pursuit of multiple objectives. SOE is a mixed enterprise with a predominant private shareholder; usually state ownership is diversified, but 'golden shares' are retained by the government to ensure control over the SOE. This is oftentimes synonymous to *corporatization* or *partial privatization* of state assets. *Examples*: Portugal's Galp Energia, Kuwait's United Arab Shipping Company, South Korea's Hanna Financial Group

Source: Nem Singh and Chen (2018, 1083) adapted from Bruton et al. (2014, 101).

[a] The OECD and World Bank recommend the centralized model of control as a way of reducing the multiple-principals problem, by enabling governments to introduce ex-ante procedures to monitor SOE state managers' behaviour, and to standardize financial reporting, procurement rules, and so on.
[b] The decentralized approach was used in the 1960s and 1980s because it allowed states to pursue industrial policy as a result of corporate autonomy. However, decentralized control also exacerbated the multiple-principals problem and non-standardized procedures over financial reporting and auditing.

professional managers, often through a CEO and Board of Directors, according more emphasis on profit-making as the fundamental driving force behind the management of the SOE. In highly sensitive industries like mining, the state might seek to still extend influence even if only indirectly. An important policy in such circumstances includes the issuance of 'golden shares', which are special capital shares providing national governments with the right to outvote or block specific decisions of private shareholders as typically outlined in company charters (Nem Singh and Chen 2018, 1082). However, unlike majority ownership structures, these golden shares do not grant the state any right to influence the day-to-day management and decision-making of the company. It is worth pointing out that Codelco—the Chilean case study in this book (see Chapters 5 and 6)—maintains 100% state ownership despite the successive waves of privatization in Chile, giving the government direct and full control over the company's assets and management decisions. Petrobras, the Brazilian case study (see Chapters 7 and 8), has a majority shareholder structure, while former mining SOE giant Vale, airplane manufacturing company Embraer, and steel giant CSN all have a minority shareholder structure (Döring et al. 2017; Goldstein 2002; Guimarães, Eduardo. 2003; Foncesca Monteiro 2011; Massi 2014; Massi and Nem Singh 2016; 2020).

In the second set of reforms (axe 2), states have adopted reforms to solve their dilemma of how to insulate their SOEs from political interference, specifically by exploring alternative options to monitor and control the day-to-day management of the company. Here, states are faced with the need to adopt either a centralized or decentralized control-monitoring scheme. In a centralized control-monitoring scheme, the state exercises direct control through a state-owned holding company (SOHC),[21] central ministry, or regulatory agency to coordinate control across a range of SOEs in the economy, or exercise indirect control through state-owned financial institutions holding equity investments. The most prominent examples include the Temasak Holding Company in Singapore (SOHC), the BNDES' portfolio of investments (state-owned financial institutions) and the accompanying Department of State-Owned Enterprises (DEST) in Brazil, and the range

---

[21] An SOHC is defined as 'a parent company that either directly or individually controls the composition of the board of directors of its subsidiaries, or as a professionally managed institution owning a portfolio of stocks in public and private companies with the purpose of influencing them' (Kim 2019, 142). Crucially, an SOHC does not produce goods and services, but instead is involved in the management of SOEs as both a *financial intermediary* and an *active stakeholder*.

58 Business of the State

of policy finance institutions (PFIs) in Korea, notably the Korean Development Bank (Kim 2019; Maciel and Arvate 2010; Massi 2014; Thurbon 2016).[22] Most conspicuously, China's State-owned Assets Supervision and Administration Commission of the State Council (SASAC) represents the most successful example of centralized monitoring of state enterprises of various sizes across numerous sectors under a single government entity (Chen and Chen 2019; Nem Singh and Chen 2018). Overall, the idea is that national states seek to exercise control and monitoring through either a state company (SOHC), a centralized financial institution, or a regulatory agency, which effectively provides the government with a variety of instruments to influence SOE decision-making.[23]

By contrast, under a decentralized control-monitoring scheme, the government leaves the monitoring, evaluation, and supervision of SOEs to its professional managers and CEOs, offering managers very wide latitude over reporting and pursuit of multiple objectives. As Nem Singh and Chen (2018) note, a decentralized approach to SOE management enables specialization of knowledge and a closer working relationship between specific agencies and SOEs. Historically, this was justified as an effective way to pursue industrial policy given that policy coordination and sectoral learning can take place through the local networks of experts, entrepreneurs, and local state managers. As Table 2.1 shows, using the 2×2 matrix along the axes identified above, we can therefore establish four types of SOE reforms: (1) *centralized state control with majority ownership*, (2) *decentralized state control with majority ownership*, (3) *centralized state control with minority ownership*, and (4) *decentralized state control with minority ownership*, which the typology maps out using the work of Bruton et al. (2014), which encompasses a range

---

[22] PFIs are state-owned financial institutions whose main purpose is to lend or invest in Korean companies to advance government-set goals. PFIs provide low-interest loans to, or make investments in, Korean companies operating in 'strategic' sectors. Historically, such industries included steel, automobiles, and semiconductors; recently, the list encompasses renewable energy, intelligent robotics, and industrial components for smart devices (Thurbon 2016, 95, 186; Weiss and Thurbon 2020). The Korean Development Bank is one such PFI, which supported industrial policy by financing major industrial projects guided by the government in power since its inception in 1954. The Bank was also instrumental in financing the nationalized sectors under President Park Chung Hee (1963–1979). After the 1997 Asian Financial Crisis, the Bank was instrumental in supporting traditional large conglomerates—*chaebols*—and in providing financial support to non-chaebol companies. While financial liberalization between the 1980s and 1990s fractured the coherent system of financing under the developmentalist state, strategic industries and methods of financing potential winning sectors have remained heavily monitored and influenced by the Korean state (see Thurbon 2016, Chapters 6–9; Wade 2018).

[23] Since state-led financial activism encompasses the activities of both SOEs and private companies, Kim (2019, 148–149) argues that there are three different types of SOHCs: (1) corporate investor type, where the SOHC functions like a private institutional investor whose primary objective is profit maximization, and therefore bears no social or political mandate; (2) shadow investor type, where the SOHC focusses on operational efficiency but is concerned with both profit maximization and other policy goals mandated by the state; and (3) submissive investor type, under which the government has almost complete control over the subsidiaries and the SOHC is run like a government entity.

of sectors including natural resources, energy, finance, transportation, and manufacturing.[24]

In brief, the range of corporate governance reforms detailed above concern changes related to the institutional development of SOEs in strategic sectors. For example, at the macro-institutional level, reforms focussed on government ownership and control provide the rules and regulations to establish an arms-length relationship between the SOE and national government. At the micro-level, corporate governance reforms might also induce *internal* organizational changes within the SOE, such as enacting procedures to strengthen the office of the CEO whose authority and mindset influence the operations of the company, vis-à-vis the Board of Directors, which often comprises professionals and government ministers. These reforms are important in creating institutional environments that shape the corporate behaviour of state enterprises (see also Hall and Soskice 2001; Hancké et al. 2007).

However, these reform efforts to induce a private company mindset in a public entity only indirectly impact on the performance of SOEs. As the *Lava Jato* scandal vividly illustrates, corporate governance reforms seeking public actors to perform on par with private companies do not induce incentives for productivity. Because SOEs are ultimately public entities, more attention should be paid to the role of the government in setting the direction of SOEs, implementing industry-wide regulations to promote an equal-level playing field, and driving their techno-industrial competitiveness. As Chapter 9 will detail, we need to use a wider criterion in evaluating the performance of SOEs beyond profit maximization and, in so doing, a broader understanding of why states persistently reform SOEs without resorting to privatization.

Conclusions

The literature on the resource curse and rent-seeking has failed to account for the persistence of SOEs in strategic industries; generalized convergence towards neoliberalism within political economy scholarship likewise neglects the process of institutional change in resource-rich states. This theoretical chapter has outlined why we need to study patterns of institutional stability and change in order to understand why strategic extractive

---

[24] Bruton et al. (2014) deliberately chose the cases to include a diverse range of industries with mixture of ownership and control. Unlike the cases I examine here in this book, all their case studies are based on three important criteria: (1) all cases are not directly linked to national security, thereby giving the option for governments to divest state assets without considerable political opposition; (2) all cases are subject to market competition and industry concentration is modest; and (3) all the companies can be compared in the same industry, while showing variations of ownership and control.

SOEs like Petrobras and Codelco have developed specific relationships with their national governments and, with their historically constituted role, have enabled elites to craft a hybrid development strategy in the mining (Codelco) and O&G (Petrobras) sectors. Chapter 3 presents the evolution of the Latin American developmental state, taking the case of Venezuela as an example of resource-based industrialization strategy. In Chapter 4, I present the historical construction and the politics of managing SOEs in Chile and Brazil throughout the 20th century. Chapters 5–8 analyse the regulatory reforms undertaken in Chile (Chapter 5) and Brazil (Chapter 7), as well as the internal restructuring of Codelco (Chapter 6) and Petrobras (Chapter 7 and 8) in response to the globalization strategy of their national governments. In so doing, the book will show the rise of a hybrid development model, which combines continuity of regulatory reforms in the mining (Chile) and O&G (Brazil) industries and changes to SOE governance to enhance their competitiveness and to respond to the challenge of economic globalization between the 1990s and 2010s.

PART II

STATE OWNERSHIP IN BRAZIL AND CHILE

3
The Rise and Fall of Public Enterprises in Latin America in the 20th Century

This chapter aims to address two questions: first, why and how did states in Latin America consolidate an SOE-led growth model in their strategic natural resource sectors; and second, what were the hard limits of this SOE-based growth that paved the way for the implementation and dominance of neoliberalism in the region between 1980s and early 2000s? To answer these questions, this chapter places an emphasis on the central role of natural resources in Latin America's history of industrial development, specifically the significance of SOEs in developing *indigenous* industrial capacity and human capital stocks in the region. Historically, Latin America's large endowments of oil and mineral resources (and export-oriented growth centred on natural capital) were considered a given; however, considerable variation existed as regards the political choices regarding the extent on which to rely on foreign versus national ownership, and to incorporate labour movement campaigns for the outright nationalization of natural resource endowments (Bergquist 1986). Hence, the extent to which developmental states were successfully consolidated in the Southern Cone in Latin America[1] was a direct result of the configurations of political power between the state, foreign capital, and a narrow but highly organized labour movement.

This chapter, then, analyses how the logic of state action became compatible with emerging development strategy within Latin American states centred on extractive industry exports. Political elites pursued the structural transformation of their national economies by emphasizing institution-shaping reforms and the creation of public SOEs. In particular, SOEs can be understood as containers of policy ideas, in which developmentalism as an organizing logic for state action and a framework for economic development found its institutional home. Through SOEs, the idea of *national autonomy*

---

[1] The Southern Cone refers to the physical shape of the southern portion of the continent. It includes Argentina, Brazil, Chile, Paraguay, Peru, and Uruguay.

Business of the State. Jewellord T. Nem Singh, Oxford University Press. © Jewellord T. Nem Singh (2024).
DOI: 10.1093/oso/9780198892212.003.0003

became consolidated as a developmental mindset,[2] and, over time, the proliferation of state bureaucrats sharing a belief in their developmental role has provided them with the capacity to assert the political autonomy of SOEs vis-à-vis the national state. The presence of an institutional home, in turn, shaped the survival strategies of public enterprises when neoliberal reforms swept the continent and would seek to dismantle the developmental state. By offering a nuanced history of state activism during the 20th century, the chapter highlights the importance of institutional continuities and changes between SOE-driven growth models and neoliberalism, which played a vital role in mediating state–capital and capital–labour relations in the natural resource sector.

Natural Resources as the Building Blocks of Latin America's Development Model

The post-colonial economic history of Latin America from the 1880s until the Great Depression of the 1930s is often characterized as the export expansion phase, when Latin America's integration into the world economy took place through the exports of primary commodities (Furtado 1970, 32–34, 36–39). The region had been dependent on commodity production for its economic growth and development strategy before gaining independence, shaped by what Bulmer-Thomas (2014) refers to as the 'commodity lottery', in which the distribution of natural resources was based on natural endowments, geographical and geological limitations, and demand characteristics based on the changing global economy. Political elites pursued their comparative advantages through export production. Some commodities faced greater competition (e.g. sugar), while others had a monopoly or greater share of global markets (e.g. metal minerals). The evolution of commodities from luxury to basic consumption likewise affected the growing importance of specific commodities in the national economy. For example, coffee was radically transformed into a major commodity export in Brazil as American consumers steadily increased demand between the 1880s and 1945. Such external factors meant that coffee elites in the South would play a large role in Brazilian political economy, especially during industrialization in the inter-war years (Bulmer-Thomas 2014; Topik and Samper 2006).

---

[2] The concept of 'developmental mindset' refers to a 'worldview that is focussed on a desire for national techno-industrial catch-up and export competitiveness via strategic interventions by the state in economic life to promote national strength in a hostile and competitive environment' (Thurbon 2016, 2).

Latin America's phase of export-propelled growth—or *crecimiento hacia afuera*—lasted up until the Great Depression and was then replaced by growth via domestic markets—or *crecimiento hacia adentro*—which commenced after World War II and flourished between the 1950s and late 1960s (Hirschman 2013, 104–105). Further, the transition between externally driven growth and domestic market expansion is marked by two phases of industrialization. In phase 1, alongside export-propelled growth, primary production specialization facilitated increased productivity and purchasing power of the population, which consequently permitted the formation of a domestic market of manufactured goods and expanding infrastructure. Additionally, as rising productivity sought to replace highly efficient producers operating in world markets rather than low-productivity companies, the formative industrial sectors produced non-durable consumer goods supplied to the world market through the expansion of exports (Furtado 1970, 75–77, 82–83). Without exception, economic performance until the late 1920s remained heavily dependent on the fortunes of the export sector and the world markets. In this way, Latin American economies were exposed to the effects of the 1929 global financial crisis, which led to the collapse of their capacity to import, the contraction of the export sector, and a rapid fall in export profits. This was mainly the result of tensions between production for the internal market and the global economy, alongside a prolonged difficulty in strengthening domestic industrial capacity, and the strong presence of foreign capital in the most important sectors of regional economies (Cardoso and Faletto 1979; Furtado 1970). The contraction of the export sector motivated regional elites to proceed with phase 2 of industrialization, which was more commonly associated with *crecimiento hacia adentro*—a focus on structural change, industrialization, and diversification of the non-export economy (Cardoso and Faletto 1979; Tandeter 2006).[3] In the language of historical institutionalists, the collapse of the export economy brought by the 1929 financial crisis served as a critical juncture for Latin American elites to embrace a new pathway for long-term economic development: import substitution industrialization (ISI).

The ISI strategy took place in countries that completed the initial stage of industrialization or those where a significant nucleus of non-durable consumer goods industries was already established. The international context is important to note here: emergent protectionism across the US and Europe

---

[3] The prices of primary commodities fell dramatically, in which the unit value of exports dropped by 50%, and those with a modest plunge in prices such as bananas and oil were sectors dominated by foreign capital. Import prices also went down as a result of free-falling world demand, resulting in a sharp decline in export volumes across the region (Bulmer-Thomas 1994, 196–199).

encouraged regional elites to shift away from export-based growth strategies. Additionally, with World War II further restricting international trade, Latin America experienced very modest growth in volumes of exports. The turbulent years of the Great Depression after 1930 compelled elites to make a choice between, on the one hand, inward-looking ISI to reduce vulnerability from flux in external economic conditions and, on the other hand, the retention of export-oriented growth based on natural resources with an emphasis on export intensification and export diversification.

With the exception of Peru, Southern Cone states in Latin America embraced the ISI model through a wide array of credit and fiscal policy devices designed to pressure foreign importing companies to set up local manufacturing bases and to establish SOEs, development corporations, and development banks to promote specific ventures. The states that had begun to build industrial bases—Argentina, Brazil, Chile, Colombia, Mexico, and Uruguay—decisively embarked on ISI due to the possibilities for rapid growth in output and employment in manufacturing. Although there was no single ISI model, it was best characterized in terms of 'tightly separate stages' of industrialization, beginning from the manufacture of finished consumer goods, through to imitation and importation of available foreign technology, towards more complex sectors, as observed in the shift from light to heavy consumer goods and towards capital goods industries (Cardoso and Faletto 1979; Furtado 1970).

Notably, Peruvian elites chose to continue with a natural resource export strategy while the rest of the Southern Cone pursued an ISI strategy. To this extent, Peru stands as an exception in the regional trend. Most countries in Latin America responded to the financial crash of 1929 by using it as the stimulus for a pivot towards development premised on industrial policy; however, from 1930 onwards, Peru opted to uphold the free trade principles and reinforce its liberal export-oriented model (Bulmer-Thomas 2014; Crabtree and Durand 2017, 46). Consequently, political elites missed the construction of a coherent developmental project, which meant the absence of a coherent ISI strategy to overcome commodity dependence and elite capture of the state. The absence of a project for structural transformation, in turn, reinforced multifaceted inequality inherited from the colonial era. Peru alongside Bolivia and Ecuador were drawn back to primary commodities and failed to spur institution building based on national ownership (Orihuela and Thorp 2012, 35–38). The 1950 Mining Code offered generous tax incentives to medium- and large-scale mining projects and increased Peru's export base from traditional mining (copper, silver, and gold) towards industrial minerals like zinc, lead, and iron. The drive to increase mineral production incentivized American capital to invest, leading to rising mineral export figures—from 33% in 1948 up to 50% in 1960 (Crabtree and Durand 2017, 48).

The military dictatorship under Juan Velasco (1968–1975) pursued expansionary state capitalism through nationalization of O&G and mining assets, secondary import substitution, and large public infrastructure investments. The military also adopted a strategy of building alliances with industrialists based in non-natural resource sectors, whose support would prove vital for the industrialization policy. Velasco created '*empresarios dialogantes*' to bring government closer with willing business elites, thereby creating formal and informal channels of cooperation. Such political coalitions were supported by concrete economic policies, including monetary, tax, and credit incentives, protection from foreign competition (especially in banking and manufacturing), and easier access to credit through state control over the national banks. Yet, despite all such efforts, the military regime failed to carve out an effective role for the state as a motor of development or mediator of societal conflicts (Crabtree and Durand 2017, 57–58; Wise 2003, 11–12, 14). SOEs neither developed niche markets nor pursued technological innovation. Without efficiency, SOEs became easy targets for privatization during the liberalization years. Its main legacy was the solidification of a cluster of problems related to the inefficiencies of state-led development, which in turn induced a radical neoliberal programme.

The Latin American Developmental State

From a Latin American perspective, natural resources and industrialization have been opposite, if not competing, sources of economic development. While natural resources can be utilized as a means of creating linkages between the resource and the productive economies (Hirschman 2013, 156–194), industrialization is conceived as a counter developmental strategy to that of commodity production. Thus, Latin American economic history does not necessarily lend credence to the resource curse argument,[4] although scholars have long recognized the tendency of resource specialization to generate perverse economic incentives in directing capital and labour away from national industrialization. Thus, criticism of commodity-based export

---

[4] For example, oil wealth in Venezuela was present in periods of both productivity and severe economic crises throughout the 20th century; instead, political strategies in managing conflicts interacted with economic development strategies, which points to political institutions—not oil wealth—as the explanation to better economic performance during 1930–1980 compared to the post-1980 period (Di John 2009).

68   Business of the State

development is rooted less in the incapacity of natural resource wealth to complement industrial development and more in the trade-off between export specialization and manufacturing expansion.[5]

Throughout the 1950s and 1960s, during which time the ISI model was implemented, Latin American economies remained dependent on the expansion of commodity exports and infrastructure investments financed by foreign capital. Therefore, so long as primary exports played a role in Latin American economies, the instability of raw material prices affected the internal coherence of the state. The answer to this externally driven export dependence was to undertake steps to control foreign economic and financial relations—Latin American elites saw the crucial role of internal integration of their national economies and reduced dependence on international division of labour (Furtado 1970, 152). In this context, industrialization efforts can be viewed as national responses to the international division of labour across the developing world.

The rise of developmental states can be attributed to the historical necessity of cohesive industrial planning, with domestic capitalists lacking financial and technological capabilities and who were often less willing to undertake high-risk projects (Bulmer-Thomas 1994, 277–288). As such, it was the state who stepped in to undertake large-scale investments, offered infant industry protection against international competition, and socialized risks and rewards to promote capital accumulation. On the one hand, Latin American countries passed key legislations to delimit the operations of foreign-owned enterprises in the O&G industry, as observed in Mexico, Venezuela, and even Argentina and Brazil, and, to a limited extent, increased state control in mining, as noted in Chile. On the other hand, international financial institutions—including the World Bank and Inter-American Development Bank—played a major role in financing infrastructure projects, though their significance to overall investments remained of secondary importance (Furtado 1970, 166–168). Furthermore, access to modern technology was supposedly facilitated by foreign investments in the manufacturing industries. As Table 3.1 demonstrates, the bulk of US investment in Latin America was destined for Argentina, Mexico, and Brazil, those same countries who had passed legislation to delimit foreign-owned enterprises in their O&G industries. This US investment was directed to finance the vigorous expansion

---

[5] Recently, the idea of resource-based industrialization has begun to make traction—i.e. countries with prior history of earlier industrialization and deepening of capital goods markets helped promote substantial upstream and downstream industrial linkages, enabling the creation of many positive externalities between the resource and productive economy (Brooks and Kurtz 2016, 28; Massi and Nem Singh 2018; Nem Singh 2014; Priest 2016).

Table 3.1 US investments in Latin American countries' manufacturing industries (in million US$).

Country	US investments in Latin American manufacturing industries (in million US$)		
	1950	1965	Percentage increase
Argentina	161	617	280
Brazil	285	722	153
Mexico	133	752	466
Chile	29	39	34
Colombia	25	160	540
Peru	16	79	393
Venezuela	24	248	933
Latin America	780	2,741	251

Source: *Survey of Current Business* in Furtado (1970, 172).

of manufacturing subsidiaries, as US corporations sought to reinvest their undistributed profits and raise local funds. Overall, the effect was greater foreign participation in the manufacturing sectors.

Let us take the case of Brazil as an example. An overall survey of 276 business groups printed in 1965 showed that more than half of the capital invested in Brazilian industrial sectors was held by foreign groups. In addition, foreign control increased from consumer non-durables towards consumer durables and heavy capital goods (Furtado 1970, 175). In the private sector, out of the 55 consortia with a total capital of 4 billion cruzeiros and more, 29 were foreign-controlled, 2 were mixed, and 24 were nationally owned companies. In the consumer durables and capital goods sectors, 16 were foreign-controlled and 8 were nationally owned companies. At that time, US multinationals dominated the whole of the Latin American market, as the potential to transfer technology, marketing strategies, management skills, and access to financial markets provided the developmental justification for allowing foreign control. Such loose state control over strategic industries was described by Evans (1979) as dependent development, in which a 'triple alliance' between the national state, domestic industrial capitalists, and foreign-owned enterprises limited Brazilian industrial transformation.

Unlike the East Asian developmental states, in Venezuela, oil revenues played a central role in generating political stability and in financing industrial policy. The case of Venezuela is also an extreme case of how tensions between natural resource-led growth and industrialization played out in the institutional development of a petro-state and is worth discussing in more detail, as the following section describes.

Venezuela: Development of a Petro-State

Between the 1920s and 1970s, Venezuela was transformed from a poor, agricultural-based economy into a petro-state and the second richest country in Latin America, and yet, its growth performance remains erratic. The petro-state can be traced back to autocrat President Juan Vicente Gómez (1908–1935) who deliberately fused state power with the oil industry. Alongside the arrival of Shell in 1913, Gómez's Development Minister, Gumersindo Torres, implemented far-reaching regulatory changes which increased the state's participation in windfall profits as a means of asserting state rights to participate in the oil industry's profits. The so-called subsoil rights previously conferred to private landowners were transferred to the national state, transforming its role into a 'landlord' who can levy ground rents for the extraction of oil (Coronil 1997, 81; Mommer 1986, 65–73). Specifically, new oil legislation was enacted to assert resource sovereignty that required, above all, safeguarding oil from foreign companies, and thus incorporating natural resources into the country's national history and political identity. Between 1908 and 1935, Gómez managed to overcome local caudillos and established a strong executive, created a national army, built a road system leading to the territorial integration of the nation-state, and, importantly, developed a public bureaucracy capable of negotiating with oil companies. Yet the centralization of power under Gómez simply restricted the social base of his regime and severely limited the benefits of oil rents within his small clique. After 1935, limited democracy pushed the Venezuelan state into the centre of political conflicts, wherein clientelism and personal enrichment clashed with demands from below to expand state income from the oil industry towards stronger public participation in political life and in the nation's oil wealth. In other words, Venezuela's rentier liberalism sought to break the association of oil and politics with the autocratic regime; democracy became a transformative liberal project galvanizing mass politics, underpinned by the distribution of oil rents.

The Venezuelan petro-state sought to maximize benefits from a geopolitically significant commodity through nationalization. The 1943 Hydrocarbons Act transformed Venezuela into a full-pledged petro-state. Pérez Alfonzo, Minister of Development, through this law, implemented the 50:50 principle which limited concessions for IOCs, created the NOC *Corporación Venezolano del Petróleo* (CVP), and facilitated the incorporation of organized petroleum workers (Karl 1997, 85–87). A major change involved the passage of the clause requiring all foreign oil companies to build refineries in Venezuela rather than overseas. The law fully recognized the subsoil as national property to which the ultimate role of the state was to safeguard the country's natural resource wealth on behalf of the collective. The state gradually increased income taxes and higher royalties in the oil industry, the effect of which was to enhance state participation in industry profits and promote an economic policy of state-initiated industrialization (Coronil 1997, 107–108). Venezuela's economic policy focussed on 'sowing the oil' (*sembrar el petróleo*) by supporting export diversification through widespread expenditure of natural resource rents. However, the military dictatorship of Marcos Pérez Jiménez (1948–1957) that followed pursued greater concentration of power within the executive and centralization of state machinery to achieve industrialization. His regime collapsed in 1958 when he expressed his desire to stay in power. Marked by overspending and corruption, Pérez Jiménez tried to hold onto power, but such efforts brought together various segments of society clamouring for political change, including the Catholic Church, factions of the armed forces who felt excluded from his government, and the growing urban masses and middle classes (Karl 1997, 97).

The 1958 pact of *Punto Fijo* under President Romulo Betancourt (1959–1963) bound all political parties into the same economic and political programme, irrespective of electoral outcomes, and sought for a cross-party consensus on the governance of natural resources. The petro-state bolstered a top-down, selectively inclusive pattern of state–society relations which limited social mobilization, weakened the autonomous organizational capacity of radical actors (notably labour), and restricted the policy agenda. Pacted democracy (*democracia pactada*) ensured the dominance of political parties to selectively meet demands from below while limiting the scope of representation to guarantee the hegemonic position of the dominant classes. As the oil industry expanded, mineral wealth surpassed agriculture and manufacturing in the national economy. Such industrial reorganization weakened the landed oligarchs and industrial groups became clienteles of the state. Karl (1997, 112) describes the institutionalization of oil wealth management in Venezuela as follows: (1) governing parties followed the maxim of extracting as much oil taxes as possible from the oil companies;[6] (2) all policymakers pursued a common strategy of 'sowing' petroleum and expanding the state through state-directed oil-based industrialization simultaneously with ISI in the private sector (see also Coronil 1997, 282–285); and (3) in maintaining political stability, state actors sought a policy of appeasement by way of distributing the spoils of the oil industry across all politically relevant

---

[6] For example, in 1957 the Venezuelan government obtained 52% of oil profits and was paid US$968 million; by 1970 the government retained 78% of oil profits and received US$1.4 billion (Tugwell 1975, 150).

72   Business of the State

actors. Thus, the flow of oil wealth into the treasury had transformative effects on the state as political machinery for redistribution. In practice, however, the tensions around how to manage natural resource wealth were complicated by the desire to create an emerging manufacturing sector, as per the policies promoted by the Cepalistas as the solution to overcome the natural resource dependency and structural heterogeneity that hindered Latin American industrial development.

Venezuela: Industrial Policy During the Oil Boom

The Latin American petro-state would have been the exemplar of a successful developmental state. In the context of two periods of oil bonanzas in the 1970s, Venezuela and Mexico both experienced unprecedented economic growth and within the span of a decade had concentrated state investments in manufacturing. While East Asian states, notably Korea, Taiwan, and Japan, pursued industrial policy through domestic savings, petro-states financed their growth strategies through oil revenues (Di John 2014, 327). As Table 3.2

Table 3.2 Fiscal revenues of Venezuelan governments, 1917–1978 (in million bolivares).

Government	Regime type	Total income	Average/year
Gen. J.V. Gomez (1917–1935)	Military dictatorship	476	25
Gen. E. López Contreras (1936–1940)	Democracy	471	94
Gen. I. Medina Angarita (1941–1945)	Military dictatorship	971	194
Acción Democrática (1946–1948)	Democracy	2,337	779
Government junta (1949–1952)	Military dictatorship (junta)	4,963	1,241
Gen. M. Pérez Jimenez (1953–1957)	Military dictatorship (junta)	9,615	1,923
Government junta (1958)	Military dictatorship (junta)	2,713	2,713
Rómulo Betancourt (1959–1963)	Democracy	16,285	3,257
Raúl Leoni (1964–1968)	Democracy	25,573	5,114
Rafael Caldera (1968–1973)	Democracy	36,952	7390
Subtotal[a]		**100,356**	
Carlos Andrés Pérez (1974–1978)[b]	Democracy	14,8640	29,728
Total revenue		**228,758**	**45,752**

Source: Banco Central de Venezuela (1979; 1987b) cited in Karl (1997, 117).

[a] Revenues are calculated in current prices due to negligible effects of inflation until the early 1970s.
[b] Constant 1973 prices.

shows, during the five years of the oil boom, Venezuela under President Andrés Pérez (1974–1978) received more oil revenues than all previous presidents combined, since 1917. As much as US$800 million was each month pouring into the treasury thanks to the quadrupling of world oil prices (Karl 1997, 116). Between 1972 and 1975, oil prices jumped from US$2.10 to US$10.90 per barrel, an increase of roughly 419%, and Venezuela's fiscal income per barrel of exported oil rose by 587% from US$1.65 to US$9.68 (Banco Central de Venezuela 1978, cited in Karl 1997, 120). Between 1973 and 1974, Venezuela's government income jumped from US$4,418 million to more than US$14,418 million (Baena 1999, 41). Overnight the rapid climb in fiscal income had dramatic expansionary effects on monetary liquidity, aggregate demand, imports of consumer goods, and expenditure on industrial goods for manufacturing. These changes in the economy, in turn, changed Pérez's political decision-making capacity and ambition as the sudden influx of windfall profits transformed the institutional setting.

Prior to 1973, presidents were forced to strike a bargain with other parties—a coalitional constraint to check presidential powers—and compromises with Congress were vital for passing key legislation. Given the wide margin of Pérez's election victory and soaring fiscal income, Pérez was neither bound by coalitional bargaining nor minority status in Congress (Karl 1997, 121). To prevent the overheating of the economy and mitigate the anti-inflationary effects of exceptionally high volumes of petrodollar income from crude oil sales, Pérez created the Venezuelan Investment Fund (VIF) as a counter cyclical economic measure, and expanded his political vision, from a modest development programme for the country towards promoting *La Gran Venezuela*, instantaneously propelling the country towards modernity to catch up with the industrialized West. The public sector expanded dramatically and government expenditure soared by 250%. Terry Karl (1997, 120) puts this transformation in comparative perspective: 'Venezuela's fiscal income rose from VEF 12,546 million in 1972 to a whopping VEF 41,001 million, roughly 40% of its GDP, which is equivalent to four times the percentage in Brazil (3.6), more than four times in Mexico, and twice the percentage in Yugoslavia in 1976.'

Oil in Venezuela was associated with the so-called 'big push, natural resource-heavy industrialization' strategy (Di John 2014, 321) focussed on the development of large SOEs in steel, petrochemicals, aluminium, and hydro-electric power. When oil was fully nationalized on 1 January 1976, Petróleos de Venezuela, S.A. (PDVSA) became responsible for the modernization and expansion of the oil industry, including the refinery segment of the value chain, and alongside the establishment of non-oil state enterprises, the state became the key producer of the country, the largest source of foreign exchange, and the main employer of the workforce (Di John 2014, 337). The state's primary objective was two-fold: to diversify the export structure of the economy and to promote industrialization by deepening the manufacturing sector. While everyone agreed that oil wealth should be distributed more widely, growing partisan divisions and competing models of oil nationalization mired industrial policymaking in Venezuela. Worse, Pérez felt his power was unchallenged—he overlooked the draft bill produced by a commission he set up, and instead submitted his own version to Congress with support from selected factions across the party spectrum. His bill specifically included a new clause allowing foreign capital to participate in the newly nationalized industry through the formation of enterprises with a joint or mixed ownership structure. Congress narrowly passed the bill, albeit with opposition from major parties who walked out of the ceremony of the bill passing (Karl 1997, 152–153). But it was not only the state that had borne the rentier mentality—mass politics was underpinned by a belief in citizens' right to enjoy oil wealth. They were used to highly subsidized lifestyles, especially the middle classes seeking consumption goods from abroad. Additionally, given the difficulty of passing painful economic reforms in Congress, foreign borrowing as opposed to domestic taxation became the norm. The Venezuelan state and its citizens pursued a policy of enormous spending, subsidies, and unrestricted foreign borrowing. Figures 3.1 and 3.2 illustrate the unfettered

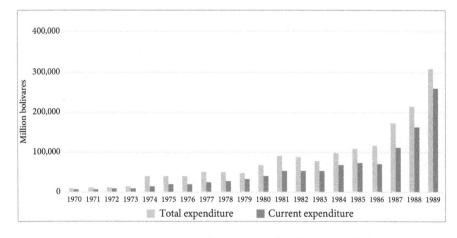

Figure 3.1 Central government expenditures in total and current values, 1970–1989.

Source: Banco Central de Venezuela, Oficina Central de Estadística e Informática, various years in Karl (1997, 165) (adapted).

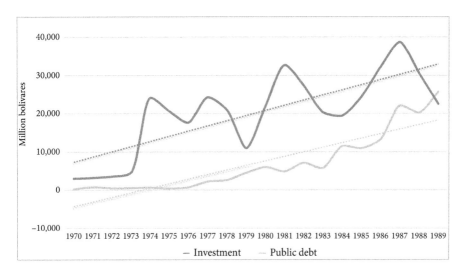

Figure 3.2 Central government investment and public debt, 1970–1989.
Source: Banco Central de Venezuela, Oficina Central de Estadística e Informática, various years in Karl (1997, 165) (adapted).

fiscal expansion, using various metrics such as total and current expenditures, investments, and public debt throughout the boom years all the way to the fiscal crisis in the 1980s. While current spending declined as a percentage of total government spending during the Pérez presidency, total government spending by 1992 was about thirty times more than in 1970.

For these reasons, by the time the second oil boom (1979–1980) occurred,[7] rapid, chaotic, and unplanned growth led to a missed opportunity for industrialization. Without disciplined bureaucrats and domestic capitalists checking each other with the state, Venezuelan industrial policy was haphazardly implemented (Coronil 1997). To put it bluntly, state reforms were not meant to strengthen the autonomy of SOEs and bureaucrats away from organized interests; rather, policies sought to concentrate power towards the Presidency. Informal channels became the norm to incorporate private sector interests—notably in the steel, cement, and automotive sectors—into decision-making; non-oil capitalists also wanted petrodollars to subsidize their businesses,[8] rather than to become internationally competitive

---

[7] The second oil boom of 1979–1980 was caused by the temporary closure of Iran's oil industry, a direct outcome of the revolution against the Shah's regime. Iran's position as the Organization of the Petroleum Exporting Countries (OPEC)'s second-largest oil producer and exporter after Saudi Arabia caused ripple effects in world oil prices. The sudden supply glut doubled the price of oil to about $30 per barrel by early 1980 (Thee 2012, 90).

[8] Between 1974 and 1978, the most important contracts were awarded by the Pérez administration to the so-called Twelve Apostles, a group of wealthy second-level entrepreneurs who had access through

76 Business of the State

companies. Furthermore, SOEs had very little capacity for self-financing and relied very heavily on oil subsidies from the central government. The outcomes were clear—wasteful spending and several miscalculations on project planning resulted in crucial investments in ports, airports, and internal transport systems being left unfinished or inefficiently constructed. Despite the stream of capital investments from oil revenues of the Venezuelan government, export diversification towards capital-intensive manufacturing failed spectacularly. The cycle of taxing foreign companies, exorbitant spending through oil industry profits, and borrowing loans from abroad continued until oil prices collapsed.

Oil revenues plunged from 1982 onwards, and by 1986 prices had fallen to less than 40% of their 1982 peak. With exorbitant foreign borrowing—reaching over US$30 billion—the petroleum industry could not produce enough rent, leading to a widening gap between the value of oil exports and government expenditure. This in turn, stymied Venezuela's big push, oil-financed industrialization model as the Organization of the Petroleum Exporting Countries (OPEC) lost control over pricing powers in world oil markets throughout the 1980s (Roberts 2003, 257). The Venezuelan state's strategy of augmenting taxes by constraining supply was deemed ineffective. Additionally, while most developing countries derived their tax income from goods and services (27.93%) as well as import duties (24.98%) (Karl 1997, 171),[9] Venezuela was overly reliant on corporate taxes (70%) as opposed to individual taxes (4%), domestic taxes on goods and services (6.75%), and import duties (9.78%). By 1988 the budget deficit was above 9% of GDP and artificial price controls to avert public panic encouraged hoarding and widespread shortages (Roberts 2003, 257). In this context of declining oil prices and a highly uncompetitive non-oil sector, plunging foreign reserves, spiralling budget deficits, and a collapse in economic growth, the demand for economic reform—debt restructuring and structural adjustment—began to brew.

Venezuela's oil boom failed to produce a strong, coherent national state. If the failure of its big push, oil-financed industrialization model rests on the quality of the state, then we cannot discount the role of rent-seeking. Few controls existed on public spending and mechanisms of bureaucratic

---

prior political ties. Some high-profile contracts included the Guri Dam, the Zulia steel mill, construction of Parque Central, and Cementos Caribe (Karl 1997, 146).

[9] However, Moreno and Shelton (2014) offer an alternative argument: Venezuela actually carried out substantial fiscal adjustment after the onset of the debt crisis. Falling oil revenues generated new efforts at raising new sources of revenues and cutting expenditures. However, these cuts were insufficient to curb the gap and the oil revenue deficit was simply too large to cover. Rather than blaming the flaws of the fiscal response, the magnitude of excessive spending prior to 1983 was the main cause of the growth collapse.

accountability were virtually absent during the oil boom, both of which fostered low-level corruption and mismanagement. The proliferation of SOEs in the mining and oil sectors provided very little capacity in other segments of the state in building a cadre of professionals, enhancing productivity and commercial profitability of resource-based SOEs, and creating incentives for business groups to become internationally competitive. As for its NOC, PDVSA was an island of efficiency and productive capability with an international orientation that did not always necessarily align with state objectives (Baptista and Mommer 1987; Karl 1997, 140–142).

Worse, growing incompatibility of the big push industrial strategy with existing power structures limited the scope of state action. Thus, growing factionalism, clientelistic politics, and populism that characterized Venezuelan state–society relations seemed highly ineffective when compared with the military dictatorship governments of Brazil and South Korea—both of which are known for *dirigiste-corporatist* states. By exerting state power through co-optation and coercion, the state maintained a coherent developmental strategy leading to structural transformation (Amsden 1992; Massi 2014; Schmitter 1971; 1974). While Coronil (1997, 271–278) attributes the failed undertaking of Venezuela's oil-financed industrialization model to the fractures within the state apparatus between political leaders and technocrats as well as the power of American multinationals in shaping the responses of the government, Karl (1997, 139–142) argues that the oil boom exacerbated the dynamics of rent-seeking, state disorganization, and regime decay leading to the deterioration of pacted democracy.

By 1988 when oil prices slumped and citizens had to choose a new president, neither political candidate wanted to face the reality of debt servicing or the pressures from the International Monetary Fund (IMF) on structural adjustment. When Pérez's *Acción Democrática* government won a second term in 1989, Venezuela was reneging on state-backed spending and was desperate to secure the IMF loan. The collapse of oil prices came together with the neoliberal development model. As a consequence of the implementation of these economic reforms, within weeks of taking office, Pérez faced a popular backlash. In February 1989, citizens in Caracas and other cities took their grievances to the streets after a plan to increase bus fares triggered a spontaneous five-day rebellion—known today as *caracazo*—to which the government responded by sending military troops to suppress the rioters and looters (Roberts 2003, 258–259). This tumultuous period marked the nadir of the most stable democracy in Latin America since 1958.

Until 1998, as Di John (2014, 345–347) explicates, factionalism exacerbated the politics of rent distribution, which in turn fuelled politicization of state-initiated industrial policies and political polarization in an era of two-party rivalry. When the economic crisis occurred, economic liberalization worsened the political divide. Yet its most important consequence was the delegitimization of the dominant party, *Acción Democrática*, as the champion of the working classes and advocate of developmentalism. The 1990s were characterized by rotating ministers, failed economic rescue plans, and a series of corruption scandals as the state's dangerously fragile distributive apparatus began to unravel as the oil rents typically greasing the wheel of corruption and patronage dried up, which narrowed down the policy space for elites and led to the imposition of unpopular economic reforms. However, strong, disciplined parties failed to sustain market reforms in the 1990s, largely due to their excessive reliance on oil rents for political stability and their incapacity to maintain legitimacy amidst growing costs of economic adjustment. The political consequences of this failure to manage the economic crisis proved to be very costly: the collapse of one of Latin America's most highly institutionalized party systems and a rupture in its most stable democratic regime. As Roberts (2003, 249) aptly phrases it, Venezuela represents an extreme case of a nation with a consolidated democracy and entrenched political parties that was so discredited that a former coup leader, Hugo Chávez, was elected as president.

Developmental States in Latin America Versus East Asia

While petro-states had an exceptional experience, East Asian developmental states and Latin American bureaucratic authoritarian states sought to overcome their dependence on foreign borrowing and insecurity brought about from relying on US support for financing industrial policies. A developmentalist mindset—a belief on national techno-industrial catch-up and export competitiveness as an imperative or even prerequisite for state survival—was instrumental in the formulation of an activist state in Latin America and East Asia during the 20th century (Amsden 1992; Sikkink 1991; Wade 1990). East Asia was more successful in industrial policy compared to Latin American counterparts. While similar logics of state intervention were applied to both regions, Latin American states were less coherent, social conflicts around class cleavages prominent in the political arena, and bureaucratic autonomy of major planning ministries less secured to pursue bold industrial strategies. Importantly, a strong alliance between national elites and domestic capitalists served as the foundation of industrial policy, whereby political leaders and industrial elites were bound by a mutual threat credible enough to discipline capital from excessive profiteering and to deploy machine politics as a way of coping with a potentially unstable political environment—riddled with factionalism, plagued by political infighting, and suffering from deep polarization—where ideological factors and shared identity are insufficient to bind competing interests towards a stable ruling coalition (Amsden 2007, 94–99; Kang 2002a, 2002b; Wedeman 2012, 181). Put differently, industrial policies in Latin America and East Asia had widely varying outcomes due to the different character of national states and the logic of coalition building across social and economic forces, which subsequently influenced the calculus of state elites in distributing rewards and risks among industrialists and social groups.

Beyond the state–industrial elite dynamics playing out in policymaking during this period, the role of SOEs in facilitating national industrialization must not be overlooked (Randall 1993; Trebat 1983). In Latin America, there was wide variation in success rates, and Bulmer-Thomas (1994, 283) argues that countries with larger markets—Argentina, Brazil, and Mexico—were more successful in experimenting with state-led development compared to smaller countries like Chile and Colombia. SOEs often operated in basic and infrastructure industries characterized by high risks and large-scale operations in potentially rent-rich sectors linked to the extraction and production of crude oil, metal minerals, steel, railroad and transport, telecommunications, and power generation. These sectors were deemed too important to be left out of the hands of the centralized state. Hence, SOEs reflected the long-standing efforts of political elites to expand the scope of state intervention and increased bureaucratic capacity in a period of rapid socioeconomic and political change in the 20th century. In particular, the consolidation of SOEs in Latin America's natural resource sector was promoted as the prevailing answer to the dominance of foreign ownership in the O&G and mining sectors. The logic of resource nationalism—often implemented via expropriation of assets and establishment of public enterprises—was deemed compatible with the general tendency towards state intervention. What was perhaps unsurprising was the pivotal role of militant labour unions in the nationalization of natural resources.[10] For one thing, organized workers were campaigning in defence of national monopolies in rent-rich sectors and technology transfer towards domestic industries controlled by foreign

---

[10] Labour unions played a pivotal role in the emergent corporatist framework in the Southern Cone. The militancy and sustained capacity of the trade unions to mobilize required state and economic elites to respond to this 'political question' by gradually incorporating trade unions into formal political structures as a means of channelling disruptive labour conflicts through institutional mechanisms (Collier and Collier 1991).

80 Business of the State

compaies. As Sikkink (1991) rightly demonstrates, state enterprises were not simply abstract creations of national elites; public ownership was an institutional design rooted in popular struggles and demands for greater control over natural resources. SOEs were the embodiment of national sovereignty, reflected some radical ideas about autonomous economic development, and represented attempts at crafting institutional capacity.

Chapter 4 serves as an introduction to the case study chapters of this book. An examination of the rise of Codelco and Petrobras contextualizes the emergence of SOEs as instruments for state-building in Brazil and Chile between the 1930 and 1970s, illustrating how SOEs adapted to the crisis of state developmentalism in the 1980s. In both Chile and Brazil, the establishment of relatively successful SOEs in the 20th century meant that the arrival of neoliberalism in the region became subject to intense contestation, and, consequently, significant adaptation of neoliberal reforms had to be made to accommodate the presence of state companies in the mining and O&G industries.

4
Developmental States in Chile and Brazil

This chapter serves as a way of framing the two case studies that follow, providing detailed analysis of the rise of the developmental state in Brazil and Chile using a historical institutionalist framework to consider how political conflicts drove elites towards consolidating an SOE-based growth strategy in major industries. It traces the co-evolution of an activist state in the commodities sector and the necessity of creating a public enterprise to achieve industrial development. The chapter likewise traces the early successes of Chile's Codelco and Brazil's Petrobras, which in turn enabled these companies to survive privatization and thrive during the heyday of neoliberal reform years.

The Chilean Developmental State, 1925–1973

The Chilean developmental state finds its origins around the mid-1920s, becomes consolidated in the late 1930s, and is punctuated by the military coup d'état in 1973. Its performance was quite successful until the late 1940s, but began to decline in the 1950s and 1960s as frictions between political and economic actors grew and accommodation and political agreement among parties failed to materialize. The emergence of the Chilean developmental state was a reaction to the limitations of the liberal export-expansion economic model that had been consolidated after independence in the 19th century. Chile's political system developed a very wide spectrum of ideologically oriented, mass-based political parties marked by a long tradition of democratic pluralism. The creation of a viable export economy in which silver, copper, and wheat were the main sources of state revenue sustained this relatively stable democratic political system. There existed a stable political pact between the dominant class of exporters and importers in Central Chile who were divided in several respects but were united behind the maintenance of a liberal political economy (Bergquist 1986; Collier 1993). After the successful annexation of Northern Chile after the War of the Pacific against Bolivia and Peru (1879–1883), Chile took over the nitrate fields, or *oficinas*,

---

Business of the State. Jewellord T. Nem Singh, Oxford University Press. © Jewellord T. Nem Singh (2024).
DOI: 10.1093/oso/9780198892212.003.0004

in the North, which had previously been owned by Peru. This acquisition necessitated the development of a more complex economy—encompassing agriculture, nitrate, and mining industries—as well as the construction of a centralized state. Chile's fairly developed taxation system allowed for the gradual expansion of the reach and scope of the state whilst maintaining an open export-oriented economy[1] as the Chilean state and the upper classes of the Central Valley exercised direct control in the political sphere, and through its firm hand over the peasants in the countryside, the political classes managed to employ clientelistic tactics to retain elite and state cohesiveness (Collier and Collier 2002, 104, 169–195).

The acquisition of the nitrate fields after the War of the Pacific also represents a critical juncture for state-building and highlights the prominence of nitrate in the Chilean export economy (see Figure 4.1). Crucially, export taxes on nitrate (or *salitre*) and iodine (a by-product of nitrate processing) served as direct revenues for the state, which therefore placed the burden of managing production on the state. However, this did not result in the nationalization of the nitrate fields. As Table 4.1 illustrates, British capitalists and merchant houses—the main financiers of the transport and commercialization

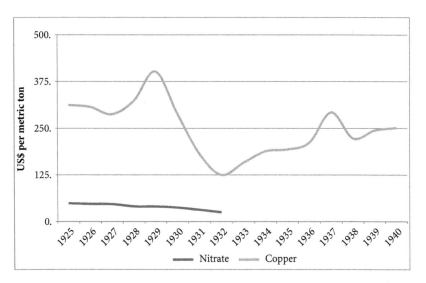

Figure 4.1 International prices of key exports (nitrate and copper) in Chile, 1925–1940.
Source: Braun-Llona et al. (2000, 132) (adapted).
Note: There were no available data in 1933–1936.

---

[1] One indicator of state capacity was the ability of the Chilean state to administer taxation on the nitrate fields and use export taxes to finance not just the war but also the development of state infrastructures (Gallo 2008; Kurtz 2009).

Table 4.1 Ownership of the Chilean nitrate economy (in percentage).

Country	1878	1895	1926
Britain	12	60	41
Chile	22	13	42
Germany	7	8	–
Peru	52	8	1
Others	7	11	16

Source: Bergquist (1986, 35).

of the Peruvian-owned nitrate and guano—had been given a privileged position, which they maintained even after the annexation.[2]

By 1913, nitrate and copper accounted for 78.3% of Chile's exports (Bulmer-Thomas 2014, 59) and Chile's insertion in the world economy was underpinned by primary commodities which were controlled by British and American capitalists. Capital in Chile, *ipso facto*, was foreign and therefore its economic fortunes depended on volatile global markets. As such, the nadir of the nitrate economy was punctuated by a global decline in demand for natural resources proceeded by intense state protectionism as a way of recovering from the devastating human effects of the 1929 Wall Street Crash and the Great Depression.

The transition to copper as Chile's primary export occurred when the nitrate export economy collapsed after 1929 (see Figure 4.1). Coincidentally, this coincided with Chilean political forces realigning themselves, as the military government—first led by General Altamirano in 1925 and then by Carlos Ibañez (1927–1931)—began to espouse ideals of economic nationalism and implement large-scale programmes of public works. These works were funded by the last years of the nitrate boom and ranged from building roads, drainage, bridges, barracks, prisons, airfield, port facilities, and railways. This period is also known as the early years of the Chilean developmental state, in which Ibañez staffed ministries and public agencies with technocrats, civil engineers, and middle-class professionals, removing those

---

[2] The dominance of foreign ownership in the nitrate sector also indirectly affected workers' mobilization. The emergent autonomous working-class culture of *salitre* workers was a reaction to the harsh working conditions in nitrate production and led to the emergence of a new set of cultural values and attitudes in the North that were distinct from other sectors of the Chilean working classes. The cultural and social activities held by working-class men led to the emergence of working-class institutions called *mancomunal* (Cruzat 1981; González Miranda 2002). Furthermore, the infamous 1907 workers' strike in the *oficinas*, though it ended in bloodshed, recognized the legal, public nature of working-class institutions (Bergquist 1986, 38).

84 Business of the State

in the civil service appointed through political patronage (Loveman 1976, 249). President Ibañez strengthened the state through the expansion of the public administrative apparatus, creating offices including the *Contraloría General* in 1927 to oversee fiscal spending and bureaucratic professionalism, as well as specialized development banks—*Caja de Crédito Agrario* (Agrarian Credit Bank) and *Caja de Crédito Minero* (Mining Credit Bank)—all of which had the effect of deepening state influence in the provision of welfare for the working classes (Collier and Slater 2004, 216–220). Ibañez's political downfall was punctuated by the 1929 economic crash and the collapse of the international economic order as a new paradigm coalesced around Keynesianism that legitimized state intervention as a development strategy.

To understand the rise of Codelco as Chile's state-owned copper company in 1971, copper politics must be placed within the context of Chile's industrial impulse between 1930 and 1970, national debates around the taxation of copper mining, and the extent to which foreign mining companies contributed to Chile's economic development. As early as 1940, the question of copper nationalization had been raised by some leaders (e.g. *nacista* Jorge González von Marees). By the 1950s, copper had fully replaced nitrate as Chile's principal export, and the country's export economy was again tied to a primary commodity subject to the harsh, volatile flux of international prices and global demand. However, there exist two fundamental differences between the nitrate and copper industries. First, although Chile's economic fortunes still relied on foreign capital, copper was now in the hands of American capitalists. Second, unlike the labour-intensive production of nitrate, modern production of copper mining reduced the labour force through the use of mechanization, which reduced employment from 18,390 in 1940 down to 12,548 in 1960 (Collier and Slater 2004, 269). Yet with urbanization rapidly taking place and the countryside not offering any possibilities for employment, Chile turned to state-led industrialization as the solution.

In terms of state building, key state agencies were established to promote national industrialization. Under the short-lived *Popular Frente* government (1938–1941), President Pedro Aguirre Cerda narrowly passed a legislative proposal for the creation of *Corporación de Fomente* (CORFO) to oversee the reconstruction process of ravaged communities after an earthquake hit the South in 1939.[3] This special development agency—initially proposed to

---

[3] Under Aguirre Cerda, Marxist parties were also finally integrated in the political system, which galvanized coalition building in Chilean democracy. The reforms rewarded the middle classes through job employment in the burgeoning bureaucracy and granted them a disproportionate share of social security compared to the needy. His greatest achievement is perhaps the institutionalization of the Radical party

Developmental States in Chile and Brazil **85**

be financed through a tax against the wealthy—became tied to American capital since it was financed by foreign loans and broad lines of credit from the US Export–Import Bank (Silva 2018, 294). This ushered in a close relationship between the US and CORFO, which was consequential for domestic politics as the hard-line anti-imperialist discourse of Leftist parties in the 1950s was mitigated by the desire to strengthen US–Chile relations. The successful creation of CORFO was driven by the strong support of an emergent industrialist elite, which established the *Confederación de la Producción y el Commercio* in 1934. The *Confederación* was backed up by the leading economic group *Sociedad de Fomente Fabril* (SOFOFA), which advocated for a technical voice to inform governmental decision-making (Orihuela 2018, 112–113). Hence, CORFO served as the engine of import substitution industrialization by establishing state enterprises in key industries and financing private initiatives in manufacturing.

Several SOEs were created to support Chile's national industrialization to secure the country's energy needs. These include the *Empresa Nacional de Electricidad* (ENDESA) (National Electricity Enterprise), established to generate low-cost power and to develop hydroelectric plants. By 1965, the company succeeded in providing electricity across the national territory. To develop the petroleum reserves discovered in Magallanes, CORFO funded the creation of *Empresa Nacional de Petróleo* (ENAP) (National Petroleum Enterprise) with a core function to coordinate the development of the oil industry and build a refinery in Concón, Valparaiso. Finally, Chile sought to develop an industrial complex through the establishment of a national steel company—*Compañia de Acero del Pacífico* (CAP) (Pacific Steel Company)—which began production in 1950. With respect to manufacturing, CORFO lent money to the private sector to produce home appliances, copper tubes, alloys, and brass fixtures, as well as to other companies involved in wire, electrical goods, motors, radios, and automobile tires. Additionally, as Collier and Slater (2004, 271) noted, CORFO did not ignore the countryside, as evidently shown in the establishment of the Mechanized Agriculture Equipment Service (SEAM)—an SOE importing and then renting tractors to small-scale farmers. This expanding reach of the state in the national economy was made possible through close alignment with the US and the increasing fiscal importance of copper revenues (see Table 4.2).

For Silva (2018, 295–298), CORFO's success was achieved by way of simultaneously promoting compromise and autonomy. Despite rejecting

---

as a formidable political force in Chile, evidently reflected in the successive election of Left and Centre parties between 1938 and 1952.

86 Business of the State

Table 4.2 The Chilean economy, 1938–1952 (in US$ million).

Year	Export revenues	Import expenditures	Foreign investment[a]
1938	329	240	–
1945	406	187	847
1952	547	430	1,025

Source: Drake (1993, 119).

[a] Note that nearly 70% of foreign investment was from the US.

an activist state, the Chilean Right accepted CORFO but demanded close scrutiny of its activities through strict parliamentary oversight. The Chilean Left, seeking autonomy for the agency to urgently respond to the imperatives of national industrialization, wanted CORFO to report directly to the president. A political compromise was reached by adhering to the strict technical nature of CORFO: its day-to-day activities would be run by highly trained technocrats (mostly civil engineers) and who would be given wide policy latitude and a high degree of autonomy in daily decision-making (Silva 2018, 296). In exchange, CORFO technical staff maintained fluid relationships with representatives of the industrial sector and other government agencies. This 'embedded autonomy' (Evans 1995) created an institutional culture centred on technocracy, which over time became a powerful tool to protect CORFO's professional and working interests within the developmental state apparatus (Ibáñez Santa María 2003; Orihuela 2018, 115–116). This search for accommodation and compromise characterized the political system in Chile between the 1930s and early 1960s. The emerging consensus was to support state-led industrialization and the containment of popular sector mobilization through technocratic-led governance—the outcome of a political tie between the Left, Right, and Centre parties or the so-called *Estado de Compromiso* (State of Compromise) (Silva 2008; 2018, 299). However, this consensus was, at best, fragile and tenuous and would periodically be challenged during every presidential election when popular mobilization could trigger a change in the balance of power (Cavarozzi 1992, 214; Silva 2018, 300).

The CORFO initiatives led to a substantial increase of Chile's industrial output. From 1940 until the mid 1950s, industrial production increased at an annual rate of 7.5%, while in the same period the industrial sector's share in the GDP grew from 13.4 to 23% (Silva 2018: 300). However, the production of new factories increasingly relied on local raw materials. By the early 1950s, the industrial base was overconcentrated in furniture, food, clothing, textiles, and footwear, which were produced at inefficient rates because they were more expensive than imported products from the US or Latin America. From the mid-1940s onwards, spiralling inflation and macro-economic difficulties began to change public opinion about state expansion. Between 1953 and 1956, annual industrial growth fell by 60% compared with the previous three-year period and never recovered to the 1953 level thereafter (Collier and Slater 2004, 276). Despite Chile's industrialization efforts, the country had a limited domestic market, became dependent on copper, and the economy was tied to American capital. While the US government mounted strong pressures to retain control over the Northern mines, the Chilean state consistently failed to strike a bargain between the workers and foreign capital. This was complicated by a crisis in Chilean copper, with growing competition in the world market from African copper mines (Vergara 2008).

General Carlos Ibañez (1952–1958) won a second presidential term as a public reaction to the shortcomings of the Radical governments that preceded him. Ibañez issued *El Nuevo Trato* (New Treaty) through *Decreto Lei* (Decree Law) (DL) 11.828, which defined the relationship between the Chilean state and foreign copper companies between 1955 and 1964. In this treaty, a new tax on large-scale mining was imposed which consisted of a 50% tax based on profit and an adjustable 25% tax on investment and production. It also eliminated exchange rate regulations and government control over pricing and marketing. In 1955, Ibañez created the *Departamento del Cobre* (Department of Copper) under the control of the Ministry of Mining (created itself only in 1953), which was responsible for making studies on copper policies, international prices, and mechanisms for foreign companies to outsource their supplies locally (Vergara 2008, 94). As Moran (1977) explains, the Department of Copper trained a new generation of professional bureaucrats who played a critical role in the *Chileanización* (1964–1970) and nationalization (1971) of copper. However, ultimately this *Nuevo Trato* failed to resolve the limitations of the ISI model through increased copper revenues and private investment at a time when copper production and investment were declining and American copper companies were pressuring the Chilean state for a more favourable environment as well as to eliminate state control of price and commercialization (Vergara 2008, 95).

In this context, Ibañez's adjustments to domestic taxation were made despite him knowing full well that an economy based on declining copper revenues could not sustain the reforms. Consequently, the cost of living in Chile jumped by 50% in 1953, the year after by 58%, and in 1955 by 88%; GNP likewise plummeted by 8% (Collier and Slater 2004, 278). As a defensive strategy, workers waged sustained protests as unemployment

88   Business of the State

figures doubled, while copper workers in the North demanded their right to maintain and protect their standard of living, the recognition of the unique characteristics of large-scale copper mining, and a share of benefits from the new copper prosperity (Vergara 2008, 100). Such activism from the newly founded *Confederación de Trabajadores del Cobre* (CTC) (Copper Workers Confederation) organized in 1951 was a stark contrast to the conciliatory position of the Chilean government with foreign capital. This radicalism of the copper unions reflected the politicization of labour issues at a national scale. Chilean miners rejected the *Nuevo Trato*, which posed a serious problem in a country dependent on a single commodity. In response, Ibañez enacted the Statute of Copper Workers—a labour deal that recognized the distinct and influential position of copper workers and consequently reframed labour relations in the copper industry. It shortened the bargaining period, strengthened the power of local unions by ensuring cooperation between permanent and professional unions, and reinforced the role of the state in mediating labour conflicts. In labour negotiations, the state guaranteed the participation of the Minister of Labour and Mining in the special arbitration board alongside the legalization of CTC as the official union— serving as a bridge between local unions and national authorities across the three large mines (Chuquicamata, El Teniente, and Portrerillos). Put simply, the Statute was a means to decrease political conflicts in the copper mines and a second attempt at incorporating the organized working class into a controlled system of labour relations.

During the government of Jorge Alessandri (1958–1964), the question of the nationalization of copper became more prominent as labour tensions continued to escalate in the copper mines. Alessandri sought to retain the political alliance of the state with American capital, and ultimately had a hands-off approach towards the question of copper nationalization, and as such foreign ownership became the fulcrum of escalating conflicts. As the question of agrarian reform and copper nationalization became very politicized in the context of growing nationalism and labour tensions, US private company Anaconda bought Chile's fourth largest mine—El Salvador— in an effort to modernize its operations as a competitive strategy in the world economy.[4] Three American companies—Kennecott, Phelps Dodge, and Anaconda—owned and produced most of Chile's copper and their

---

[4] The company introduced two aspects of corporate restructuring. With respect to productivity, Anaconda sought to improve production processes through cost reduction by way of building new facilities and introducing technology in several phases of the operations. With respect to the rationalization of the administration of mining camps, Anaconda replaced or introduced new machines alongside an increase in subcontracting as a response to the changing labour structure of the world economy. Ultimately, intermediate companies emerged to provide contract workers and services (Vergara 2008, 138–140).

ownership of *La Gran Minería* (the four mines together are referred to as la Gran Mineria in Chile. Prior to El Salvador, it was only the three mines) now expanded to four mines—El Salvador, El Teniente, Andina, and Chuquicamata—and this shaped worker dissatisfaction as well as national mood towards foreign capital. In this political climate, President Eduardo Frei Sr. (1964–1970) was elected under a social reform agenda that did not necessarily win the hearts of the labour movement, particularly the copper workers. Lacking a traditional support base within the union movement, Frei Sr. had sought to gain political support from the non- or less-organized sectors of society, leading to a popular mobilization of the urban poor, women, and peasants.[5] Once he became president the developmental state also expanded under Frei Sr., creating new state enterprises and establishing the National Planning Office (ODEPLAN) in 1967 to formulate plans for economic and social development (Silva 2018, 304).

Amidst growing failure to maintain a political compromise, Frei Sr. approved DL 16.425, or the *Chileanización del Cobre* (Chileanization of Copper) in January 1966. DL 16.425 promised copper companies that copper policies would remain stable for the following 20 years while negotiations took place in order for the state to acquire 51% control of large-scale copper mines, along with a promise of improved conditions in the copper mines, better health and safety measures, and increased state participation in copper production. However, Chileanization did not resolve the escalating labour conflicts and social polarization, and in the copper mines, the intensity and length of labour conflicts—e.g. solidarity and industry-wide strikes—ignored legal frameworks. The CTC protested against DL 16.425 and demanded an improvement in workers' legal and economic status, and crucially sought full nationalization of the copper industry in Chile as the only solution to foreign dependence, while President Frei Sr. portrayed the workers as unreasonably demanding higher wages beyond the capacity of the country and industry. At the national level, the Left and national union *Central Única de Trabajadores de Chile* (CUT) strongly supported the demands of copper workers and opposed the general contracts in the copper industry.[6] In sum, the limitations of the national economy, the shortcomings of copper policy

---

[5] Frei Sr.'s last three years were marked by wage and stabilization programmes alongside a *mano dura* (firm hand) policy against the labour and popular sectors (Vergara 2008, 146).

[6] *Central Única de Trabajadores de Chile* (CUT) functioned from 1953 to 1973, but the national union was dissolved after the fall of President Allende. The union was refounded as *Central Unitaria de Trabajadores de Chile* (CUT) in September 1988 as representative of labour in the opposition movement against the Pinochet dictatorship. CUT was legally recognized after the transition via *Ley Numero* 19.049. As a result, CUT sat in tripartite negotiations to discuss labour issues, including minimum wages, with the *Concertación* government and big business.

90 Business of the State

and its dependence on foreign companies, and the rapidly escalating tensions between foreign capital and labour unions prevented the creation of stable labour relations—all of which contributed to the nationalization of the Chilean copper industry.

With these escalating tensions as a backdrop, in 1970 President Salvador Allende (1970–1973) and his socialist government coalition, *Unidad Popular* (Popular Unity), were elected with a radical proposal of income redistribution, reallocation of public investment, and the reorganization of the national economy centred on the nationalization of Chile's copper industry. On 11 July 1971, for the first time, a cross-party agreement was reached transferring Chile's Gran Minería to 100% state ownership, without any form of compensation to foreign companies.[7] For Vergara (2008, 157–158), copper nationalization was the culmination of a long historical battle to radically decrease the influence of US capital in Chile in a context of extreme economic dependence. For copper workers, nationalization was the realization of their long-standing demand for political autonomy, rooted in the lived experiences of workers and policies of segregation among workers imposed by US management of the copper mines. Allende's nationalization required restructuring the copper economy in terms of both the state role in management of mining and labour participation in decision-making. Through the creation of SOEs—Codelco and *Empresa Nacional de Minería* (ENAMI) (National Mining Enterprise)—the centralized state now directly participated in the economy and the organization of production, coordinated through the Ministry of Mines. A massive training programme was established to effectively integrate workers within the administrative structure of the state companies, while mine workers were given seats in the Board of Directors, General Workers' Assembly, in several production councils linked to the SOEs. The success of the training programme has been debated, specifically the extent to which participation brought about economic benefits rather than productivity in the copper mines (see Barrera 1981; Petras 1972; Zapata 1975). In conclusion, copper nationalization and the establishment of a public enterprise not only diffused class conflict but also was a solution to foreign capital dominance in the Chilean export economy.

Copper nationalization as a central policy of Allende's reorganization of the national economy generated contradictory responses from all sides. Despite Allende's political alliance with labour, nationalization failed to prevent the explosion of labour conflicts, which contributed to a crisis of

---

[7] Nationalization without compensation was a break from the past policies of negotiation between the state and multinational capital. As such, American companies, specifically Kennecott, launched a serious campaign to damage the reputation of Chilean copper (Vergara 2008, 158).

legitimacy and of democracy as wildcat strikes and work stoppage became a common feature of the political landscape. Labour conflicts are rooted in wage policies, internal political strife, and a traditional pattern of conflicts in an industry marked by high rates of absenteeism, labour turnover, and illegal work stoppages (Vergara 2008, 171). The radicalization of the copper mines during this period, of which the most emblematic case was the long strike in El Teniente in April and June of 1973, ultimately became an instrument in the fall of Allende. With the support of the Chilean Right and the US government, the military successfully launched a bloody coup d'état on 11 September 1973, which ended the socialist experiment and broke the tradition of party politics in Chile.[8] As Collier and Slater (2004, 359) describe it, *El Once* ('the eleventh') represented the worst political breakdown in Chilean history as General Augusto Pinochet Ugarte (1973–1989) consolidated his power base and took over as a dictator. Under his 17-year rule—a record length of tenure among Chilean leaders, the most since 1540—a new development model was implemented in Chile—neoliberalism—characterized by depoliticized, technocratic governance of the economy.

Codelco and the Consolidation of Neoliberalism in Chile, 1973–1989

While the creation of Codelco as an SOE became the answer to unresolved political conflicts with its ideological roots in developmentalism, ironically it was consolidated under Pinochet's neoliberal authoritarianism. Pinochet drew his economic strategy from a group of conservative economists educated at the University of Chicago, experimenting on monetarism and unrestrained laissez faire economics. These 'Chicago Boys', who moved into the state planning agency ODEPLAN, aimed to reverse all of Allende's economic policies, particularly the nationalization of key industries, the universal welfare system, and the excessive tools of state protectionism such as trade tariffs and quantitative restrictions. The neoliberal programme privatized more than 400 state-owned, state-controlled, or state-intervened companies since 1974, although SOEs considered 'strategic' remained in the hands of the

---

[8] In particular, Valenzuela (1978) argues that the key to the coup is the failure of Centrist forces to incorporate themselves in the Allende government: the deliberate sabotage of the Right and Centre of *Unidad Popular* government's economic programmes, the breakdown of the coalition between the Christian Democrats and Government in Congress, increased polarization in a context of intensified popular mobilization (a result of President Frei Sr.'s social programmes), and the constitutional crisis due to failure of the Christian Democrats to compromise that led to the crisis of democracy. For other references see Garretón 2003; Taylor 2006.

92   Business of the State

military. While the Chilean state reoriented economic production across its whole industrial portfolio by withdrawing the state from direct management and allowing the collapse of industries like textiles and traditional agriculture, Chile's investment policy in its natural resource sectors accommodated the presence of public and private enterprises. Pinochet's greatest legacy was perhaps the retention of full state ownership of SOEs Codelco and Enami in the country's main export sector—mining—where the role of the state was redefined in terms of a *regulator* aimed at enforcing the rule of law in favour of entrepreneurship and maintained 'liberal neutrality' in the emerging import and export regimes (Kurtz 2001).

This reorganization of Codelco was complemented by a liberal, pro-FDI mining regime, with Pinochet issuing DL 1.349 and DL 1.350 on 1 April 1976 to consolidate the administration of copper production by centralizing the operations and control of Codelco across the four large mines. On the one hand, Pinochet kept Codelco directly in state hands to manage the persistent factional tensions within the military regime. The nationalist faction of the military viewed the potential privatization of Codelco as an act of betrayal to the country, largely mirroring nationalist sentiments of resource sovereignty, so Pinochet keeping La Gran Minería away from foreign hands was used as a method to consolidate his political control. Specifically, he issued a law automatically transferring 10% of Codelco's profits to the armed forces' budget with the explicit goal of modernizing the armed forces. On the other hand, new mining laws were codified to attract—and more importantly legitimize—foreign investment in Chile. Two landmark policies set in motion a fundamental change in mining governance. Firstly, DL 600, also known as the Foreign Investment Statute, offered foreign companies generous tax breaks by way of a 15% reduction in corporate taxes (from 35%) and adjusting for the depreciation of imports defined as 'investments' across sectors. Secondly, the Mining Code of 1982 was issued to accord private mining companies similar property rights to state-owned mining companies. At its core, this Mining Code was a guarantee to foreign capital that in acquiring concessions contracts to operate in Chile, the state cannot discriminate against economic entities based on the national origins of the investors. In this case, state ownership—historically conceived as an obstacle to foreign participation in the export sector—was at best seen as a neutral force in economic development.

The economic and social costs of neoliberalism were very high in Chile, at least during the initial stages of its implementation. The Chilean economy nearly collapsed in the 1982 economic crisis, leading to massive political mobilization by trade unions between 1983 and 1984. Yet, the authoritarian

Chilean state remained strong in suppressing opposition and remarkably, despite the repression of the labour movement and its demobilization, the Chilean economy experienced a miraculous recovery from 1985 onwards. In the copper sector, Codelco survived the lack of state investments and dramatic restructuring of the sector as the economy shrank, and from 1987 onwards, private capital returned in the mining sector—an apparent indication of the success of the pro-FDI mining regime (see Figure 4.2). In 1976, public investment in Chilean mining measured US$111 million and foreign capital contributed a mere US$2 million. By 1990, as Chile transitioned towards political democracy, the eclipse of productive investments in Codelco and Enami by the state (stagnating at US$386 million) was compensated by soaring foreign investment in mining worth US$762 million. In 1989, Minera Escondida, operated by Anglo-Australian company BHP Billiton, was the single biggest investor in the sector and today stands as the second biggest mining company after Codelco.

Chile's successful political democratization incorporated political parties and trade unions in the democratic system, although the military government dictated the terms of the transition (Garréton 2003; González 2008). Pinochet had failed to secure another seven years in office during an intense plebiscite in 1987; and in the 1990 election that followed, a coalition of restored Left and Centre parties, known as *Concertación por la Democracía*, won against the Right-wing coalition. Moreover, the *Concertación* coalition inherited a very peculiar political arrangement in Chile's mining sector: on the one hand, Codelco had survived and retained its full state ownership

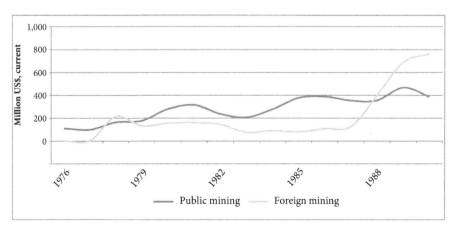

Figure 4.2 Public and private (foreign) mining investment under Pinochet, 1976–1990.
Source: Cochilco (2009, Table 30) (adapted).

94   Business of the State

amidst neoliberal authoritarianism; on the other hand, mining governance promoting foreign capital investment had legitimized the private sector as the new engine of growth for Chile. The following Chapters 5 and 6 examine the tensions and challenges associated with the *political continuity of neoliberal mining governance* under the *Concertación* government in Chile, in which mining governance in Chile became—and still remains—associated with a highly technocratic style of management. The Chilean case study demonstrates that whilst Chile's resource strategy still adheres to some of the theoretical axioms laid down by neoliberalism, the politics of state enterprise governance and labour relations require scholars to revise their expectations about the stability of institutions and political relationships.

The Brazilian Developmental State, 1930–1964

The Brazilian developmental state finds its origins in the Vargas era (1930–1945) and the creation of the *Estado Novo* (New State), and is followed by two further phases—during a democratic interlude (1945–1964) and an authoritarian military government (1964–1985). Unlike the Chilean or other Latin American variants of developmentalism, in Brazil elite consensus around the significance of the centralized state in leading and shaping modernization persisted throughout the 20th century. However, the creation of *desenvolvimentismo*—state developmentalism—as a dominant paradigm emerged in the context of failed modernization. The post-independence Brazilian state lacked political centralization and concentration of power—a problem exacerbated by the territorial size of Brazil. Throughout the rule of the monarchy (1822–1889), Brazil's political institutions were at best continuities of a colonial administration with a 'weak sense of national purpose' (Kohli 2004, 133). Even after the First Republic (1889–1930) was established based on a liberal export economy of primary commodities, the persistent lack of state centralization and the immense control exercised by regional oligarchs over the vast rural populations hindered the establishment of effective institutions to manage volatile commodity prices and to address political reforms of state institutions (Carvalho 1996; Guimarães 2003, Chapter 3; Kohli 2004).[9] As a consequence, two attempted coup d'états were launched against the oligarchic democracy in 1922 and 1924, which signalled the dissatisfaction of the military against a failing state. The military opposition sought to mobilize

---

[9] The system was characterized as *coronelism*, in which the governors of states maintain political control by giving local landowners—or *coroneis*—access to public posts and arms in exchange for electoral support.

various sectors of society in favour of a strong state in direct contravention to the liberal export economy model. It was during the first 15 years of Getúlio Vargas's rule (1930–1945) that significant political and institutional mechanisms were put in place that ushered a new period of state-building, characterized by state intervention in the economy, centralization of political and administrative institutions, and political incorporation of urban workers (Nunes 1997; Sola 1998).

Vargas faced two major problems: firstly, for 150 years since colonial times cycles of primary commodity production had exposed Brazil to volatile international market prices and a chronic dependence on export revenues from sugar and coffee (Machado and Figueiroa 2001, 9); and secondly, the conflict between a homogenous political elite with mercantilist traditions and land-owning groups with financial resources in regional territories which constrained the development of the national state and a professional bureaucracy (Carvalho 1996). When the 1929 global financial crisis hit Brazil, the export economy based on coffee collapsed, and this provided Vargas, who saw himself as a 'candidate of a country in protest rather than a candidate of a segment of dissident oligarchies' (Faoro 1998, 692), with a justification for his armed revolution to bring forth the creation of the modern state in a clean break from the past oligarchic democracy.

Two key conditions paved the way for the *Estado Novo*. Firstly, the *Estado Novo* benefitted from social discontentment—mainly from labour and the urban middle classes—which was used to justify the early provision of social policies and the implementation of a corporatist system to contain social conflicts and incorporate societal demands in the new institutional order (Leão 2018, 159).[10] The Varguista state had imposed restrictions on labour activities which included only recognizing one trade union per industry, creating regulatory bodies and state agencies linked to the Ministry of Labour to monitor labour activities, and financing trade unions directly through taxes (*imposto sindical*). Vargas saw the mobilization of popular classes as an obstacle to national industrialization; however, the *Estado Novo* could not simply ignore the 'labour question'. Accordingly, Vargas created a pension system to incorporate workers, fixed the working day to eight hours, and structured the organization of business associations (Collier and Collier 2002; Schneider 2004a). Secondly, Vargas's aims of strengthening state autonomy through SOEs and expanding the administrative machine were aligned with the post-1930 elite consensus to build an indigenously inspired, populist-flavoured,

---

[10] Corporatism is a system of representation that allowed the Brazilian state to shape class relations and determine the ways that labour and business organizations had access to decision-making structures of the centralized state (Schmitter 1971; 1974).

96 Business of the State

autonomous direction for economic development (Diniz 1978). In this context natural resources were conceived by Vargas and the military as a key pillar of national security, which meant dispossessing the private sector of ownership in the mining sector and reserving ultimate subsoil rights for the federal government. In this way, mining policy received renewed attention with the intention to shift subsoil rights from surface owners to the state (Triner 2011).[11] The new 1934 Constitution of the *Estado Novo* was a centralizing force that transferred decision-making powers to the federal government to authorize private companies to search for and develop oil and mineral resources (Randall 1993, 9), through the 'progressive nationalization of mines, mineral veins and waterfalls or other sources of hydroelectric energy deemed basic or essential for national economic or military defence of the country' (Article 119 §4).[12] The 1934 Constitution was followed by the nationalization of petroleum in 1937, and in 1938, General Horta Barbosa—committed to securing Brazil's energy needs for industrialization—created the *Conselho Nacional do Petróleo* (CNP) (National Petroleum Council) to oversee the governance of oil in Brazil.[13] Additionally, and despite the lack of capital and technological capacity of local entrepreneurs to explore oil blocks, nationalist restrictions on any foreign exploration of petroleum development in the country were put in place (Guimarães 2003, Chapter 4; Wirth 1970).

Between 1938 and 1945, a centralized state apparatus began to emerge, whose main purpose was to exercise political authority over strategic natural resources and to enhance state capacity to effectively regulate the national economy. For example, Vargas funded the National Coffee Council to conduct studies on marketing and production of coffee to bring back the prices to competitive levels. His government raised the tariff levels, devalued exchange rates, and sought for controls in imports. By the end of the 1930s, available financing for industrial investments increased alongside the creation of *Carteira de Crédito Agrícola e Industrial do Banco do Brasil* (CREAI) (Bureau of Agrarian and Industrial Credit of the Bank of Brazil). Vargas also sought to create SOEs, or at least began the discussion to establish them, in the steel, mining, and petroleum industries. With the outbreak of World War II in 1939, a national steel industry became a necessity and the need for

---

[11] See *Constituição da Republica dos Estados Unidos do Brasil*, Article 72, 1891. The Old Republic Constitution of 1891 changed mining rights, which then passed from the federal government (or from the imperial crown) to landowners. The Constitution further allowed foreigners the right to mine in Brazilian soil.

[12] See *Constituição da Republica dos Estados Unidos do Brasil*, Article 119, §4, 1934.

[13] Incidentally, the CNP was inspired by Argentina's state-owned oil company (YPF, formerly *Yacimientos Petrolíferos Fiscales*), though Barbosa thought petroleum was better suited to be a state enterprise that was not to be entrusted to anyone, including the Brazilian industrialists (Smith 1976; Wirth 1970).

self-sufficiency in the oil and mineral sectors drove the actual creation of SOEs. Vargas commissioned a study on how to create a 'big steel industry', which led to establishment of the *Companhia Siderúrgica Nacional* (CSN) located in Volta Redonda in 1946. During the same period, the *Companhia Vale do Rio Doce* (CVRD) was created in 1942 in Minas Gerais, with the company immediately becoming responsible for 80% of Brazilian iron ore exports. As Vargas committed to nationalizing natural resources in Brazil, his corporatist framework also provided industrial groups with the appropriate channels for lobbying to secure their private interests (Fonseca 1989; Guimarães 2003, 94–105; Wirth 1970).[14] By 1945, Vargas had centralized power in the *Estado Novo* with the capacity for state-led developmentalism. This was a state significantly different to the one that existed during the First Republic.[15]

In 1945, Vargas was overthrown by the military and democracy was reinstalled. The democratic period (1945–1964) was a period of continuity, whereby the role of the state as the leading agent of national modernization was reinforced. Several practices remained intact, such as the federal government retaining the right to intervene in labour unions, creating government agencies subordinate to the Executive together with the bureaucratic insulation of key state agencies, and creating SOEs for the state to retain control in the national economy (Evans 1995; Leão 2018, 163–166). Additionally, developmentalism provided the ideational glue for the state to link the 'oil question' with national industrialization. In April 1947, the military was involved in debating whether foreign participation in oil development was consistent with national security or not. On the one hand, General Juarez Távora advocated for the participation of foreign companies in the oil sector to secure Brazil's energy needs, in which concessions were seen as a way of funding oil exploration led by the government. On the other hand, General Horta Barbosa argued for state monopoly on the grounds of national security. Although the military was deeply divided over the nationalization of oil, a significant portion of the military backed General Horta Barbosa's nationalist position, perceiving oil control as a means of political control and extra

---

[14] As Guimarães (2003, 98) points out, corporatism was aimed at regulating and intervening in the economy. Vargas created several institutions across an array of sectors, such as the *Ministerio do Trabalho, Indústria e Comércio* (Ministry of Labour, Industry and Trade—1931), the *Conselho Nacional do Petróleo* (National Petroleum Council—1938), the *Conselho de Águas e Energia Elétrica* (Council of Water and Electrical Energy—1938), the *Conselho Nacional de Minas e Metalurgia* (National Council of Mining and Metallurgy—1940), *Comissão Executiva do Plano Siderúrgico Nacional* (Executive Commission of the National Steel Plan—1940), the *Comissão Executiva Têxtil* (Textile Executive Commission—1942), and the *Comissão de Mobilização Econômica* (Commission of Economic Mobilization—1943).

[15] In the First Republic, political power was distributed among four main poles—São Paulo, Minas Gerais, Rio Grande do Sul, and the army (Leão 2018, 158).

98 Business of the State

leverage for the military to move towards the centre of the political arena. As Philip (1982, 235–236) observed, the nationalist campaign produced an unlikely alliance between the military, students, the press, and the Communist Party. Their call for oil nationalization became famous with the slogan *O Petróleo é Nosso* (The Petroleum Is Ours), and was their rallying call between 1947 and 1953.

Oil exploration, then, had three policy alternatives: first, through a government monopoly with no Brazilian or foreign capital participation; second, through a monopoly on oil exploration including the minority shareholding participation of Brazilian and foreign capital; or third, concurrent oil development by government and private enterprise, although preference was to be accorded to Brazilian companies. When Vargas was re-elected in 1951, state intervention in the O&G sector (and beyond) as a national development strategy was consolidated. During the nationalization debate, Vargas had manoeuvred between the *Escola Superior da Guerra* (ESG) (Superior School of War),[16] his own Left-wing supporters, and civilians, which made the debate more ideological than economic. Once he was re-elected Vargas set up a commission composed of technocrats, headed by Rómulo de Almeida, to come up with a technocratic answer. The model that was proposed and implemented reflected the nationalization project of Brazilian steelworks— i.e. the Volta Redonda project—in which a government holding company rather than a state monopoly would be granted broad powers and discretion to seek foreign financing and technology to support oil development in Brazil. The subsequent bill sent to Congress proposed the creation of a 51% government-owned holding company for oil development and refining, in a model where private capital could play a large role in subsidiaries and associated enterprises. The NOC Petrobras would be financed by the transfer of existing state property, by selling 49% of the shares to the private sector and by a set of taxes on certain luxury goods. Petrobras would become a publicly owned trading company that would be free from congressional approval if the company was to pursue overseas oil exploration activities (Philip 1982, 237–241; Randall 1993, 9–11).

However, the technocratic solution was not palatable politically and, despite the multiple options outlined above, the 'oil question' was difficult to resolve. The *Petróleo é Nosso* campaign rejected the bill sent to Congress, to prevent 'backdoor dealing' with foreign companies, advocating instead for nationalist restrictions on foreign capital in exploration activities. When

---

[16] The ESG was an influential institution responsible for defining national security and in educating the military.

Congress passed DL 2.004 in October 1953, it became clear that the national state would establish *absolute monopoly* over oil exploration and production while Petrobras was created as a mixed public–private company. In April 1954, Petrobras inherited existing government oil holdings and state assets managed by the CNP which were valued at US$165 million. These included two refineries—in Mataripe (Bahia) and Cubatão (São Paolo)—a certain amount of drilling equipment, and a tanker fleet (Evans 1979, 90–92; Randall 1993, 9–12). Capital ownership of Petrobras was divided between domestic private shareholders (49%) and the federal government (51%). It is important to note that while Petrobras was born in a wave of nationalist fervour, its objective and outcomes were radically different from other NOCs. Latin American oil exporters created PDVSA and PEMEX to manage the large rents accrued from oil production operated by foreign oil companies. However, Petrobras began with an imperative to transform Brazil into an oil producer like its neighbours to meet domestic consumption for national industrialization (Priest 2016, 54).

As detailed above, the nationalization campaign to form Petrobras was forged through an unlikely alliance between the military and the Communist Party (among others), which unsurprisingly unravelled after the Brazilian army took a generally pro-US position after the Cuban Revolution in 1959. In this context, the real winner of the oil debate was the military, which had asserted its control over the petroleum, mining, and steel sectors by defining these industries as key pillars of national security. Beyond the oil industry, Vargas established the *Comissão de Desenvolvimento Industrial* (CDI) (Commission of Industrial Development) to increase the interaction and coordination between business and public agencies. He likewise established *O Banco Nacional do Desenvolvimento* (BNDE) (Brazilian Economic Development Bank) in 1952—an investment bank with its own resources, administrative structure, and internal statute that was autonomously managed for the sole purpose of financing long-term loans for efficient allocation of investments and to serve as a central agent for the coordination of economic management (Massi 2014; Sikkink 1991).[17] Put simply, oil nationalization became compatible with the developmental state.

Since its creation, Petrobras was embedded in the political system and, therefore, subject to periodic government intervention up until the 1964 military coup d'état. For example, Petrobras's profitability was achieved not through earnings from operations but through supportive public policies,

---

[17] BNDE was renamed as *Banco Nacional de Desenvolvimento Econômico e Social* (BNDES) (Brazilian National Economic and Social Development Bank).

100 Business of the State

most notably government support for gasoline prices, tax exemptions and earmarked sources of revenue, and direct government protection of the refining sector (Philip 1982, 368–369). But as Table 4.3 shows, Petrobras's earnings gradually increased as profitability became its central objective. With greater financial independence, the company also developed corporate autonomy from both Congress and the federal government.

Petrobras's strategy in its early years was centred on strengthening its refining capabilities and utilizing revenues from oil derivatives to finance oil exploration activities within Brazil. However, the ISI model implemented during the 1950s–1960s placed enormous pressure on Petrobras to meet the energy needs of a rapidly industrializing country. Oil accounted for one-fifth of Brazil's imports in 1954 and oil price increases had debilitating effects on its economic growth. While Petrobras was producing more oil, it was simply insufficient to meet demand. The company raised production from 2,721 barrels per day (b/d) in 1954 to 80,910 b/d in 1960; but consumption was at an astounding 263,844 b/d (Philip 1982, 372). There were also concerns that Brazil might not really have significant oil reserves to meet demand, which would severely limit the ISI model (Smith 1976). In the so-called Link Report (1960), Walter Link—an American consultant hired to survey potential oil reserves in the country—suggested Petrobras focus on finding offshore reserves and intensifying its overseas operations due to fewer prospects for onshore oilfields.

Around the early 1960s, Petrobras's involvement in politics was rapidly growing. Under nationalist pressures, President Juscelino Kubitshek (1956–1961) appointed Colonel Janari Nunes as head of Petrobras, which began the politicization of the state enterprise. Corporatist mechanisms were frequently used to control labour unrest in Petrobras, which at the time of the Cuban Revolution became controversial among the populace. In

Table 4.3 Petrobras's finances, 1955–1960 (in million cruzeiros).

Finances	1955	1956	1957	1958	1959	1960
Sales income (less costs)	1,021	2,817	4,705	7,766	13,333	15,477
Reinvested profits[a]	n.a.	166	1,577	3,492	4,687	7,522
Earmarked taxes	936	1,300	2,557	3,042	4,575	6,118
Vehicle levy	446	472	416	7	11	2
Total	2,403	4,755	9,255	14,307	22,606	29,119

Source: Petrobras Annual Report 1960, in Philip (1982, 369).

[a] Previous year.
n.a. Data not available.

exasperation, President Goulart (1961–1964) made political appointments in state enterprises to replace technocratic modes of leadership as a means to build political coalitions. This, in turn, compelled Petrobras managers and workers to search for a political base outside of the organization to utilize as a weapon in the internal conflicts developing within the state enterprise (Randall 1993, 27–29). The labour unions increased their control over some operations; for example, regional efforts to obtain investments were subject to political rather than strict economic criteria. In 1961, the departure of foreign advisers in Petrobras further weakened technocratic management and appointments became political battlefields between the Left and the politicians who wanted to gain control of the oil company (Randall 1993; Smith 1976). Consequently, Petrobras became a political arena between technocrats and the trade unions, which was only resolved with installation of the military government (1964–1985). The raison d'être of the coup d'état was clear: to provide overall societal guidance by exercising the capability of the military to quell social polarization and the need to reorient the state towards a more pragmatic stance, which would allow domestic business and foreign capital in the oil industry, albeit still to a limited extent (Schmitter 1972; Stepan 1971; 1973).[18]

The Military Period (1964–1985): From Strengthening to Weakening Petrobras

Under the authoritarian military government, Petrobras was depoliticized and achieved corporate autonomy to rededicate itself to oil exploration. General Castelo Branco's government (1964–1967) eliminated labour resistance, eased foreign exchange controls, and allowed private investment in petrochemicals, and, in a turnaround, the military government also rescinded the law nationalizing private refineries (Priest 2016, 59; Trebat 1983, 107). In 1963, the Petrobras Board of Directors established the company's centre for human resource training and development, the Centre of Oil Upgrade

---

[18] Such congruence between the state and capital is neither a natural nor static process. The changing conception of the military of national security and the role of Brazil in the international system was shaped largely by the international context. The 'Doctrine of National Security', as promoted by the influential ESG, was particularly not quite antithetical against giving the private sector (including foreign capital) important roles in strategic industries. The ESG did not advocate for a full monopoly of oil exploration and accepted the participation of domestic and foreign capital, which reflected the peculiar beliefs of this faction in power vis-à-vis the large segment of the military (Stepan 1971, 246). From the position of conceiving the production of basic goods—e.g. steel, oil, and coal—as crucial elements of national security, the military leadership altered its perspective after World War II towards further engagement with the Western world and participation in the international system (Guimarães 2003, 185).

102   Business of the State

and Studies (CENAP, known today as CENPES), while, coincidentally, off-shore oil development in the North Sea in the UK generated strong interest in technological learning in Brazil. Petrobras began to assimilate industry advances in offshore technology to improve its geophysical exploration capa-bilities, and in 1968 Petrobras drilled its first significant offshore wells in the Espiritu Santos and Sergipe–Alagoas Basins, using foreign contractors (Priest 2016, 60). As other small but important oil discoveries were achieved in 1969–1970, Petrobras set a new pathway to achieve energy self-sufficiency by moving into offshore exploration, although its main strategy was to focus on downstream investments through the company's subsidiaries. Hence, Petro-bras expanded the scope of its operations, and achieved complete vertical integration of its O&G industry with the creation of Petroquisa refinery as a majority government-owned SOE in 1967, and from 1969 onwards Petroquisa inherited Petrobras's rubber and fertilizer factories. At its peak, Petrobras had integrated several new subsidiaries into its operations, includ-ing Petroquímica União, Copene, Copesul, and Norquisa (Randall 1993, 32), with the objective of developing indigenous technology and to gradually replace foreign specialists with Brazilian professionals in the O&G sector.

The major transformation of Petrobras occurred between 1969 and 1973, during the authoritarian government of General Emílio Garrastazu Médici, who appointed General Ernesto Geisel as president of the state company. Geisel accepted the position with a tacit agreement that he would operate autonomously from the Ministry of Mines and Energy. Armed with inde-pendent decision-making powers, Geisel reorganized the directorate of the company to strengthen Petrobras's capacity to finance its expansion without relying on government budget. In hindsight, three major factors conditioned the success of Geisel's strategy. First, Petrobras's refining sector gave the company its comparative advantage and was a major source of profitabil-ity through its monopoly over the modern and larger refineries in Brazil. Petrobras benefitted from substantial market share and brought in bud-get surplus for the company. Second, the world oil market oversupplied, yet a reduction in the posted price of oil was impossible. Consequently, IOCs responded by offering discounts on posted prices, which, combined with Petrobras's oil import monopoly, had forced import prices to go down. Additionally, with North Africa and the Middle East entering the world oil market, Brazil was freed from its dependence on traditional suppliers like Venezuela. Third, Giesel expanded Petrobras's participation in downstream activities in the O&G value chain, where the main consumers of oil deriva-tives were government agencies, ensuring a constant demand for its products. This was achieved through the modification of DL 2.004 in 1968, which allowed Petrobras to set up subsidiaries with budgets beyond the oversight of Congress and compelled the subsidiaries to focus on costs and profits. In 1971, Petrobras created its subsidiary *Distribuidora* on the grounds of national security and profitability in the downstream sector. Petrobras's move to control the downstream sector also benefitted the private sector, which had previously supplied government agencies and which was unhappy with their delayed payments, and the modified law DL 2.004 also gave Petrobras authority to establish joint ventures and public–private partnerships with foreign and domestic oil companies. This strategy to expand Petrobras's activities into downstream sectors proved so successful that Petrobras's final market share jumped from 10.4% in 1965 to 15.2% in 1970, 22.1% in 1971, and 27.5% in 1973 (Philip 1982, 381; Randall 1993, 31–32).

Geisel's most controversial decision was to involve Petrobras in oil exploration. By 1970 the Brazilian government was wary about its dependency on the Middle East to supply oil, which could endanger the viability of the ISI model. Dias Leite, then Minister of Mines and Energy, proposed that foreign investment was necessary and Petrobras should sign service contracts with foreign oil companies to allow foreign exploration within the country. However, Geisel blocked Leite's proposal and maintained that oil exploration was to be a strictly Brazilian affair. As a compromise, in 1972 Petrobras set up an overseas exploration subsidiary, Braspetro, to find and import oil to Brazil, particularly from the Middle East. The creation of Braspetro was controversial because it was a recognition of the Link Report's main findings—that Brazil should abandon its objective of making the country self-sufficient in oil and Petrobras, originally set up to refine oil to generate funds to finance exploration and support the ISI model, was now being forced to change its objectives. If Petrobras was to move towards the downstream sector, the company ought to find a new criterion and a new purpose for its operations. In this way it was profitability, then, that became the most important measure of Petrobras's economic performance. Braspetro successfully found oil in Colombia, Iraq, and Algeria, though it failed to secure supply of the oil through contracts. Under a 1972 contract with Iraq, Petrobras operated in the oilfields discovered in Majnoon in 1976 and Nahr Umr-North in 1978 (Randall 1993, 33). In 1979, however, Iraq abrogated its initial agreement with Brazil and Petrobras was forced to absorb Braspetro's losses in order to maintain the viability of the subsidiary. However, despite its financial weakness, Braspetro had acquired technical and commercial experience in global oil operations, which helped the company to formulate risk contracts. In sum, domestic exploration within Brazil was neglected based on Petrobras's economic, technical, and bureaucratic logic and the government encouraged the expansion of Petrobras as it coincided with a relatively long period of stable economic growth, known as the 'Brazilian miracle' (1969–1974).

Ernesto Geisel went on to become president of the authoritarian military government (1974–1978), which then supported Petrobras's move to invest in upstream activities. Firstly, Petrobras had already replaced the military officers in management positions with civilian technical specialists. Secondly, building on the initial success of the Guaricema field—the company's first off-shore discovery in 1968 off the coast of Sergipe—Petrobras began to acquire marine seismic data on the Campos Basin. After eight failed attempts at the Campos Basin, Petrobras geologists were advised by French oil company Elf-Aquitaine to drill deeper. On its ninth attempt, Petrobras discovered oil in the Albian carbonate prospect called Garoupa, located about 120 metres below water and 100 kilometres from shore, and the Garoupa deposit became the first major discovery in the Campos Basin (Priest 2016, 62). The Garoupa and then Pargo fields were identified as potential oil reserves, with an estimated area of 100,000 square kilometres to be drilled at the depth of 100 metres.[19] With Petrobras's limited technological capability, which remained at the hands of IOCs, President Geisel made an unprecedented move to force IOCs to sign service contracts with Petrobras to finance the exploration of Brazil's oilfields. Under this arrangement, IOCs would be reimbursed through the revenues generated from discovered oilfields, while Petrobras would assume the role as sole operator of any oilfield eventually found (de Oliveira 2012, 528; Priest 2016, 62).

By the end of 1977, Petrobras had contracted 26 offshore drilling vessels to accelerate oil exploration in the Campos Basin, and by 1980, Petrobras had a total of eight commercially viable offshore oilfields (Priest 2016, 63). At the same time, Petrobras was experiencing unprecedented expansion and diversification. In 1976, Petrobras expanded into the fertilizer industry, creating its subsidiary, Petrobras Commercial International SA (Interbras), aimed at obtaining improved trade deals with oil-producing states in the Middle East. Meanwhile, Petromín (later called Petromisa) was set up in 1977 to enable the company to operate and develop in the domestic minerals market (Randall 1993, 34). As Petrobras expanded, its organizational structure also changed to reflect that of an IOC (de Oliveira 2012, 523).

Petrobras's corporate restructuring was complemented by a stronger alliance with the federal government, whose arms-length relationship with the SOE proved to be highly successful. The authoritarian military

---

[19] The discussion here is based on Petrobras's own account of its corporate history: https://www.petrobras.com.br/quem-somos/trajetoria (accessed 26 January 2011).

government provided generous financial incentives, such as exemption of import duties and royalties, tax relief on sales of equipment earmarked for Petrobras projects, international parity pricing for oil products, and a scheme to give Petrobras 80% of the foreign currency 'saved' from domestic production of oil (Alveal 1993). Petrobras was put in charge of setting the conditions for the joint ventures with IOCs whose officials were opposed to risk-service contracts, refocused its investment budget towards the upstream sector, and redoubled its efforts in offshore exploration (Priest 2016, 62). To overcome its technological fragility, Petrobras offered incentives for Brazilian offshore service and equipment suppliers to develop and share new technologies with the company, designed to support its intention to expand the participation of Brazilian companies in offshore platform production. As such, technological innovations were rapidly achieved in the offshore oil sector due to the opportunities for oil exploration and production in the Campos Basin (de Oliveira 2012, 530).

By the end of the authoritarian military government in 1985, Petrobras had made several key offshore discoveries (amounting to more than 600 million barrels in Albacora and 2.3 billion barrels in Marlim field). Facing formidable technological hurdles, Petrobras embarked on an unprecedented multi-billion-dollar industrial mobilization that required, above all, creating an in-house research and development (R&D) programme called PROCAP[20] coordinated by CENPES located in Rio de Janeiro. This six-year programme aimed to establish production capabilities in 1,000-metre-deep waters and to design production facilities to float or bob in the water. PROCAP, consisting of Brazilian and foreign universities, technology centres, engineering consultants and associated industries, was the largest undertaking to develop deepwater production.[21] This alliance—between an SOE and industry participants—was at the heart of the industrial and technological mobilization that swept the O&G industry in Brazil which saw Petrobras contract out drilling and well services, as well as fabrication, installation, and diving/subsea engineering (Priest 2016, 67). In other words, Petrobras's technological advancement was a by-product of the company's international orientation to acquire and learn from IOCs, which was only possible due to its arms-length relationship with the military government.

---

[20] In Portuguese, *Programa Tecnológico Empresarial de Desenvolvimento em Exploração de Águas Ultraprofundas.*
[21] Deepwater production is defined as water depths greater than 400 meters (1,300 feet).

Petrobras, Offshore Development, and Brazil's Lost Decade

Petrobras's success and attempts at pursuing technological advancement coincided with the so-called lost decade of the 1980s in Latin America. Like its neighbours, Brazil was engulfed by unsustainable debt and macroeconomic instability, leading to a sharp decline in the general contribution of state enterprises towards fixed capital formation. Given that Brazil remained heavily reliant on oil imports, to combat the crisis the Ministry of Finance took over the policy of pricing crude oil, diesel and gasoline, ethanol, and other oil derivatives. Its primary objective was to strike a balance between industrial growth and controlling inflation. The political transition to democracy in Brazil was principally (though not exclusively) facilitated by the failure of the autocratic military government to deal with the country's looming debt, hyperinflation, and economic stagnation as the cohesive developmental state experienced a profound crisis of legitimacy. Under President José Sarney de Araújo Costa (1985–1990), the 1986 Cruzado Plan was implemented to address the capital transfers and fiscal imbalances in the economy; however, its failure was a critical factor in the implementation of a more drastic macroeconomic stabilization strategy implemented under the 1987 Bresser Plan.

Petrobras is without qualification a success story. As Figures 4.3 and 4.4 demonstrate, Petrobras through its national monopoly was responsible for Brazil's steady increase in crude oil production, refining capacity, and amount of recoverable petroleum reserves, from its origins in the post-war years.

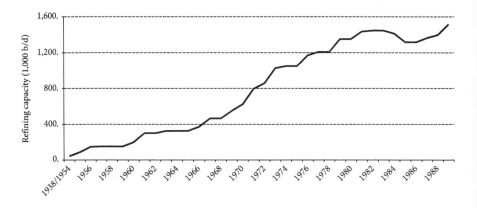

Figure 4.3 Petrobras's refining capacity, 1938–1990.

Source: Petrobras Annual Reports in Randall (1993, 13) (adapted).

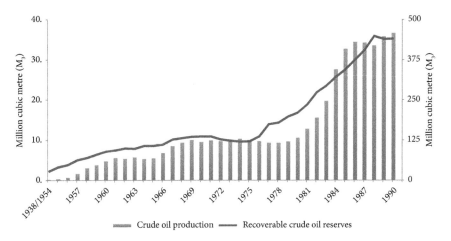

Figure 4.4 Petrobras's oil exploration and production capacity, 1938–1990.
Source: Petrobras Annual Reports in Randall (1993, 13) (adapted).

Production in the Campos Basin grew past 300,000 b/d at the end of 1982, which enticed Petrobras officials to pursue further deepwater exploration. Petrobras benefitted from technological learning and industrial collaboration with foreign oil players, developing a culture of innovation within the company, and a strong sense of corporate autonomy from the national state.

Nevertheless, Petrobras was subject to intense politicization during the economic crisis of the 1980s. There were political demands for the company to invest and employ locally, compelling Petrobras to expand its oil services and capital goods sector. Additionally, as a direct consequence of the balance-of-payments crisis, proposals arose to privatize Petrobras and other state enterprises to reduce the federal government's budget deficits as a means to attract foreign investors in the hope of introducing market competition in the Brazilian economy. In an unprecedented move, President Fernando Collor de Mello (1990–1992) proposed to sell the assets of Petrobras to allow the company to reorganize its operations focussed on its core business areas, and the National Congress approved the full privatization of Interbras and Petromisa, while Petrofertil and Petroquisa were partially privatized. In March 1992, Petrobras announced its reorganization to reduce levels of hierarchy and streamline its business activities to focus on oil production and processing. In April 1992, Petrobras President Ernesto Weber announced the company's 10-year strategic plan, which envisaged the end of Petrobras's monopoly in transport, refining, and imports. The financial and commercial directors were also replaced by individuals with extensive experience in the private sector and international operations. The reorganization

108 Business of the State

cut costs from US\$4.2 billion to US\$3.2 billion as the Petrobras system was eventually trimmed down to Petrobras and its subsidiaries Braspetro, Petroquisa (its subsidiaries were privatized), and Petrofertil (its subsidiaries were privatized). Petrobras, however, retained its minority ownership of the naval repair company *Empresa Brasileira de Reparos Navais* (RENAVE) (Randall 1993, 42–46).

Conclusions

Overall, similar to the fate of most SOEs across Latin America and globally in response to steady dominance of neoliberal economic orthodoxy from the 1980s onwards, Petrobras was exposed to demands for its privatization in order to attract foreign IOC investments, leading to the restructuring of the regulatory framework to accommodate competition and private participation. As in the rest of Latin America, neoliberal reforms were conceived as the antidote to the balance of payments crisis, indebtedness, and hyperinflation of the 1980s. It was also the solution preferred by governments in the region in lieu of the 'apparent failure' of the ISI model. In an unprecedented move, Petrobras's monopoly in oil exploration and production ended in 1997 and its company shares were sold to private investors and enlisted in the New York Stock Exchange in 2000 (see Chapter 7); and after witnessing the success of the company in deepwater exploration and production, IOCs began to take an interest in Brazil's oil reserves, notably the Santos, Campos, and Espiritu Santos salt-turbidite basins. The Brazilian case study (see Chapters 7 and 8) will critically discuss how developmentalism remained powerful in shaping the O&G industry in Brazil between the 1990s and 2010s, as Petrobras's governance model remained firmly intact despite waves of market-opening reforms in the succeeding three decades. As this chapter has demonstrated, Brazil and Chile experienced some success in pursuing sectoral development through the creation of SOEs. It has also shown that SOEs respond to their political environment. To pursue an argument examining the politics of SOE governance, the following chapters examine the continuity and changes between resource developmentalism and neoliberalism using the cases of Codelco in Chile and Petrobras in Brazil. Through empirical analysis, I seek to challenge two key ideas: (1) that developmentalism was eclipsed by the introduction of neoliberal reforms in the O&G sector; and (2) that SOEs in strategic resource industries were subject to an ideological warfare leading to the delegitimization of SOEs as engines of economic development.

5
Chile's Mining-Led Growth Strategy, 1990–2020

> The role of the state in Chile is to regulate mining ... not to do the business by itself. The role ... is subsidiary. The state should leave business where the private sector can do it.
>
> **Senior Official, Cochilco**[1]

Chile is exceptional in Latin America for many reasons. On one account, political economists have often described Chile as the poster child of neoliberalism, particularly given the staggering pace and scope of economic liberalization in production, finance, and social welfare provision under General Pinochet (1973–1989). Additionally, the Left and Centre governing coalition *La Concertación por la Democracia* (*Concertación* governments) (1990–2009) and succeeding governing coalitions in the 2010s have pursued political continuity with limited changes from Pinochet's authoritarian neoliberalism (Bril-Mascarenhas and Madariaga 2019; Bril-Mascarenhas and Maillet 2019; Madariaga 2020). However, as this chapter elucidates, the ideational reification of Chile as a neoliberal state completely overlooks a crucial element in the country's post-dictatorial development strategy: the overwhelming presence of the centralized state—and state ownership—in copper mining, the country's most strategic industry.

This chapter seeks to answer two key questions. Firstly, how do we account for Chile's hybrid mining model—discursively sustained by private sector governance but materially embedded in Codelco's (the state-owned mining company) presence in the sector—and secondly, to what extent has this governance model pursued structural transformation in Chile? In this way, the chapter offers a nuanced reinterpretation of Chile's state transformation and its development model. In the literature, the Chilean resource

---

[1] Author interview with Senior Official, Foreign Investment Department, *Comisión Chileno del Cobre* (Cochilco), Santiago de Chile, 1 October 2009.

Business of the State. Jewellord T. Nem Singh, Oxford University Press. © Jewellord T. Nem Singh (2024).
DOI: 10.1093/oso/9780198892212.003.0005

110 Business of the State

governance model is characterized as either unabashedly neoliberal or, in the terms of *Cepalistas*, neostructuralist[2] (Kirby 2009; Leiva 2008).[3] However, neither description captures the hybrid nature of the resource governance model in Chile. On the first question of *continuity and change* in this hybrid mining model, I argue that Pinochet's neoliberal model was fiercely defended by the post-dictatorial governments, leading to gradual, incremental changes in the institutional framework. Indeed, Chilean political elites maintained a contradictory strategy of reifying and retaining state ownership in its most critical sector while embracing neoliberalism as a hegemonic paradigm, as Codelco's overwhelming presence in copper mining—as Chapter 6 illustrates—provided the political resources for *Concertación* governments (1990–2009) and succeeding coalitions in 2010s to craft a narrative of 'private sector-driven growth'.

Secondly, considering the capacity of this hybrid development model to deliver industrial development, there are recent assessments about the apparent limitation of Chile's hybrid model (Madariaga 2020) and, as this chapter argues, have gradually escalated leading to profound questions about the future of Chile's neoliberal governance architecture. Specifically, the turbulent second decade of the 21st century, characterized by social protests and mass mobilizations, combined with a period of low commodities prices after the end of the commodities super-cycle in 2017 has slowly compelled the centralized state to accommodate institutional change. Nevertheless, growing demands for a new institutional arrangement favouring stronger state participation—through the passage of a new foreign investment law in 2016 and a shift away from the subsidiary role for the state in the economy—are yet to be completed.

With limited change, Chile's export-led growth model reflects the institutional continuity of Pinochet's neoliberal mining governance, which privileges private (foreign) capital as the driving force of economic growth and advocates for a minimalist role for the state in economic governance. By emphasizing the significance of private over public actors, the scope and range of development policies becomes limited, which consequently constrains the national state from pushing industrial development and moving away from commodity export-based growth. At the same time, by also emphasizing high-quality technocratic institutions with clearly delimited

---

[2] *Cepalistas* are heterodox economists based in the ECLAC (CEPAL in Spanish) who argue that structural heterogeneity and dualistic economies are the main sources of persistent underdevelopment in Latin America, and who from the late 1980s advocated neostructuralism as policy paradigm premised on the logic of international competitiveness.

[3] Oddly, most studies on Chilean mining have focussed on private mining interests and the ways business groups wield political and market power in shaping the resource sector (Bril-Mascarenhas and Maillet 2019; Leiva 2019).

boundaries as regards the role of state in the economy, state ownership in mining serves as a buffer against hyper-privatization. Hence, gradual institutional change—as opposed to a rupture from the Pinochet model—is likely to remain the pathway for Chile.

This chapter is structured in three main sections. The next section analyses continuity with change under *Concertación* governments from a historical institutionalist lens. A following section then explores incremental changes through the limited success of introducing new royalty taxes in the mining sector and calls to reform the 1974 Foreign Investment Statute (DL 600) with a new labour reform bill. Finally, in the concluding section, I examine attempts at introducing innovation policies in response to challenges to the neoliberal export-oriented model through the World Class Supplier Programme.

Phase I: Neoliberal Continuity with Changes (1990–1999)

Chile's peaceful transition to democracy was shaped by the political and economic rules of the Pinochet dictatorship constitution (1980) writ large, which meant that structural constraints for a new development model had domestic rather than international origins. In delineating the difference between Pinochet and *Concertación* governments' policies in copper mining, the starting point is to define primarily what kinds of political and economic institutions have survived in the post-dictatorial years. Below, I outline four contours of *institutional continuity* in mining governance.

Firstly, DL 600 sets out the rights and responsibilities of foreign investors through a special foreign contract. It offers generous tax rebates by allowing foreign companies to deduct 15% in their corporate taxes (at a rate of 35%) to adjust for the depreciation of imports declared by companies as investments. DL 600 remains a major pillar of Chile's pro-FDI regime, which throughout the 1990s prevented heterodox economist reformers within the *Concertación* coalition persuading Congress to introduce any royalty tax for mining. Even after a new Royalty Law was introduced in 2006, higher royalty fees were politically infeasible, and a transition period was put in place to reduce their impact on large mining operations.[4]

Secondly, the 1983 Mining Code and DL 18.097 institutionalized private property rights for natural resources by defending non-discrimination

---

[4] As will be discussed in section on Royalty Law, the tax clauses in DL 600 would be the basis of the new Royalty Law, particularly the option to stay within the DL 600 fixed taxation scheme or progressively apply a new variable tax rate. See Guajardo (2008, 2012), Libertad y Desarollo (2002; 2004; 2005), and Riesco (2005; 2008) for technical and political discussions of the Royalty Law.

112 Business of the State

between Chilean and foreign capital when applying for contract licences to exploit, develop, and produce mineral reserves. Whilst the Chilean state remains the ultimate owner of subsoil rights with the right to revoke mining concessions,[5] this was not exercised in practice. Political elites in Chile have repeatedly deployed the 'small state' rationale by emphasizing the power of international investors and their preference for tax stability, of which the latter has been considered as the country's source of competitiveness in mining.[6] Beyond the discursive power of neoliberalism, institutional constraints likewise prevented *Concertación* governments from introducing reforms. Specifically, the 1983 Mining Code belongs to the *Leyes Organicas* (Organic Laws) that refer to special legislation issued by Pinochet requiring a quorum of four-sevenths (4/7) of the acting members of Congress in order to be enacted, modified, or even discussed.[7] To further lock in succeeding governments, Pinochet also created an electoral system aimed at securing the interests of Right parties in Chile. He introduced the so-called binomial system—an electoral mechanism making it difficult for the creation of legislative majorities—and gave the Right several veto points alongside an outright majority in the Senate (González 2008, 109–110, 152–156). Formal rules adopted under the 1980 Constitution thus remained unchanged even after the return of democracy. *Concertación* governments failed to challenge these authoritarian enclaves because the coalition was unwilling to delegitimize the hybrid mining model skewed in favour of neoliberalism (Bril-Mascarenhas and Madariaga 2019; Madariaga 2020). In this context, that 20 years passed without an effective alteration in the model should not come as a surprise.

Thirdly, Chilean elites continue to reify the dual but contradictory role of the state as *regulator* and *producer* in the mining industry (Nem Singh 2010; 2014). To depoliticize copper governance, the Chilean state emphasizes the *technocratic* role of its specific state agency, the *Comisión Chilena del Cobre* (Cochilco) (Chilean Copper Commission), whose principal task is to perform annual audits on Codelco, thereby pushing the state enterprise to perform *at par* with private copper companies. As a regulator, the Commission is responsible for issuing foreign contracts and checking that

---

[5] The 1983 Mining Code Article 4 states: 'Should the State consider it necessary to retain the exclusive right to explore or to exploit substances subject to concessions, it shall act through companies and enterprises in which it holds an interest and said companies shall create or acquire corresponding concessions, provided they are empowered to act, under constitutional provisions, in said manner.'

[6] Author interviews with Juan Carlos Guajardo, Executive Director, CESCO, Santiago de Chile, October 2009; and Carlos Gajardo Roberts, *Sociedad Nacional de Minería* (SONAMI), Santiago de Chile, 14 September 2009.

[7] For a detailed explanation see http://www.law.edu/ComparativeLaw/Chile/.

all licences for operating mining companies are in compliance with Chilean laws. Crucially, Cochilco also exercises an oversight function in determining the copper prices on which the profits and sales of private companies are calculated for tax purposes. By assigning a technical position for Cochilco, *Concertación* governments upheld their widely acknowledged preference for dealing with conflicts through bureaucratic technocracy. This, in turn, depoliticizes highly contentions policy reforms, channelling political discontentment into expert-led commissions that seek for detailed policy solutions rather than challenging the political character of policy problems (Madariaga 2020; Nem Singh 2010).

For policymakers in Cochilco and at the Ministries of Finance and Mining, 'mining governance' is strictly defined as policies fostering stable macroeconomic conditions for investment, the promotion of export capacities by the private sector (and ironically, not Codelco), and setting performance standards to benchmark the state enterprise vis-à-vis private mining.[8] As such, more critical and politicized issues are left outside institutional channels or are watered down upon arriving in National Congress. The issue of royalty taxes is an excellent example of this: at the height of the taxation debate in 2004, Cochilco dismissed contentious claims of organizations critical to the royalty proposal, notably the *Centro de Estudios Nacionales de Desarrollo Alternativo* (CENDA) and *Universidad de Artes y Ciencias Sociales* (ARCIS), who accused *Minera Escondida* and other mining companies of creative accounting, tax evasion, and other unscrupulous business practices in Chile (Riesco et al. 2005).

Economically, Pinochet's legacy of maintaining the power of big business has stayed the course of post-dictatorial politics, becoming more entrenched in the democratic political game. The wider access of organized private interests in state policymaking, most notably *grupos económicos*, and in mining, the *Consejo Minero* (Mining Council) and *Sociedad Nacional de Minería* (SONAMI), have been far more institutionalized under the *Concertación* governance style.[9] One stark example of this relationship between the state and big business is the approval of National Service Customs Resolution No. 2757, which established the requirement to certify the weight and quality

---

[8] Author interviews with Senior Official, Foreign Investment Department, Cochilco, Santiago de Chile, 1 October 2009; Gustavo Lagos, Consultant, Santiago de Chile, November 2009; and Nicolas Majluf, Codelco, October 2009.

[9] *Consejo Minero* represents the interests of big mining companies; its membership includes the foreign companies operating in La Gran Minería, and Codelco is part of the council. Codelco's interest clearly runs against other companies, since the former aims to produce for the state whilst the latter is simply for profit. This was demonstrated in the royalty debate where Codelco threatened to withdraw from the Council due to conflicts of interests. SONAMI is the national grouping of miners in Chile; the organization goes back as far as 1883 and has therefore long been engaged in policy consultations.

of all copper concentrates leaving national ports, and a range of maximum acceptable variations was established regarding the content levels present in concentrate upon arrival at destination.[10] The resolution was the result of a joint effort by the *Ministerio de Minería* (Ministry of Mining), the National Customs Service, the Internal Revenue Service, and Cochilco, with the technical collaboration of *Consejo Minero* (Ministry of Mining et al. 2002 in Riesco et al. 2005, 51). Crucially, discourses of economic efficiency and productivity also added a cloak of legitimacy to the policies of *Concertación* governments that protected the interests of the mining business community.

Finally, the Chilean state upheld labour flexibility as a core principle in managing labour relations, leading to the atomization of unions and a shift from collective to individualized negotiations (Cook 2007; Winn 2004). Like other pro-FDI reforms, Chile's labour policy has failed to substantially move away from Pinochet's *Plan Laboral* issued in 1979. While centralized trade unions were demobilized as a result of neoliberal continuity, mining workers—historically insulated from political weakening—have avoided demand-making beyond narrow economic benefits such as negotiation of bonuses (Nem Singh 2012a; 2012b). Put simply, the 'labour question' often associated with politicization was by and large divorced from other national policy debates by moving contentious issues into the realm of technocratic commissions and the Department of Labour (Crocco 2017, 192). In the absence of protective labour legislations, the global division of labour favouring specialization of mining companies towards their core business operations has resulted in the unfettered subcontracting of mining operations. As the sector embraced widespread subcontracting, stratification between contractual and permanent workers contributed to widening divisions within the labour movement, leading to the fragmentation of a once-strong centralized union movement in the strategic mining industry (Donoso 2017).

The continuity of the hybrid model was legitimated by the success of placing Chile as a magnet for trade and investment at a time characterized by unfavourable external conditions across Latin America, notably low commodity prices and low economic growth rates. As Figure 5.1 shows, DL 600 brought in US$762 million in 1990 (as opposed to public investment in Codelco and ENAMI of US$386 million). By 1999, private investment jumped up to US$1,337 million, whilst public mining investment fell to US$369 million. An inevitable consequence of *Concertación* governments'

---

[10] If the levels in an operation fall outside of this range, the National Customs Service adjusts the figures regarding the contents actually present in the concentrate and reports this to the Internal Revenue Service (IRS, or SII in Chilean), which takes the relevant action to correct and fine the violating party.

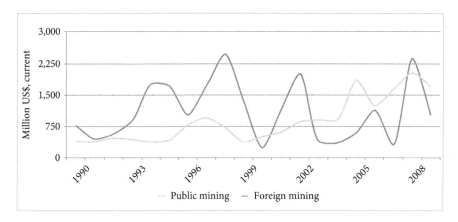

Figure 5.1 Public and private (foreign) mining investment in Chile, 1990–2009.
Source: Cochilco (2010, Table 30) (adapted).

pro-FDI strategy was the steady decline of Codelco's share of mining investment, which suffered from continuous disinvestment from the Chilean state. With its corporate governance structure under the tight control of the state (see Chapter 6), the *Concertación* governments' hybrid mining strategy built on neoliberalism left Codelco with severely limited financial capital to reinvest in the company. This, in turn, provided some evidence for the argument that Codelco was unproductive compared to its private sector counterparts.[11]

Phase II: Incremental Changes (2000–2010)

The election of Ricardo Lagos (2000–2006) from the Social Democratic faction of the *Concertación* coalition marked a hope to break away from Pinochet's development model. However, the hegemonic discourse of neoliberal continuity made any radical reforms in mining extremely difficult to push forward. The position of mining companies was clear—that political continuity of the economic model is the source of Chilean economic growth.[12] Hence, Lagos came to power with a powerful institutional constraint, as the Centrist faction within the *Concertación* coalition was working closely with private mining companies to avoid introducing new legislations on mining.

---

[11] Author interviews with Jonathan Barton, Santiago de Chile, 3 November 2009; and Ricardo Ffrench Davis, Former *Concertación* technocrat, Santiago de Chile, 18 August 2009.

[12] Author interviews with Javier Cox, Santiago de Chile, Secretary General, *Consejo Minero*, 22 October 2009; and Carlos Gajardo Roberts, SONAMI, 15 September 2009.

As historical institutionalists often posit, exogenous factors are vital in opening pathways for incremental institutional changes, and in the case of Chilean mining, soaring commodity prices driven by China's hunger for natural resources provided an opportunity for some shifts in the overall growth model (Nem Singh and Bourgouin 2013), opening up new development spaces and policies asserting greater state control to be articulated (Jepson 2020; Nem Singh 2010; 2019). While mining unions—especially subcontracted workers' movements—have remained critical of *Concertación* governments' apparent privatization of mining (Donoso 2017),[13] Figure 5.2 shows the dramatic rise in copper prices that enabled heterodox *Cepalista* economists within the *Concertación* coalition to reintroduce a new royalty bill and pass it into law.

The 2005 new Royalty Law as well as the 2007 Subcontracting Law passed under Chile's New Left Bachelet government (2006–2010) are notable examples of incremental institutional changes away from neoliberalism. Through the concerted efforts of *Cepalista* technocrats and organizations seeking greater state control (e.g. CENDA and ARCIS), mining governance has slowly pushed beyond a pro-FDI institutional framework. By analysing these two legislations, I depart from strict interpretations of the Chilean model as neoliberal. If hegemony is constituted through the use of coercion and consent (Cox 1981), then the dissatisfaction—if not cautious rejection—by Chilean technocrats and labour unions of neoliberal ideas as the foundation of its growth strategy indicates the gradual breakdown of the unfettered

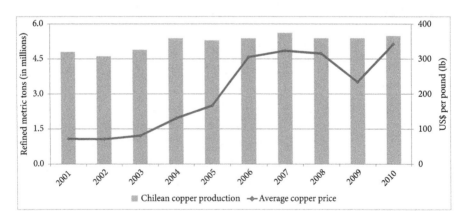

Figure 5.2 Chilean copper production in relation to copper prices, 2001–2010.
Source: SERNAGEOMIN (2010).

---

[13] Author interviews with labour unions, Antofagasta, November 2009.

pursuit of competitiveness. Under Lagos and Bachelet, Left-led *Concertación* governments' push for gradualism is an explicit attempt to ameliorate market excesses in order to 'make mining contribute for Chilean development'.[14]

The New Royalty Law of 2005

The move to increase taxation in the mining sector was a major revision in the neoliberal mining framework. As early as the mid-1990s, *Cepalista* economists such as Ricardo Ffrench Davis proposed the idea of a royalty tax, but this was immediately rejected, as discourses of global competitiveness and comparative advantage were powerful arguments to dissuade President Frei Jr's government from introducing any significant changes in the neoliberal model. The persuasive power of these pro-business discourses was rooted not only in the threats coming from the Right, but also from low commodity prices between the 1980s and 2002, leaving *Concertación* governments with limited policy options. Without an alternative institutional option away from neoliberalism, a debate on royalty taxes did not take off and the agenda faltered for another five years.[15] However, in 2001, the *Superintendente* of Antofagasta—the country's mining capital—boldly proclaimed that 'mining can and should contribute more in Chile's development', and on 19 June 2001, a new legislative bill was introduced for debate, the *Ley de Evasión y Elusión* (Ley No. 19.738) which sought to investigate and establish new laws against business practices related to tax avoidance in Chile. One principal change was to amend existing laws to give more powers to tax agencies to seek ways of penalizing both legal (tax avoidance) and illegal (tax evasion) forms of skirting around tax payments. This was, in hindsight, a precursor to the larger debate aimed at introducing further changes in the mining taxation regime.

In April 2002, during the *Expomin*, a major gathering of mining companies and state agencies, the Ministry of Mining clearly expressed its position on the need for Chile's mining industry to contribute more substantively to Chile's development. The Ministry proposed to strengthen the 'sectoral clusters' and create a Sustainability Fund for the state to finance research, innovation, and sustainability. While discontentment from factions within the *Concertación* coalition was not entirely new, such public statements drew

---

[14] The quote is from the *Superintendente* of Antofagasta in 2001.
[15] Author interview with Ricardo Ffrench Davis, Former *Concertación* technocrat, Santiago de Chile, 18 August 2009.

118   Business of the State

more attention due to an increasingly politicized climate resulting from investigations of the business practices and tax payments of mining companies (Forum on Royalty, Cluster, and Innovation 2005; Punto Minero 2005, 6–7). The tipping point was, however, when Exxon attempted to sell its subsidiary, *Disputada de Las Condes*, to Anglo-American to avoid capital taxes. Political discussions within Chile intensified, leading some critical organizations to question how much private mining had contributed to Chile's economic development (Punto Minero 2005; Riesco et al. 2005). Subsequently, Lagos affirmed his desire for a new legislation introducing a new specific tax on mining. The Senate responded by establishing a special commission to study fiscal policies of the foreign-owned mining companies that make up *La Gran Minería*. Between mid-2003 and early 2004, Finance Minister Nicolás Eyzaguirre pursued mining companies to voluntarily give up some of their tax benefits established in DL 600 (Punto Minero 2005, 7).

On 19 April 2004, at the *Expomin* meeting of private mining and politicians, President Lagos announced the royalty legislative project aimed at establishing royalty charges in metal and non-metal mining activities, with the end goal of financing initiatives to expand Chile's technological and innovation capacity. On 5 July 2004, the new legislative agenda sought to create (1) an *ad valorem* mining royalty and (2) the *Fondo de Innovación para la Competitividad* (Innovation Fund for Competitiveness). The proposal generated important political support, for example from Joaquín Lavín, the Mayor of Santiago, with a vote split of 61 in favour and 41 against the bill on 21 July 2004. Yet, this majority vote was not sufficient for its passage through the National Congress, which required a quorum of a four-sevenths vote to pass the bill, as stipulated in the 1983 Mining Code. Subsequently, Lagos used his *facultad presidencial* (special presidential powers) to compel Congress to retake the initiative. However, on 10 August 2004, the Right-dominated Senate then rejected the presidential decree to take up the royalty bill again (Punto Minero 2005, 7). In this way, thanks to the institutional constraints imposed by the 1980 constitution, the Right was able to safeguard the neoliberal economic model and effectively deter mining reforms proposed by the *Concertación*.

Despite losing the political battle, President Lagos announced he would insist on passing the legislation to enhance the contribution of the mining sector to Chilean development. After going through intensive coalition bargaining, on 14 December 2004 Lagos introduced a new royalty bill—Royalty II or the *Impuesto Específico a la Minería* (Specific Tax on Mining)—after the municipal elections, and the *Cámara de Diputados* (Chamber of Deputies) passed the new bill with an overwhelming majority—86 in favour and 14 against—before it was then taken up by the Senate who passed the bill with 28 votes in favour, 5 against, and 6 abstentions (Senate Press 2005). As SONAMI director Alfredo Ovalle argues, President Lagos' decision to use his presidential powers to reintroduce a second bill indicates not just the delivery of a *Concertación* electoral promise, but also the popularity of this economic reform (Senate Press 2004), given that it also reflected guarantees sought by private mining companies including fiscal resource transfer to non-mining regions, the protection of small and medium mining companies (SMEs), and advancing a system of mining patents to ensure competitiveness (Senate Press 2005).

The Royalty II law stipulates that mining companies with annual sales of more than 50,000 metric tons of fine copper are subjected to a maximum of 5% tax. Those companies with sales of equal to or below 50,000 metric tons but more than 12,000 metric tons are taxed at a variable rate from 0.5 to 4.5%. All companies producing equal to or less than 12,000 metric tons are in equal measure exempted from the additional taxation. As Figure 5.3 shows, the law directly impacts on the profits of the group of mining elites (also known as *gran minería del cobre productores* or GMP-10). The government also gradually modified the law in three key aspects: (1) by requiring taxes to be paid in Chile in the case of sales of foreign companies which directly or indirectly control more than 10% of Chilean companies;[16] (2) by eliminating the accelerated depreciation for the purposes of additional taxation; and (3) by introducing 'royalty' taxes. Furthermore, there were outstanding legal conflicts between the fiscal benefits for companies derived from DL 600 and the new mining tax, which meant that negotiations between business groups and the Ministry of Mines took place.[17]

The passage of the Royalty II law adds a level of nuance against generalized claims of Chile's staunchly neoliberal style of economic management. Although the Right repeatedly challenged the societal and public benefits of a new mining royalty by stressing the long-term costs for Chilean competitiveness (especially for large-scale mining companies),[18] the Royalty II tax law was—as argued by *Concertación* technocrats—an important economic measure to improve Chile's absorptive capacity to cushion commodity price

---

[16] This was a specific response to the controversy on corporate malpractices of mining companies to avoid tax payments in sales in 2001.

[17] DL 600 has a specific clause exempting companies from future taxes by deducting a further 8% of their operational costs. The IRS can contest copper prices that have been used to calculate the annual sales of companies. Cochilco, then, has the ultimate right to determine referent copper prices to make sure that companies do not sell fine copper at undervalued prices for the sake of tax evasion. Cochilco performs a special function whereby it supervises and inspects full and correct compliance with laws, regulations, and norms regarding procedures that are specifically applicable to the mining sector and to the relevant companies in the public and private sectors (Riesco et al. 2005, 50).

[18] Author interviews with Javier Cox, Santiago de Chile, *Consejo Minero*, 22 October 2009; and Carlos Gajardo Roberts, SONAMI, 15 September 2009.

volatility and external shocks.[19] It was deemed necessary to finance research and innovation towards export diversification and long-term fiscal stability, which could only be done through a special mining tax. While the additional tax is not a substantial windfall, given the veto power of the Right in the Senate, its impact on the Chilean public treasury is apparent, especially when combined with the fiscal contribution of publicly owned companies. Figure 5.3 and Table 5.1 both provide a clear picture of mining taxation—where Codelco clearly plays a role in maximizing rent capture—as a key policy instrument in managing and legitimizing copper as the engine of economic growth.

By the end of the *Concertación* government in 2009, this growth model was by all means successful. The astutely crafted model of continuity was credited with delivering economic growth based on Chile's natural comparative advantage, gains in poverty reduction, and long years of political stability based on consensual party politics. While the rest of Latin America that transitioned towards the 'pink tide' saw their party systems collapse and established institutions challenged by social movements, notably in Bolivia,

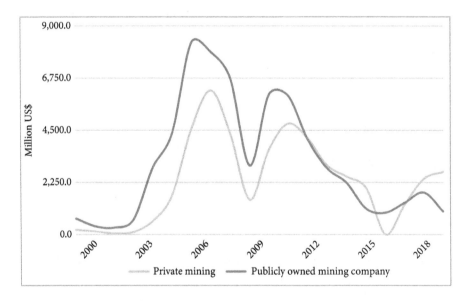

Figure 5.3 Fiscal contribution of the mining sector in Chile, 2000–2019.

Source: Cochilco (2019, Table 30) (adapted).
Note: Public mining enterprises include Codelco and ENAMI. Private mining includes the group of 10 large copper companies that had subscribed to a DL 600 Foreign Investment Contract in 2001; these companies account for 90% of total private mining production (also called *gran minería del cobre productores* or GMP-10).

---

[19] Author interview with Ricardo Ffrench Davis, Former *Concertación* technocrat, Santiago de Chile, 18 August 2009.

Chile's Mining-Led Growth Strategy, 1990–2020   121

Table 5.1 Selected data on the tax contribution of copper mining in Chile, 2000–2019.

	2000	2004	2008	2012	2015	2019
Total fiscal revenue[a]	15,918.0	21,047.0	43,468.0	59,036.5	51,277.8	60,515.5
Gross specific mining tax reported by GMP-10 companies[b]	–	–	416.0	442.0	94.0	217.0
Mining contribution to total fiscal revenue	909.1	3,491.0	11,093.3	8,306.7	3,129.5	3,708.1
Codelco's share of fiscal revenue, in percentage of total revenue	4.4	13.7	15.5	6.9	3.9	1.7
GMT-10 companies' share of fiscal revenue, in percentage of total revenue	1.3	2.8	10.0	7.1	2.2	4.5

Source: Cochilco 2019, Table 30 (adapted).

[a] Fiscal revenues in Chilean pesos (CLP) are converted to US$ at the observed exchange rate.
[b] Adjusted figure, to exclude Codelco's participation in El Abra (49%) and Anglo-American Sur (2012: 8.2%, and since 2013: forgard 20%). Actual payment of this tax is included and part of the Business Tax GMP-10 (Letter A). The source for 2015's figure is the Provisions of Companies Financial Statements (for previous years, the source is Sales Reports).

Ecuador, and Venezuela, Chile—together with Brazil—embarked on gradual institutional change emphasizing moderate transformative politics delivered through coalition building and inter-party consensus (Altson et al. 2016; Nem Singh 2014).

The Subcontracting Law of 2007

Concertación governments believed that economic growth could deliver gains in poverty reduction and resolve employment-related problems in Chile (Sehnbruch 2006, 137). The goal was to combine labour flexibility with worker protection, with an emphasis on a moderate and gradualist course in policy reforms (Donoso 2017, 105–107). Pinochet's 1978 Labour Code institutionalized outsourcing (*subcontratación*),[20] not just of non-core business activities, but also of the core functions and operations of a company, and

---

[20] Outsourcing is defined as 'the triangular employment relationship where a worker ("contract" worker) employed by an enterprise (the "provider") performs work for a third party (the "user") to whom their employer provides labour or services' (Duran-Palma and López 2009, 247–248). In the mining sector, the user is often referred to as the principal company, while the provider is often the subcontracting company.

122 Business of the State

this remained in place throughout post-dictatorial Chile. This was largely due to the social contract among elites to retain the neoliberal model, which in return delivered political stability in the 1990s (Cook 2007; Frank 2002; Sehnbruch 2006). However, outsourcing was poorly regulated and unions called for more critical discussions on how to address workers' rights in Chile. During the presidential election of 2005, the 'contractual labour question' emerged in the national political debate. Spurred by the collective action of a national contractual workers' movement originating from the mining industry, in 2006 newly elected Michelle Bachelet (2006–2010) reintroduced a labour reform bill that was shut down during the previous Lagos government. Known as the 'Outsourcing and Supply of Labour Act' (DL 20,123), herein the Subcontracting Law, the legislation claims to serve as a 'definitive, decisive and clear step in terminating the division between first- and second-class workers' (Duran-Palma and López 2009, 249). In the words of former Labour Minister Ovaldo Andrade, the new law aims to protect the workers' rights and minimum benefits and its immediate effect will directly benefit 'more than one and a half million workers who are under a subcontracting regime'.[21]

Subcontracting law DL 20,123 introduced five new articles into the 1978 Labour Code. Firstly, it requires that the contract worker establishes a direct and legal employment with the provider (the subcontracting company); if, on the contrary, the worker does not have any contract with the subcontracting company, it is understood that the principal company *directly* employs the worker (Article 183-A).

Secondly, it makes the principal company accountable by introducing the principle of joint and several liability (*responsibilidad solidaria*), whereby the contract worker is allowed to sue the principal company and all those who may be held liable for breach of their rights (Article 183-B). Under the existing Labour Code, user enterprises (the primary company) were only liable for the action of subcontracting companies/providers (*responsibilidad subsidaria*), leaving workers very little legal recourse for upholding their rights.

Thirdly, to avoid joint liability, the principal company must ensure subcontracting companies are fully compliant, and the Subcontracting Law gives the principal company the power to request and access information from providers on how they fulfil their labour obligations. This can be achieved by either securing a certificate issued by the *Direccion del Trabajo* (Labour

---

[21] For a general overview see http://www.dt.gob.cl/1601/w3-article-93827.html (accessed 15 February 2012).

Bureau) or 'other suitable methods guaranteeing the validity of the information' (Article 183-C). Any breach of labour obligations by the provider gives the principal company the right to withhold payments to the provider until the rights of contract workers are fulfilled.

Fourthly, the recourse of the principal company is restricted only to access to information and withholding payments to the provider (Article 183-D).

Fifthly, the Subcontracting Law obliges the principal company to adopt all necessary measures to protect the life and health of all workers employed irrespective of their contract status (Article 183-E). In practice, however, to enforce the law the contract worker must pursue a court case to extract liability from provider companies as the 'user enterprise', which in practice can be long, complex, and expensive (Duran-Palma and López 2009, 250, 254).

To understand the passage of the Subcontracting Law requires a broader analysis of the Chilean political economy. The growth of outsourcing had become widespread as a direct result of Pinochet's 1978 Labour Code. Chilean companies' use of third-party contracts increased from 43% in 1999 to 50.5% in 2005—a seven-point jump within six years (Ministerio del Trabajo 2006, 7). In manufacturing, the percentage of contract workers increased from 32.9% in 1999 to just under 5% in 2006 (Duran-Palma and López 2009, 248). Since the 1980s, Codelco began to outsource its non-core activities and, gradually, moved towards subcontracting its core functions and operations. Subcontracted mine workers increased from 12% in 1990 to a staggering 60% in 2000 (Manky 2018, 582). Outsourcing was justified by the government and private sector as a labour efficiency practice and, therefore, legitimate for mining companies.[22] The overall effect is the creation of a dual structure of employment relations in the copper mining industry encompassing both permanent workers—*trabajadores de planta*—who became part of the corporatist pact with Codelco and large private mining companies to guarantee labour stability in the sector; and temporary contract workers—*trabajadores subcontratados*—who must accept worse labour conditions and less pay than their counterparts.

This labour flexibility was enshrined in Chile's post-dictatorial employment relations as Chile embraced global competitiveness as the driving force of its export-oriented commodity strategy. This, in turn, meant that the labour question was silenced and conspicuously swept under the carpet. Any serious reform efforts with regard to labour policy were thwarted either within the *Concertación* coalition itself or in the halls of Congress

---

[22] Author interviews with Pedro Marin, President, *Federación Minera de Chile* (FMC), Antofagasta, 2 November 2009; and Lariza Palma, *Centro Unita de Trabajadores* (CUT), Santiago de Chile, 16 October 2009.

124 Business of the State

where the Right is firmly embedded in policy decisions (Cook 2007).[23] The *Concertación* labour reform sought a balance between employers' demands for maximum flexibility in the labour market—contracts, rules in hiring and firing, and working hours—and the concerted attempts of workers and unions to recuperate their economic gains prior to the dictatorship.[24] Thus, the pursuit of economic continuity with marginal changes is reflected in the shortcomings of the labour reforms achieved in the 20 years of democratic rule (Cook 2007; Frank 2002; 2004; A. Vergara 2008, 190–193; Winn 2004).

The move to challenge labour flexibility, unsurprisingly, came from contracted mining workers. Firstly, copper—and especially mining by Codelco which produces at least 11% of the world's supply—is not only the country's principal export (hence its name, *el sueldo de Chile* or the Chilean wage), but also central to the construction of Chile's natural resource-based economy (Nem Singh 2010). The technology-intensive and capital-driven requirements of large-scale mining imply that the sector generates high wages without creating mass employment even during periods of rapid expansion in production. This accords miners structural power vis-à-vis the state and business. Secondly, despite the point above, mining experienced the most significant increase in subcontracting practices. In Codelco, as Table 5.2 shows,

Table 5.2 Permanent and subcontracted workers in Codelco, 1995–2015.

Workers	1995	1998	2001	2004	2007	2010	2013	2015
Company personnel[a]	19,753	18,258	17,166	16,778	18,211	19,347	19,242	19,117
Operating contractors[b]	8,913	9,206	13,773	19,929	26,210	23,138	26,523	23,098
Investment contractors[c]	4,720	6,307	5,346	8,683	17,079	18,103	21,214	23,250

Source: Codelco Annual Reports (1998, 1999, 2001, 2004, 2007, 2009, 2010, 2013, 2015, 2018, 2019).

All figures are calculated as of 31 December of every year.
[a] Company personnel are defined as those included on the company payroll.
[b] Operating contractors represent personnel used by subcontractors who support normal operations, e.g. mining work.
[c] Investment contractors are personnel employed by subcontractors as part of new investments, e.g. investments to develop underground mining in Chuquicamata and many other mining projects.

---

[23] The two failed referendums on constitutional change in September 2022 and December 2023 tried to address the technocratic and party-centred nature of decision-making and the balance of power across the political spectrum.
[24] Author interviews with Pedro Marin, President, FMC, Antofagasta, 2 November 2009; Lariza Palma, CUT, Santiago de Chile, 16 October 2009; and Agustin Latorre Risso, *Sindicato de Empresa de Trabajadores Xstrata Copper AltoNorte*, Antofagasta, 4 November 2009.

in 2015 those without permanent contracts constituted more than double the total workforce in the company, with 46,348 contracted and 19,117 permanent workers, as Codelco hired contract workers on an ad-hoc basis to perform core functions and operations while maintaining labour stability through a social contract with permanent workers (see Chapter 6 for details). Put crudely, labour flexibility constitutes one of the defining features of Chile's resource governance model.

Finally, given the corporatist employment relations in the mining sector, contract workers are able to draw from the long tradition of labour militancy, linkages with Leftist parties, and mobilizational capacity distinctive to copper workers, making it possible for workers to organize and coordinate to place localized grievances into a collective defence of equal pay to equal work (Fermandois et al. 2009; Manky 2018; A. Vergara 2008). In this way, framing workers' economic benefits as a form of labour justice has become politically feasible in mining but not in other segments of the Chilean economy.[25]

The prelude to the passage of the Subcontracting Law was the mobilization of contract mining workers between 2003 and 2007, which brought back into national politics the labour question that had been buried since the Allende years. In 2006, 12 organizations linked to the Communist Party formed a National Committee of Subcontracted Workers with more than 50 union leaders across Chile. This committee was formalized on 8 June 2007 into a new umbrella organization representing contractual workers in both state-owned and transnational private mining companies. The movement took the name the *Confederación de Trabajadores del Cobre* (CTC)—the same as the copper workers' union of permanent workers formed in 1951. Led by Cristian Cuevas, the CTC created a national network of contract workers' unions that reshaped policy discourse on labour relations.[26] Known as the *Contratistas*, the workers of Codelco staged a 37-day-long strike beginning 25 June 2007, under the banner 'Equal Pay for Equal Work' (Donoso 2017; Duran-Palma and López 2009, 252–253). The strike involved 25,000 workers across Codelco's five mining divisions and cost the company US$10 million a day. Codelco attempted to co-opt the movement by signing an agreement with three unions involved in the conflict after 27 days; however, the CTC rejected the validity of the agreement and it was not until 10 days later that a framework agreement between Codelco, the CTC, and subcontracting companies was agreed.

---

[25] However, Duran-Palma and López (2009) compare labour mobilization in the copper and forestry sectors, suggesting that episodes of labour militancy in resource sectors are a critical exercise of political agency of workers—largely a direct effect of the country's export-oriented economic strategy.

[26] For a historical overview of the links between the CTC, the Communist Party, and its predecessor union Sindicato Interempresa de la Gran Minería y Ramas Anexas (SITECO) see Manky (2018).

126 Business of the State

The issue, however, did not end here. The National Labour Bureau published its inspection reports into the industrial dispute five months later and its main ruling was that Codelco was at fault and must internalize nearly 5,000 contract workers, granting them personnel status. But, in an unprecedented move for the state company, Codelco went to court to challenge the decision, arguing that the National Labour Bureau did not have the authority to instruct the company to absorb the contractual workers. As Donoso (2017, 119–120) points out, Codelco's defiance caused an open conflict within the *Concertación* government—with the Ministry of Mining and the Ministry of Finance supporting Codelco on the one hand, and the Ministry of Labour and the National Labour Bureau supporting the workers on the other. In May 2008, the Supreme Court ruled that employment relationships cannot be determined solely based on National Labour Bureau inspections, but through an employment tribunal. This ruling had the simultaneous effect of weakening the spirit and the provisions of the Subcontracting Law and legitimizing the hard-line stance of private companies for outsourcing (Duran-Palma and López 2009, 250). In response, President Michelle Bachelet, embattled after public sector protests and strikes by students in 2006 and contracted workers in 2007, decided to intervene. She endorsed the agreement between Codelco and the CTC; however, this ruled out the possibility of regularizing 5,000 workers in the state enterprise.

One significant effect of this contentious episode between state and labour was a cascade of social conflicts within the mining sector, this time in the private sector. Since 2006, contract workers had already mobilized against BHP Billiton's *Minera Escondida*, Chile's largest private mining company and the second largest copper producer in the world. Mining workers decided to reject the company's offer in the collective bargaining, which had the net effect of ramping up and compelling *Minera Escondida* to reach a compromise to avoid a similar outcome to the Codelco dispute. Among many things, workers' demands included a 5% increase in salary, a bonus to prevent future labour strikes, and further health and education plans for workers' families. These demands are conspicuously depoliticized—especially given that contracted workers want more concrete economic benefits—and therefore limit the capacity of unions to play a wider role in Chile's post-*Concertación* days. In a significant way, social mobilizations throughout the 2010s were led by students and environmental justice movements precisely because the equal wage campaign was decidedly narrow and specific.

Overall, the Subcontracting Law was fraught with compromise within the *Concertación* coalition and was severely diluted in Congress. President Bachelet's *Concertación* government embraced Pinochet's Labour Code, struggled to make peace with unions, and strengthened individual worker protection at the expense of collective rights (Leiva Gómez 2009; Ugarte Cataldo 2006; Winn 2004). In this way the Subcontracting Law is a vital, yet reactionary measure aimed at managing labour conflicts. By refusing to reject the pillars of labour flexibility, the *Concertación* government was in a double bind: on the one hand, it was beholden to big business who continuously argued that 'companies buy goods and services from third parties, thereby making labour rights the primary responsibility of contracting firms'.[27] On the other hand, the social debt incurred by the working classes under neoliberalism could not be ignored easily, and neither could the recognition that reducing poverty without addressing social inequality is insufficient as a sustainable growth strategy. These dynamics reflect the tensions in the mining sector, whereby Codelco and transnational private companies have extensively practised outsourcing their core business operations—a strategy crafted in pursuit of competitiveness at the global scale.[28]

The Subcontracting Law succeeded in partially protecting individual rights, but this came at the expense of workers' collective rights. The gulf between unionized permanent staff in Codelco—the *Federación de los Trabajadores del Cobre* (FTC) (Copper Workers' Federation)—and contracted workers under the CTC underpins the fundamental contradiction of the mining governance model. As an activist from the national union CUT argues, there is simply no interest for the FTC to wholeheartedly join other workers in solidarity.[29] This brings us back to the central issue of workers' political identity: subcontracting—and the principle of labour flexibility— has not only broken down the traditional relationship between the principal company and the worker, but also produced fragmentation, tensions, and conflicts between unions and workers who are at different positions in the structure of production (Nem Singh 2012a).

Phase III: The Growth Model Amidst Turbulent Times (2010–2020)

The election of Sebastian Piñera (2010–2014) yielded neither major policy shifts nor fundamental changes in the structure of political power in Chile. If the hegemonic position of neoliberalism remained unchallenged

---

[27] Author interview with Javier Cox, Santiago de Chile, *Consejo Minero*, Santiago de Chile, 22 October 2009.

[28] Author interviews with Javier Cox, *Consejo Minero*, 22 October 2009; and Juan Saldivia, Independent Consultant, August 2009.

[29] Author interview with Lariza Palma, CUT, Santiago de Chile, 16 October 2009.

128   Business of the State

under the Centre-Left *Concertació* governments, the Centre-Right governments that followed enjoyed the benefits of institutional continuity. The main
thrust of the Chilean mining model remained untouched: the promotion
of foreign direct investment and the central role of resource exploitation—
as opposed to shifting towards manufacturing and industrialization—as the
dominant economic strategy. Consistent with neoliberalism's emphasis on
natural comparative advantage, trade and investment policies in mining were
guided by Chile's export-oriented strategy (Bril-Mascarenhas and Madariaga
2019). For two decades, Chile's mining model has financed poverty reduction and social welfare expansion, even catapulting the country to become
an OECD member, and Chile's copper mining governance model appeared
to be an unqualified success.

Yet, the Chilean model was also showing signs of fragility. While piece-
meal reforms—notably the Royalty II law and Subcontracting Law—were
successfully introduced in the 2000s, the structural problems of neoliberalism caught up as the commodity super-cycle ended, signalling hard times
were about to come. With the benefit of hindsight, the period of the 2010s
can be more accurately described as the years of turbulence and politicization of neoliberalism (Donoso and von Bülow 2017; Grugel and Nem Singh
2015; Roberts 2016). In 2006 and 2011, high-school and university students
led sporadic yet concentrated protests, questioning the privatization of education and rejecting inequality as a natural consequence of neoliberalism
(Grugel and Nem Singh 2015). Additionally, anti-dam building protests,
Mapuche resistance, and contracted workers' strikes added pressures on
elites to contain the rising political discontentment (Donoso and von Bülow
2017; Manky 2018). These protests would culminate in the so-called *estallido
social* of October 2019—a series of social mobilizations marked not only by
the construction of a national protest movement in which critiques against
neoliberalism were articulated in different forms across social movements,
but also by the unprecedented violence against citizens from the democratically elected state. We cannot fully comprehend these turbulent years without
also examining the exhaustion of Chile's neoliberal mining regime.

Chile's mining model promoting its comparative advantage was presumed
highly successful, requiring very little modification from its original blueprint
based on the sustained export of refined copper in world markets, facilitated by a swathe of trade agreements across North America and the Pacific.
Chile's dominance in world copper supply, however, is an outcome of a geological lottery—that is, its copper reserves are of the highest quality and
cost less to extract compared to Peru, Mongolia, or Zambia, for example.

By comparison, advanced industrialized countries with substantial mineral endowment such as Australia, Canada, and the US emphasized the importance of linking mineral extraction with value addition to dominate the supply chain. In these countries, mining was pivotal in building spillover effects and sectoral linkages, as well as in facilitating the creation of domestic mining suppliers—meaning that mineral extraction was seen as an engine for building knowledge-intensive capabilities suitable for industrialization (Atienza et al. 2018; Lebdioui 2019; 2020).

By contrast, the changing patterns of control in the global supply chain of mining show the limited advancement in innovation systems in Chile. Overall, Chile's share of global copper production dropped from 33.6% in 2010 to 28% in 2019. While over the same period traditional mining producer Peru has increased its share of production from 7.7% to 11.9%, China—a new participant in the supply chain—has more or less maintained its share (from 7.3% to 7.7% of production) (Cochilco 2019, Table 78). As Nem Singh (2019) argues, China is now moving from merely importing metals and commodities towards being an active participant in the world supply. Thanks to its industrial strategy, China has transformed itself as the dominant player in global copper refining and in copper smelter production (see Table 5.3 and Figure 5.4). Hence, Chile's traditional comparative advantage through its natural resource endowment has been slowly eclipsed by Chinese emphasis on investing in value-added activities in the commodities sector.

Table 5.3 Global refined copper and smelter production (in kMT of copper content), 2010–2019.

Country	2010	2011	2012	2013	2014	2015	2016	2017	2018	2019
China	4,540	5,163	5,879	6,667	7,649	7,964	8,436	8,889	8,949	9,447
Chile	3,244	3,092	2,902	2,755	2,729	2,688	2,613	2,430	2,461	2,269
Japan	1,549	1,328	1,516	1,468	1,554	1,483	1,553	1,488	1,595	1,495
US	1,098	1,031	1,001	1,040	1,095	1,141	1,221	1,079	1,111	1,057
Russia	900	912	891	875	894	876	867	949	1,020	1,020
Democratic Republic of the Congo	254	349	453	643	742	793	707	699	821	842
South Korea	556	593	590	604	604	595	607	664	665	638
Germany	704	709	682	667	673	678	672	695	670	600

Sources: Cochilco, 2019.

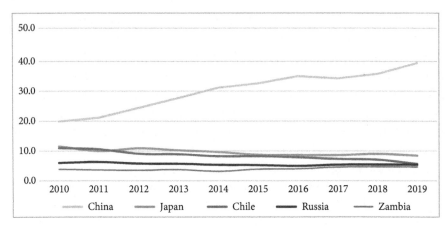

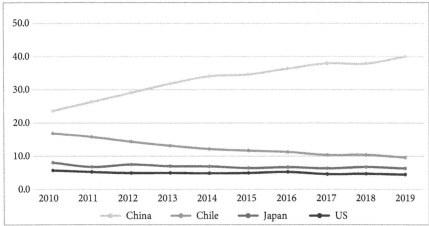

Figure 5.4 Percentage share of global copper smelter (top graph) and refined copper production (bottom graph), 2010–2019.
Source: Cochilco (2019).

That the trend is moving towards Chinese control over value-added activities in the natural resource chain should not come as a surprise. Chinese industrial strategy in the 20th century mirrors the regulatory tactics and control exercised by the US government during its catch-up phase in the 18th and 19th centuries (Gallagher and Porzekanski 2010; Jepson 2020; Klinger and Muldavin 2019). As the literature demonstrates, successful mineral producers have often linked industrial policies with the export sector to diversify export baskets, create vertical and/or horizontal spillover effects in the supply chain, and reorient mining as a knowledge-intensive, research-driven sector suitable for seeking new value-added activities (Di John 2009; 2011; Lederman et al. 2008; Massi and Nem Singh 2018; Wright and Czelusta 2004).

The World Class Supplier Programme

Two key trends have altered the policy perspective of Chilean decision-makers from 2008 onwards. Firstly, the sustainability of mining requires the achievement of productivity gains, development of new technologies, and adaptation of existing ones—all of which can only be addressed through a coherent innovation policy. Secondly, despite the challenges above, mining underwent a process of vertical *disintegration*, whereby large mining companies followed the international trend in organizational change by focussing on their core activities and outsourcing the services and goods indirectly related to mineral extraction and production (Navarro 2018). According to Fundación Chile (2014), about 60% of the operating costs of Chilean large miners are provided by outsourcing companies—a trend that is comparatively higher than Australia, Canada, and Finland (Korinek 2013). Consequently, the apparent spillover effects to the productive economy that could be generated from mining are weak, leading to uneven development and lack of innovation within the sector (Atienza et al. 2018). As Figure 5.5 shows, total factor productivity in Chilean mining dramatically dropped in the 1990s and 2000s, spurring elite motivations to create a supplier programme to support the internationalization of Chilean domestic companies.

The development of domestic suppliers with high technological innovation and managerial capabilities became the cornerstone of Chile's new resource growth strategy. A new programme was launched in 2008,

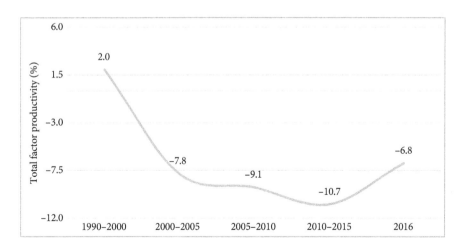

Figure 5.5 Total factor productivity of the mining sector in Chile, 1990–2016.
Source: Fundación Chile (2019, 23) (adapted).

132 Business of the State

Programa de Proveedores de Clase Mundial (PPCM) (World Class Supplier Programme), which aims to contribute to reducing information asymmetries, coordination, and transaction costs between lead mining companies and their suppliers. Initially sponsored by BHP Billiton Minera Escondida, followed by Codelco, the PPCM seeks to provide technological solutions to specific challenges detected by large companies in their operations. Consistent with the Chilean approach of state minimalism, Fundación Chile, a public–private partnership, serves as a broker between mining companies and suppliers. Although some public funding eventually became available through the Corporación de Fomente (CORFO) and the Ministry of Mining, the bulk of financial support for the PPCM has remained in the hands of mining companies.

Additionally, through the National Council of Competitiveness and Innovation (NCCI)—the same agency created for supporting mining innovation and financed by royalty fees (see discussion on Royalty Law above)—the National Commission for Mining and Development (NCMD) was created. In 2014, it presented its first systematic report to President Bachelet (elected for a second term as president, 2014–2018), containing key guidelines for a long-term mining development strategy that was underpinned by innovation and technological investments ranging from policies on how to reduce greenhouse gas emissions (GHG) to improving water and energy efficiency (Comisión Minería y Desarollo de Chile 2014).

Returning to the PPCM, the two main participants, large mining companies and their suppliers, undergo a three-phase process: first, the mining company identifies the technological problems in its operations; second, interested suppliers apply to the Fundación Chile website and a selection process by mining companies takes place to find the supplier with the best fit to deliver technological solutions; and third, the mining companies provides technological, managerial, and financial support for the scaling up and internationalization of these solutions. Suppliers' participation lasts between 15 and 27 months after the selection process; however, there are still no clear guidelines about the scaling up and internationalization (phase 4). The project investments range from US$100,000 to US$20 million, and by November 2013, collaboration between major mining companies, suppliers, and universities was accelerated to develop a coherent strategy to accelerate the internationalization of suppliers' technological solutions. In 2014, 17 contracts were signed between suppliers and universities for acceleration and consulting, and by 2015, Fundación Chile in coordination with the sector produced a detailed report, the *Technological Roadmap to the Mining Sector*, to offer guidelines on how to tackle the main challenges of the mining sector regarding innovation and internationalization (Navarro 2018, Table 1, 53).

Using data on 2010–2014, Navarro (2018, 54–58) evaluated the initial success of PPCM. Firstly, that the two biggest copper producers in the world—BHP Billiton's Minera Escondida and state enterprise Codelco—embraced the programme was crucial in supporting domestic suppliers to enhance their participation in the global value chains. Secondly, out of the 6,000 suppliers in mining, 51% of suppliers that participated in the PPCM have exported their products in 2012, while only 34% of the suppliers not aligned to the PPCM had successfully exported to the global market. Thirdly, calculating the annual average of the value of exports, percentage of exporters, and average number of exported products by exporting companies, there is an increase in the value of exports and the number of shipments, a slight reduction in the participation of exporters in the programme, and no clear trend in the number of products exported. Finally, an important measure of R&D is the number of patent applications. Table 5.4 details the percentage of projects with intellectual property rights (IPR) applications in the final year (2016) of the programme. The last column of the table shows the suppliers' previous experience with IPR applications and their potential to generate new innovations. Based on these data, 41% of the total sample of suppliers in the programme had applied for patents, indicating a large innovation potential among companies with experience. Put differently, these suppliers were able to provide technological solutions to the specific problems faced by large mining companies in their operations. Where any doubt lies is in the capacity

Table 5.4 Suppliers' IPR applications, 2011–2016.

Final year	Number of PPCM projects	Percentage of PPCM projects with IPR applications	Percentage of companies with previous IPR applications
2011	1	0	100
2012	16	13	25
2013	16	6	31
2014	33	27	52
2015	17	35	47
2016	9	11	33
Total	92	–	–

Source: Navarro (2018, Table 6, 58).

134 Business of the State

of suppliers to scale up and internationalize these solutions—future studies are needed to measure and document this more effectively.

In 2017, as copper prices dropped and the super-cycle ended, PPCM was renamed as *Programa de Innovación Abierta en Minería* (PIAM),[30] which later became absorbed by a larger public–private initiative called the Alta Ley National Mining Programme (ALNMP). Led by CORFO and the Ministry of Mining, the ALNMP aims to promote innovation, productivity, and international competitiveness of mining companies, considering the volatility of international market prices.

What these findings indicate overall is that supplier participants show themselves to be skills-intensive and export-oriented. The programme successfully appears to choose potential winners that can become internationally competitive in the long term. Despite the neoliberal character of the state, the Chilean government's objective of achieving US\$4 billion in exports for participant suppliers reflects a political will for technological innovation similar to Korea in the 1970s and other developmental states. Whether this can be realized is a matter of empirical investigation for future scholars. For now, it is critical to note the shift in public policy in Chile—whereas the state was often hands-off in supporting mining companies or suppliers in the past, the challenge of competitiveness and innovation is slowly reformulating Chile's growth strategy in the 21st century.

Neostructuralism and Its Discontents

Chile offers a hybrid development strategy for resource-rich states—the so-called neostructuralist state—which coheres around a policy paradigm aimed at engaging with, not isolating from, the global political economy and, in so doing, embraces the logic of international competitiveness (Kirby 2010; Leiva 2006; 2008; Taylor 2010). The overarching principle of the exports-led growth model is *productivism*, or the discourse of global competitiveness and private sector notions of efficiency. The logic of productivism and competitiveness ensured institutional cohesion around neoliberalism. The productivist discourse abandons the traditional statist developmentalist elements of managing production and gives priority to entrepreneurial initiatives as the driving force of economic growth. This is exemplified in economic projects enhancing 'public–private partnerships', for example, the 'clusters' concept where state-financed private sector projects are seen as the more efficient way

---

[30] For details about PIAM see Meller and Parodi (2017).

to use fiscal policy towards economic growth. The state role was defined by creating the National Council for Innovation and Competitiveness (NCIC) to enhance public–private initiatives through direct access to state funds of private companies. In a 2010 evaluation report on Chile's national innovation strategy, it was noted that:

> Returning to high levels of economic growth is a critical policy concern for Chile. Since 1998, growth rates have been only half of the 7.1% achieved from 1984–97 ... Despite a favourable environment and significant investment, *Chile has not succeeded in diversifying its economy or becoming an innovation driven competitor.* Its competitiveness has stagnated recently. *Improving business innovation in private sector firms* in the short and medium term is a central challenge. Policy options exist that could provide a significant stimulus to business innovation. *Major government investments in innovative capacity* through such agencies as CORFO, CONICYT, and through the tertiary education sector have yielded some progress ... but *are hampered by significant coordination failures and weaknesses in institutional capacity* (NCIC 2010, 3, emphasis in original text).

However, around the end of the era of *Concertación* governments, Leiva (2008) criticized the Chilean government's *neostructuralist* strategy as neoliberalism with a veil of social equality. Indeed, despite the market power of Chile, the state insists it is not a price maker and, therefore, could not— and ought not—to artificially reverse low copper prices (Riesco 2005, 13). In an interview with a senior official at Cochilco, he summarized the role of the Chilean state in mining:

> There is an argument around why the state did not directly participate in mining activities under Concertación. First, the state simply had no money to do it, to invest and to control the sector. If the government invests in mining, you cannot invest in education, healthcare, and other welfare functions. Secondly, there is a long-held view now among Chilean elites that the role of the state in Chile is to regulate markets in times of failure and crisis, to promote growth through private enterprise, and to take care of the poorest in society through social welfare. The state should not do the business by itself ... hence, its role ... is *subsidiary*. By history, the country made this definition [under Pinochet]. The state must step aside when the private sector can do it.[31]

Of course, and as discussed above, this argument has been questioned by trade unions, students, and environmentalists, to name a few. Chile's *estallido*

---

[31] Author interview with Senior Official, Foreign Investment Department, Cochilco, 1 October 2009.

136 Business of the State

social in October 2019 is a sober reminder of the uneven costs of Pinochet's 17-year neoliberal dictatorship. While social protests led by unions and social movements between 1981 and 1983 paved the way for a smooth transition to a political democracy in 1989 through a *Concertacion* pact between the Centre-Left forces and social movements,[32] the tradition of compromise appears to be over now. Chile's image as a tutelary democracy or *estado de compromiso* (compromising state) has been eroded (Barton 2002; González 2008; Heiss and Navia 2007) and a new era of more contentious politics has arrived. To summarize briefly, economic policy continuity in mining (and elsewhere) was not just a result of the structural problems associated with mining-based development; it is a by-product of the *Concertación* coalition's embrace of neoliberalism as a growth strategy.

By 2010, the *Concertación* coalition had ended, with very strong results with regard to poverty reduction and economic growth; however, it had failed to offer an alternative development paradigm beyond tinkering with the neoliberal model. Notwithstanding copper mining as a successful resource extractive industry in the developing world, Chile has locked itself in a natural-resource-based economy. Chilean exports, whether copper, lithium, gold, molybdenum, wine, salmon, cash crops, export fruits, or forestry, are governed through the logic of competitiveness and private sector standards of efficiency. This analysis has shown important shifts in policy thinking around innovation; this does not alter the overall orientation of the neoliberal state. As Madariaga (2020) reminds us, the tripod between neoliberal ideas, interests, and institutions makes this growth model highly durable and resistant to change. Nevertheless, the on-going constitutional debates to decide on the appropriate role of the state in the economy, social welfare, and environment continue in Chile The extent to which neoliberalism can be regulated under new institutional conditions remains to be seen.

Conclusions

The political choices in favour of political continuity in Chile are the product of a combination of structural constraints imposed by mineral dependence and the political choice made by elites towards natural resources specialization, the institutional and political legacies of Pinochet's neoliberal dictatorship, and the congruence of elite beliefs around the legitimacy

---

[32] Author interview with Union Leader, Sindicato de Empresa de Trabajadores Xstrata Copper AltoNorte, and Federación Minera de Chile (FMC) Member, 4 November 2009.

of the private—as opposed to public—logic of development processes. While high commodity prices gave Chile an extraordinary opportunity to finance social welfare policies, leading to critical poverty gains, its neostructuralist approach towards global competitiveness, as Robert Cox (1981) puts it, was reproduced through a combination of consent and coercion which inadvertently led to the hegemony of neoliberalism. Hence, perhaps my distinction between neoliberal and neostructuralist policies may appear superficial for some scholars. My departing viewpoint, however, starts with a more complex and nuanced understanding of growth models—development policies are intrinsically hybrid.

Thus far, the analysis in this book has examined the power of neoliberal ideas and policy practices as constraints to the reorientation of the state in managing the economy and how consensual decision-making has led to conservative reforms in the realms of mining policy and labour relations. Based on this chapter, Chile has pursued a self-reinforcing, path-dependent sequencing of a hybrid development strategy favouring neoliberal ideas. As *Concertación* governments embraced continuity, the political costs of this model increased, and, therefore, any choices were 'locked in' to sustain the logic of global competitiveness and the hegemony of neoliberalism. By promising political stability and legal certainty, mining governance in Chile became—and remains—associated with this highly technocratic style of management. Nevertheless, Chilean state governance has proven itself relatively successful in embracing global competitiveness. Chapter 6 explores state–state (SOE) relations between the Chilean government and Codelco as an SOE, and how Codelco weathered the pressure for global competitiveness and the extent to which the company succumbed to the dictates of market forces. I emphasize the *politics* of state ownership from the point of view of state managers of SOEs and mining unions. I shall discuss the consequences of neoliberalism for corporate autonomy and labour management and, in so doing, demonstrate the variegated effects of neoliberal reforms in SOEs.

6
The Politics of Managing Codelco and Its Labour Force

> Codelco is a strategic company for Chile. Overcoming extreme poverty and transforming the country in a modern and fair society depends to a large degree on the success of its management. This very reality imposes greater demand for efficiency and competitiveness.
>
> **Marcos Lima, Codelco President, 1994–2000**[1]

Marcos Lima acknowledges the place of Codelco in Chilean politics and history, and how the future of the company is interlinked with the country's economic success. Hence, the politics of restructuring state enterprises in the mining sector reflects one of the most contentious policy agendas for the Chilean state. The *Concertación* coalition's view of state enterprise restructuring centred on subjecting Codelco to the efficiency performance standards of the private sector. Put simply, SOEs were viewed as an instrument for maximizing fiscal capture on behalf of the state, not as a source of technological innovation. Hence, corporate governance reforms were aimed at maintaining a technocratic state by way of depoliticizing the management of the company (Nem Singh 2010). Ironically, however, Codelco is at the heart of political conflicts and remains a subject of political intervention. Importantly, its contractual workforce became the engine of renewal for labour rights, leading to the construction of a national contractual movement (Donoso 2017; Manky 2018).

To what extent does Codelco exercise autonomy from the Chilean government? What are the consequences of limited autonomy for its performance as an agent of economic development? The chapter examines the dynamics and consequences of state ownership in state–state (SOE) relations and capital–labour conflicts. As Chapter 5 demonstrated, widespread marketization in the Chilean economy produced a hybrid development strategy in

---

[1] 'Letter of the President'. *Codelco Annual Report 1999*, 10. Santiago de Chile: Codelco.

Business of the State. Jewellord T. Nem Singh, Oxford University Press. © Jewellord T. Nem Singh (2024).
DOI: 10.1093/oso/9780198892212.003.0006

the mining sector, whereby public and private production co-exist with a regulatory framework privileging private property over national ownership. This chapter makes two claims: firstly, that Chile's hybrid development strategy in the mining sector exists alongside neoliberalism is a direct result of the country's political conflicts over defining state ownership; that is to say, Codelco's role is to serve as a buffer between the public and private, and, therefore, it is also an indirect *mediator* of the conflicts inherent in the neoliberal regime. Secondly, Codelco's relative autonomy is often compromised as the company is expected to compete with private companies and to adopt corporate governance reforms reflective of international companies' standards of productivity and efficiency. As Codelco responds to these demands by internalizing the logic of the market—through the professionalization of its day-to-day management and embrace of labour flexibility—the contradictions of Chile's hybrid development strategy likewise become apparent. Unlike O&G, the mining sector is driven by private companies and Chile's neoliberal model locks the state in a self-reinforcing trajectory of legitimizing private participation. Crucially, however, it also leaves sufficient room for policy contestation (Nem Singh 2014).

The chapter is divided into four sections. The first section examines the role of Codelco as the country pushed for a globalization strategy based on subjecting the state company to private sector standards of productivity and efficiency. The second section probes into the performance of Codelco and its competitive strategy. The third section explores the world of labour relations and conflicts in both public and private mining, as a case of political intervention which is arguably a net effect of the contradictions within Chile's resource governance model. The dynamics of Chile's hybrid development strategy in the mining sector are most pronounced in the copper industry but are equally prevalent in the renewable energy sector surrounding lithium mining, which is explored in the final section of the chapter.

The Myth of Neoliberal Chile

My starting point is to demystify the image of Chile as the neoliberal poster child. As demonstrated in Chapter 5, regulatory mining policies in Chile clearly signal a preference for co-existence between public and private extraction as post-Pinochet governments refused to privatize—or are incapable of privatizing—the national mining company. Instead, rather than corporatizing or partially privatizing Codelco like other companies in Chile (see Chapter 2 for SOE reforms), *both ownership and regulation* remain under

The tight control of the national state. Put differently, Codelco remains 100% state-owned, with its Board of Directors appointed mostly by the Chilean state (see Table 6.1).

At face value, maintaining state ownership over Codelco amidst the slew of privatization across various sectors in the 1980s and 1990s appears inconsistent from a neoliberal viewpoint. The free-market logic dictates a strategy conducive for public-asset-selling and pursuing comparative advantage through exports-led growth strategy. Yet, even the military dictatorship government avoided privatizing Codelco. Instead, the SOE was conceived as

Table 6.1 Corporate governance reforms in Codelco.

	Organic Law of Codelco/DL 1.350 (1976–2008)	New aspects of Codelco Law/DL 20.392 (2009–present)
Board structure	No formal shareholder role	Shareholders represented by Finance and Mining Ministers
	Seven directors: • Mining Minister (Chair) • Finance Minister • 2 Representatives of the President of the Republic • 1 Representative of the President of the Republic (member of the Armed Forces) • 2 Union Representatives	Nine directors: • 4 Directors selected by the Council of Senior Public Management • 3 Representatives of the President of the Republic • 2 Workers' Representatives
Term	Presidential period	Four years rotating with partial renewal of members
Roles and responsibilities	• Setting general policies • Approval of investments above US$50 million • No civil or criminal responsibilities for its actions • Not subject to corporation law	• Appointing and dismissing the CEO • Approval of three-year business plan, investments, and main contracts • Civil and criminal responsibilities for its actions • Faculties established in corporation law • Obligations set under corporation law

Source: Bande (2011, 6) (adapted).

142 Business of the State

a source of rent-seeking, forcing the company by law to contribute 10% of its profits towards the armed forces (Barton 2002; Nem Singh 2010). As labour leader Pedro Marin notes, Codelco not only was a strategic asset for extracting rents to sustain elite support for the authoritarian neoliberal project, but also became a source of political dividends within the military, thereby projecting an image of coherence and absolute state power.[2]

Thus, President Patricio Aylwin (1990–1994), from the Christian Democratic side of the *Concertación* coalition and Chile's first post-dictatorship president, unsurprisingly sought to reform Codelco without privatizing it. Instead, Codelco was subjected to technocratic governance, alluding to a globalization strategy emphasizing a limited state and minimal industrial policy in the mining sector. The Aylwin government had immediately removed the military generals from the Board of Directors through DN 146 of 1991. By retaining 100% state ownership—a strategy totally divergent from the partial privatization enacted in countries with large SOEs like Brazil—the national state would be reticent at relinquishing political control to make *economic* decisions on behalf of the national company. In May 1992, DL 19.137, also known as Codelco Law, was approved, but it did not overturn the 1971 copper nationalization law. Instead, following the globalization strategy of competitiveness, the Codelco Law provided the company with the freedom to sign up to joint ventures with third parties to explore and develop new mines. By enabling the state company to act as if it is a private enterprise, Codelco was given *relative autonomy* to expand its mining activities overseas as well as gain access to international trading and commercial efforts (Codelco 2010).

In so doing, the *Concertación* coalition did not have to work very hard to push for partial ownership of Codelco shares in the National Congress. Additionally, Codelco managers allude Codelco's role as reflecting a historical legacy of economic nationalism that reminds the public of the country's struggle to assert public control over natural resources since 1930.[3] In other words, full state ownership is a political choice—a compromise with *Concertación*'s growth strategy—whereby Codelco's shareholders are ultimately Chilean citizens and society writ large.[4] Such a perspective diverges from the standard neoliberal narrative in Chile and, in fact, appears more aligned with how SOEs are perceived in Brazil and China (Z. Chen and Chen

---

[2] Author interview with Pedro Marin, President, FMC, Antofagasta, 2 November 2009.

[3] Author interview with Luis Galdames, Codelco Andina Division, Andina, 27 October 2009.

[4] Author interview with Ricardo Ffrench Davis, Former *Concertación* technocrat, Santiago de Chile, 18 August 2009.

2019; Massi and Nem Singh 2018; Nem Singh and Chen 2018). Therefore, Codelco as an SOE has become subject to constant political interference—first through appointments to the company's Board of Directors that dictate its day-to-day management; and second by regularly summoning Codelco managers to congressional committee meetings to pressure the national company to answer to public inquiries.[5]

The Consequences of State Ownership for Codelco

If Codelco's state ownership is a political choice to negotiate its globalization strategy aimed at enhancing competitiveness and the consolidation of Chile's hybrid development strategy in the mining sector, what are the consequences of state ownership for the company? I argue that retaining full control over Codelco has three implications.

Firstly, state ownership reinforced the discourse of *competitiveness* and logic of *productivism*, which is subsequently internalized by managers of SOEs. From the vantage point of business, Codelco holds rich and vast mining reserves—a result of the nationalization of Chile's four large copper mines in 1971—but its alleged incapacity to compete with private mining companies represents wastefulness. Conversely, the private sector is deemed more 'dynamic and capable' of transforming the copper industry into a world-class sector of production (see Figures 6.1 and 6.2).[6]

By embracing foreign investment as crucial for Chile's globalization strategy, Codelco's state ownership is constructed as a check and balance on foreign capital in the sector and the SOE has remained an instrument for state control over Chile's natural resources. A Senior Official at Cochilco describes the relationship of Codelco and the Chilean state:

Codelco was milked like a cow during the dictatorship. With privatization, Pinochet needed as much mineral revenues he could muster from Codelco ... but he also refused to invest in [the firm]. By the 1980s, the country plunged into debt and no investments on Codelco were made except rudimentary projects to maintain production. Hence, for Concertación, foreign investment is the solution against an interventionist state ... There is a more ideological rationale for insufficiently investing on Codelco: The Chilean state saw Codelco as a threat to the private

---

[5] Author interview with Marcos Lima, Former CEO, Codelco, Santiago de Chile, 13 November 2009.
[6] Author interview with Javier Cox, Secretary General, *Consejo Minero*, Santiago de Chile, 22 October 2009.

144 Business of the State

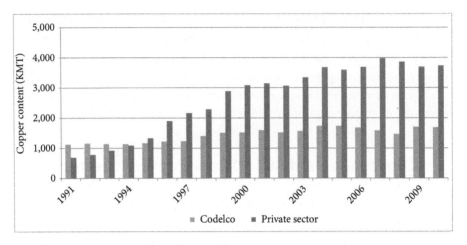

Figure 6.1 Public vs. private copper mining production in Chile, 1991–2010.
Source: Cochilco (2010, 18–19) (adapted).

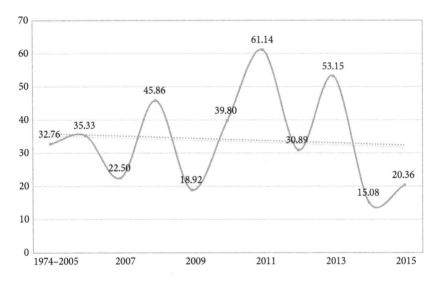

Figure 6.2 Share of Mining to Total Actual FDI in Percentage.
Source: Cochilco (2019, Table 27) (adapted).

sector. If the state invested heavily, the state would become reliant on one huge company. Furthermore, private firms saw Codelco as a threat, and fears abound if other companies would come and invest in Chile. What, then, is the sense of a pro-FDI law?[7]

---

[7] Author interview with Senior Official, Foreign Investment Department, Cochilco, 1 October 2009.

State officials were not alone in thinking Codelco must compete with private mining capital. Codelco managers themselves have also internalized the logic of competitiveness. For example, the Codelco Law in 2009 was passed and welcomed by SOE managers as a way of enhancing the 'professionalization' of the state enterprise. Codelco President Marcos Lima (1994–2000) pushed for corporate governance reforms to depoliticize the SOE and the Codelco Law aims to reduce the influence of the ministers by eliminating the automatic seats in the Board of Directors, replacing them with independent/professional directors. Their terms of office were likewise changed to avoid being co-terminus with electoral cycles. Such reforms are deemed attempts at depoliticizing the state enterprise. Yet, former CEO Nicolas Majluf (2010–2014) also notes that the law was hardly significant in improving Codelco's overall economic performance.[8] The Codelco Law simply formalized the influence of the Ministry of Mining and Finance, effectively rendering the conflict of interest between state regulation and mining production unchanged.

Secondly, state ownership fails to resolve the principal-agency dilemma inherent among SOEs. In a modern corporation, business decisions affecting company performance are typically reserved to shareholders who have voting rights to alter corporate governance rules and business decisions for the company. The CEO and the Board of Directors (agents) are thus held accountable to their private shareholders (principal). In Codelco, the President of the Republic is the principal, responsible for naming the Chair of the Board as well as approving and modifying the corporate by-laws, while the CEO and the Board of Directors (second principal) are expected to manage the company on a day-to-day basis.[9] However, the President and the Board are only *indirectly* accountable to Codelco's ultimate shareholders, the Chilean citizens and society who are the real owners of its natural resources. As per the principal-agency dilemma inherent in SOEs, with no private shareholders in an SOE, whenever problems of accountability arise, it is very difficult to penalize the mistakes on behalf of the company, and citizens suffer when SOEs are underperforming but no one is held to account for such decisions.

Thirdly, state ownership generates conflicts in the mining sector, especially around labour management. As Codelco moved towards a business model incorporating the subcontracting of core business operations and services, these neoliberal reforms created two kinds of workers with radically opposing

---

[8] Author interview with Nicolas Majluf, Former CEO, Codelco, Santiago de Chile, 21 October 2009.
[9] See summary of the Code of Corporate Governance in Codelco at https://www.codelco.com/prontus_codelco/site/docs/20110701/20110701122544/codigo_conducta_negocios_codelco.pdf (accessed 21 April 2023).

146 Business of the State

interests. Firstly, organized and powerful miners with permanent contracts were incorporated within the Codelco corporate governance framework. Their main union, the *Federación de los Trabajadores del Cobre* (FTC), sits on the Board of Directors and effectively keeps the veto power of unions in management reforms. By participating in the corporatist framework, these permanent workers enjoy unparalleled economic benefits such as higher salaries, secured pensions, and employment security for the ageing workers of Codelco. Secondly, contractual workers are employed outside the corporatist framework and must work without similar benefits from Codelco. As Chapter 5 explains, subcontracted workers organized the 'Equal Pay for Equal Work' campaign in 2007, which led to a 37-day work stoppage in the mining sector. While the National Labour Bureau released a report making a case for 5,000 contract workers to be absorbed into permanent workers, Codelco refused to follow the directive of the Labour Ministry. Instead, in an unprecedented move for the SOE, Codelco challenged this ruling in court. Subsequently, the Supreme Court ruled in favour of the state enterprise, although this did not prevent labour unions in private mining from organizing themselves and making similar demands to their employers. To put it simply, labour issues, despite the narrow scope of their claims, have been politicized and mobilized for contentious actions. That collective action occurred in an SOE in the most strategic industry elevated concerns about the ensuing instability and social disruption. It also became clear that unions remain powerholders as they could sustain the politicization of labour issues and immediately faulted the Chilean state for its unwillingness to uphold its function as mediator of labour conflicts.

While it is tempting to think of Codelco's governing structure as a state of exception in Chile, strategic control over companies remains prevalent in neoliberal Chile; worker representatives likewise serve on the Board of Directors in Chilean SOEs, including the largest ones—ENAMI, ENAP, and *Banco Estado*.[10]. In many cases, workers are given the right to speak and discuss with management, and Codelco and *Banco Estado* are unique in that these SOEs accord workers voting rights to influence company management. More compellingly, the *state* view of ENAMI is that it has a developmental role in promoting the production of copper by small mining producers by buying, processing, and selling copper as a means of cushioning the effects of volatile copper prices. This political logic also justifies the presence of two representatives of the National Mining Association (SONAMI) on ENAMI's

---

[10] ENAMI is a minerals processor with a developmental mission of supporting small and medium enterprises. ENAP is the state company in charge of oil exploration and refining and production of natural gas for Chile's energy security. *Banco Estado* is the national development bank.

board, with the aim of building a consensus on policies impacting local miners (OECD 2011, 51).

Overall, despite the speed and pace of privatization of state enterprises in Chile, there exist 32 Chilean SOEs that are under the supervision of the Public Enterprise System (SEP), 26 of which are fully state-owned while others possess private shareholders. In four cases involving water and sewerage utilities, the state owns minority shares (29–45%)—which is equivalent to the centralized control, minority ownership governance model discussed in Chapter 2. In this model, the Chilean state retains 'golden share rights', which refer to voting rights allowing the state-elected board members to veto the transfer of ownership of water rights and drinking water and sewerage concessions of these companies. Issuing golden shares was a political instrument used in the 1990s to put a brake on privatization, as an attempt to ensure all essential services may continue in all circumstances (OECD 2011, 36). As such, far from the orthodox market-conforming prescription of neoclassical economics for developing countries, the Chilean state is at best a believer of *pragmatic neoliberalism*, whereby hybrid developmental strategies enable elites to combine pro-market logics with the retention of state control over important industries.

The Role of Codelco in 21st-Century Chile

While Codelco exists as an SOE for political and economic reasons, it is also very clear that the Chilean state rejects public ownership as the only means of managing the copper industry. The hybrid development strategy in the mining sector was crafted precisely to create a balance between public and private forms of capital accumulation. Thus, a fundamental question arises about the role of Codelco in the mining sector. Unlike Brazil's Petrobras, for example (see Chapter 8), Codelco was not conceived as an engine of innovation. While copper nationalization emphasized the importance of accruing rents for the state, it was not linked to industrial development in any meaningful way. Throughout the 20th century, Codelco was always expected to maximize the fiscal revenues from the sector, and elite consensus on the fiscal role of Codelco stems from the particular ways in which conflicts between foreign capital and the state have played out historically. Between 1930 and 1970, Chilean political elites had a very difficult relationship with foreign capital and the US government, as both the Washington Agreement in 1951 and *Chileanización* project in 1966 failed to satisfy public outrage against the outflow of copper profits from Chile to Washington (Vergara 2008). Therefore,

Codelco was a direct and popular instrument for the Chilean state to increase mining revenues for the country. In the post-Pinochet years, Codelco and ENAMI contributed between 5 and 20% of the country's total fiscal revenue (see Figure 6.3).

In significant ways, Chile's heavy reliance on copper revenues makes the state vulnerable to contentious politics just like Peru, Bolivia, and Ecuador. These three Andean countries share two common features: (1) unacceptably high levels of socioeconomic and political inequalities; and (2) general ineffectiveness of neoliberal policies in delivering economic growth and equality (Grugel and Riggirozzi 2018; Weyland et al. 2010). Indeed, these characteristics became the central driving force for contentious actions among social movements and the electoral victories of Leftist parties during the 2000s, in which political elites sought to centralize power and promote redistributive politics by way of linking mineral rents directly with anti-poverty and social welfare programmes to compensate for the high costs of extraction (Gudynas 2016). Regional governments in Latin America are thus subject to the extractive imperative underpinned by the logic of productivism.

But while Chile faced similar social movement pressures from below to those of other Latin American governments, the governments of the *Concertación* coalition were remarkably successful at placating social conflicts through economic growth and Codelco is at the heart of this political

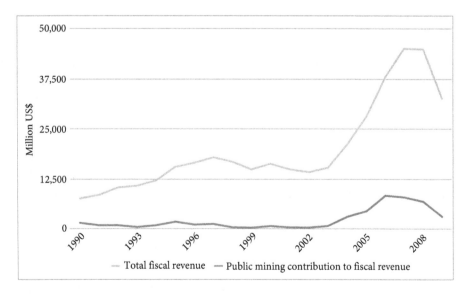

Figure 6.3 Contribution of public enterprises (SOEs) to total fiscal revenue, 1990–2010.
Source: Cochilco (2010, 76–77) (adapted).

strategy. By securing higher taxes and directly extracting revenues through Codelco, the Chilean state can transmit mineral wealth towards societal goals, for example, by financing higher education and several social pro- grammes throughout the 1990s and 2000s (Grugel and Nem Singh 2015, 358–359). The state *directly* extracts revenues through Codelco and also *indi- rectly* captures rents by levying corporate taxes on private mining capital. Thus, Codelco serves as the linkage between the state and citizens and, conse- quently, the buffer between public and private mineral extraction. If the SOE fails to yield high fiscal resources for the state, then Chilean elites would need to tax private companies at a higher rate. Codelco guarantees windfall profits for the national government, which are then utilized for education, health, poverty reduction, and importantly innovation, research, and development. With its immense state capacity and the effectiveness of its institutionalized politics, Chile has been very successful at creating a resource governance model that apparently strikes a balance between public goods provision and the embrace of private property rights. In other words, Codelco not only rei- fied but also made possible the success of Chile's governance model and its resource-led development strategy.

By contrast, the absence of SOEs in the countries of the Andean region has been consequential to their political stability. National governments in Peru, Bolivia, and Ecuador have constantly attempted to mitigate social conflicts in the mining sector as their elites struggled to strike a balance between taxation and giving incentives for private mining to retain investment in the coun- try. Hence, the cyclical nature of export prices has weakened the bargaining position of Andean states vis-à-vis foreign mining capital, and in times of low prices, elites were forced to sell their state assets and adopt low corporate tax- ation regimes to attract foreign investment. Without a strong state enterprise that can be mobilized by the state, resource-led strategies based on foreign capital extraction have fuelled economic grievances within society and ulti- mately created the social conditions for radical social mobilization against the state (Arce 2014). Popular protests thus become symbolic of demands for redistributive politics, calls for reforms to improve state oversight over the industry, or lack of political support for excessively marketized mining regimes (Bebbington and Bury 2013; Bebbington et al. 2008; Gustafson 2020; Riofrancos 2020).

A final note can be made about Codelco's political role in Chile. While the Chilean state through a commercially efficient Codelco is relatively success- ful at containing political dissent in the mining sector (Silva and Rossi 2018), Codelco itself has not escaped contentious politics. In fact, Codelco since the 1990s until the 2010s has faced two contending issues—firstly, governance

150 Business of the State

reforms; and secondly, the 'labour question', most notably subcontracting and precarious working conditions. As regards corporate governance reform, the main challenge for Codelco hinges upon the success of its state (SOE) managers at resisting political interference in its day-to-day management and in making strategic investment decisions, including the international expansion of its operations,[11] because the legal framework binding the state and Codelco, in which the national government, especially the executive (presidential) power, makes these commercial decisions, has barely changed since the Pinochet years (see Table 6.1). Unlike Petrobras, Codelco failed to achieve the corporate autonomy necessary to enhance its role in producing a competitive national innovation system, while it also had significant shortcomings in placating uneven development between the capital and peripheral mining regions of the country (Atienza et al. 2018; Stubrin 2017). With respect to labour management, Codelco's political relationship with its workers and the state is contentious. By embracing labour flexibility and global competitiveness as the logic of Codelco management, the state becomes entangled in what is an inherently conflictual capital–labour relation. This theme is discussed further in the next section.

The 'Labour Question' in Chilean Mining

This chapter has so far illustrated the complex process of managing Codelco as an SOE. In this section, I move away from a managerial perspective of corporate reforms towards the politics of labour management in the mining sector, demonstrating the significance of labour contention as a source of critique against Chile's resource governance model. The *Concertación* coalition governments' successful embrace of neoliberalism in the mining sector as a globalization strategy required labour acquiescence. As Donoso (2017) notes, we cannot look at labour contention in mining without a clear understanding of the political constraints imposed by the *Concertación* and union leaders themselves in managing capital–labour relations. As Chapter 5 shows, the gradual institutional embedding of subcontracting practices in the mining sector meant that labour was divided between workers within the corporatist framework of Codelco and big private companies on the one hand, and contractual workers who demanded equal pay for equal work because of their precarious working conditions on the other. Added to the economic costs associated with work stoppage, that labour contention emerged first and

---

[11] Author interview with Nicolas Majluf, Former CEO, *Codelco*, Santiago de Chile, 21 October 2009.

The Politics of Managing Codelco and Its Labour Force   **151**

foremost in the mining sector should not come as a surprise. Chile's tradition of labour militancy stands in contrast to the strong anti-union legacy of neoliberalism. Labour politics did not completely wane during the 1990s and 2000s. While labour unions have been weakened and atomized, public perceptions remain strong as regards the pertinent role of workers' collective action in a neoliberal democracy. Table 6.2 demonstrates that even among dominant parties across the political spectrum, unions are still key political actors in negotiating social policy choices to ameliorate the costs of neoliberal restructuring. Although the Centre and Left parties in Chile (PPD, PS, and PDC) give more importance to the labour movement than the Right parties (UDI, RN), the neoliberal assumption that class politics has waned is not necessarily accurate. While it has been student leaders that have led popular protests from 2006 onwards, their success in creating a national movement to dismantle the authoritarian enclaves that were left institutionalized in the 1980 constitution has required the acquiescence if not tacit agreement to build a national social coalition between labour unions and social movements (Crocco 2017; Gonzalez and Morán 2020; Manky 2018; Sehnbruch and Donoso 2020).

This continuing legitimacy of labour unions in Chile's national politics has implications for arguments about neocorporatism and contentious politics in Latin America. Scholars have noted the apparent decline of trade unionism and the disarticulation of labour politics brought about by the shift in contentious politics even in cases of resource nationalizations (Haarstad 2009; 2012; Oxhorn 1998; Yashar 2005). The Chilean labour movement, however, shares more similarities in terms of its mobilization tactics and trajectories with highly institutionalized democratic regimes like Brazil and

Table 6.2 Legitimacy of trade unions from political parties' viewpoints.

Political parties	Unions are obsolete	Unions are not obsolete	No response
UDI	24	67	9
RN	17	64	19
PDC	6	85	10
PPD	9	86	5
PS	9	84	7
Others	23	75	2

Source: *Barómetro de la Política*, May 2011 (El Mostrador 2011d, 24) (adapted).

Poll question: There are distinct opinions about unions. Some say that unionism is an obsolete institution in defending workers' rights. Others think that unions are necessary in defending workers' rights. Which of the following positions do you think express your opinion? (1) Unions are obsolete; (2) Unions are not obsolete.

Uruguay (Levitsky and Roberts 2011; Nem Singh 2012a; Oseland et al. 2012). In neoliberal Chile, political parties reconstituted their political relationships with class-based movements in an attempt to compromise in the name of political stability. Specifically, from 2000 onwards, Chilean parties have sought to mitigate conflicts by channelling labour grievances into institutionalized politics. It is for this reason that the Subcontracting Law was passed in 2006, as a means of taming the labour forces and retaining an image of Chile as a highly competitive export-based economy.

That union politics remains important in a highly class-based society should not come as a surprise. As some public opinion polls affirm, worker politics is a vital ingredient in mobilizing grievances in Chile. Figure 6.4 indicates the high levels of public support for forming unions to represent collective workers' interests in wage negotiations. Contractual workers themselves, who had to fight the corporatist framework of large mining companies, have offered a rallying point to advance a social justice agenda but are still confined to demands for higher wages and bonuses. Of course, there is general disenchantment in the unrealized potential of labour unions in terms of social justice demands, and even more for mining workers whose decision to strike and stop work often forces mining companies to return to the negotiating table (Crocco 2017; Donoso and von Bülow 2017; Nem Singh 2012a).[12]

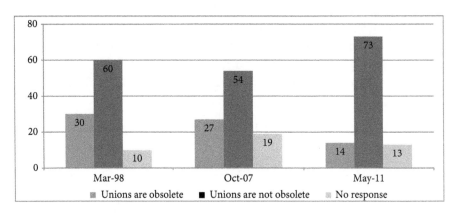

Figure 6.4 Public opinion on the legitimacy of trade unions.

Source: Barómetros Cerc (2011, 23) (adapted).

Poll question: There are distinct opinions about unions. Some say that unionism is an obsolete institution in defending workers' rights. Others think that unions are necessary in defending workers' rights. Which of the following positions do you think expresses your opinion: (1) Unions are obsolete; (2) Unions are not obsolete? (Numbers are in percentages.)

---

[12] Author interview with Lariza Palma, CUT, Santiago de Chile, 16 October 2009.

On the one hand, neoliberal reforms have significantly affected copper workers because of attempts at modernizing Codelco and exposing the industry to foreign competition and multinational production. Indeed, as discussed in Chapter 5, labour flexibility became the organizing logic of capital–labour relations in Chile's mining industry, which brought forth efforts to reorganize production by way of closing mines temporarily or permanently and through mergers and joint ventures among private companies (Nem Singh 2010; 2012; Vergara 2008). On the other hand, the fate of unions was not left in the invisible hands of the market; the power of labour—enhanced through decades of concrete social struggles against foreign capitalists—has produced an intense push back against further erosion of state control in the mining sector. Mining unions, for instance, have launched a counter-offensive against the modernization plans of Codelco and private companies. By using the right to strike in the heartland of Chile's natural-resource-based economy, mining unions averted the same debilitating effects of economic restructuring that other trade unions in the production and services sectors suffered. More crucially, the mining unions' qualified support to the *Concertación* coalition provided them a veneer of legitimacy in electoral politics and policymaking domains. This labour pact—though fragile and fraught with contention—remains critical in explaining how the *Concertación* coalition governments managed labour conflicts while also deepening their commitment to neoliberalism. In the next section, I discuss the two worlds of labour: the corporatist framework for permanent workers and the contentious politics of contractual workers in state-led and also private mining in Chile.

Alianza Estratégica as a Corporatist Pact

The so-called *Alianza Estratégica* (Strategic Alliance) represents the political compromise to promote the modernization of Codelco while also ensuring harmonious labour relations. In 1994, Codelco President Juan Villarzú established *Alianza Estratégica* in the context of the perceived loss of Codelco's competitiveness and scepticism as to the state's capacity to achieve its goal of making it the best copper company in the world (Villarzú 2005). While Codelco's attempt to 'modernize' implied closing mines, laying off workers, and further outsourcing of services, the central union negotiating collective bargaining agreements with Codelco, the FTC, was enticed into the alliance by way of Codelco's co-optation of strategies aimed at 'democratizing corporate governance'. This was achieved through a series of agreements detailing

154 Business of the State

the goals and specific targets to improve productivity and efficiency, reached as a compromise between unions and management.

In its early days, *Alianza Estratégica* was a technocratic attempt at guaranteeing stable labour relations to avoid further losses in productivity in the mining industry. In the 1990s, the Chilean mining sector was largely controlled by Codelco despite the lack of state investments for the expansion of its operations. As Chapter 2 asserts, as neoliberalism became embedded in institutions and policy practices, *Concertación* coalition elites and Codelco managers simultaneously implemented corporate governance reforms and labour flexibility. But by also recognizing the popular appeal of Codelco as a fully owned state enterprise, reforms towards the professionalization and modernization of company management—not privatization—became the only acceptable policy choice. *Alianza Estratégica* was a neocorporatist articulation of this policy choice (see below), deemed necessary for the *Concertación* coalition to maintain a balance between public and private forms of capital accumulation.

From a business perspective, the first 10 years of *Alianza Estratégica* is considered successful. Based on the agreements and the results detailed in Table 6.3, in phase I (1994 and 1999) Codelco increased its production, lowered direct cash costs, and boosted productivity by 84%. During its second phase (2000–2006), Codelco doubled its value and generated an increase in surplus for the Chilean state by 100%—from US$5,900 million in phase I to US$10,400 million in phase II. In many ways, this strategic compromise between the owner (the Chilean state via Codelco) and the workers was successful. Codelco remained state-controlled while achieving labour stability, competitiveness, and profitability. However, phase III of *Alianza Estratégica* (2007–2010) encountered serious tensions and pressures that directly impacted on its success. What was transpiring, then, in public mining was uneasiness between state (SOE) managers and workers because of the extraordinary profits generated during the commodity boom. Whilst in private mining this was only resolved through militant action, such as the infamous strike in Minera Escondida in 2006, in Codelco the paternalistic relationship between state (SOE) managers and workers constrained any possible illegal action that workers could take. While the FTC wanted more share of the profits from mining, state (SOE) managers viewed such demands highly unreasonable, especially given that a huge pool of contractual workers are employed by the state company.[13]

---

[13] Author interview with Nicolas Majluf, Former CEO, Codelco, Santiago de Chile, 21 October 2009.

The Politics of Managing Codelco and Its Labour Force 155

Table 6.3 *Alianza Estratégica* and its corporatist framework.

	Phase I (1994–1999)	Phase II (2000–2006)
Business strategy	Modernization of Codelco	Common project of state enterprise
Objectives	Recover competitiveness, profitability, and credibility of Codelco	Maximize economic value and profits (dividends) to the state
Goals and agreements	Reduce real costs to at least 10 cents per pound; increase production up to 500,000 tonnes; and enhance productivity by 50%	Double the (economic) value of Codelco; and generate surplus for the state
Results	Reduced real costs to at least 24 cents per pound; increased production up to 368,000 tonnes; and enhanced productivity by 84%	Completed (preliminary results); increased surplus from US$5,900 million in 1994–1999 to US$10,400 million (projected) in 2000–2005

Source: *Alianza Estratégica*. Fase III (Villarzú 2005) (adapted).

Beyond a modernization plan, *Alianza Estratégica* aimed to reconstitute labour ties within Codelco by offering plant miners a social status above other members of the workforce. As was enshrined in the Washington Agreement of 1951, the *Concertación* coalition governments recognized the strategic and historical importance of copper workers and the importance of labour acquiescence in maintaining the success of Codelco. As a measure of success, the index of conflictivity waned from 3.3 between 1990 and 1993 to 1.4 between 1994 and 2005. There was also a decline in the frequency of accidents from an average of 7 per 10 million hectares in 1993 to 5 per 10 million hectares in 2005, which signifies the improving standards of health and safety measures in large-scale mining operations (Villarzú 2005, 10–12).

Overall, state–labour relations in the Chilean mining sector is neocorporatist: *corporatist* simply because the pact does not really divert from the traditional tools of co-optation typically deployed by state (SOE) managers to prevent labour conflicts and social tensions, for example through higher wages, more comprehensive benefit and retirement plans, and expensive bonuses to avoid strikes; *neo* because the instruments in acquiring workers' support are deployed in the neoliberal context wherein state intervention in labour conflicts is deemed obsolete or unnecessary. As economic

156 Business of the State

competitiveness shapes the logic of Codelco governance, a strong tendency to depoliticize mining via technocratic management and union demobilization is observable in the sector.

One way in which neocorporatism was consolidated was through political pacts between the mining unions and the presidential candidates of the *Concertación* coalition. Through social dialogue, a formal agreement served to bind the party and the unions towards common goals and strategies in the copper industry. Prior to the electoral victory of Michelle Bachelet in 2006, a meeting between the *Concertación* and FTC on 17 November 2005 laid down in detail the FTC National Proposal (2006). The proposal was Bachelet's policy programme for the future of Codelco—topics included investment plans, labour rights, detailed national proposals on key management issues, social welfare, and pension reforms, and the social pact for Chile's development through collective bargaining. Crucially, in this programme there is overwhelming support for retaining Codelco as fully state-owned, and therefore in the FTC retaining their bargaining position vis-à-vis contractual workers (FTC 2006, 9–11). To a significant degree, *Alianza Estratégica's* emphasis on labour stability, competitiveness, and profitability highlights the growing divide between the two kinds of workers—permanent and contracted—in the sector.

In this context, neocorporatism only favours a very small segment of the mining workforce—those with permanent contracts in Codelco and large private companies—as labour flexibility became the answer to pressures of cost reduction and increasing labour productivity in the sector. As Codelco embraced subcontracting, private mining companies since the 1990s also engaged with such practices. Thus, as Chapter 5 explains, the precipitous fragmentation of workers between those with permanent contracts (*trabajadores de planta*) and those with temporary contracts (*trabajadores contratistas*) became a source of political conflict in the sector. Unlike the paternalistic relationship between smanagers of SOEs and permanent workers, contractual workers receive far less salary, have fewer benefit plans, and endure substandard general working conditions compared to permanent workers.[14] As Table 5.2 shows, Codelco gradually shifted towards outsourcing most of its workforce as a cost-cutting and competitiveness strategy. Its main effect was to institutionalize the divide between the different classes of workers in the sector.

---

[14] Author interviews with Pedro Marin, President, FMC, Antofagasta, 2 November 2009; Lariza Palma, CUT, Santiago de Chile, 16 October 2009; and Agustin Segundo Latorre Risso, *Sindicato de Empresa de Trabajadores Xstrata Copper AltoNorte*, Antofagasta, 4 November 2009.

Rising Conflicts in Private Mining

In private mining companies, the paternalistic relationship seen between state SOE managers and permanent workers in Codelco was never consolidated. Instead, company–worker relations in private mining are characterized by ephemeral tranquillity and permanent friction, as exemplified by the frequency of workers' strikes compared to Codelco.[15] Collective negotiations have constantly failed to achieve harmonious social relations between unionized workers and mining companies. From a labour perspective, the *patrones* (private employers) have a 'mountain of faculties to negotiate whilst workers possess no means to confront them'.[16] From a business point of view, private companies have followed the rules and requirements on subcontracting as established in Chile's Labour Code. However, they also recognize that the minimal worker protections and a pro-employer bias of the labour law are serious limitations.[17] This structural problem between individual and collective rights is often a source of conflict in the mining sector.

As Chapter 5 explains, consolidation of the Contractual Workers' Movement occurred in the context of the passage of the Subcontracting Law and the concerns of union leaders over how contractual workers are treated by mining companies. The flexibilization and subcontracting of the neoliberal labour model was untenable, and yet most elites and unions supported such policy framework to maintain a semblance of stable labour relations under a highly segmented corporatist arrangement in which the political legacies of Pinochet's Labour Code and his assault against labour rights became a barrier to unionized workers playing a larger role in Chile's contentious politics. For Chilean elites, there is an implicit assumption of the productive and efficient nature of private capital vis-à-vis public (state-owned) mining enterprises. As expressed by Pedro Marin, president of FMC in 2009,[18] the division between permanent and subcontracted workers has consequences

---

[15] Note that Codelco workers have not rejected their collective bargaining agreements between 1994 and 2007. By comparison, work stoppages in the private mining sector are common and have been time-tested strategies of unions to retain their bargaining power.

[16] Author interviews with Agustin Segundo Latorre Risso, *Sindicato de Empresa de Trabajadores Xstrata Copper AltoNorte*, Antofagasta, 4 November 2009; and Pedro Marin, President, FMC, Antofagasta, 2 November 2009.

[17] Author interviews with Javier Cox, Santiago de Chile, *Consejo Minero*, October 2009; and Carlos Gajardo Roberts, SONAMI, September 2009.

[18] The Mining Federation of Chile or FMC is a confederation of 21 mining unions in the private sector. One must remember that it is very unusual in Chile to find organized workers beyond the company level, and therefore the power of organized miners has historically remained the same. This is backed up by interviews with representatives of SONAMI and *Consejo Minero* who view mining workers as highly unionized, powerful labour aristocrats.

158 Business of the State

for the uneven distribution of labour rights and worker protection schemes within sectors and between working classes:

> Collective negotiations in private mining are very hard … Codelco has a good paternalistic administration while in the private sector, things are different … the only form of advancing … [causes] to fight for the lack of social benefits [from subcontracting] is through hard bargaining in collective negotiations. The signed agreement we have achieved is the best in both public and private mining but not for all, Minera Escondida—the largest employer in the sector—has 2,253 unionised workers, and we only secured benefits for us … For other unions, they must have the organisational capacity … to protest and stop work whenever necessary … to advance their interests … I led a twenty-five-day strike, and we won through brute force against private capital.[19]

The statement above reflects a broader trend in class politics, i.e. the systematic fragmentation and atomization of working-class solidarity and the decline of labour politics in 21st-century Latin America. While union strikes today can still promote better wages and social benefits, there are clear obstacles to workers advancing a wider campaign for social justice, and the call for a change in the institutional framework, for example, has been carried by students and other social movements since 2006.

From Copper Mining to Lithium

The dynamics of Chile's hybrid development strategy in the mining sector is most pronounced in the copper industry but is equally prevalent in the renewable energy sector linked to lithium extraction. As demands soar for renewables, notably energy from wind turbines and for EV cars, pressures for the upstream sector to respond to perked-up demand also build. Specifically, climate mitigation strategies around renewables are now set in stone, with the Conference on Climate Change (COP26) in Glasgow setting the goal to limit temperature rise within 1.5 degrees Celsius. Such pledges on carbon emissions reduction, in turn, accelerate the demand for energy transition metals that are needed to construct green infrastructure—metals such as cobalt, nickel, lithium, and REEs, to name a few (Ballinger et al. 2020; Barandiarán 2019; Kumar et al. 2016; Nem Singh 2021). Lithium is the main raw material for manufacturing lithium-ion batteries, and thanks to a geographical lottery, Chile holds two high-grade deposits—in Salar de Pedernales and Salar

---

[19] Author interview with Pedro Marin, President, FMC, Antofagasta, 2 November 2009.

The Politics of Managing Codelco and Its Labour Force   **159**

de Maricunga located close to the Atacama administrative region These two major lithium operations are known for their large-size deposits, high-quality grades, proximity to accessible and reliable infrastructure, and competitive pricing (Maxwell and Mora 2020, 58). Table 6.4 demonstrates Chile's position as the world's largest lithium producer until 2012, when Australia took the title.

There are similarities between copper and lithium. Both metals are considered strategic by the government, who consequently place some limitations on its extraction. While copper is viewed as an influential mineral for Chile's fiscal health, lithium bears a special status as a 'non-concessionable' mineral because it can be used for nuclear fusion. Hence, new contracts to explore reserves and produce lithium require the approval of the Chilean Nuclear Energy Commission.

But unlike copper mining, lithium is largely controlled by the private sector. Pinochet preferred new mines to be developed by the private sector and to only leave the nationalized copper mines to Codelco. Today, the industry is highly concentrated or horizontally integrated at the extraction stage, wherein private companies successfully consolidated market power through mergers and acquisitions. As Table 6.5 shows, between 2012 and

Table 6.4 Lithium World Production, 2022-2023 (in metric tons, lithium content)

Country	Mine Production	
	2022	2023 (e)
United States of America	W	W
Argentina	6.590	9,600
Australia	74,700	86,000
Brazil	2.630 (e)	4,900
Canada	520 (e)	3,400
Chile	38.000	44,000
China	22.600 (e)	33,000
Portugal	380 (e)	380
Zimbabwe	1030 (e)	3400
Other countries*	-	-
WORLD TOTAL (rounded)	146.000	180,000

Note: All units in metric tonnes. E refers to estimated. W refers to withheld data due to proprietary reasons. – means zero

Other countries include Austria, Congo (Kinhasa), Czechia, Finland, Germany, Ghana, Mali, Mexico, Namibia, Serbia and Spain.

US Geological Survey (2024) *Mineral Commodity Summaries 2024.* Reston, Virginia: US Geological Survey.

Source: United States Geological Survey 2024: pp. 111.

160 Business of the State

Table 6.5 First-stage lithium production in Chile (in lithium carbonate equivalent tonnes).

Company	Location	2011	2016	2021	2026 (projected)
Albemarle SCL	Salar de Atacama	19,000	33,000	87,000	87,000
SQM	Salar de Atacama	40,000	60,000	118,000	118,000
Codelco	Salar de Maricunga				25,000
Errazuriz-SIMBALIC	Salar de Maricunga			20,000	20,000
Minera Salar Blanco	Salar de Maricunga			20,000	20,000

Note: Estimated production in 2011 and 2016 with prediction in capacity in 2021 and 2026.

Source: Maxwell and Mora (2020, 64).

2018, the sector became dominated by four corporations, controlling about 83% of world supply—Albemarle SCL (*Sociedad Chilena de Litio*) (US), *Sociedad Química y Minera de Chile* (SQM) (Chile), FMC (US), and Tianqi Lithium Corporation (China). All three companies except SQM are vertically integrated along the supply chain, meaning that these companies produce lithium compounds at later stages of manufacturing. The companies signed contracts with the Chilean state to extract a specified amount: Albemarle SCL was allowed up to a maximum of 200,000 tonnes of lithium on or before 2021; SQM up to 180,000 tonnes on or before 2030. Further opportunities arise as demand for lithium steadily increases over time, and more opportunities might arise for companies to enter the downstream market as providers of goods and services to large companies. This, in turn, can become a catalyst for a natural-resource-based manufacturing strategy. But, for the present, Chile's domestic capitalists both in copper and lithium mining are unable to undertake high-value-added activities like those in Australia, Canada, and the US.

Michelle Bachelet's second government (2014–2017), called the *Nueva Mayora* grand coalition, implemented a wide-ranging tax reform agenda, including abolition of the Foreign Investment Law (DL 600) and creation of a National Lithium Commission (Maxwell and Mora 2020, 67; O'Brien 2014; Reuters 2014). Composed of 22 members, the National Lithium Commission launched an extensive consultation process typical of commission-based, technocratic governance styles in Chile throughout the second half of 2014, which highlighted several issues related to the need for Chile to benefit more from lithium extraction:

(1) the recognition of the environmental fragility of the salt flats where lithium is extracted;

The Politics of Managing Codelco and Its Labour Force   161

(2) the maintenance of lithium as a non-concessionable metal, which would retain the power of the Chilean Nuclear Energy Commission to carefully regulate and control the exploitation, commercialization, and trade of lithium and its derivatives;

(3) strong institutional oversight in managing the salt flats;

(4) a state-owned enterprise to exploit these reserves consistent with the strong role of the Chilean Nuclear Energy Commission in lithium management; and

(5) the creation and strengthening of a sectoral lithium cluster, which would expand the participation of Chilean companies from upstream to midstream and downstream segments of the value chain.

In January 2016, President Bachelet accepted the main tenets of the Commission's recommendations and used the findings to formulate a National Lithium Strategy. Nevertheless, the recent history of lithium mining in Chile is mired by conflicts including accusations of fraud in the treasury, environmental damage, anti-union practices, breaches of contracts, and illegal brine export, among many others (Jerez et al. 2021, 5). Furthermore, in 2016 Chile's state development agency CORFO sued Chilean private mining company SQM for breach of contract to expand the company's refining facilities, thereby accelerating tensions between public and private actors amidst a politically sensitive environment. A second controversial point refers to taxation. Salar de Atacama offers the lowest costs for producers of high-grade lithium carbonates, and as such, private companies Albemarle SCL (US) and SQM (Chile) were paying less than US$3 per kilogram while other deposits cost between US$4 and US$4.7 per kilogram (Maxwell and Mora 2020, 67). Instead of paying more taxes due to the high profit margins, these companies only paid ad valorem and corporate taxes.

In this context of growing tensions, Codelco formed a subsidiary in the lithium sector in early 2017—Salar de Maricunga SpA—to develop and extract new lithium production facilities and Codelco entered joint ventures with private companies in order to operate in the Maricunga and Pedernales salt flats. There are also ongoing discussions about how to move downstream segments of lithium production into Chile to add value in the domestic supply chain. As the following Chapter 7 on Brazil demonstrates, the use of local content requirements and the development of a domestic goods and services sector are potential pathways for the Chilean state to promote export competitiveness and domestic innovation through natural resources.

162 Business of the State

Conclusions

The key question to be asked about capital–labour relations in contemporary Chile is whether existing models of corporate governance and modes of controlling labour conflicts will continue to produce stable growth. In the post-commodity boom era, mining policies and Codelco–worker relations apparently point towards an unsustainable growth strategy. For example, Sebastian Piñera, despite his popular appeal to centrist forces, has consistently faced vehement opposition from unions and students. In July 2011, a nation-wide mining workers' strike took place in support of university student protests (Donoso and von Bülow 2017; Grugel and Nem Singh 2015). On the 40th anniversary of copper nationalization, the union leadership in Codelco rejected the offer for a bonus and went on work stoppage. The 24-hour stoppage of 15,000 permanent and 30,000 subcontracted workers completely paralysed Codelco, leading to a loss of US$41 million (El Mostrador 2011b). The planned modernization of Codelco—interpreted by unions as gradual steps towards privatization—met heavy protests from the workers. Piñera's Minister Laurence Golborne accused Codelco workers of launching an illegal strike, describing their demands as a danger to the fiscal viability of Codelco (El Mostrador 2011a; 2011c). This strike in the biggest private copper company, Minera Escondida, in July 2011, also highlights the fragility of neocorporatism in state-run enterprises. To sum up briefly, the turbulence of 2010s is not just confined to highly conflictual sectors like environment and education; the labour unions' relationship with the political establishment also became more complex and less predictable in this period.

Additionally, global attention in the infamous mining accident trapping 33 miners for 70 days in the San José mine in Copiapo in 2010 generated popular pressure for Piñera to save the trapped miners (El Mostrador 2010). One year after the accident, 31 out of the 33 miners sought justice by filing a lawsuit against the Chilean state—and not the mining company—for its failure to carry out proper inspections of the mine's safety and working conditions. The miners argued that the Chilean government has constantly and iteratively applied minimal standards, which makes it hardly surprising that two other deaths had occurred in 2005 and 2007 even before this tragedy came to pass (Nem Singh 2010).[20] These incidents demonstrate that after many years of silence, mining workers have become more politicized, demanding that the Chilean state should guarantee their labour rights over individual benefits.

---

[20] They are requesting a total of CLP 7.7 million or CLP 250,000 for each miner as compensation (La Nación 2011).

This period of renewal, hope, and popular contestation has been born out of three decades of silence. The idea of pursuing growth without social equity is now well challenged in Chile and elsewhere, as demonstrated most forcefully in the *estallido social* in 2019 and also in the discussions surrounding the post-pandemic recovery.

This chapter has shown the complexity of corporate governance and labour reforms distinctive to Chile's hybrid model of public–private production in the mining sector and that, consistent with historical institutionalist perspectives, the relationship between the state, SOE Codelco, and workers cannot be assumed. Instead, to understand and explain the seismic changes that swept the country in October 2019 and challenged the neoliberal tripod despite its durable and enduring institutionalization in Chilean political economy (Madariaga 2020), we must pay attention to the small shifts in political and economic decisions. The role of the state is most visible in copper mining—and perhaps it will soon be in lithium also—and the presence of Codelco in the mining sector is likely to remain in the coming decades. However, the extent to which a new developmental state can be born amidst the crisis of neoliberalism in Chile and worldwide remains to be seen. What is certain, I suggest, is that the logics of competitiveness and productivism are very likely to shape future mining policies in Chile. As these case study chapters have shown: (1) Chilean mining policy is far from the standard neoliberal narrative of depoliticized, technocratic governance, given the idiosyncratic ways Codelco has adapted to economic globalization and the political role of mining unions in reshaping capital–labour relations; (2) the corporate governance reforms in Codelco are ideal political compromises in the absence of privatization as a solution to SOE problems; and (3) labour conflicts continue to be pervasive in the mines, and therefore labour flexibility, which has silenced workers in the early years, is now being challenged by workers. Whilst Chile's resource strategy still adheres to some of the theoretical axioms laid down by neoliberalism, the politics of state enterprise governance and labour relations require scholars to revise their expectations about the stability of institutions and political relationships. The following chapters present the Brazilian case study, examining regulatory reforms and SOE restructuring in the O&G industry.

7

Brazil's Oil-Based Industrial Strategy, 1990–2018

> We need to think whether we want to become like Saudi Arabia—a major oil exporter—or Norway—an oil producer that managed its oil sustainably.[1]

> Despite the local content policy under Lula da Silva, Brazilian companies remained uncompetitive. Even with local financial support ... Local content failed at generating investments.[2]

In Brazil, the O&G industry as a strategic sector for industrialization remained firmly in place despite waves of market-opening reforms in the post-military government era. While Brazilian policy reformists aimed to introduce competition in the upstream segment of the industry, in practice three decades of market liberalization yielded a development strategy based on renewed state ownership. Since the administration of President Fernando Henrique Cardoso (1995–2002) of the Brazilian Social Democratic Party (PDSB), succeeding governments adopted *institutional layering* to adjust the oil governance model to accommodate a strong NOC and a pragmatic economic role for the state. Although Cardoso ended the monopoly of Petrobras in the upstream exploration and production (E&P) segment,[3] an institutional framework supporting the corporate autonomy of Petrobras persisted under both the Workers' Party (PT) administrations of Luiz Inácio Lula da Silva (2002–2010) and Dilma Rousseff (2011–2016) and the conservative governments of Michel Temer (2016–2018) and Jair Bolsonaro (2019–2022). In so doing, the state charted an institutional pathway

---

[1] Author interview with Senior Official, BNDES, Department of the Oil, Gas and Supply Chain, Rio de Janeiro, 14 June 2018.

[2] Author interview with Senior Representative, *Federação das Indústrias do Estado de São Paulo* (FIESP), São Paulo, 7 June 2018.

[3] The O&G industry can be divided into three segments: exploration and production, or upstream; transport and refining, or mid-stream; and production of hydrocarbon derivatives and petrochemicals, or downstream. The chapter will use these definitions interchangeably.

Business of the State. Jewellord T. Nem Singh, Oxford University Press. © Jewellord T. Nem Singh (2024).
DOI: 10.1093/oso/9780198892212.003.0007

166 Business of the State

accommodating competition and foreign participation while maintaining the market power of a single, large NOC in the O&G sector. This, in turn, became a catalyst for rent-seeking in the O&G sector and beyond, leading to the infamous *Lava Jato* (Car Wash) scandal.

This chapter examines the institutional continuity of state developmentalism in the Brazilian O&G industry by tracing Brazil's institutional pathway since 1985, based on strong state ownership forged through a combination of pragmatic market opening towards foreign companies and a persistent logic of state developmentalism. Brazilian elites introduced competing visions over the role of the state in economic development: firstly, a pragmatic shift from traditional state developmentalism towards segmented neoliberalism under Cardoso; and secondly, a shift towards new developmentalism under the PT governments (2002–2016). The persistence of state ownership in the Brazilian O&G sector derives its legitimacy not only from the limits of private companies to deliver economic growth in the strategic sector, but also from the undeniable technological capability and market-conforming behaviour of Petrobras.

The chapter is structured in three main sections, beginning by using a historical institutionalist approach to explain why state ownership in the sector persisted throughout the 1990s. It subsequently details the consolidation of a regulatory framework in the 2000s that set out a stable institutional arrangement between the state, Petrobras, and IOCs, where Petrobras plays a pivotal role. In the final section, it examines the shift from state developmentalism towards a more pragmatic model of *novo desenvolvimentismo* (new developmentalism) to accelerate Brazil's efforts towards industrialization, and which retains Petrobras as a key economic actor in developing pre-salt reserves.

Neoliberalism as a (Partial) Post-Crisis Strategy (1985–1996)

The logic of state ownership in the O&G sector is a political legacy of Vargas (1930–1945),[4] although *desenvolvimentismo* (developmentalism) articulated under the military government (1964–1985) consolidated the role of

---

[4] President Getúlio Vargas's *Estado Novo* (1930–1945) modernized the national economy through the centralization of political authority away from oligarchical elites and towards the state as a direct participant in the economy. While the 1934 Mining Code nationalized mineral assets which restricted foreign ownership in oil and mining, Vargas also financed research to build technocratic expertise and enhance the competitiveness of primary commodities. He consolidated the right of the federal government to regulate the petroleum industry and confined the ownership of refineries to Brazilian nationals. The *O Petróleo é Nosso* (Petroleum Is Ours) campaign in 1947–1953 set further limitations on foreign exploration of petroleum in domestic territories, and in 1953 Vargas gained congressional support to create Petrobras as an NOC through DL 2.004. Whilst debates ensued on Petrobras's capital ownership structure, it was

Petrobras in Brazilian economic development (Trebat 1983; Triner 2011). At this time, oil nationalization and the creation of Petrobras emerged as a technocratic-political solution by elites who distrusted foreign oil companies. *Desenvolvimentismo* thus encompassed oil nationalism and justified government policy to grant Petrobras total monopoly in the domestic energy market (Massi and Nem Singh 2020; Phillips 1982; Randall 1993). Petrobras's mandate to achieve self-sufficiency in oil pushed the company to invest in deepwater engineering from the 1970s onwards—a high-risk commercial strategy that only became possible when the state mustered its financial power and political capital in support of the company (Dantas and Bell 2009; Furtado 1995). However, with the global debt crisis and general exposure to free-market orthodoxy putting pressure on Petrobras's oil monopoly and state ownership model during the 1980s, the O&G industry adopted market-opening reforms to accommodate the entry of IOCs.

During the 1980s, the Brazilian state was incapacitated and unable to effectively respond to an economic crisis of hyper-inflation, macroeconomic instability, and insurmountable debt. Under the short-lived Collor de Mello government (1990–1992), the developmentalist orientation of the Brazilian state began to unravel, under the *Programa Nacional de Desestatização* (PND) which sought to resolve the fiscal crisis by dramatically reducing the scope of public sector activities and selling key state assets. This involved the BNDES, whose organizational identity was based on the cadre of technocratic elites with expertise across all industrial sectors (Schneider 1991), being tasked to provide institutional oversight over the privatization process to ensure its credibility and smooth execution. The BNDES coordinated studies and hired external consultants to define minimum auction prices (Baer 2008), but it also began to acquire minority ownership through state-related entities like BNDESPAR (a subsidiary BNDES) and the pension funds of SOEs, and to extend loans to domestic groups in order to form winning consortia to purchase the SOEs (Hunter 2010; Randall 1993, 41–46). In the O&G industry, as Table 7.1 shows, a total of US$2.6 billion worth of assets were privatized. BNDES was responsible for the restructuring of the petrochemical sector by selling off 27 state enterprises at a total value of US$3.7 billion and transferring dividends of US$1 billion between 1992 and 1996 (Montenegro 2003).[5] Cardoso inherited a relatively economically

---

eventually agreed to have 51% public and 49% private shares—a technocratic solution to compel the state enterprise to achieve private sector efficiency (Evans 1979, 90–92; Nem Singh 2012

[5] The petrochemical sector is part of the downstream activities of the Petrobras system. No reforms were introduced in this sector except the company reorganization, and the sector was not directly affected by the Petroleum Law, which focussed on generating more investment in the upstream activities.

168 Business of the State

Table 7.1 Sales from privatization of the petrochemicals industry in Brazil, 1992–1996.

Year	Amount (in US$ million)
1992	1,330.3
1993–1994	551.8
1995	604.04
1996	212.9
Total	2,699.04

Source: BNDES data from Montenegro (2003) (adapted).

stable government in 1996 when he assumed the presidency, though this balancing of the state budget through extensive privatization came at the cost of facilitating the decline of industrial sectors after the economic crisis.

Under the government of Itamar Franco (1992–1995), Cardoso as Finance Minister implemented the 1994 Real Plan, which sought a dual strategy of maintaining inflation and controlling wages. With its success in bringing down inflation, Cardoso secured the presidency and reoriented his policy towards the privatization of strategic state enterprises, including in the steel, oil, and mining sectors, as a central plank of his economic recovery plan. Cardoso's rationale for his ambitious programme of corporate restructuring and privatization of SOEs was competitiveness and necessity, with market-opening reforms presented as the inevitable alternative to developmentalism, irrespective of the performance of state enterprises. The state appeared unstoppable at its privatization agenda[6] and was highly successful in breaking the monopoly and privatizing steel and mining (Hunter 2010), while also aiming to dismantle the market power of Brazil's NOC Petrobras (Massi and Nem Singh 2016, 163).

Petrobras was dramatically impacted by a series of stabilization plans; its assets were sold, and the public company was restructured to ensure its survival. In 1992, Petrobras's reorganization reduced its operating costs from US$4.2 billion to US$3.2 billion. This was achieved through decentralizing administrative tasks, offering incentive programmes for retirement to slim the labour force, and selecting subsidiaries to extinguish or privatize (Randall 1993; Trebat 1983). In line with the BNDES restructuring of the Petrobras system, Brazil's National Congress decisively voted to eliminate Interbras and

---

[6] For a balanced critique on privatization and the strategic direction of the PND during the 1990s see the following newspaper articles of Damasceno (1995); Folha de São Paulo (2003); and Landau 1995

Petromisa as well as to privatize subsidiaries controlled by Petroquisa, all of which were justified as poorly performing.

Yet, attempts at privatizing Petrobras failed despite the mass support for Cardoso's highly successful neoliberal programme. One explanation draws on the timing and sequence of privatizations in Brazil. By the time Petrobras was being prepared for privatization, it already had a niche in the global oil industry through its deepwater engineering technology,[7] unlike, for example, mining company *Companhia Vale do Rio Doce* (CVRD), which was privatized despite a legal battle and its record as a successful mining company,[8] because, from the government's viewpoint, it had less chance of promoting technological innovation. Another crucial explanation for the failure to privatize Petrobras was that privatization in O&G was very politicized and heavily contested. Organized oil workers defended Petrobras against privatization through the *Federação Única dos Petroleiros* (FUP), the largest and most organized labour union affiliated with the national-based *Central Única dos Trabalhadores* (CUT). Labour mobilized to retain state ownership of Nitrofertil, which was eventually incorporated in the Petrobras system as *Fábrica de Fertilizantes Nitrogenados* (FAFEN) (FUP 2011). The peak of political mobilization between the reformist government and the combative unions was the 1995 oil workers' strike in defence of state monopoly in the oil and telecommunications industries, during which Cardoso called for military troops to occupy the refineries in Paraná, Paulínia, Mauá, and São José dos Campos and enforce law and order on the streets (Folha de São Paulo 1995; FUP 2011). The 31-day strike brought public sector workers' rights to the centre of national politics and received expressions of solidarity from a broad range of actors. In the end, Cardoso fell short in fully liberalizing the highly strategic O&G sector and Petrobras remained state-owned, albeit subject to extensive corporate restructuring (see Chapter 8). Instead, market competition became the overarching logic of reform in Brazil, in which the state was conceived as both a *regulator* and an *oil producer*. Table 7.2 summarizes the politics, institutional arrangements, and corresponding development policy/industrial strategy of the market competition agenda, together with the external conditions and outcomes, under the Cardoso (1996–2002), PT (Lula and Rousseff) (2003–2015), and Temer

---

[7] Author interview with Nogueira da Costa Jr., Deputy Secretary, Secretariat of Geology, Mining, and Mineral Processing, Ministry of Mines and Energy (MME), Brasília, September 2011.

[8] It is worth mentioning that a legal battle regarding the privatization of state-owned mining giant CVRD (now Vale) reflected the public discontent over the economic reform agenda. Further, the Brazilian state continues to exercise indirect influence through its golden shares in the company (Nem Singh and Massi 2016, 167–168).

170   Business of the State

(2016–2018) administrations. It affirms that state ownership and incremental changes in the regulatory framework of oil-based development are a core feature of Brazilian economic strategy.

Table 7.2 Continuity and change in Brazilian O&G sector governance, 1996–2018.

	Fernando Henrique Cardoso (1996–2002)	Luiz Inácio Lula da Silva (2003–2010)	Michel Temer (2016–2018)
Politics • Logic of state action • Orientation of state	• Introduce market competition and encourage IOCs to invest in E&P sector	• Introduce industrial strategy to promote Brazil as an oil producer and supplier of high-quality equipment for deepwater oil production	• Emphasis on Brazil as an oil producer with the objective of attracting foreign investments in pre-salt oil production; emphasis on the need for *competition* with Petrobras
	• State as *regulator* of market competition and as *oil producer*	• Maintain previous roles, but emphasis on state as oil producer and greater role in industrialization	• Maintain previous roles, but emphasis on state as regulator; smaller role for state in oil production
Institutional Arrangements • Regulatory functions • Fiscal regime • Domestic financing	• Tripartite regulatory framework between federal government (state), Petrobras (SOE), and ANP (regulator)	• Tripartite regulatory framework remained unchanged; creation of a new SOE (PPSA) to represent federal government in contracts and joint ventures	• Tripartite regulatory framework remains; greater autonomy for ANP to guarantee competition in contract bidding
	• Concessions grant fiscal regime to secure private property rights of IOCs	• Concessions grant fiscal regime remained in place; a new production-sharing agreement (PSA) fiscal regime was introduced for pre-salt oil reserves	• All existing legislations remain in place; PSA as dominant fiscal regime due to size of pre-salt offshore reserves

	Fernando Henrique Cardoso (1996–2002)	Luiz Inácio Lula da Silva (2003–2010)	Michel Temer (2016–2018)
	• 'Free' competition between Petrobras and IOCs	• Upon discovery of pre-salt reserves, new law allocated 30% minimum participation share for Petrobras in *all* offshore oilfields	• Due to economic and political crisis, Petrobras's 30% minimum participation share requirement was scrapped
	• BNDES' role was to oversee privatization of SOEs	• BNDES' role shifted towards financier of investment projects for public and private enterprises; investments in O&G industry mainly through ship-building	• As a direct effect of *Lava Jato* crisis, BNDES' role focussed on financing initial investments, specifically in infrastructure, taking a 'transversal' rather than sectoral view of development

Development Policy/Industrial Strategy

	Fernando Henrique Cardoso (1996–2002)	Luiz Inácio Lula da Silva (2003–2010)	Michel Temer (2016–2018)
• Capital ownership of SOE • Approach towards sectoral linkages • Capital reinvestment	• Introduction of international shareholders within Petrobras (change in capital ownership structure; state remains dominant shareholder)	• Petrobras ownership structure remained unchanged	• Petrobras ownership structure intact; privatization of refineries debated
	• Flexible local content policy with low percentage requirements to utilize domestic suppliers	• Rigid local content rules with high percentage requirements to *accelerate* expansion of domestic supply chain	• Flexible local content requirements with priority to attract investment for oil production; *de-emphasis* on 'thickening' or expanding domestic equipment supply chain

Continued

172 Business of the State

Table 7.2 *Continued*

	Fernando Henrique Cardoso (1996–2002)	Luiz Inácio Lula da Silva (2003–2010)	Michel Temer (2016–2018)
	• Obligatory R&D expenditure through special tax	• Obligatory R&D expenditure remains; heavy investments in infrastructure development via BNDES credit lines, specifically pipeline network and new refineries	• Earmarking of taxes towards R&D remain in place; reliance on IOCs for infrastructure development and for oil E&P
External Conditions			
• Oil price volatility • Macro-economic conditions	• Low oil prices in 1990s and early 2000s	• High commodity prices between 2003 and 2013 followed by dramatic oil price crash in 2014; pricing policy implemented under Dilma as anti-inflation measure	• Slowly recovering oil prices (2015–2018); gasoline prices were pegged at international market prices
	• Debt crisis (1980s) and macro-economic instability until 1995	• High average annual GDP growth rates from 2.10% in the 1980s and 1990s to 3.28% from 2001 to 2013 (Carvalho and Rugitsky 2015: 2). Based on commodity boom and expanding domestic consumption	• Gradual recovery from economic crisis
	• Neoliberalism as a worldwide ideology	• Discovery of pre-salt oil reserves in offshore fields in 2007	• *Lava Jato* scandal challenged consensus on 'state developmentalism' and industrial policy was perceived as *rent-seeking* by PT government

	Fernando Henrique Cardoso (1996–2002)	Luiz Inácio Lula da Silva (2003–2010)	Michel Temer (2016–2018)
Outcomes			
• Competitive-ness in sector	• Entry of IOCs in E&P sector but only to work in joint ventures with Petrobras	• Significant expansion of oil E&P under Petrobras	• Increasing number of IOCs in oil E&P; joint ventures with Petrobras remain the norm
• E&P capacity of sector	• Petrobras remains a dominant market player in oil E&P	• Modest success in bringing global players into equipment supply, with pre-salt as potentially largest offshore supply market for offshore O&G production	• Growing productive capacity of IOCs; declining refining capacity in Brazil
• Degree of vertical and horizontal integration	• Refining and downstream segments remain largely dominated by Petrobras	• Failed investments in further supply chain and ship-building due to corruption and falling oil prices	

Source: Author's summary, compiled from various sources (Musacchio and Lazzarini 2016; Massi and Nem Singh 2018; Priest 2016).
FMC Technologies Inc, General Electric (GE), Pré-Sal Petróleo S.A. (PPSA).

The 'Norwegian Model' in the Brazilian Oil Industry (1997–2002)

Table 7.3 summarizes the four major kinds of fiscal regimes in the O&G industry. The principle of *risk sharing* between private capital and the Brazilian state is central to the political choice over how to organize the relationship between states, state-controlled companies, and IOCs. Cardoso's fiscal regime—built at a time of low oil prices, slow recovery from external debt, and a fragile economy—recognized market competition as the only means to generate the necessary investments in the E&P sector. He sought a concession grant contract regime, where risks in oil exploration and development are shouldered by private capital and Petrobras was to seek its own capitalization. By 1997, the Brazilian O&G industry was opened for global oil players. National Congress initially ratified Constitutional Amendment No. 5, which

174 Business of the State

Table 7.3 Risks and rewards in E&P sector contract regimes.

Contract type	Oil company	State	Description
Concession	All risk and high reward	Low risk and low reward	Oil company holds exclusive rights to explore, develop, sell, and export oil and minerals extracted from a specified area within a fixed period of time. The successful bidder takes all the risks of exploring and developing oilfields
Production-sharing	All risk and low reward	Low risk and high reward	Ownership of natural resources rests on the state but permits foreign corporations to manage and operate the development of oilfields. Foreign capital takes the risks of developing oilfields, and the model typically works when a national state-owned and/or private company joins the consortium as interest holders. Often the state has the cost of its initial contribution carried by the other companies, which would be repaid from the state's future profits. Intense negotiations between the sharing of costs and capital exist here. Contracts play a critical role because the legal system is the only guarantee that the state will not renounce its previous commitment. It is also in this system that the state is at its most conflictual role because it acts both as profit maximizer and as enforcer of the rule of law
Pure service	No risk and low reward	All risk and high reward	Under this contractual arrangement, the oil company is engaged by the regulatory authority or state-owned company as state representative to conduct petroleum exploration for a fee or share of production. It can either be pure service contract or risk service contract. The oil company has neither any exploration or production title nor ownership of petroleum produced at any stage of the commodity chain
Joint venture	Share in risk and reward	Share in risk and reward	By definition, it refers to an arrangement where two or more parties wish to pursue a joint undertaking of oil exploration and development. However, there is a long list of issues that need to be resolved before any joint venture can be negotiated, especially as regards risk, costs, or potential liabilities (e.g. in cases of accidents or environmental damage). The state is directly responsible in resource extraction

Sources: Lima (2009a; 2009b); Radon (2005) (adapted).

broke the monopoly of Petrobras in the lucrative E&P upstream segment of the oil industry. This was followed by the 1997 Petroleum Law (Lei 9.478) approved on 6 August 1997, which ended Petrobras's monopoly in the oil industry.

The 1997 Petroleum Law had two important effects. Firstly, it established the concessions regime, allowing IOCs to participate and compete with Petrobras in O&G E&P. During this period, Petrobras's commercial strategy was mainly to fund the production of existing offshore oilfields, notably in the Campos Basin, so there were limited resources to explore new reserves.[9] Cardoso perceived oil exploration with scepticism and preferred a conservative approach in extending government support to Petrobras. In many ways, Petrobras's necessity to become self-sufficient created the conditions to assert its political autonomy from the state, in particular its capacity to finance its expansion in the E&P sector through profitable refining and downstream segments of the oil value chain. By contrast, Cardoso had a more optimistic view on foreign capital's interest in oil exploration as a source to make the O&G industry competitive.

The second effect of the Petroleum Law is linked to the consolidation of a tripartite regulatory framework patterned after the so-called Norwegian model. This refers to an institutional arrangement where the national government, the state company, and an autonomous regulatory agency have clearly identified and distinctive functions in the sector (Thurber and Istad 2012). The 1997 Petroleum Law established the *Agência Nacional do Petróleo* (ANP) (National Petroleum Agency) as an independent regulator to facilitate auctions of the oilfields for E&P, to ensure compliance of oil companies in environmental rules and fiscal obligations, and, crucially, to protect the private property of capital in Brazil. The creation of ANP is, by itself, a political decision to weaken the power of Petrobras. Indeed, it was a break away from the historical role of Petrobras as the agenda-setting organization within the state (Randall 1993; Trebat 1983).[10] For private oil companies, ANP was initially conceived as the guarantor of the reformist government's commitment to establish market competition through the entry of IOCs in the sector as the new rule of the game to curb Petrobras's sectoral dominance.[11] David

---

[9] Author interview with Senior Member, Executive Board, Petrobras, Rio de Janeiro, 28 May 2018.

[10] Author interview with Former Senior Officer, ANP, Rio de Janeiro, August 2010.

[11] Author interviews with three Senior Officers, *Instituto Brasileiro de Petróleo, Gás e Biocombustíveis* (IBP), Rio de Janeiro, August 2010.

176 Business of the State

Zylberstajn, the first ANP Director, reflected on these early reforms as an ideological shift away from oil monopoly:

> We had reforms [in the O&G industry] because the sector drastically needed foreign investment ... [this] was a consensus among politicians ... a constitutional amendment was passed ... [so that] the state will retain ownership ... but [allow] other operators [to partake] ... We had to break the monopoly of Petrobras, create a more competitive oil sector, and instil a culture of independent regulation ... Our greatest achievement as a regulator is to bring in new companies, consolidate a sector with new players, and develop expertise and independence of people outside of Petrobras.[12]

The 1997 Petroleum Law provides a legal basis for ANP to maintain total control over its own budget, establish fixed mandates for its Board of Director (Kasahara and Botelho 2019, 394), and exercise its discretionary powers in formulating sectoral policy (Mueller and Perreira 2002). The ANP set out a plan to strengthen Petrobras's professional bureaucracy because it was the principal source of expertise and technical capacity within the O&G sector. It sought to break the loyalty of bureaucrats and engineers within the sector away from Petrobras by building a new system of training personnel through direct agreements with 36 universities to train new professionals in the O&G and biofuel sectors. The ANP drafted its own postgraduate training schemes, systems of public procurement, and regulations in the energy sector—all aimed at consolidating technical capacity as a way to assert its organizational autonomy from the state and from Petrobras.[13] In other words, ANP emulated an ideal model of a regulator characterized by functional autonomy and a provider of critical technical services and advice—the Norwegian Petroleum Directorate (NPD) being a prime example—which is protected from undue interference from the Ministry or the NOC (Thurber and Istad 2012). Nevertheless, Brazil's lack of history in independent regulation has shown to be an obstacle in realizing this goal. Musacchio and Lazzarini (2016, 122) express concern that 'the ANP is relatively weak, with past allegations of corruption and with direct influence by the government; the President of Brazil and the Minister of Mines and Energy remain as the de facto "regulators" of Petrobras'. The creation of a formal regulatory

---

[12] Author interview with David Zylberstajn, Former Executive Director, ANP, Rio de Janeiro, 15 July 2010.

[13] Author interviews with Victor Martin Souza, Executive Director, ANP, Rio de Janeiro, 25 August 2010; and Former Senior Officer, ANP, Rio de Janeiro, 05 August 2010.

institution, thus, did not necessarily transfer policy competence and independence to the ANP or the Ministry of Mines and Energy (MME); and Petrobras's continued market presence has reflected its power and influence in policymaking.

As part of the broader institutional arrangement in energy governance, the 1997 Petroleum Law likewise created the *Conselho Nacional de Politíca Energética* (or CNPE) (National Council for Energy Policy) as a way of generating policy proposals directly to the president. The CNPE draws from technical expertise of other state agencies—mainly the *Empresa de Pesquisa Energética* (EPE) and ANP—in crafting policy proposals, which includes the submission of legislative bills in Congress for subsidies for regions requiring federal support to finance energy consumption (Chapter 2, Article 2, 1997 DL 9.478). While ANP explicitly draws legitimacy from its technocratic expertise, CNPE can be interpreted as an intermediate institution to provide an avenue for ministers and experts on an ad hoc basis to provide strategic advice to the president as regards energy policy.[14] By implication, their advice often becomes government policy only through presidential decrees rather than set in legislation. However, despite the apparent restructuring in political decision-making, the CNPE played a minor role during the market-opening process. Expectations for setting the new rules of the game were pinned on the ANP.[15] Put crudely, regulatory governance fell between ANP and Petrobras, with the MME having little steering role in designing sectoral policy.

In a nutshell, market-opening reforms under Cardoso reflect the shifting coalition of economic and political actors in favour of market competition and privatization of strategic industries (Almeida and Moya 1997; Kingstone 1999). Privatization was conceived as a challenge to create a new 'compact' between state and market actors in ways that accommodate national interests in open-economy settings (Goldstein 1999, 679; Musacchio and Lazzarini 2016).[16] The ANP initially sought to assert its autonomy as a regulator and to establish an organizational identity distinct from the national

---

[14] Beyond the O&G industry, the CNPE provides an avenue for inter-ministerial coordination as regards energy policy more generally; sensitive issues related to hydropower, electric generation, and thermonuclear are extensively discussed to guarantee the protection of consumers, free competition, and internationalization of energy (Chapter 1, Article 1, 1997 DL 9.478).

[15] Author interviews with Ildo Sauer, Petrobras, São Paulo, August 2010; Roberto Schaeffer, Academic Consultant, UFRJ, Rio de Janeiro, July 2010; and David Zylberstajn, ANP, Rio de Janeiro, July 2010.

[16] Some countries have designed privatization as grand strategies to recast economic relations and the role of the state, for example in the UK and Chile; others have sought privatization as a gradualist strategy to delineate incoming governments from previous administrations, such as in France; and still others have used privatization as a macroeconomic management strategy to deal with a crisis, as in Italy and Argentina (Goldstein 1999, 679).

178 Business of the State

state to provide credibility in the reform process. Nevertheless, an alternative reading suggests that neoliberal reforms were only implemented in partial, segmented forms due to political resistance and business demands for a recalibrated industrial policy in the era of economic globalization (Montero 1998; Pinheiro et al. 2004; Schneider 2004a; 2009b). As such, rather than fully relinquishing control in strategic industries, the Brazilian state adapted to external forces by embracing liberal economic discourse alongside state intervention (Ban 2013; Döring 2017).

Institutional Continuity of *Desenvolvimentismo* Under Cardoso

While there is a general assumption that Cardoso's market reform agenda was largely embraced to dismantle Brazil's developmental state, I argue that key continuities in *desenvolvimentismo* persisted in the O&G industry under neoliberalism. In this section I reexamine two vital aspects of the 1997 Petroleum Law to illustrate this argument: first, the range of obligatory payments attached to taxes in the O&G industry; and second, specific details on the local content requirements (LCRs) for oil companies. To begin with, the 1997 Petroleum Law institutionalized four types of payments to be made by the concessionaires for O&G E&P activities: (1) the signature bonus from production contracts; (2) royalty payments earmarked among oil-producing states and municipalities; (3) special participation fees; and (4) payments for occupation or retention of area (see Table 7.4). Only the royalty fees existed prior to the passage of the law, albeit at a lower percentage.

Therefore, the extensive fiscal regime crafted under the 1997 Petroleum Law has important implications not only for redistributive politics but also for the general orientation of the Brazilian state in transforming the O&G industry as an engine for national industrialization. Firstly, the Law reflects the decentralization of fiscal revenues at subnational levels, thereby ensuring fair distribution of oil rents towards municipalities and regions producing and impacted by hydrocarbon activities (see Table 7.5). This meant that while most Latin American countries implemented retaxation of their extractive industries during the commodity boom (2002–2012), Brazil was advanced and had already set measures in place to avoid redistributive conflicts emerging from a resource bonanza. Secondly, the Law is extremely clear about two complementary logics on the rules over state spending of oil rents. Royalty payments and special participation fees outline very specific rules about the share of the Ministry of Science and Technology to

Table 7.4 Distribution of fiscal revenues according to Brazil's 1997 Petroleum Law.

Onshore activities	Percentage share
Oil-producing states	52.5
Oil-producing municipalities	15
Municipalities impacted by landing or shipment of O&G production	7.5
Ministry of Science and Technology	25
Offshore activities	
Oil-producing states	22.5
Oil-producing municipalities	22.5
Brazilian Navy	15
Special Fund for non-oil producing regions	7.5
Ministry of Science and Technology	25
Special participation fees	
Ministry of Mines and Energy	40
Ministry of Environment, Hydro-resources, and Amazon	10
Oil-producing states	40
Oil-producing municipalities	10

Source: DL 9.478 (1997 Petroleum Law).

finance studies and exploratory projects aimed at technological innovation in the sector.[17]

Another key feature of this innovative legislation rests on the earmarking of funds to support the protection of the environment and to offset the ecological costs of hydrocarbon extraction. Hence, the 1997 Petroleum Law was a highly advanced redistributive mechanism set in motion by the Brazilian state despite the limited amount of discoverable oil reserves, aimed at facilitating regional development and sectoral innovation. Indeed, this institutional innovation in the absence of large oil reserves is reflective of the state's developmentalist logic that characterized similar trends during the formative years of Petrobras in the 1950s. Finally, Brazil's legislation mirrors the experience of successful natural-resource producers like Norway and Malaysia, which institutionalized rent maximization and measures prior to the commodity boom to mitigate against the negative development outcomes of the resource curse (Barbier 2012; Barma et al. 2011).

The second continuity of *desenvolvimentismo* can be observed in the way Cardoso adopted local content (LC) policy as a means to establish a social

---

[17] In addition, 40% of oil rents from offshore activities received by the Ministry is earmarked to finance scientific R&D to be applied to North and Northeast Brazil.

180   Business of the State

compact with industrial elites. Taking advantage of ANP's organizational autonomy, its first director, David Zylberstajn, commissioned studies to evaluate the technical and engineering capacity of Brazilian national suppliers to provide local goods and services for the O&G sector, and whether a local content policy in Brazil would violate its obligations under the World Trade Organization (WTO) agreements, especially on government procurement (Kasahara and Botelho 2019, 395). This was a response to the efforts of two groups who wanted to increase the market share of domestic suppliers in the sector. One group, based in Rio de Janeiro headed by Anthony Garotinho, lobbied at the federal level to bring Petrobras's construction of oil platforms within the state, given its proximity to offshore activities. He campaigned and won the election to become the governor of Rio de Janeiro in 1998, and upon taking office he established tax exemptions as an incentive for shipyards to become competitive.[18] The second group known as *Compete, Brasil* was an action group comprised of eight business associations in the manufacturing industry, demanding credit and tax incentives to level the playing field between foreign and domestic suppliers. They feared that Brazilian manufacturing would lose out as global oil players would continue to rely on foreign suppliers of equipment and services, while at the same time Petrobras would increasingly outsource its projects to foreign contractors. The first Rio de Janeiro-based group represented a more inward-looking perspective on industrial policy, while *Compete, Brasil* was more concerned with international competitiveness and was thus aligned to a more outward-looking perspective, similar to Cardoso himself (Kasahara and Botelho 2019). In 1999, through the active lobbying of *Compete, Brasil*, Zylberstajn adopted the LCR clause in the first concession bidding. The clause stipulates that oil companies are free to voluntarily set the local content percentage and can decide which equipment and services will be outsourced among suppliers, while the ANP calculates the signature bonus to be paid by oil companies (see Table 6.4). As an incentive, the LCR bid can also be used as a tiebreaker among competing bidders (Kasahara and Botelho 2019, 395). Cardoso adopted a more flexible local content policy in the O&G sector, recognizing information asymmetry and unconventional barriers to entry in the industry.

Finally, in 1999, following the organizational model of the *Compete, Brasil* movement, the ANP supported the creation of the *Organização Nacional da Indústria do Petróleo* (ONIP) (National Organization of Petroleum Industry). ONIP created a space to 'build consensus among various national

---

[18] While the federal government committed to finance the construction of new ships under the Naval Transportation Promoting Fund, Petrobras in negotiation with Cotinho and MME agreed to use 40% local suppliers in constructing two new oil platforms (Kasahara and Botelho 2019, 394).

producers across the O&G value chain in order to broaden the domestic capabilities of Brazilian companies, maximize the participation of suppliers in the value chain, and to stimulate innovation for productivity gains and export performance.'[19] Therefore, in the era of economic globalization, the Brazilian state reestablished its corporatist framework by incorporating business and labour interests into the state apparatus, ensuring that state presence in the strategic O&G sector was maintained, despite calls for weaker government intervention (Kasahara and Botelho 2019).

The PT (Workers' Party) in Power: More Continuity Than Change?

The end of Cardoso's presidency was marked by the electoral victory of Lula da Silva (Lula) in 2002 and the beginning of the PT reign in power. Although Lula often portrayed himself as a radical alternative to Cardoso and the PDSB, policy continuity rather than change characterized his first term in office. There are two key continuities between Cardoso and Lula prior to the discovery of pre-salt reserves. Firstly, Lula committed to promote and attract foreign investment as a central pillar of his development strategy. Upon taking power in 2003, Lula adopted a conservative set of policies marked by stringent fiscal policy to obtain a budget surplus, inflation targeting, and maintenance of high interest rates (Amann and Baer 2009; Artestis and Saad Filho 2007). He appointed Antonio Palocci as Finance Minister and a well-known market-oriented economist from the PDSB, Henrique Meirelles, as Head of the Central Bank to ensure that the Brazilian government would avoid reneging on its international commitments. These appointments signalled Lula's commitment to bind the government to the institutional framework inherited from Cardoso's PDSB, and in the O&G industry, the concession grant model remained in place as the fiscal regime. Secondly, Petrobras was maintained as a dominant player in the O&G industry. While Cardoso retained state ownership in Petrobras due to his failed attempt at privatizing the company, Lula was more committed to transform Petrobras into a major energy player to support his industrialization agenda.

Nevertheless, there are important differences between Lula and Cardoso as regards O&G policy. In 2002, Lula denounced Petrobras's policy of buying from the cheapest supplier and its lack of an active strategy to support

---

[19] See https://www.onip.org.br/institucional/apresentacao (accessed 26 August 2019).

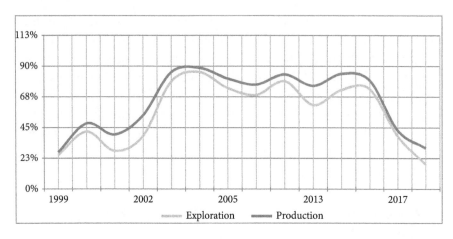

Figure 7.1 Average percentage of LCRs in Brazil's domestic industries, 1998–2018.
Source: ANP (2018, Table 5.3) (adapted).

domestic industries (Lima-de-Oliveira 2019), and by 2003, the PT government had radically increased LCRs (see Figure 7.1) as part of a broader industrial strategy (Kasahara and Botelho 2019). Lula discussed switching to a model of production-sharing agreements in the O&G sector, as an alternative model to Cardoso's concession-based regime, but this was not adopted in the end for two reasons. Firstly, oil rents coming from the O&G sector were not enough to justify an institutional overhaul in the sector, and the high costs associated with offshore oil E&P remained prohibitive for any large-scale government takeover. Secondly, the arms-length relationship between the Brazilian state and Petrobras proved effective in terms of maintaining the NOC as a profit-oriented and competitive company. By allowing Petrobras to make the strategic commercial decisions, the state company continued to assert its corporate independence and kept the state at bay from its commercial activities.

The Age of Oil in Brazil

The first critical juncture that consolidated the dominant power of Petrobras despite the pressures of market liberalization was driven by external conditions related to the international political economy. Firstly, by 2003, the advent of the longest recorded commodity price boom (2002–2012) ended the fiscal constraints on Brazil's budget. As a resource-intensive economy, high prices in iron ore, soya, and agricultural products reversed the country's trade imbalance between 2002 and 2007 (see Figure 7.2). While exports

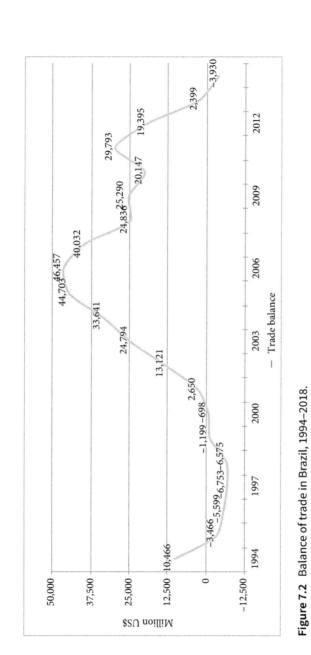

Figure 7.2 Balance of trade in Brazil, 1994–2018.
Source: IPEA (2020).

184 Business of the State

had driven growth between 2003 and 2006, other key factors such as fiscal activism, higher minimum wages, and the expansion of credit and social provision facilitated a virtuous circle of growth and redistribution supported by domestic investment and mass consumption (Saad Filho and Morais 2018, 99).

Secondly, in 2007 Petrobras announced the discovery of *pre-salt* reserves located in its coastlines. In 2002, Petrobras drilled beneath the salt layer (about 2,000 metres thick) and wells penetrated ultra-deep waters over 7,000 metres below sea level.[20] In 2005, the Tupi bloc showed indications of oil in the pre-salt layer and in late 2006 Petrobras estimated between 5 and 8 billion barrels of pre-salt oil in the Campos and Espiritu Santo Basins. At present, the pre-salt oil reservoir is approximately 800 kilometres long by 200 kilometres wide, which runs along the southern and southeastern coasts of Brazil from Santa Catarina all the way to Espiritu Santo (see Figure 7.3).[21]

Lula interpreted the oil discovery as a signal to reshape the relationship between the state, global oil players, and Petrobras. The PT revived the oil question—the strategic use of oil as a tool for industrial policy—previously resolved in the 1950s, which is essentially about whether state ownership should have a place in the era of economic globalization, and dormant suspicions of foreign capital exploiting Brazilian resources for profit. The PT envisaged the pre-salt discovery as a window of opportunity to deepen the role of the state in national industrialization through *novo desenvolvimentismo* (new developmentalism)—a shorthand used to describe the 'return of state capitalism' (Bresser-Pereira 2006; Sicsú et al. 2007) or 'international developmentalism' (Ban 2013). Lula articulated the logic of developmentalist state action to accelerate Brazil's efforts towards late industrialization. The PT drew inspiration from *desenvolvimentismo*, whereby Petrobras would play a central role in generating demand for industrial inputs to create sectoral linkages between the O&G industry and the rest of the national economy.[22]

However, there are sharp distinctions between these old and new *desenvolvimentismos*. Firstly, the traditional fusion of the regulatory and entrepreneurial functions of the state, as outlined by Trebat (1983), is

---

[20] Using its years of geological information, including data on the nature of rocks in the salt layer, Petrobras developed a new version of its Basin Simulator to accurately map the oil deposit and extraction site—a task deemed difficult due to the distortions created by the salt. Equally, a new process had been developed to deal with the corrosiveness and instability of the salt (Petrobras 2007, 4–5).

[21] Technically, light hydrocarbons refer to 30 API (American Petroleum Institute) oil, natural gas, and condensate.

[22] Author interviews with Margarete Gandini, *Ministério do Desenvolvimento, Indústria, e Comércio Exterior* (MDIC) (Ministry of Development, Industry and Foreign Trade), Brasília, 4 June 2018; and two Senior Officials, (SEST), Ministry of Planning, Brasília, 4 June 2018.

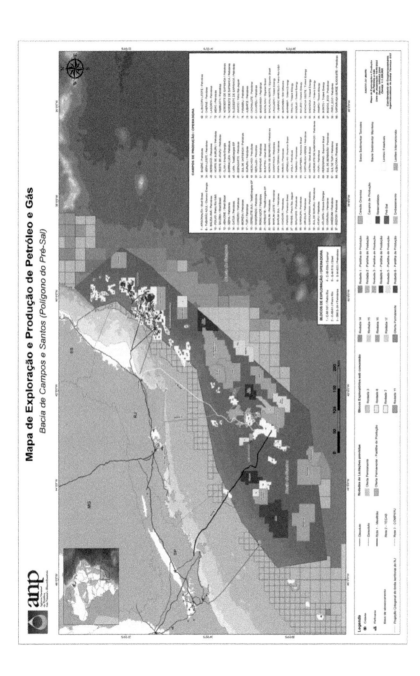

Figure 7.3 Pre-salt O&G exploration and production—Campos and Santos Basins.
Source: ANP (2022).

impossible to sustain in the era of globalization because international competitiveness drives states to limit excessive state intervention in markets. Under Cardoso's economic strategy, the Brazilian state had shifted its role from being an owner of productive capital towards a provider of finance capital. For example, the Brazilian state owns voting capital stocks in previously state-run enterprises, most emblematically in Petrobras, CVRD, and CSN, but their corporate governance decisions now lie in the hands of their company CEOs. In the steel and mining sectors, the state has retained control through golden shares,[23] which is an indirect way of exercising strategic influence in privately run enterprises (Massi and Nem Singh 2016, 166–168; Musacchio and Lazzarini 2014, 218–232). The peculiar privatization of strategic sectors in Brazil is reflective of what Musacchio and Lazzarini (2014, 99, 211–215) describes as the Leviathan playing a dual role as an 'entrepreneur and majority investor on the one hand, and a minority shareholder on the other' as a means of gatekeeping strategic domestic assets from foreign capital.

Secondly, an important distinction between old and new developmentalism stems from how the PT interprets the role of natural resources in industrialization. While the military government (1964–1985) consolidated the role of Petrobras in Brazilian economic development, it clearly envisaged manufacturing as the engine of development. However, the PT came to power when Brazil was experiencing slow de-industrialization and the decline of manufacturing amidst a commodity boom. The PT had to decide whether to pursue Brazil's comparative advantage to become a major resource producer, or to undertake a complex industrial strategy which would require transforming Brazil into a supplier of high-technology equipment and complex services for offshore oil production activities. While the PT was confident that the risks were lower for oil exploration, a natural-resource-based industrial policy is equally mired with a high risk of failure. However, the pre-salt reserves have been branded as one of the biggest offshore discoveries in modern history and, subsequently, policymakers understood that Brazil could become more than just an oil exporter, by transforming the country into the largest supply market for offshore production.[24] The challenge was to develop the supply chain for subsea, submarine, and offshore wells in a cost-effective

---

[23] Golden shares are special voting rights that accord the majority shareholder, in this case the Brazilian state, some veto power over any significant changes in corporate governance, such as changes in the company's name and purpose, headquarters' location, liquidation, and closure or sale of major operations (Schneider 2009a; 2009b; 2013).

[24] Author interviews with three Senior Officials, BNDES, Rio de Janeiro, 14 June 2018; Margarete Gandini, MDIC, Brasilia, 4 June 2018; but also corroborated by José Ricardo Roriz Coelho, FIESP, São Paulo, 7 June 2018.

way so as to realize the objective of linking the O&G sector to industrial capital goods production. Therefore, Lula's new developmentalism is crucial to understand the strengths and limitations of the PT government's strategy to promote oil-based industrialization.

Institutional Change in the Age of Pre-Salt

Under Lula, the role of the state in Brazil's development trajectory deepened and Petrobras was placed at the apex of national politics, as three important institutional changes were introduced in preparation for pre-salt production. In 2010, Lula enacted Law 12.350—the Pre-Salt Law—which established a production-sharing arrangement for the pre-salt field and other strategic oilfields (see Table 7.4). While the concession grant model assumes high uncertainty and high risks that deter the state from directly investing in O&G E&P, the production-sharing regime assumes that risks and uncertainties are lower and justifies a direct role for the state as an investor and market participant. This production-sharing model is the one that Lula had previously considered for the O&G sector when he first became president, but had not pursued. The new Pre-Salt Law sharply diverges from the conventional role of the state in governing risk; the new assumption is that the sector bears lower risk upon Petrobras's discovery of oil reserves. The Brazilian state retains its subsoil rights and controls the participation of foreign players as service contractors. By maintaining ownership rights, the PT guarantees future oil rents for the state and clearly favours the NOC over IOCs by establishing a minimum participation share for Petrobras. When the law was passed, Petrobras was accorded 30% minimum participation stake in every E&P contract in the pre-salt field.

By contrast, participants in the consortia formed under a concession grant model do not own mineral rights and merely serve to provide services in oil exploration on behalf of the state (Lima 2009a; 2009b; Radon 2005). The creation of the production-sharing regime triggered a second institutional change—the establishment of a new state enterprise, Pré-Sal Petróleo S.A. (PPSA) (Petró-Sal), whose mandate is to represent the federal government in all production-sharing contracts (PSCs), joint ventures, and consortia. This new SOE is itself a by-product of Petrobras's complex corporate governance arrangement. The Pre-Salt Law requires state interest to be represented in all contracts in the pre-salt region, but Petrobras's hybrid ownership structure implies that the NOC operates independently from the national state. In this context, the PPSA also functions to reduce information asymmetry

188 Business of the State

between public and private actors. By obtaining and producing technical and financial knowledge in all aspects of oil production, such as costs of wells, platforms, and equipment for offshore exploration, PPSA protects the long-term financial and economic interest of the Brazilian state in the strategic industry.[25]

Finally, pre-salt production under the PT government actively utilized the BNDES in supporting an industrial strategy based on deepening LCRs and expanding state-backed finance in infrastructure building in O&G and related sectors. While the BNDES had taken a back seat under Cardoso in terms of financing projects aimed at supporting manufacturing and industries, the PT administrations of Lula and his successor Rousseff aggressively pushed the BNDES to increase investments in large-scale infrastructure aimed at enhancing the supply chain of services and goods—all of which were focussed on supporting the expansion of pre-salt production. As a consequence, the role of the BNDES shifted from an institution overseeing the privatization process under Cardoso, to a provider of finance capital aimed at disbursing loans and credits for huge infrastructural projects under PT governments.[26] This new role of the BNDES was underpinned by the conviction of Brazilian elites that the pre-salt reserves could be transformed into the largest offshore supply market for offshore O&G production.[27] Therefore, the institutional reorientation of BNDES as a source of domestic investment is aligned with the PT's strategy of using sectoral intervention—notably LC policy—to support the O&G sector as Brazil's 'winning' bet in the globalization race. The following section will discuss how this institutional framework complements the PT government's industrial strategy.

Attempts at Oil-Based Industrialization Under the PT

The most significant change in Brazil's development strategy under PT governments is the promotion of technological innovation within the O&G supply chain and the establishment of sectoral linkages. This strategy became possible only through the integral role of Petrobras in the transformation of the sector. Petrobras made strategic commercial investments to develop deep-sea E&P with an excessively optimistic projection of the world economy (see Chapter 8). While sectoral policy under Cardoso aimed to introduce private investment in the O&G industry, Lula sought to deepen state capitalism

---

[25] Author interview with Antonio Cláudio Correa, PPSA, Rio de Janeiro, 14 June 2018.
[26] Author interview with André Pompeo do Amaral Mendes, BNDES, Rio de Janeiro, 14 June 2018.
[27] In 2013, the Lula field was in the top five largest offshore oil reserves in the world (Pentland 2013).

during his second term. There were two key components in this approach: first, heavy state investment in infrastructure in O&G and related sectors to generate new demand in the domestic market; and second, the utilization of LCRs to bolster the local supply chain while fostering linkages between O&G and productive sectors (Massi and Nem Singh 2018, 1138–1139).

In 2007, the government aggressively earmarked funding for infrastructure projects with the objective of creating jobs through public spending. Off the back of windfall profits from a commodity boom, Lula launched a two-phase major infrastructure programme—the *Programa de Aceleração do Crescimento* (PAC) (Growth Acceleration Programme). An initial US$349 billion was invested through PAC 1 (2007–2010), followed by PAC 2 with an estimated spending of US$526 billion between 2011 and 2014 (SECOM 2010). And overall, public expenditure rose from 0.5% in the 1990s to 5% of GDP in 2007–2010 (Resende 2009, 32). Investment under PAC was divided into three categories: (1) logistical infrastructure; (2) energy infrastructure, which includes generation and transmission of electricity, as well as the production, exploration, and shipping of petroleum, natural gas, and renewable fuels; and (3) social and urban infrastructure (Pardelli 2010, 54–57). The energy infrastructure projects funded by BNDES were concentrated in O&G and were aimed at exploring the pre-salt oilfields, with Petrobras as the direct beneficiary.

The second aspect of PT government policy was focussed on LCRs, which refer to the percentage of domestically produced goods and services used in O&G projects. Although Cardoso de-emphasized industrial policy, seeking instead to promote macro-economic stability, privatization, and deregulation, several of his policies might be considered as de facto sector-specific industrial policies. Cardoso established LC rules and procurement policy through the ANP in 1999 as a way to expand the capacity of the domestic supply chain, and this approach to sectoral development is intimately linked to the evolution of Petrobras and its long history of supporting domestic suppliers. This began during the era of import substitution after 1930, when its policy of favouring domestic producers was strategically used to develop the capital goods sector in Brazil. Petrobras successfully created a network of local suppliers as it worked to enhance the quality standards of the inputs of Brazilian companies into the supply chain. LC policies continued to be widely used in the following decades and Petrobras's purchases peaked at 80% in the 1980s. However, during the 1990s, LC dropped substantially, falling to about 40%, although the policy was then reestablished in response to growing business concerns regarding the competitiveness and capacity of the domestic industry to meet the challenges of an open economy. Since

190 Business of the State

1999, companies taking part in O&G exploration are required to acquire local goods and services. Contracts signed between the ANP and oil companies also required that companies give preference to Brazilian suppliers in cases where prices, quality, and delivery were equivalent to those of international suppliers (Xavier Junior 2012).

Under Cardoso, there was no minimum or maximum level of LC; but during Lula's government, LC requirements became obligatory. In 2003, the government imposed a minimum share. In 2005, the ANP established a minimum and a maximum level of LC and a certification process through an independent organization accredited by the regulatory agency for each concession bidding round. The results were apparent (see Table 7.5); the average of LC increased from 33.5% in exploration phases and 42.25% in development phases in the first four rounds to 79.6% and 85.3% respectively in the following bid rounds. Under the conservative government of Temer (2016–2018), the compulsory use of local suppliers was reversed and the average of LC dropped to 18% in exploration phases and 30% in development phases in 2018.

The PT government saw the potential of local inputs as a way to accelerate development of the local supply chain and LC policies and to compel multinational capital to support linkage development between the O&G sectors and the productive economy. Lula's strategy was to extend LC requirements across oil and related sectors, thereby artificially setting the percentage use of domestic suppliers to consolidate and extend the vertical integration of the O&G supply chain in Brazil, using Petrobras as the main driver. Given the size of Petrobras and the importance and contribution of the O&G sector to domestic GDP, the establishment of a procurement policy that gave priority to domestic suppliers had the potential to significantly impact the supply chain and productive structure of the Brazilian economy. For instance, in the pre-salt area, Petrobras was expected to invest US$128 billion in E&P between 2012 and 2015 (BNDES 2012). In 2014, the government estimated that until 2020, US$400 billion would be invested in equipment, services, maintenance, and production expansion (PWC 2014). This would, in theory, facilitate an increase in domestic demand of machinery and equipment, trade, and services, as well as oil tankers, support ships, and marine services.

Consistent with Hirschman's staple linkages theory, Brazilian elites viewed the pre-salt exploration and supply chain expansion as the new source for further sectoral linkages between commodities and manufacturing. One concrete effect of Cardoso's 1997 Petroleum Law was the revitalization of Brazil's shipbuilding industry. In the 1970s, Brazil's shipbuilding industry ranked among the largest in the world. Since the late 1970s, however, the

Table 7.5 Bidding rounds and LC percentages in Brazil's O&G sector, 1999–2018.

Bidding rounds	R1	R2	R3	R4	R5	R6	R7	R9	R10	R11	R12	R13	R14	R15
Year	1999	2000	2001	2002	2003	2004	2005	2007	2008	2013	2013	2015	2017	2018
Exploration phase	25.0	42.0	28.0	39.0	78.8	85.7	74.0	68.9	79.0	61.5	72.6	73.1	38.8	18.0
Development phase	27.0	48.0	40.0	54.0	85.6	88.8	81.0	76.5	84.0	75.6	84.5	79.5	43.0	40.0

Source: ANP (2019, 207).

Percentages are averages per round.

192　Business of the State

industry experienced a drastic decline. At the height of trade liberalization, this decline was intensified as domestic shipyards were exposed to increased global competition. Unable to compete, most companies went bankrupt, and employment fell from over 39,000 in 1979 to only 1,880 in 1998 (Araujo et al. 2011). The 1997 Petroleum Law brought competition (although limited) into the sector through concession grants and free competition between Petrobras and IOCs, which in turn yielded a gradual recovery in outputs and brought forth new demands for drill rigs, support vessels, and marine services.

The industry was further boosted by Petrobras's programme of modernization and expansion of its fleet Programa de Modernização e Expansão da Frota (Promef), which the PT promoted as a substantial part of the PAC infrastructure package, calling for investment in support vessels, platforms, and related services that was expected to reach R$135 billion (approximately US$41.5 billion at current exchange rates) by 2020 (da Silva and Neto 2014). Petrobras served as the largest contractor of vessels and marine support services, which consequently shaped the fate of the shipbuilding industry.

In the industry, LC rules were also applied to shipbuilders, equipment manufacturers, and service providers. According to the *Sindicato Nacional da Indústria da Construção e Reparação Naval e Offshore* (SINAVAL)—the organization that represents Brazilian shipyards—in 2011, the local industry aimed to supply over 70% of the inputs required for the construction of tankers and over 64% of the inputs for floating production storage and offloading (FPSO) vessels (SINAVAL 2012). Petrobras demand for new vessels was expected to assure work in Brazilian shipyards up to 2020. The direct effect of the LC rules was a significant increase in sectoral employment—reaching over 82,000 in 2014—as Petrobras investments in offshore production fuelled new demand for ships (ABENAV 2016). Nevertheless, these positive results were undermined profoundly by the combination of the flaws in the institutional design of the PT's industrial policy and the devastating impacts of the *Lava Jato* scandal both to the sector and to Petrobras's autonomy (discussed further in Chapter 7).

Brazil's Oil Governance Model in Summary

This chapter concludes by outlining the contours of the consolidated governance model in the Brazilian O&G sector. Firstly, it is without question that continuity with change around state ownership accommodated the entry of global players in both offshore oil exploration and equipment supply, thereby strengthening the supply chain in Brazil.[28] While Cardoso's strategy successfully attracted FDI and created the conditions for competitiveness in the O&G sector, Lula's industrial policy was an ambitious attempt to tap the potential of pre-salt oil to expand the oil supply chain and overcome its fate of only being an oil producer. Table 7.6 provides indicative data for this claim. Between 1999 and 2002, Brazil successfully attracted 25 new operators as ANP auctioned a total of 47 sedimentary basins and 88 awarded oilfield blocs. Other relative measures of industrial growth are also positive. The average LC that oil companies applied in exploration activities increased from 25% in 1999 to 39% in 2002, while oil development and production soared from 27% to an impressive 54% (see Figure 7.1). Cardoso was extremely successful in both attracting new economic players and raising the profile of domestic suppliers in the O&G sector. The PT maintained its commitment to private investment, in which the numbers of oilfields auctioned and granted are consistently close to each other; Petrobras by virtue of its geological knowledge and ultra-deepwater engineering capability has remained a major player in pre-salt E&P.

Nevertheless, both Cardoso and Lula failed to expand private investment in the refining and distribution downstream segments of the O&G industry. By 2011, 12 out of 16 national refineries operating in Brazil were owned by Petrobras, which is equivalent to 98.1% of total refining capacity of the country (ANP 2011, 97). As Table 7.7 details, the downstream segment is also controlled by Petrobras's main subsidiary, and despite the rhetoric of market liberalization, the O&G sector remained largely dominated by a single company, the NOC Petrobras. It was only after 2014 that Petrobras began to sell its refineries and petrochemical processing plants, in response to a lack of cash flow, in order to continue investing in its E&P expansion activities. The lack of competition in mid-stream and downstream segments is due to Petrobras's ownership of major pipelines and refining plants as well as the lack of interest among foreign oil players to invest beyond the E&P sector.[29] Consequently, policymakers justified the costly infrastructure projects as a way of providing public goods to encourage domestic and foreign private investment.[30]

Finally, a crucial question posed in Brazilian politics is the role of Petrobras in economic development, which affects public perceptions as regards the legitimacy of state developmentalism as an overarching logic of economic

---

[28] Author interviews with Luiz Henrique Bispo, ANP, Rio de Janeiro, 19 June 2018; Margarete Gandini, MDIC, Brasília, 4 June 2018; and Andre Pompeo Mendes, BNDES, Rio de Janeiro, 14 June 2018.

[29] Author interviews with José Ricardo Roriz Coelho, FIESP, São Paulo, 7 June 2018; and Nelson Simão de Carvalho Júnior, SEST, *Ministério de Economia*, Brasília, 4 June 2018.

[30] Author interviews with Cláudio Navarro, *Ministério da Economia Planejamento, Desenvolvimento e Gestão*, Brasília, 4 June 2018; and Margarete Gandini, MDIC, Brasília, 4 June 2018.

Table 7.6 Exploration and development activities in Brazil's O&G sector, 1999–2018.

Bidding rounds	1	2	3	4	5	6	7	9	10	11	12	13	14	15
Year	1999	2000	2001	2002	2003	2004	2005	2007	2008	2013	2013	2015	2017	2018
Blocs auctioned	12	21	34	21	101	154	251	117	54	142	72	37	37	22
Blocs granted	12	21	34	21	101	154	242	108	40	120	62	36	32	22
Area offered (km^2)	132,178	59,271	89,823	144,106	162,392	202,739	397,600	73,079	70,371	155,813	163,917	122,215	122,616	94,602
Area granted (km^2)	54,660	48,074	48,629	25,289	21,951	39,657	171,007	45,329	44,954	61,259	20,371	33,513	24,887	16,400
New operators	6	6	8	5	1	1	6	11	2	6	1	3	4	–
Companies expressing interest	58	49	46	35	18	30	52	74	52	72	26	39	36	21
Winning companies (national)	1	4	4	4	2	7	14	20	12	12	8	11	10	2
Winning companies (foreign)	10	12	18	10	4	12	16	16	5	18	4	6	7	10

Source: ANP (2018, Table 5.3) (adapted).

Table 7.7 Participation share (%) in Brazilian distribution segment, 2010 and 2017.

| Company | Diesel oil[b] | | Gasoline C[c] | | Combustible oil[d] | |
Year	2010	2017	2010	2017	2010	2017
Petrobras BR Distribuidora	40.63	31.07	29.67	24.26	79.64	87.90
Ipiranga	22.35	21.31	19.60	19.82	5.81	3.59
Raízen[a]	–	17.36	–	17.78	–	4.29
Shell	9.66	–	11.21	–	13.09	–
Cosan	5.75	–	6.70	–	0.76	–
Alesat	2.98	2.76	5.75	4.33	–	–
Total	1.28	1.59	1.66	2.74	–	–
Sabba	1.52	2.15	1.18	1.68	0.09	–

Source: ANP (2011, 137, 140, 145).

[a] Raízen was formed as a joint venture between Shell and Cosan in 2011.
[b] Total of 127 distributors in 2010 and 133 in 2017.
[c] Total of 140 distributors in 2010 and 128 in 2017.
[d] Total of 20 distributors in 2010 and 12 in 2017.

governance. The prominent reformist Ildo Sauer argues that Petrobras became competitive not *because of* the 1997 Petroleum Law, but *despite* market reforms.[31] By recognizing Petrobras's leadership in transforming the O&G industry, political economy scholarship directly challenges the often-held assumption on the virtues of market-led governance (Massi and Nem Singh 2018; 2020; Nem Singh 2014; Priest 2016). This is not to deny the efficiency- and productivity-enhancing effects of markets. As argued by Felipe Dias, Executive Secretary of the *Instituto Brasileiro de Petróleo, Gás e Biocombustíveis* (IBP)—a business organization that brings together domestic and foreign oil companies in Brazil:

> While Petrobras remains a major oil player, the presence of private companies has changed its behaviour … it is very difficult to defend the position that it has not benefited from market competition. From exploration, production towards downstream segments, the [competitive] environment has transformed Petrobras into a more efficient state company. Our participation has had [positive] consequences.[32]

To put it differently, the persistence of a state ownership model in the Brazilian O&G sector derives its legitimacy not only from the limits of capitalist companies in delivering economic growth in a strategic sector, but also from the undeniable technological capability and market-conforming behaviour

---

[31] Author interview with Ildo Sauer, Petrobras, São Paulo, August 2010.
[32] Author interview with Felipe Dias, Executive Secretary, IBP, Rio de Janeiro, August 2010.

of Petrobras. The Brazilian O&G industry is at best described as a 'contestable market', whereby a dominant market player with a high concentration of ownership, capital, and productive capacity acts *as if* there exists a competitive market (Bridgman et al. 2008). By implication, the governance model enables the state to implement an outward-looking industrial policy through an arms-length relationship with Petrobras, while also maintaining a veil of legitimacy for the eyes of private investors by guaranteeing their (limited) access to profits of the oil industry.

Conclusions

The institutional framework consolidated during the period between Cardoso and Lula emphasized state ownership in the era of economic globalization. That the state should remain a developmental actor was a political consensus among Brazilian elites. This chapter has argued, quite controversially, that the state transformed its role and institutional architecture in response to economic globalization. Rather than embracing privatization of the NOC and unfettered market competition, Cardoso and Lula were sufficiently pragmatic to adopt key market-enhancing reforms not only to ensure the survival of Petrobras, but also, perhaps more controversially, to steer the Brazilian economy to adapt to the pressures and changes brought forth by neoliberalism.

The strategic role of the O&G sector in Brazilian industrial development and the historically constituted autonomy of Petrobras conditioned elites to usher the return of industrial policy during the commodity boom. However, favourable economic conditions for Brazil came together with new incentives that restructured state–NOC relations. With soaring prices and increasing resources revenues pouring into state coffers, some political elites, industrial companies, and state managers within Petrobras colluded to form the most systematically corrupt rent-seeking scheme in the developing world. Chapter 8 analyses the role of Petrobras in the corrupt rent-seeking scheme that was uncovered in 2014, as well as the short- and long-term impacts of the *Lava Jato* scandal in the Brazilian political landscape. In a somewhat ironic way, the scandal did not lead to calls for privatization of Petrobras. While state managers and technocrats argued that Petrobras was a victim of politicization and extreme state interference, they only demanded more corporate autonomy for Petrobras from the conservative government. Put simply, this critical juncture reinforced the centrality of Petrobras in Brazilian politics, rather than weakening state ownership as a governance model.

8
Petrobras and Brazil's Political Crisis

> The discovery of heavy oil in the 1970s was an opportunity for Petrobras to develop technology to solve a specifically Brazilian problem ... Since then, Petrobras learned to do everything independently either from the IOCs or the state.
>
> **Senior Member, Petrobras Executive Board**[1]

> Petrobras was a victim of the [*Lava Jato*] criminal scheme—in not one moment was it a beneficiary.
>
> **Pedro Parente, Petrobras CEO**[2]

The persistent dilemma of an SOE was, and remains, the need to make vital corporate decisions for commercial profits while retaining its identity as a political subject of the national state. Most observers would often default to corruption and rent-seeking as the explanation for Petrobras's fate. Indeed, how can a company that emerged as the fifth largest in the world with market capitalization valued at US$310 billion in 2009 fall so spectacularly down to a net worth of US$39 billion in 2015?[3] When the *Lava Jato* (Car Wash) investigations commenced with an effort to target Petrobras executives, the global and Brazilian media outlets portrayed the NOC as a vessel of rent-seeking, a typical SOE with weak corporate governance structure lacking a credible internal audit mechanism (Bajpai and Myers 2020, 108).[4] In some sense, this assessment is correct. The reports and police investigations point to a complex web of contract bid rigging, bribery, and embezzlement among Petrobras directors, the major political parties, and a cartel of construction companies. In whatever way one looks at this corruption, it all leads the

---

[1] Author interview with Senior Member, Executive Board, Petrobras, Rio de Janeiro, 28 May 2018.

[2] Cited from Leahy (2017).

[3] Consolidated Fourth Amended Class Action Complaint, United States District Court Southern District of New York, Case 1:14-cv-09662-JSR, Document 342, filed 30 November 2015, Preliminary statement p.5.

[4] Bajpai, R and Myers, B (2020) *Enhancing Government Effectiveness and Transparency: The Fight Against Corruption*, 108. Washington, DC: World Bank.

Business of the State. Jewellord T. Nem Singh, Oxford University Press. © Jewellord T. Nem Singh (2024).
DOI: 10.1093/oso/9780198892212.003.0008

198 Business of the State

investigators back to Petrobras. However, as this chapter demonstrates, the *Lava Jato* scandal does not fully explain the fate of Petrobras. Instead, we need to place Petrobras and its quest for its corporate autonomy in relation to government policy.

This chapter makes two key claims. Firstly, government policy— specifically President Dilma Rousseff and the PT's response to Brazil's economic stagnation from 2010 and 2014—was largely responsible for Petrobras's rapid accumulation of debt. Rousseff's policy of increasing government intervention, forcing Petrobras to subsidize gasoline prices and divert investments into unproductive assets, while increasing the state's share of control in the company had negative cumulative effects amidst an economic crisis. Secondly, political interference by the PT in the management of Petrobras constrained the ability of the NOC to make investment decisions based on the logic of the market. Petrobras's business strategy would fall apart as oil prices collapsed in 2014. In a significant way, 'external' interference drastically constrained the NOC's investment and production strategy in the O&G industry, and given the size of Petrobras this had devastating consequences for the Brazilian economy. This does not in any way refute the argument about the negative effects of political corruption in Brazil. Indeed, the chapter concurs with the claim that the developmental alliance built around corruption, and the subsequent *Lava Jato* scandal, can be traced back to the underlying political basis of industrial policymaking. The developmental alliance collapsed as senior party officials, business tycoons, and executives of Petrobras involved in the scheme were punished by spending years in jail, thereby shaking the coalitional foundations of state-based developmental interventions that had guided Brazilian industrial policy since the 1930s.

Petrobras and Its Performance Before *Lava Jato*

The *Lava Jato* investigation exposed Petrobras as an SOE captured by the accumulation of private wealth and abuse of power for political purposes. This is, of course, not something new. On 8 October 1957, the daily newspaper *O Globo* published '*Suspeitas de corrupção na Petrobrás*' (Suspicions of corruption at Petrobras). Denouncing suspicious activities within Petrobras, the article constitutes the first public accusation against Brazil's NOC. Back then, Petrobras produced just 11,000 barrels of oil equivalent per day (BOE/D), each barrel priced at US$2.92. Established in late 1953,[5] it was

---

[5] Law no. 2004 of 3 October 1953 (Petrobras Law), passed under President Getúlio Vargas.

not until 1957 that political activities within Petrobras began to affect the company's activities. Petrobras president Janary Gentil Nunes[6] 'reportedly used the company to further his own political ambitions, and political activity was used to disguise inefficiency and scandal' (Smith 1969). Yet, despite this widely acknowledged problem of political interference in Petrobras, the company has maintained—at least up until 2014 before the *Lava Jato* scandal broke—a unique position as a model for SOEs in Brazil. Indeed, Petrobras is known for its niche in the global O&G sector as a provider of ultra-deep-sea drilling equipment and services, its internationally recognized governance standards (an outcome of the company going public in the stock exchange), and its contribution to technological innovation driven by sustained investments in human capital and R&D (Brooks and Kurtz 2016, 37–40; Lima-de-Oliveira 2019; Nem Singh 2014, 341–347; Priest 2016, 59–67). Additionally, Petrobras was often cited as evidence of 'pockets of state efficiency' within the sea of corruption and inefficiency in the Brazilian bureaucracy (Randall 1993; Trebat 1983).

The emphasis on Petrobras's success is critical because oil and industrialization are two sides of the same coin. The O&G sector as a target for industrial policy is by no means an accident. Rather than being pushed by other sectors, the industry acts like a centripetal force, pulling other economic activities towards the centre by generating demands for goods and services around offshore oil production. The specificity of the parts and equipment needed in oil operations also means that manufacturing companies must fit their engineering capability around these demands. The risk of failure is higher, the environmental and financial costs of oil leakage more expensive, and Petrobras's demand for precision for product inputs higher.[7] Brazilian manufacturers have worked very closely with Petrobras and various research institutions to gradually improve the quality of goods and services in offshore production. The rigour in offshore oil is thus more comparable to aeronautics and nuclear energy than the simpler technological breakthroughs in automobile and primary commodities exports.

Looking at the basic indicators of financial performance of the company demonstrates that NOCs can be well managed under particular conditions. In the global media, Petrobras's debt was erroneously reported as a direct effect of the *Lava Jato* scandal. However, the accumulation of the company's debt took place over a five-year period (see Figure 8.1) and its main cause was largely due to the PT government's economic policy mistakes and Petrobras's

---

[6] Appointed by Juscelino Kubitchek, then President of Brazil, from 1956 to 1958 as Petrobras's third president. Mr. Nunes was an army captain and a politician.
[7] Author interview with Andre Pompeo do Amaral Mendes, BNDES, Rio de Janeiro, 14 June 2018.

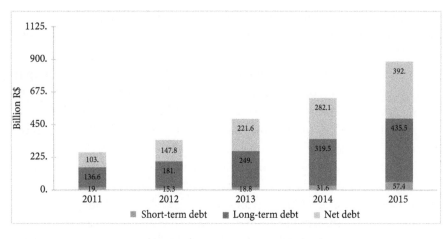

Figure 8.1 Petrobras's gradual accumulation of debt, 2003–2015.
Source: Petrobras (2015b, 8) (adapted).

overly optimistic business strategy from 2010 to 2015. As per Figure 8.2, the company's net income rose from R$17,795 million in 2003 to R$35,189 million in 2010, before plunging to a loss of R$–34,836 million in 2015. In a similar trajectory, market capitalization[8] (see Figure 8.3) climbed from R$87 billion in 2003 to R$380 billion in 2010, plummeting to R$101 billion in 2015; and Petrobras's net equity[9] soared from R$49 billion in 2003 to R$349 billion in 2013, again falling to R$258 billion in 2015.

In 2015, Petrobras's consolidated debt (see Figure 8.1) reached R$492,849 million, which included overpayments to contractors and suppliers worth R$6,194 million and impairment charges of R$47,676 million (Petrobras 2015b, 52, 59), alongside a spectacular plummet in expected future operating revenues. This is evidence of the cumulative impact of the international oil prices collapse, the application of the geological revision of the Papa-Terra field, and the application of a higher discount rate as a direct effect of Brazil's loss of investment grade (Petrobras 2015b, 52–53). In other words, Petrobras's business strategy mistakes, which had also allowed the corruption scheme to operate, were exposed by the *Lava Jato* investigation, and this was more damaging to the company's reputation as an efficient NOC insulated from rent-seeking than the actual loss of income.

However, profitability is not the best measure for the effectiveness of an SOE because its role is both to secure commercial profits for its investors and to pursue long-term economic development for Brazilian society. For

---

[8] Market capitalization refers to the total US$ value of a company's outstanding share of stocks.
[9] Net equity value is the fair market value of a business's assets minus its liability.

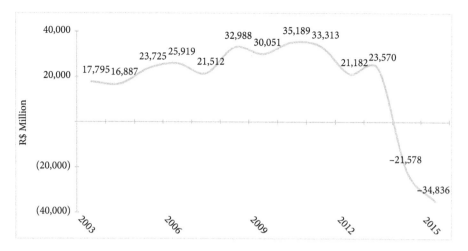

Figure 8.2 Petrobras's net income and losses, 2003–2015.
Source: Petrobras (2007; 2010; 2015b) (adapted).

Figure 8.3 Petrobras' market value and net equity, 2003–2015.
Source: Petrobras (2007; 2010; 2015a) (adapted).

many observers, the production capacity of an energy company is a more reliable indicator of its competitiveness. Several years after the *Lava Jato* scandal and low oil prices, Petrobras's O&G production surpassed the mark of 3 million barrels per day (Petrobras 2019, 1). We can also examine Petrobras's performance in terms of the success rate in drilling hydrocarbons in oil wells, mainly concentrated in ultra-deep waters. Figure 8.4 shows the sharply increasing success of Petrobras in finding oil wells since 2002, which indicates the sophisticated geological knowledge of the company in

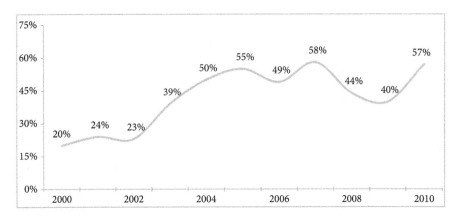

Figure 8.4 Petrobras's success rate in oil exploration, 2000–2010.
Source: Petrobras (2007; 2010) (adapted).

deciding when and where to locate pre-salt oilfields (oil reserves below the salt layer)—a feat we need to recognize given that a single exploratory well may cost around US$250 million (SEC 2002, 92). This is also complementary to our knowledge of Petrobras as a key enterprise leading R&D investments in Brazil, especially in developing ultra-deepwater engineering technology, equipment, and services.

Ultimately, one might argue that Petrobras's measure of success rests on the fact that the company alone discovered the pre-salt oil reserves through its emphasis on human capital formation and endogenous technological capacity (see Figure 8.5). Petrobras successfully increased the amount of proven oil, condensate, and natural gas reserves in Brazil up to approximately 8.78 million barrels of oil and 38.692 cubic metres of natural gas in 2018 (ANP 2019: pp. 82). The company has remained as the main economic player in O&G production (see Table 8.1). These achievements must be contextualized: Brazil—and Petrobras specifically—commenced its operations in O&G production as a company with a national monopoly possessing very few oil reserves, importing crude oil as a strategy for creating a domestic energy market. Beyond the development of the country's offshore resources, Brazil has historically used its regulatory prerogatives to promote broader industrialization objectives, especially in the context of upgrading Petrobras's capacity for innovation and expanding the domestic supply chain of equipment, services, and engineering (Lima-de-Oliveira 2019; Massi and Nem Singh 2018; 2020). The idea that energy and sectoral innovation are fundamental to industrialization is, of course, novel for neither Brazil nor leading innovators elsewhere. For countries like Israel, Taiwan, and South Korea, innovation

Table 8.1 Top O&G producers in Brazil, 2018.

Company	Barrels produced in 2018	Natural Gas in thousand M₃/cubic meters
Petrobras	878,334,599.5	878,334,599.5
Equinor Brasil	22,531,097	22,531,097
Total E&P do Brasil	13,416,336.9	13,416,336.9
Shell Brasil	13,262,736.4	13,262,736.4
Chevron Frade	6,499,624	6,499,624
PetroRio O&G	3,148,635.7	3,148,635.7
Queiroz Galvão	2,923,404.6	2,923,404.6
Total	944,117,414.2	40,857,207.1

Source: ANP (2019, 82) (adapted).

policies were largely driven by national security imperatives to catch up in the industrialization race (Amsden 1992; Breznitz 2007; M.Z. Taylor 2016).

Petrobras's Competitiveness Strategy

Firstly, this section considers how Petrobras developed the technological capability to extract offshore resources. From a global value chain (GVC) perspective, the O&G sector—particularly the upstream or E&P segment—possesses high barriers to entry and high capital requirements, with relatively few companies responsible for the production and services around the world. Although companies might look like competitors in the same market, their cost structures radically differ. While conventional oil generates high rents due to its low costs of extraction—for example, onshore crude oil extracted by NOCs in the Middle East—there is still space for Petrobras to extract costly deep-sea oil reserves through technological solutions and operational investments (Lima-de-Oliveira 2019, 287). A key contribution of Petrobras to the O&G sector is sustained investments in R&D, which became obligatory for all oil players operating in Brazil after the passage of the 1997 Petroleum Law. While oil companies have gradually invested in Brazil, Petrobras remains the principal contributor in R&D (see Figure 8.5). Petrobras always featured prominently in ultra-deepwater oil production, winning at least two innovation awards for putting together equipment and services for subsea, submarine construction, and recently spearheading oil companies to move towards remote operation fields. An official suggests that Petrobras is now at the forefront of creating an 'underwater factory', whereby the company has moved from simply producing equipment for offshore production

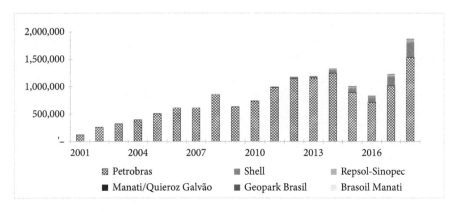

Figure 8.5 Petrobras's R&D contribution to Brazil's O&G sector, 2001–2018.
Note: Investments in R&D are in conformity to Chapter 10 of Article 8, DL 9.478, of 6 August 1997.
Source: ANP (2010, 91; 2019, 95) (adapted).

towards developing niche engineering technology to reduce production costs and gain productivity.[10] This confirms the long-standing developmental role attributed to Petrobras in developing and expanding the technological frontiers of the O&G sector.

The main driving force behind Petrobras's innovation is historical necessity. As water depths increased after the discovery of the Campos Basin fields in 1974, Petrobras was required to develop indigenous technology that was unavailable in the global oil industry mainly due to the low costs of oil extraction in the Middle East. Petrobras mobilized revenues from refining and downstream segments of the company and, through its national monopoly, production of gasoline and petrochemicals became profitable. Crucially, R&D towards deep-sea engineering systems was built over time through the creation of knowledge production networks involving universities, research centres, and government agencies (Dantas and Bell 2009, 830–831). The Petrobras innovation system was transformed from a passive learning network (1960s–1984) towards a strategic innovation network (1997–present) capable of absorbing science and technology, and subsequently applying and transferring technology to partners (Dantas 2006; Dantas and Bell 2009). But the underlying strength of Petrobras's strategy lies in its influence on Brazilian politics: government policy in the O&G sector was always crafted by Petrobras officials, thus enabling the company to make commercial decisions insulated from the excesses of politics pressures.[11] Even under Cardoso, Petrobras had a tight relationship with the government which had the effect of aligning the company's desire for profitability with the long-term energy security objectives of the Brazilian state (Massi and Nem Singh 2020).

---

[10] Author interview with Andre Pompeo do Amaral Mendes, BNDES, Rio de Janeiro, 14 June 2018.
[11] Author interview with Senior Member, Executive Board, Petrobras, Rio de Janeiro, 28 May 2018.

A second competitive strategy of Petrobras was maintaining its relative independence in labour management.[12] While members of the Petrobras Executive Board are chosen by the Brazilian President, all the engineers, geologists, and economists working for the company are selected through a highly competitive civil service examination. Hence, Petrobras not only developed a professional bureaucracy with the technical know-how to improve efficiency in its business operations, until 1997 it also created a vast network of experts in the O&G sector.[13] The company invested in the National Training Scheme[14] and other government programmes aimed at rapidly expanding the knowledge base of Brazilian universities and research institutions to meet the growing demand for engineers and geologists in the O&G sector. As Figure 8.6 details, Petrobras steadily increased its labour force across the board, and this indicates its growth of a high-skilled workforce in the O&G

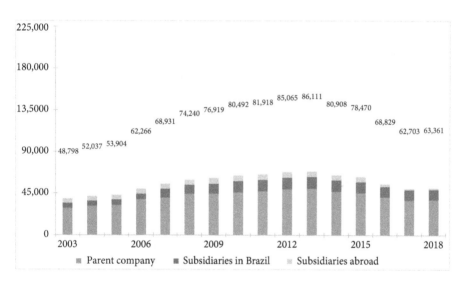

Figure 8.6 Total number of employees of the Petrobras system, 2003–2018.
Source: Petrobras (2007; 2010; 2013, 53; 2015a, 129; 2018, 18) (adapted).

---

[12] Author interviews with Heitor Chagas de Oliviera, Former Human Resource Officer, Petrobras, Rio de Janeiro, July 2010; Ildo Sauer, Petrobras, Rio de Janeiro, August 2010; and Roberto Schaeffer, Academic Consultant, *Universidade Federal do Rio de Janeiro* or *Universidade do Brasil* (UFRJ), Rio de Janeiro, July 2010.
[13] Author interviews with Heitor Chagas de Oliviera, Petrobras, Rio de Janeiro, July 2010; Ildo Sauer, Petrobras, Rio de Janeiro, August 2010; and Roberto Schaeffer, Academic Consultant, UFRJ, Rio de Janeiro, July 2010.
[14] This is part of the wider Programme to Mobilize the Brazilian O&G Industry (PROMINP). In 2007, Petrobras had invested R$40 million in this project (Petrobras 2007, 70). Equally, the Ministry of Science and Technology had poured in massive investments since 2000 to finance innovation projects at the university and company levels, particularly in the O&G sector. The specific agency of the ministry, *Financiadora de Estudos e Projectos* (FINEP), aims to promote the development of science, technology, and innovation through public funding in companies, universities, technological institutes, and other public and private organizations. For details see http://www.finep.gov.br/. Author interviews with Paulo Krahe, FINEP, Rio de Janeiro, August 2010; and Aparecida Neves, FINEP, Rio de Janeiro, August 2010.

206 Business of the State

sector—because oil extraction requires technological excellence, rising public employment in the NOC corresponds to improving technical expertise of its workforce. By 2018, 59% of 47,566 employees had university degrees and 17% received post-graduate training (Petrobras 2018, 18). Several Petrobras executives have noted the importance of maintaining a highly qualified workforce to avoid downward pressures of subcontracting and to move forward the frontiers of technological innovation in the O&G sector.[15] This is a striking difference between Petrobras and Codelco in terms of respective employment policy as a response to international competitiveness.

A final feature of Petrobras's competitive strategy is that through government policy, Petrobras was partially insulated from political pressures by way of changing its ownership structure. As Chapter 2 discusses, corporate governance reforms were implemented to prepare SOEs for global competition. In the 1990s, Cardoso pushed for Petrobras to corporatize its public assets and sell a limited number of non-voting capital shares to non-Brazilian investors on the New York Stock Exchange (NYSE) and the *Brasil Bolsa Balção* or B3 (formerly BOVESPA). In this way, the government introduced private shareholders into the ownership structure of Petrobras without relinquishing its control. Figure 8.7 provides a breakdown of the different investors in Petrobras. This trend is consistent with the reorganization of ownership and management of SOEs all over the world (Nem Singh and Chen 2018). Corporate governance reforms—partial divestment/corporatization as opposed to full-scale privatization—of SOEs has been an essential tool for policymakers who did not wish to relinquish state control over strategic industries that necessitated structural reform, to ensure not only their survival but also success in a globalized and competitive economic environment.[16]

Brazil is not alone in choosing this development strategy. Many Asian tigers, notably China, Korea, Singapore, and Indonesia, have implemented gradual liberalization and selective SOE reforms—a point I return to in Chapter 10 when discussing the uniqueness of SOE-led growth models (Z. Chen and Chen 2019; Kim 2019; Musacchio and Lazzarini 2014). To a limited extent, restructuring ownership and management functions was effective in so far as strengthening mechanisms of due diligence and internal oversight to monitor potential fraud and rent-seeking. But as the *Lava Jato* scandal indicates, the extent of political corruption in Brazil has meant that internal measures cannot mitigate the politicization of Petrobras through state

---

[15] Author interviews with Ildo Sauer, Petrobras, Rio de Janeiro, August 2010; and Heitor Chagas de Oliviera, Former Human Resource Officer, Petrobras, Rio de Janeiro, July 2010.

[16] Author interview with Senior Member, Executive Board, Petrobras, Rio de Janeiro, 28 May 2018.

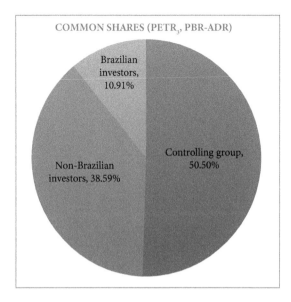

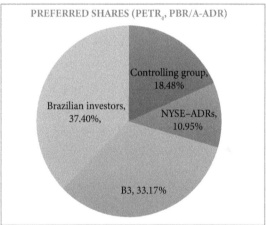

Figure 8.7 Petrobras's shareholding structure, May 2020.

Note: PETR, PBR-ADR and PBR/a-ADR are the names of stocks traded in the stock exchange.

Source: Petrobras Investor Relations 2020, https://www.investidorpetrobras.com.br/en/overview/shareholding-structure/ (accessed 19 June 2020).

interference over its affairs—a serious flaw that was only rectified through further corporate governance reforms after 2015.

To sum up briefly, prior to the *Lava Jato* scandal, Petrobras was considered a highly successful NOC, comparable to leading NOCs like Saudi Arabia's Aramco and Norway's Equinox (previously Statoil) (Stevens 2012; Thurber

208 Business of the State

and Istad 2012). Notwithstanding the reputational damage inflicted by the *Lava Jato* scandal, Petrobras remains a well-managed SOE that has survived the oil price crash in 2014 and has continuously played a vital role in human capital development and R&D investments in the O&G sector. Crucially, Petrobras has remained focussed in maintaining its role as a lead company in the offshore oil value chain. In the next section, I analyse the ways in which external factors have shaped both Rousseff's economic policy and Petrobras's commercial strategy.

Rousseff's Developmentalist Strategy

The differences between the external context of Presidents Lula da Silva (Lula) and Rousseff's administrations are important in evaluating the success of their development policies. While 2003–2007 was characterized by very favourable terms of trade—notably high commodity prices and external demand—and capital inflows, the post-2008 period was predominantly shaped by an economic crisis and external shocks (de Paula et al. 2015; Prates et al. 2017, 16–17). After the 2008 crisis, the Brazilian state responded through a series of counter-cyclical policies, which included (1) interventionist policies by the Central Bank in the credit and foreign exchange markets, (2) expansion of loans and credit operations by the BNDES to compensate for dwindling credit supply from private banks, and (3) fiscal measures by the Finance Ministry to stimulate aggregate demand (Prates et al. 2017, 24–27; Saad-Filho and Morais 2018, 108–111).

In mid-2011, during her first term, Rousseff introduced the 'New Macroeconomic Matrix' to boost growth. Her approach was more aggressive than Lula's: monetary policy to bring down interest rates to reduce speculative foreign capital, as well as devaluing the currency and lowering the cost of credit to stimulate domestic investment and consumption. Despite hopeful attempts for a private investment-led growth, the opposite occurred: GDP growth rates declined from 7.5% in 2010 to 2.7% in 2011. Furthermore, currency devaluation undermined foreign capital inflows. Under intense pressure from financial and elite interests, the Central Bank changed its approach and imposed credit restrictions in March 2013. This was meant to control inflation, which reached above 10% in 2015 but was already worrying in 2013. The Ministry of Finance under Guido Mantega responded by deploying fiscal measures aimed at improving infrastructure investment and enlarging tax exemptions. Crucially, Rousseff sought to improve infrastructure through the nominal freezing of public tariffs and a reduction of electricity prices for price stabilization purposes (Prates et al. 2017, 25; Saad-Filho and Morais 2018, 111–114), while tax exemptions—rather than public expenditures—had limited impact on production and employment. Moreover, with oil prices crashing and the *Lava Jato* investigation in full swing, Petrobras reduced its investments, which, given its size, profoundly affected overall investment in the economy (Afonso and Fajardo 2015).

By the time Rousseff was elected for her second term in 2014, the economy was rapidly deteriorating amidst negative growth rates. Rousseff responded by switching back to a more orthodox policy stance. To achieve a fiscal surplus, she implemented public spending cuts, readjusted energy prices, and increased interest rates. As a consequence, gross debt over GDP rose from 51.5% to 69.6%, which had the effect of shrinking foreign reserves and loans to public banks (Prates et al. 2017, 27). A new Finance Minister, Nelson Barbosa, sought to consolidate the fiscal condition of the state by imposing limits on government expenses, introducing tax reforms, and tackling the thorny issue of pension reforms. However, during this time, the political crisis in Brazil had already spread beyond the halls of Congress and the PT government was virtually paralyzed. Embattled President Rousseff would have to turn her attention to desperately avoiding the collapse of her governing coalition amidst an impeachment trial towards the end of 2016.

It is important to contextualize Rousseff's policy decisions vis-à-vis those of Lula. When Rousseff narrowly won the election in 2014, she had already lost the support of the middle classes by pushing forward with a redistribution agenda which raised the expectations of organized workers, Leftist parties, and the unorganized poor. For Saad-Filho and Morais (2018, 119–124), the PT's loss of control over Congress exacerbated Rousseff's incapacity to implement her development programme. In this fragmented multiparty presidentialism, the PT barely possessed 1/3 support from Congress and from the onset it was clear that corruption, rent-seeking, and flawed ways of conducting political business were integral to executive–legislative relations (Armijo and Rhodes 2017; Mello and Spektor 2018, 115). While corruption-fuelled relations already posit as an obstacle to the shift from clientelism to programmatic politics, the *Lava Jato* investigation of collusive corruption practically diluted the little credibility left in the Rousseff government. In this new battlefield, the PT would be portrayed as the harbinger of rent-seeking and the mastermind behind the unravelling systemic corruption in Brazil.

The Janus Face of Corruption

In hindsight, we can observe that President Lula's rise to power in 2003 coincided with the establishment of a corruption scheme that would link Petrobras to a complex web of illicit money laundering involving high-level

PT party officials and a cartel of construction companies. Some analysts have already hinted at my argument: that the PT's achievement of a decade-long period of economic growth and poverty reduction was only possible through the simultaneous co-existence of 'developmental' and 'degenerative' corruption (Ang 2020; Wedeman 2012). The former is associated with the rare example of East Asia, in which countries enjoyed considerable economic success despite being dogged by high levels of corruption—corruption that was deeply embedded within their political systems and became central to their smooth operations.[17] Corruption was a necessary precondition for rapid growth, not because corruption fuelled growth, but rather political instability threatened to harm, slow down, or reverse economic growth. On the other hand, degenerative—or 'predatory'—corruption was never integral to the maintenance or construction of governing coalitions. Instead, it constitutes a mechanism for individuals or a group of officials to siphon off rents or a share of the gains from economic growth. Here, corruption leads to endemic economic crisis (Wedeman 2012, 52–79).[18]

To be sure, corruption is rooted in Brazil's political history. Prior to democratization in 1986, traditional manipulation of public funds for political purposes was the norm (also known as 'pork barrel' or machine politics)—a form with clear resemblance to East Asian countries' structural corruption. Most explanations link political culture and traditionalism or backwardness, specifically the existence of a 'dualistic society' between urban, modern sectors in the centre and southern parts vis-à-vis rural, traditional sectors in the north and northeast. By the time Collor de Melo (1990–1992) was impeached, a new pattern of corruption had emerged whereby the president and their cronies engaged in private wealth accumulation (Geddes and Neto 1992, 642–643; Hagopian 1996). This has been associated with the changes in electoral rules and in the Constitution, in which the fragmented, multiparty presidentialism in Brazil is blamed for the decreased capacity of the executive to build a strong, ideology-based governing coalition and to ensure the loyalty of coalition members within Congress (Katz 2018; Mello and Spektor 2018). In a significant way, the *Lava Jato* scandal thus reflects the wider cultural and institutional history of corruption rooted in the social organization of Brazilian society around unequal access to land and stratified public

---

[17] In Japan, South Korea, and Taiwan, corruption was institutionalized and sustained through a symbiotic relationship between conservative, pro-developmental political parties and business interests.

[18] Degenerative corruption can be found in well-known examples of China under the Communist Party (1978–present), Zaire during the Mobuto era (1965–1997), post-1968 Equatorial Guinea, and the Dominican Republic during the Trujillo years (1930–1961).

goods provision, as well as being demonstrative of cultural practices such as *jeitinho* (Nishijima et al. 2019, 35–36).[19]

The *Lava Jato* investigation led to the conviction of six Petrobras executives[20] and the company was shown to be a victim of bribery and bid rigging. A criminal conspiracy was organized and run from within Petrobras after 2003—a period when former-president Rousseff was Minister for Mines and Energy and chairperson of the company's board of directors, as well as chief of staff of Lula's government. Figure 8.8 details the scheme, which lasted for at least a decade and was aimed at defrauding Petrobras through contracts upon the discovery of pre-salt oilfields. Corrupt payments totalling approximately US$349 million were made to obtain and retain business with Petrobras through overpriced contracts for oil rigs, ships, and drilling facilities, and transportation projects.[21] The scheme involved what Pei (2016, 7–12) calls 'collusive corruption', where legal and illegal activities involve multiple officials either in the same public institution or across geographical jurisdictions.[22] Since there were only a handful of companies with the technical capability and resources to complete large-scale infrastructure projects, such as those proposed by Petrobras's Department of Services and Supply and International Division, the construction companies formed a cartel to render ineffective the competitive bidding process. All the divisions or directorates within Petrobras were assigned a sponsor from a political party (within Petrobras, this is known as the *padrinho* or 'godfather'), which subsequently nominated the director and was confirmed by the Executive Board. The job security of each director, in turn, was dependent on keeping the *padrinho* and his party happy by building a 3% kickback into every major contract.

On the side of the construction cartel, a committee among the member companies was established. According to the Public Prosecutor's Office (MPF), the prices in the contracts offered to Petrobras were calculated and

---

[19] *Jeitinho* refers to the custom whereby the rules, regulations, and social customs are bent to serve particular interests. Personal favours and exceptions are given by public officials to families and friends, even if such acts imply breaking the rules, facilitating corruption, and skewing public welfare benefits towards certain social groups (Nishijima et al. 2019, 36). As Faoro (2012) suggests, this tradition stems from the Portuguese crown's tendency to conflate between public and private property.

[20] Paulo Roberto Costa, supply director 2004–2012; Renato de Souza Duque, services director 2003–2012; Nestor Cunat Cerveró, international director 2003–2008; Jorge Luiz Zelada, international director 2008–2012; Eduardo Costa Vaz Musa, international manager from 2009; and Pedro José Barusco Filho, executive manager of engineering 1997–2003 and an executive of Sete Brasil.

[21] US District Court of Eastern District of New York, *United States against Odrebrecht S.A.*, Criminal No. 16-643, p. 13, https://www.justice.gov/opa/press-release/file/919916/download (accessed 21 May 2020).

[22] Collusive corruption—as opposed to individual corruption—destroys the organizational and normative fabric of the state because the involvement of high-ranking state actors and their subordinates within public institutions and state enterprises makes corruption harder to detect, increases the financial stakes of corruption, and, due to its pervasiveness and entrenchment in the political system, limits the impacts of anti-corruption campaigns.

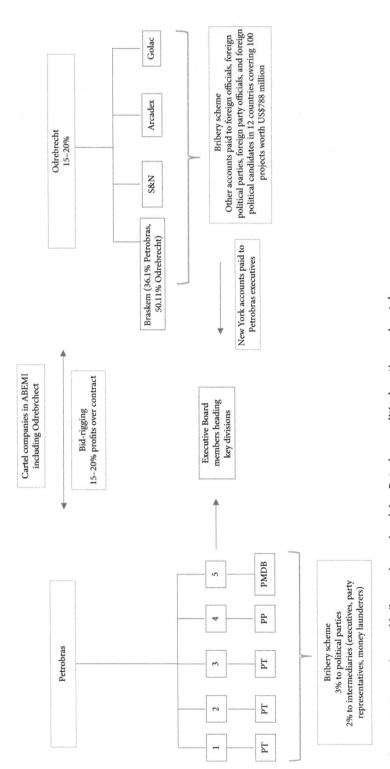

Figure 8.8 Corruption and bribery scheme involving Petrobras, political parties, and cartels.

Source: United States of America vs. Braskem SA 2016a; United States of America vs. Odebrecht SA 2016b

Note: Associação Brasileira de Engenharia Industrial—Abemi (ABEMI); PMDB, Brazilian Democratic Movement Party; PP, Progressive Party, Smith and Nash Engineering Company (S&N).

adjusted in secret meetings usually in São Paulo or Rio de Janeiro. These meetings served for the contractors to agree beforehand which company would win the contract and at what price. The cartel would coordinate their bids with the respective director, which allowed them to adjust their bids to conform with the parameters of a 15–20% profit margin and 3% kick-back to political parties and Petrobras directors.[23] If any cartel member failed to include the required 3% kickback, they would be disqualified in future bids by the cartel. Put simply, Petrobras's employees were co-opted to restrict the participation of outsiders and then negotiated unnecessary additions to contracts, raised prices at excessive rates, and leaked relevant information to favoured bidders (Massi and Nem Singh 2018, 1143–1144).

Similar to Wedeman's (2012) argument, the corruption uncovered by the *Lava Jato* investigation has a striking resemblance to the machine politics in East Asia that cemented a mutually beneficial relationship between big business and the state.[24] The misconduct of Petrobras executives was closely linked to the political nominations of their executive posts. Each of the already convicted directors represented one of three political parties, namely the PT, Progressive Party (PP), and Brazilian Democratic Movement Party (PMDB). The established norm was that 2/3 of collected bribes were destined to the respective parties while the remaining 1/3 was divided among inter-mediaries, such as executive directors, party representatives, black-market money bankers, and money laundering operators. The paybacks to the political parties were destined mainly to fund election campaigns. In the case of President Rousseff (PT) and her vice-president Michel Temer (PMDB), both campaigns in 2010 and 2014 had large chunks of the paybacks destined to marketing costs and directly paid to campaign marketers. Among those directly implicated in the scandal were the CEOs and senior executives of the major construction companies that constituted the cartel, such as the Odrebrecht Group, OAS, Queiroz Galvaão, Andrade Gutierrez S.A., and Camargo Corrêa.

This scheme, however, goes beyond Petrobras and extends to the wider political system. A second pillar of corruption uncovered by the *Lava Jato* investigation was the involvement of financial operators who became responsible not only for the payment of bribes, but also for laundering

---

[23] US Department of Justice, Petrobras Non-Prosecution Agreement, Petrobras Securities Litigation Case No. 14-cv-9662 (JSR).
[24] Machine politics operates through two mechanisms: (1) transactive corruption, whereby exchanges and deals between the machine (through political parties) and business interests are conducted through the manipulation of power for money; and (2) redistributive politics, in which money is deployed and reallocated for political purposes, including coalition building, purchase of political loyalty, and drawing support for industrial policy (Wedeman 2012, 52–53).

214   Business of the State

and distributing the money to key beneficiaries in the legislature and executive branches. In 2015, the Attorney General of the Republic presented to the Federal Supreme Court 28 petitions for the opening of criminal investigations on 55 people, 49 of whom were holders of *foro privilegiado* (privileged forum). This is a special status granted to individuals with high positions in the public administration. In practice, these are office holders in the executive, legislative, and judiciary branches of government to which only the Supreme Court has the power to prosecute. As the investigation unfolded, most of the people charged were related to political parties responsible for nominating and maintaining the directors of Petrobras. It is estimated that over US$2 billion was redistributed through the corruption scheme, to the benefit of its operators and to politicians, mostly from the PT and its main coalition partner the PMDB. And, in a further twist, the *Lava Jato* investigation also discovered corruption in Odrebrecht's international operations, through its involvement in the domestic politics of countries in which it sought to obtain contracts. Odrebrecht together with its co-conspirators paid more than US$788 million in bribes to illegally secure projects in 11 countries, with systematic corruption schemes—e.g. embezzlement, bribery, and slush funds—extending payments to foreign political parties, government officials, and foreign political candidates (see Figure 8.8).[25]

Greasing the Wheels of Development?

The corruption scheme uncovered by the *Lava Jato* investigation reflects the political story of developmental states outside East Asia. Moneyed influence was an effective instrument to oil the wheels of the political system and to buy political support, sustaining electoral victories for politicians in power and consolidating a permanent coalition that would generate institutional equilibrium. What made developmental corruption effective in Japan, South Korea, and Taiwan was that both political and business elites perceived these exchanges of corrupt and collusive transactions—both legal and illegal—as beneficial, with politicians gaining and securing power on the one hand, and business interests earning profits on the other hand. In Brazil, the construction cartel benefitted from lucrative contracts funnelling profits away from Petrobras while profiting from large infrastructure projects

---

[25] US District Court of Eastern District of New York, *United States against Odrebrecht S.A.*, Criminal No. 16-643, p. 7, https://www.justice.gov/opa/press-release/file/919916/download (accessed 21 May 2020).

domestically and abroad. Within the dysfunctions of the Brazilian party system, kickbacks and side payments were channelled from private agents towards the political parties—a precondition that allowed the PT to keep political power and to continue promoting its expensive industrial policy. Since 1997, companies involved in the graft secured around US$20 billion in subsidized credit from the BNDES (Mello and Spektor 2016, 107). As in East Asia's structural corruption, the system in place was meant to cement a stable political relationship. The *Lava Jato* investigation showed that the PT sought to create a mutually beneficial political arrangement that would mitigate regional factionalism, clientelism and patronage, and party fragmentation. Worse, it also showed that opposition parties likewise profited from corruption despite their casual protest against government policies, citing economic crisis and corruption to attack the governing coalition (Castro and Ansari 2017, 354).

Another important question to ask is why and how corruption is linked to Brazilian economic growth. Even in cases of structural corruption, corruption itself is not the cause of growth, and it is only one of the many variables that affect development. To answer the larger question as regards why Brazil achieved stable growth during this period, we must be sensitive to the other factors, including fiscal activism, stable macro-economic conditions, the expansion of credit and social provision to the middle classes, considerable reduction in poverty (from 35.8% of the population in 2003 down to 13.3% in 2014) and income inequality, high commodity prices, and, importantly, a renewed relationship between China and Brazil that provided the PT government with foreign reserves to shift its position towards a net creditor (Jepson 2021, 86–90; Prates et al. 2017, 20–21; Saad-Filho and Morais 2018, 93–103). Faced with an inefficient and corrupt system, both Cardoso and Lula sought reforms not to transform Brazilian politics, but to work cleverly around them by enacting growth-oriented policies. The expansion of welfare—Brazil's hallmark of successful poverty reduction—was delivered by Cardoso through the consolidation of the Family Health Strategy, and under Lula, the dramatic expansion of *Bolsa Familia* at a cheap cost of 0.8% of GDP (Mello and Spektor 2016, 108). Under both presidents, the Central Bank and Ministry of Finance gained substantive autonomy from interest groups and factions of state elites, giving their leaders room for policy manoeuvre to pursue macro-economic stability and pro-poor growth. These Brazilian presidents greased the wheels of the patronage system to maintain a governing coalition and, in so doing, successfully formulated a cohesive developmental vision for Brazil.

216 Business of the State

The *Lava Jato* investigation exposed how industrial policy—and development strategies more generally—are profoundly embedded in political corruption. A quick glimpse at the spending priorities of the BNDES supports this claim. Under Lula, Brazil's development strategy involved subsidized credit to big business in order to enhance the competitiveness of domestic companies and expand the industrial sector. Energy-related spending dominates BNDES's loan portfolio between 2002 and 2011—six of the eight largest loans were meant to generate, produce, and distribute energy, and the seventh loan paid for the construction of oil tanker ships by Transpetro. The O&G industry—notably Petrobras and its subsidiaries—benefitted from these loans in lieu of the high capital requirements to develop offshore oilfields, though a substantive amount went to large energy plants, including wind, ethanol, and sugarcane (Hochstetler and Montero 2013, 1490–1491). Key investments within the sector were focussed on its rapid expansion, including pipelines, platform support vessels, and a huge supply chain to provide services for offshore oil production equipment. In addition, building linkages between oil and the naval industry meant that Petrobras contracts were used as a guarantee to justify the construction and financing of platform construction equipment.[26] So, while financial viability and capacity to meet debt obligations were crucial to BNDES's lending policy, the PT government and its bias towards infrastructural spending drove the Bank towards these commitments.

In Table 8.2, the 10 largest loans listed comprise 35% of BNDES disbursements between 2009 and 2011 and all are related to 'national champion' SOEs originating from the ISI period. The largest loan was allocated to the construction of the controversial *Abreu e Lima* oil refinery plant costing US$5.2 billion (see the next section). The loans are less about nudging companies into new industries than supporting a vision of globally competitive large companies. These projects also have a secondary objective: to generate jobs and redistribute income towards the North and Northeast. Three out of four refineries were geographically located in poorer regions to promote Lula's regional development strategy. Despite the technical reports used to justify the decision to build them in Maranhao and Pernumbuco, the financial case to support the PT strategy overall was weak.[27] For Petrobras, such large financial transfers left the NOC vulnerable to rent-seeking, and the corruption uncovered by the *Lava Jato* investigation cast serious doubt over BNDES's

---

[26] Author interview with Andre Pompeo do Amaral Mendes, BNDES, Rio de Janeiro, 14 June 2018.

[27] Author interviews with Celso Knijnik, *Ministério de Planejamento, Desenvolvimento e Gestão*, Brasilia, 4 June 2018; and Nelson Simão de Carvalho Jr., *Secretaria de Coordinação e Governança das Empresas Estatais*, 4 June 2018, Brasilia.

Petrobras and Brazil's Political Crisis 217

Table 8.2 BNDES loans to O&G and infrastructure companies.

Company	R\$ million (US\$ million)	Year	Project detail
Abreu and Lima Refinery (Petrobras and PDVSA)	9,890 (5,235)	2009	Petrobras refining plant
Petrobras	9,410 (4,981)	2009	Investment in O&G upstream sector
Electronuclear	6,146 (3,680)	2011	Build Angra 3 nuclear power plant
Transportadora Asociada de Gas (Petrobras)	5,700 (3,017)	2009	Pipelines for Petrobras midstream segment
Norte Energia	3,680 (2,238)	2011	Build Belo Monte hydroelectric plant
Energia Sustentável do Brasil	3,635 (1,866)	2009	Build Jirau hydroelectric plant, localized transmission lines
JBS	3,480 (2,000)	2009	Internationalization of meatpacking
Santo Antonio Energia	3,094 (1,267)	2009	Build Santo Antonio hydroelectric plant
Vivo	3,031 (1,715)	2011	Improve infrastructure for new telecommunications technologies
Marfig Alimentos	2,500 (1,418)	2010	Assistance with issue of debentures by food processor

Source: BNDES data from Hochstetler and Montero (2013, 1492).

capability to remain autonomous and competent and, subsequently, its ability to perform its functions of financing high-risk projects, developing new industrial leaders, and fostering national champions to compete globally. From a business perspective, the scandal shook the established mechanism for industrial financing in Brazil in ways that were damaging to the long-term prospects of the manufacturing sector via BNDES support.[28]

To put this into perspective, BNDES assets were worth R\$871.41 billion and disbursements amounted to R\$187.8 billion (US\$70.7 billion) in 2014, which is equivalent to 3.4% of GDP. Nearly 80% of BNDES lending goes to infrastructure and manufacturing projects, while large Brazilian companies receive most of the subsidized loans (see Table 8.3). Massi (2014) argues that the bank lending policy favouring low-default risks is skewed in favour of large companies. In turn, large companies provide the most significant share of electoral campaign donations, notably JBS, the Odrebrecht Group, Camargo Corrêa, and Andrade Gutierrez–the latter three construction companies are implicated by the *Lava Jato* investigation. Fears of political capture

---

[28] Author interview with Ricarado Roriz Coelho, FIESP, São Paulo, 7 June 2018.

Table 8.3 BNDES loans under the PT government, 2004–2014.

	2004	2005	2006	2007	2008	2009	2010	2011	2012	2013	2014
Assets (R$ billion)	161.87	171.43	184.53	198.67	272.09	379.28	520.85	603.70	693.85	762.95	871.41
Liabilities (R$ billion)	147.76	155.72	165.44	173.74	246.83	351.65	454.95	542.69	643.86	702.33	805.13
Disbursement											
R$ billion[a]	39.8	47.0	51.3	64.9	90.9	136.4	168.4	138.9	156.0	190.4	187.8
US$ billion	15.01	20.08	23.99	36.64	38.90	78.34	101.07	74.05	76.34	81.28	70.70
As percentage of GDP	2.1	2.2	2.2	2.4	2.9	4.1	4.3	3.2	3.3	3.7	3.4
Composition (%)											
Manufacturing	38.9	49.0	49.9	39.1	39.2	44.2	45.8	28.9	29.3	28.2	25.0
Services	3.3	4.4	4.5	5.4	5.4	6.8	8.4	10.7	18.2	18.0	19.9
Construction	3.1	3.6	3.0	4.8	4.5	4.8	3.9	5.2	5.1	5.1	5.5
Infrastructure	34.5	31.6	29.4	37.4	37.5	32.7	28.6	37.4	30.3	27.7	29.7
Large companies	68.4	75.2	78.3	75.2	76.0	82.5	70.2	57.7	62.6	61.1	62.6

Source: BNDES Balance Sheets, 2004–2014, adapted from Sztutman and Aldrighi (2019, 24).
[a] Disbursement at 2014 constant prices (nominal value deflated by IPCA).

of BNDES led to a parliamentary inquiry in July 2015 looking into contracts and loans between 2013 and 2015 (Sztutman and Aldrighi 2019).

The Impacts of Corruption on Petrobras

For Petrobras, the damage of the *Lava Jato* scandal quickly eroded its reputation as a highly professional and autonomous state enterprise, with corruption having constrained Petrobras in two ways—first, collusive corruption within the company led to investment decisions not serving Petrobras's interest; and second, corruption undermined internal compliance mechanisms and due diligence controls. Between 2003 and 2014, Petrobras made several overpriced purchases of refineries and equipment during the oil-construction boom, of which the most notable examples are the Crown refinery in Pasadena (2006), *Complexo Petroquimica do Rio de Janeiro* (COMPERJ) (2008), and Abreu e Lima refinery (2009). Overexpenditure in oil exploration and production was a principal flaw in its investment strategy—the company Board approved these projects that brought little financial returns. The spending bonanza facilitated the corruption within the company to transfer illicit funds from Petrobras to the political parties. This is not to say that Brazil should not build more refineries; in fact, companies seek more refining capacity, but through the private sector to enhance competition in the mid-stream segment of the O&G sector.[29] However, the complicated story of corruption and flawed business planning caused the deterioration of Petrobras's commercial performance.

The overpriced construction of the Abreu e Lima refinery in Pernambuco is an excellent case to illustrate how Petrobras was a victim of collusive corruption (see Figure 8.8). The refinery initially costing US$4 billion was eventually built for US$18 billion, through add-on contracts with the construction cartel. Venina Velosa da Fonseca, former manager of downstream operations at Petrobras and who worked under Paulo Roberto Costa, testified under police protection about the inflated contracts and payments for services connected to this project. On 8 March 2007, Costa asked Fonseca to design a plan to accelerate the construction of the Abreu e Lima refinery before the original scheduled date, with an additional cost of US$328.7 million. Fonseca reported several problems on contracts, bidding, and other practices through the internal mechanisms of the company since 2008. On 3 April 2009, Fonseca created the 'Internal Document of the Petrobras System' (DIP)

---

[29] Author interview with Ricarado Roriz Coelho, FIESP, São Paulo, 7 June 2018.

which officially reported and concluded the administrative irregularities in the downstream unit, in addition to R$58 million worth of contracts that may have been potentially embezzled. Fonseca sought the advice of Maria Foster da Graça (who became Petrobras president in February 2012). Despite warnings from mid-level management, Petrobras proceeded with its construction and contracts with the construction cartel. Almost simultaneously, in May 2009, opposition parties led by the Brazilian Social Democratic Party (PDSB) gathered 32 signatures from senators to create a parliamentary committee hearing to investigate cases of corruption including Petrobras's Abreu e Lima refinery.[30] The anomalies were increasingly becoming controversial— the link between Petrobras and the political parties was gradually being revealed. In June 2012, Petrobras finally conducted an internal audit on the Abreu e Lima refinery. Incidentally, these investigations coincided with the Board's approval of a debt-driven strategy to expand Petrobras's operations in pre-salt exploration, refineries, and petrochemicals segments. In the same month, Petrobras posted its first quarterly loss in 13 years—a result of Rousseff's refusal for the company to raise fuel prices in line with global market prices.

In July 2013, amidst rumours and growing suspicion of corruption, Petrobras implemented its Corruption Prevention Programme (PCPP) to reinforce existing mechanisms to prevent, detect, and correct fraud and corruption within the company. By September 2013, the company reported gross debts amounting to more than US$135 billion, which led to restructuring and asset sales to mitigate its growing liabilities. By March 2014, the *Lava Jato* investigation took off, and in October 2014, Costa was arrested and agreed to reveal the details of systemic corruption within Petrobras. Given the size of the scandal, Foster was called to testify in the congressional enquiry about the effectiveness of the internal corporate mechanisms in detecting and identifying corruption. In February 2015, the company faced a double blow: Foster and five other members resigned; and Moody's downgraded Petrobras's bonds to junk, which effectively stripped off the company's investment grading. Hence, as illustrated here, corruption and the company's decisions are intertwined very closely; however, government policy is undoubtedly the driving force behind these mistakes that cost the company debt and reputation.

---

[30] Petrobras launched an aggressive internal lobbying to stall the investigation, which, according to Costa's plea-bargaining statement, was resolved by organizing bribes to several opposition parties during an election year.

The Political Aftermath of the *Lava Jato* Scandal

To understand the crisis of governance in Brazil today, one must go back to the sequencing of historical events that might identify the structural and conjunctural factors that explain the fall of the PT from power and the rise of conservative governments in power. The *Lava Jato* scandal fuelled a crisis of legitimacy in Brazil, which abruptly ended Rousseff's term through an impeachment procedure. While scholars debate on the degree to which other political parties' abandonment of the PT constitute an institutional coup (Antunes et al. 2019; de Oliveira and de Souza 2016; Santos and Guarnieri 2016), the outcome is that a coalition of conservative forces emerged victorious in the political vacuum left by the PT. Michel Temer (2016–2018) completed Rousseff's remaining term and appointed Pedro Parente as Petrobras president. Under Temer, the developmental alliance completely collapsed. The *Lava Jato* investigation continued to pursue evidence to jail high-ranking party officials and business executives beyond the construction and O&G sectors. The alliance fuelled by collusive corruption spectacularly fell apart as industrial policy became synonymous with grand theft and elite-driven corruption. The leading prosecutor of the investigation, Judge Sergio Moro, became highly popular and was transformed by the Brazilian and international media into the face of anti-corruption in Brazil (Guaíra 2016; Londoño 2017; Wilson Centre 2016).

Notwithstanding the attacks against the PT, the aftermath of the crisis is best captured by two major changes in Brazilian politics: (1) a reorientation in the role of the state in economic development in favour of pro-market forces; and (2) the collapse of a coherent industrial policy. Firstly, the decline of the developmental state manifested itself with the successful attempt of Petrobras to become independent from the national state, asserting its corporate autonomy as the only antidote to corruption. Parente often claimed that the company was a victim of individual greed and his mandate as president came with an agreement from Temer that he would be given absolute control over the restructuring of the company. Parente's goal was to improve Petrobras's financial health and investor reputation. He had a wide policy latitude on how to manage debts, to sell non-performing assets of the company, and to regain investment capacity as Brazil moved towards pre-salt production.[31] One major implication of this agreement was to end government control over

---

[31] Author interview with Cláudio Navarro, *Ministério da Economia Planejamento, Desenvolvimento e Gestão*, Brasília, 4 June 2018.

pricing policy, effectively taking away state subsidies on fuel prices. Since Rousseff's anti-inflationary measure relied on state intervention in oil prices, Temer's complete policy turnaround allowed Parente to align the domestic oil price with the global market. However, in June 2018, a nation-wide truck drivers' strike paralyzed public transportation in Brazil's major cities. Faced with the consequences of Petrobras's pricing policy, social unrest and public discontentment became widespread as the poorer segments of Brazilian society paid for the adjustment cost of Parente's policy. The truck drivers' strike not only put a brake on Petrobras's pricing policy but also opened a wider debate: the dual role of Petrobras as an NOC with societal obligations and as a quasi-private company with accountability to its shareholders. As an official put it aptly, 'a delicate balance must be struck between the company pursuing its commercial profitability (or demands of the market) and fulfilling societal needs ... because the country as a whole cannot be punished for Petrobras' debts especially given that the state enterprise was built by taxpayers' income'.[32]

Secondly, Temer dismantled the instruments of national industrial policy in favour of market liberalization. The most critical policy reversal involved changing the role and scope of BNDES' lending policy and loosening local content requirements in the O&G sector. Temer did not believe in BNDES's role as a strategic arm of the national state for economic development, and, consequently, the bank's credit lines collapsed and funding was restricted immediately after the new government came to power.[33] In other words, the Bank's role became to finance highly selective and cross-cutting investments, notably in infrastructure, and less about supporting Brazilian companies to make them internationally competitive. Temer's third policy reversal involved the flexibilization of local content requirements for manufacturing and service companies working in the O&G sector. While the PT government had perceived local content policy as a vehicle for strategic sectoral promotion and improved competitiveness of domestic companies, Temer emphasized the need for more flexibility to attract multinational companies and investments in pre-salt oil production. As one official argues, no industrial policy is an industrial policy position—an argument that is also supported by the claim that Brazil's comparative advantage lies in agrobusiness and mineral commodities.[34] Thus, the objective was not so much about

---

[32] Author interview with Nelson Simão de Carvalho Jr., *Secretaria de Coordinação e Governança das Empresas Estatais*, Brasília, 4 June 2018.
[33] Author interview with Andre Pompeo do Amaral Mendes, BNDES, Rio de Janeiro, 14 June 2018.
[34] Author interview with Margarete Gandini, *Ministério de Economia Indústria, Comércio Exterior e Serviços* (MDIC), Brasília, 4 June 2018.

expanding or 'thickening' the supply chain, but a redirection towards making Brazil an oil-exporting country.[35] A shift is discernible from the PT's view of the O&G sector as a means to transform the country as both an oil producer and supplier of equipment and services in offshore production towards Brazil as a magnet of natural-resource-based FDI. To put it differently, Temer's policy is a return to an anti-statist position in an unresolved debate about industrialization and state-led growth.

For Petrobras, these changes dramatically shifted the relationship between the federal government and the NOC. After 2014, oil prices collapsed and the entire investment chain in the O&G sector was cancelled. These major externalities undermined Petrobras's aggressive expansion particularly because the 2012–2016 business plan was approved by the Board of Directors when oil prices were at US$100 per barrel and the financial health of the company appeared very promising. Apart from unfavourable market conditions, the *Lava Jato* scandal created an impossible situation for Petrobras, leading to the NOC's paralysis. The company experienced immense difficulties in signing new contracts and significant additional compliance requirements were imposed by BNDES on the company. Overall, Petrobras's strategic roles as a vehicle for investment and regional development and as a driver of economic growth were all reduced under the Temer government.

Conclusion: The End of Developmentalism in Brazil?

The eclipse of the PT's dominance in Brazilian politics marked a shift away from new developmentalism towards market-friendly policies at the national level. State-led development under the PT was portrayed as a thin veil to hide corruption and rent-seeking in Petrobras and beyond. Jair Bolsonaro's government consolidates the anti-PT sentiments, growing anti-statism, and the rise of conservative social forces in Brazil. Importantly, there is undoubtedly no question that Brazil is currently experiencing a crisis of governance and legitimacy. This chapter has shown that understanding how the developmental alliance was built in this period—through industrial policy, corruption, and rent-seeking—is important, though remains an insufficient explanation for the persistence of SOEs in Brazil. Both Chapters 7 and 8 have argued that historical path dependencies have enabled Brazilian political elites to shape strategic industries in ways that maintain the core

---

[35] Author interview with Andre Pompeo do Amaral Mendes, BNDES, Rio de Janeiro, 14 June 2018.

224 Business of the State

elements of state-driven growth models. Rather than embracing privatization and wholesale asset selling, Petrobras underwent significant corporate governance reforms, and legislation was put in place to create a regulatory framework that accommodates the strategic purpose of SOEs in economic development.

The corruption uncovered by the *Lava Jato* investigation is an exemplar of the difficult balance between the pursuit of individual greed and grand corruption on the one hand, and the consolidation of machine politics to buy off political support for industrial policy on the other. The Brazilian experience is not unique among industrializing economies catching up with the developed world. As Ang summarizes (2020, 11–18, 206–207) in her book on China, corruption impedes economic growth, but the harms of different forms of corruption manifest themselves in different ways. Petty theft and grand theft are often damaging and a drain to public and private wealth; exchange-based corruption has ambiguous effects. In some instances, bureaucratic corruption (petty bribery) may enhance efficiency by overcoming the administrative hurdles of inefficient bureaucratic apparatus. In extreme cases, as in China, *access money*—or corruption involving high-stake rewards extended by business actors to powerful politicians (such as exclusive, valuable privileges)—might be used to share the profits of economic growth.

In East Asian countries, exchange-based corruption that closely resembles the corruption exposed in the *Lava Jato* investigation has been an integral part of political coalition building: bribery and corruption have been a vital instrument for business actors to cement their political alliance with party bosses in order to sustain industrial policy in an otherwise fractious policy environment. The extent to which corruption was developmental in Brazil is, however, a separate topic for another book. What is illustrated here is that corruption and machine politics were intertwined in Brazil. The involvement of Petrobras in the scandal is also far more limited in comparison to private sector rent-seeking. And, as the latter parts of the chapter suggest, the problems associated with debt accumulation and collapse of Petrobras's investment rating were all tied to government policy and business strategy of the state enterprise. At the core of this complex story is the difficulty in maintaining corporate autonomy vis-à-vis government policy and bureaucrats who run the company.

Part III expands the arguments of the book beyond the individual contribution of the country cases. The next chapter (Chapter 9) discusses the implications of the two case studies in our theory of SOE-based growth strategies. These case studies explore two key questions—to what extent does historical path dependence matter in the survival of SOEs during privatization reforms? And, how far can SOE-growth strategies succeed in promoting long-term economic development? To answer these questions, the next chapter provides a comparative analysis of Brazil and Chile but also extends the argument to the Southern Cone region of Latin America.

PART III

COMPARATIVE AND HISTORICAL DIMENSIONS OF STATE OWNERSHIP

9

State Ownership in Comparative Perspective

This book has documented a persistent and evolving trend of state ownership in Latin America's strategic natural resource industries since the late 1980s. Despite the emerging literature on resource nationalism and privatization, most discussions fail to account for the political role of SOEs, and the scholarship makes sweeping claims about state activism without any in-depth analysis about the agency of SOEs in the reform process. By contrast, the empirical chapters in this book have documented episodes of sustained reforms in regulatory frameworks and corporate governance to support SOEs—not the privatization of state assets—in strategic natural resource industries. And these hybrid development strategies involving SOEs bear significant implications for industrial development because through SOEs, resource-rich countries have captured more windfall profits, enhanced technological innovation, and promoted sectoral development. While most studies use resource nationalism as an organizing concept to explain the range of institutional changes regarding taxation and the renegotiation of contracts with foreign capital investors, this book makes a different empirical claim: resource-rich countries have enacted dual economic reforms, namely the creation of regulatory frameworks to manage competition and the internal restructuring of SOEs to enhance their effectiveness as agents of economic development. This book, therefore, challenges a long-held view that SOEs are intrinsically unproductive, laggards in the technological race, and conduits of rent-seeking. Instead, the book asserts that in fact these dual economic reforms likewise point to the unrelenting role of purposive state intervention in managing strategic industries for long-term economic development. As such, these issues are central questions for further comparative research beyond Latin American natural resource sectors.

This chapter argues for a recognition of the significance of state ownership and SOEs in understanding fundamental debates in political economy that seek to address both critical real-world and normative questions: the relation between state capitalism and economic development, the role of state ownership in institutional capacity building and industrial policy expansion

Business of the State. Jewellord T. Nem Singh, Oxford University Press. © Jewellord T. Nem Singh (2024).
DOI: 10.1093/oso/9780198892212.003.0009

230 Business of the State

in the 21st century, and the political conditions necessary for continuity in maintaining efficient, productive SOEs that can be politically autonomous, thereby reducing the possibilities of state companies being conduits of rent-seeking and corruption. This chapter is divided into three sections. Firstly, it revisits the historical institutionalist framework and examines the comparative evidence from Brazil and Chile, exploring the important mechanisms linking the regulatory politics and SOE reforms in the mining and O&G industries analysed in the empirical chapters. By placing the history of state activism within the long durée, the book offers a strong explanatory framework of the continuities and changes in resource governance models. Secondly, the chapter examines other Latin American governance models for natural resource industries, specifically drawing comparisons with Peru and Venezuela to show the significance SOEs for industrial development in Brazil and Chile. In so doing, the analysis emphasizes the various modes of engagement with globalization in the region, while demonstrating that an SOE-based industrial strategy appears to be a superior template to secure long-term gains for natural resource producers.

Key Arguments and Case Studies Compared

After three decades of market reforms that began during the 1980s and the dual transition towards political democracy and neoliberal economics, SOEs not only survived but also thrived amidst a large-scale effort to privatize massive public enterprise systems that aimed to make SOEs competitive and on par with private mining and O&G companies. In this way, states accommodated the existence of SOEs rather than deliberately eliminating state control in strategic natural resource industries. Regulatory reforms opened natural resources sectors to foreign capital by passing legislative measures to attract FDI and rein in the overwhelming market dominance of large SOEs that had operated in oligopolistic ways. At the discursive level, national elites, bureaucrats, and civil servants, and SOE managers declared an unfathomable commitment to liberalism as the answer to the remaining vestiges of state inefficiency. In both Chile and Brazil, development planning welcomed technological innovations and engineering expertise from multinational capital as the new pathway towards economic globalization. This book characterizes this approach to economic globalization as a *hybrid* development strategy—whereby both Chile and Brazil cleverly combine market incentives with traditional state controls to find the appropriate balance between public goods provision and profit-oriented business planning.

However, rather than assuming that the rise of hybrid development strategies was a by-product of rationally calculated business decisions by domestic companies and the deliberate choice of the state to retreat from the national economy, this book argues that hybrid strategies are historically constituted outcomes, derived from the dynamics of institutional change and stability which led to the dominance of SOEs in strategic industries throughout the 20th century. Between the 1930s and 1970s, Brazil and Chile experienced convergences towards state developmentalism characterized by a mixture of export-oriented commodity production and ISI—a process mirrored across the Americas (Ferraro and Centeno 2019; Offner 2019). This developmentalist orientation is characterized by the creation of SOEs, state-led financing through national development banks, and export-promoting development agencies aimed at deepening industrialization and reducing dependence on primary raw materials. As Chapter 3 showed, the existence of a developmentalist ideology was contained and reproduced through these development-oriented institutions—a process that was only feasible whenever elite consensus was forged through a developmentalist vision (Sikkink 1991; Trebat 1983). SOEs developed their technical competencies through coordinated efforts in development planning, often led by a cadre of highly trained professional bureaucrats in pursuit of state-guided development to become highly productive companies. While variance in state capacity influenced the success of ISI model and mass support for developmentalism across Latin America, the post-war years had strong affinities for centralized, state-led growth models.[1]

Although the initial conditions and drivers of institutional change between the 1930s and 1970s were generally similar across the countries of Latin America, important idiosyncratic state and market characteristics led Brazil and Chile towards *divergent* models of natural resource governance from the 1980s onwards. In Chile, the origins of a hybrid strategy can be traced back to the dictatorship. In 1973 the military government introduced the neoliberal doctrine through a combination of an institutionalized network of technocrats—the Chicago Boys—and the overt deployment of violence to curtail labour resistance. This formidable task of social reengineering to introduce and embed neoliberalism in Chile was highly successful, so much so that its ideological power runs deeper in Chile than many parts of the developing world. Crucially, Pinochet codified a pro-FDI, pro-labour flexibility model in the strategic mining industry. However, Chile's reliance on

---

[1] However, in Colombia and the US, a developmental and welfare state model was pursued, based on decentralized, technocratic governance where private initiatives autonomous from centralized federal control were the driving force of productivity and innovation (Offner 2019, 15, 34–36, 278–280).

the rents from copper exports led him to retain Codelco as a 100% state-owned enterprise. Put differently, Pinochet and his military saw Codelco as the main source of rent-seeking for the military government. In 1976, the dictatorship issued DL 1,530, also known as *Ley Reservada del Cobre*, to compel the automatic transfer of 10% of the rents from Codelco's copper sales (at least US$90 million annually) to the armed forces. In this way Codelco remained fully state owned despite the rise of Chile as a neoliberal state and throughout the period of institutional stability (the 1990s–2000s), when the *Concertación* coalition embraced economic continuity with the gradual expansion of private sector participation in Chile's economy. Therefore, the Chilean hybrid development strategy was directly a function of political elites' efforts at maintaining institutional stability and political continuity of neoliberalism.

By contrast, the core elements of Brazil's state developmentalism inherited from the Vargas military dictatorship remained largely intact during the 20th century. Brazil's success story of state-led industrialization during the 1960s and 1970s was itself an extension of the Varguista state, characterized chiefly in terms of centralized economic planning and structural transformation through the bureaucratic competence of public administration, and a central role for SOEs. Petrobras was at the heart of Brazil's industrialization story: the NOC implemented a local content policy leading to a diversified domestic supply chain, invested in R&D, yielding world-class ultra-deep-sea engineering technology, and efficiently managed oil rents by financing offshore exploration and production activities through revenues from crude oil refining and the production of petrochemicals. Overall, Brazil's regulatory framework championed a single company monopoly which centralized O&G policy within Petrobras, resolving coordination problems between public and private actors, and creating a vertical supply chain in the O&G industry. By the 1980s, however, Brazil's SOE-centred development model had encountered huge debts, hyperinflation, and inefficiency, leading to a major readjustment in the model, in which, like Chile, market reforms were partially conceived as a solution to excessive state activism. Yet, as Chapter 7 illustrates, societal mobilization through the leadership of organized labour contested the terms and scope of neoliberalism in Brazil. Put simply, political elites and SOE managers did not fully reject the role of state ownership in the pursuit of national economic development. As such, overall, Brazil's hybrid model engenders key continuities between state developmentalism and neoliberalism through the 1990s and 2000s.

The analysis in this book has presented Brazil and Chile's institutional stability in the 1990s and 2000s as a by-product of initial conditions and shared drivers of institutional change in each country: (1) initial conditions between the 1930s and 1970s consolidated a developmental state model in Latin America, which was dismantled and transformed to varying degrees depending on domestic politics; and (2) as external factors such as debt, low commodity prices, and the persuasive power of neoliberal ideology created immense pressure for institutional change, endogenous factors stemming from domestic politics mediated the embedding of market reforms. These idiosyncratic factors have produced two divergent models which are characterized by institutional stability during the 1990s: a hybrid development model based on neoliberalism in Chile and a hybrid model based on state developmentalism in Brazil.

As Offner (2019, 15–16) rightly points out, a great deal of scholarship on the unravelling of developmental states has focussed on half a century of conflict between Left and Right as well as between capital and labour, culminating in political and institutional coups from the Right during successive crises between 1973 and 1991—namely oil shocks and stagflation, the debt crisis, and the collapse of the Soviet Union. This book takes this scholarship one step further: by documenting the new dynamics that reshaped the development models of Brazil and Chile from the 2000s onwards, it shows that, over time, neoliberalism was internalized in the public bureaucracy and management boards of SOEs, creating a political alliance and intellectual consensus on the death of *old* developmentalism of the 20th century. Neoliberalism became an endogenous, self-perpetuating force driving market liberalization in strategic industries, and natural resource sector reforms began to court private investment as a globalization strategy. At face value, market reforms delegitimized industrial policymaking and played a role in unmaking the developmental state model that ensured the traditionally strong function of SOEs in national economic development; however, the reforms in the natural resource sectors were premised on emphasizing the competitiveness of SOEs and privatized regulatory governance in the mining and O&G sectors. Hence, state ownership was refashioned as a paradigmatic response to economic globalization.

This book argues that, as Figure 9.1 shows, a combination of exogenous and endogenous factors set in motion the revival of SOEs from 2000 onwards: (1) exogenous factors include the growing presence of Chinese state-owned capital in Latin America and elsewhere, and, relatedly, soaring commodity prices in a cycle that lasted from 2002 to 2014, and which created fiscal surplus for resource-rich countries; and (2) endogenous factors include the successful election of Left and Centre-Left parties and leaders into power, thereby, reintroducing statism into national political economy debates. While scholarly accounts highlighted changes in regulatory frameworks in favour

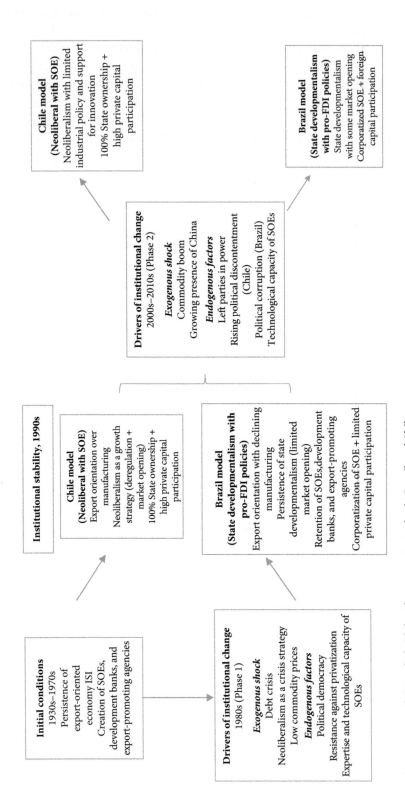

Figure 9.1 Explaining hybrid development strategies in Brazil and Chile.

of renationalization as a response to the new commodity boom since 2003, this book highlights the stable presence of highly productive SOEs as a conditional variable that shaped the governance models in Brazil and Chile. Unlike the Andean region, SOEs in the Chile and Brazil case studies were—and remain—legitimate sources of capturing windfall profits, generating innovation and technological change, and yielding productive capacity and sectoral linkages, after the successful organizational restructuring that took place throughout the 1990s. The empirical analysis chapters in this book have documented the following trends: SOEs returned to the centre of national politics during the commodity boom, but this was not because of exogenous geopolitical shifts or a consequence of the strength of societal mobilization in defence of renationalization. Rather, the history of state activism in Brazil and Chile enabled the developmental role of SOEs to be articulated in national politics more widely. Put differently, policy elites and SOE managers made strategic political choices to avoid privatization and to adopt regulatory frameworks that accommodate—not eliminate—state ownership as their primary development strategy in the era of economic globalization. Alluding to the political agency of Latin American states, Brazilian and Chilean political elites interpreted their geopolitical contexts in ways that enabled them to reformulate their development strategies. The post-crisis strategy during the 1990s reflected their willingness to adjust to the demands of neoliberal globalization without necessarily giving up absolute control over their strategic industries.

As the case study analysis in this book has shown, the mutually reinforcing effects of internal dynamics and exogenous factors can explain the variation of state activism across Latin America. Firstly, it draws out the similarities between traditional developmental states like Brazil and a neoliberal state like Chile—an unlikely comparison given the radically different ways in which neoliberalism was articulated in these countries. Secondly, through process tracing dual reforms in strategic natural resource industries, the book shows the distinct trajectories of state intervention to implement, firstly, regulatory frameworks to attract FDI and, secondly, the attendant corporate governance reforms of SOEs to ensure their competitiveness despite market liberalization. In this way, the book characterizes how institutional stability was achieved in Brazil and Chile through the pragmatic response of elites towards pressures of market reforms. By emphasizing continuity in their respective models, the governance of strategic natural resource sectors remained stable throughout the 1990s and 2000s. This stood in contrast to the rest of the region that embraced sweeping privatization of SOEs, beyond their mining and O&G industries (Haslam and Heidrich 2016).

236   Business of the State

There are important differences between the two case studies. *Firstly, the timing, sequencing, and pace of market reforms differ between Brazil and Chile,* which in turn determined how far neoliberalism could be implemented. Mining codes embracing foreign capital were adopted as early as 1974 in Chile, whereas in Brazil the Petroleum Law was adopted as late as 1997. Hence, Chilean market reforms were more closely associated with neoliberalism, while Brazilian reforms are often considered to have been done in patchwork, rather than through a consistent, ideology-based commitment to institutional change. In other words, political timing explains the depth of embedding of neoliberal reforms in the two cases. They were also adapted to fit into distinctive national contexts. Chile was the first country in Latin America, perhaps in the world, to embrace a neoliberal mining regime. Pinochet conceived neoliberalism as a social reengineering project to radically break from its socialist past, and his political project serves as the critical juncture heralding private capital as Chile's engine of growth. Politically, he was also able to secure veto powers for the military and Right-wing parties to prevent future changes in legislation through the 'Organic Laws' requiring 2/3 majority votes in Congress for any change—an arduous task as long as Pinochet's electoral system is retained (Barton 2002; González 2008). This double bind was sufficiently powerful to compel the Centre-Left *Concertación* coalition to design reforms gradually as its governments pursued institutional continuity by locking in space for institutional change for the next 20 years after the 1989 referendum and the political transition to democracy. The *Concertación* coalition governments proved their credibility to govern Chile by ameliorating the costs of neoliberalism through expansive social policies without challenging the core elements of the growth model. Pinochet's mining regulatory framework—the 1974 Foreign Investment Law (DL 600) and the 1983 Mining Code—remains intact in this governance model. As Madariaga (2020) highlights, in Chile the tripod between neoliberal ideas, interests, and institutions that became institutionally embedded in policymaking meant that post-dictatorial *Concertación* governments were severely constrained in any attempt to radically alter the governance model. Among elites and SOE managers, alternative policy discourses challenging neoliberalism were found incoherent and were only articulated in the margins of political debates, thereby reducing the actual policy choices available to manage the copper industry and the economy writ large. At best, there were sporadic societal mobilizations from mining unions contesting some aspects of neoliberal mining management.

By contrast, neoliberal reforms were rendered incomplete, partial, and contested (if not negotiated) in Brazil (Almeida 1996; Monteiro 1998; Pinheiro et al. 2004). The economic crisis in 1982 opened a space for the civilian government from 1985 to begin the sales of SOEs and the arduous process of market-opening reforms. However, it was not until 1995 when the Cardoso government fully privatized mining giant CVRD (now a multinational corporation named Vale) that a new Petroleum Law was narrowly passed in Congress. While the 1997 Petroleum Law ended the state monopoly in the O&G sector, the federal government retained strategic control through restructuring the ownership of NOC Petrobras. Requirements on local content were also introduced at the same time as market-opening reforms were codified in legislation. And, despite the tumultuous political crisis in Brazil after 2014, Petrobras withstood attacks from the political Right as its state managers challenged calls for further privatization of the company by arguing that Petrobras's corporate autonomy was quintessential to its success. They rebuked the politicization of Petrobras as it was criticized as the culprit of mismanagement, calling for politicians to respect Petrobras's technocratic expertise and meritocracy in its selection processes for its future leadership, and its business strategy. Under the Right-wing governments of Presidents Temer (2016–2018) and Bolsonaro (2019–2022), Petrobras publicly demanded its autonomy from state intervention, especially in setting gasoline prices, implementing its programme against corruption, and designing its strategy for exploiting the pre-salt reserves.

Since the PT left power in 2016, succeeding Petrobras presidents have wrestled with Brazilian presidents and governments to maintain its autonomy in making strategic decisions for the company and this highlights the indisputable role of Petrobras in Brazilian political and economic life. Notable examples include: (1) setting gasoline prices at international market levels has often generated conflicts between Petrobras and the government; and (2) inflationary pressures and rising gasoline prices often trigger social protests, as in the case of the truck drivers' strike in 2016. Put crudely, the ideological orientation of the government in power appears less relevant than the general desire for political interference in Petrobras's affairs when it comes to state–SOE relations. This should not come as a surprise— Petrobras continues to occupy a strategic role in oil policymaking in the post-liberalization era. The huge profit margins of the oil business, especially after the discovery of pre-salt reserves, have made the company a target for state intervention and mismanagement, as the *Lava Jato* corruption scandal in 2014 exposed.

Secondly, sector-specific features of strategic natural resource industries generated very different pathways of neoliberal reforms in Chile and Brazil. One metric of the reform outcome can be derived from the emergent relationship

238 Business of the State

between states and foreign capital after the restructuring period as natural resource sector reforms valorized the importance of foreign investment as the new source of economic dynamism. On the one hand, the mining industry is historically dominated by multinational capital, especially North American capital. In fact, Codelco remains to be one of the few SOEs in the minerals sector (Nem Singh 2010; Nem Singh and Chen 2018). On the other hand, the development of the O&G sector as a self-sufficient industry has been driven by energy security imperatives and, thus, was always constitutive of broader national security objectives, not simply economic development (Massi and Nem Singh 2020). As Chapter 3 demonstrated, unlike mining, oil nationalization was at the crux of foreign and economic policies in Latin America. Throughout the 20th century, the global oil market was restructured from oligopolistic control held by the Seven Sisters towards a cartel of oil-exporting states made up of NOCs, whose policies included not just nationalization of reserves but also artificial manipulation of oil prices through restrictive supply policies leading to the oil boom in the 1970s. The overall effect of such restructuring has been to substantially shift market power from multinational oil capital towards state-owned companies (Marcel and Mitchell 2006; Victor et al. 2012). Therefore, Chile's hybrid strategy is inclined towards neoliberalism due to historical antecedents and general pressure to maintain openness to foreign competition. By contrast, Brazil's developmental state strategy reflects the historical role of oil in national security debates and high levels of resource control in terms of both wealth creation and production.

Extending this sectoral variation to explain varying pathways of neoliberalism, the type of natural resource matters for the type of resource nationalist projects embraced by political elites. Because mining differs from O&G in terms of distinct organizational structures and methods of asserting control, the specific policy instruments of resource control also differ. Whereas the mining sector often restricts nationalization to the renegotiation of contracts and increasing royalty taxes to generate more windfall profits, O&G re-nationalization reforms tend to be more intrusive, if not radical, including policies taking over actual production sites, changing the regulatory frameworks for contracts from concessions towards production sharing and/or service contracts and, importantly, strengthening the market power of NOCs vis-à-vis multinational oil capital. While very few countries would be considered dependent on a single mineral commodity, a substantial number of oil exporters are entirely dependent on oil rents for wealth generation. For this reason, oil is often alluded to as 'black gold', conjuring images of modernity through resource nationalism (Coronil 1997; Gustafson 2020; Parra

2004). Hence, natural resource conflicts between the host state and foreign oil capital have been more intense and difficult to resolve, which has led to uncompensated expropriation as opposed to a stable, negotiated exit. The Brazilian governance model is arguably a successful strategy in dealing with this problem. While Brazil sought to protect its O&G industry from foreign interference in its early years despite the near absence of oil reserves, the discovery of pre-salt reserves in the current era of economic globalization has meant that Brazilian political elites have formulated a regulatory framework for the O&G industry to accommodate foreign interests, but with Petrobras as a buffer to protect its national interests. Nevertheless, there is an inherent tension in the role of the state as both a regulator of the market and a direct participant in the economy, which remains unchanged despite this strategy of accommodation.

To conclude, we can observe a shift in terms of the regulatory and entrepreneurial role of states from state intervention towards a more hybrid developmental role, in which the promotion of private initiatives melds with the continuing presence of SOEs. Consequently, states and foreign capital are reconfiguring their relationships as global market integration in natural resource sectors becomes inevitable. This book demonstrates varying patterns of natural resource governance as an outcome of political choices made to generate market incentives and to assert political authority in strategic natural resource industries.

Petrobras and Codelco Compared

The key novelty of this book lies in its empirical and theoretical contributions in explaining SOE behaviour in the post-liberalization period. Most earlier scholarship on SOE reforms during the 1990s took a teleological approach to explain SOE organizational behaviour, drawing on evidence from former Soviet states in which arguments were deployed to support privatization to achieve SOE depoliticization: SOEs are depicted as conduits of rent-seeking, highly inefficient, and lacking competitiveness vis-à-vis their private sector counterparts (Dabrowski et al. 1991; Kikeri and Kolo 2005; Kikeri et al. 1994; Sachs 1992; Yoder et al. 1991). Through international financial institutions (IFIs), most policy recommendations drawn from studies were aimed at dismantling centralized planning, strengthening market institutions, and implementing structural adjustment programmes (SAPs) in the aftermath of market stabilization (Kikeri and Kolo 2005; Kikeri et al. 1994; Ramamurti and Vernon 1991).

240   Business of the State

Throughout the 1980s and 1990s, convergence towards market liberalization meant that the role of the state in industrial development also waned. In turn, market-building institutions sought to weaken the role of SOEs in strategic sectors. The activist state nudging companies in the right direction, particularly through the deployment of selective industrial policy, has become unpopular in the heyday of economic globalization. Yet, by the mid-2000s the failure of the market reform agenda to deliver growth threatened the SOE privatization mantra. As the case of China demonstrates, the advance of the state once again became a strategy to expand markets for domestic companies. In pursuit of this strategy, Chinese policy on trade, investment, and finance centred on strengthening state companies and supporting their activities overseas. Beyond China, the World Bank and IMF likewise underestimated the political significance of these organizations in the Global South. As state bureaucrats downsized SOEs and appeared to conform to the logic of market competition as a means to access international finance, they averted the fully pledged privatization of SOE assets, much to the surprise of donors. In this context, SOEs were compelled to focus on two key reforms: to reorganize their operations around their core businesses and to design changes in their management structure and internal control mechanisms to increase their professionalization. Rather than pursuing reforms to eliminate SOEs, bureaucrats in partnership with national elites implemented reform policies to transform SOEs into hybrid organizations capable of adapting to economic globalization (Bruton et al. 2013; 2014). In Schamis's (2002) words, the state was 're-formed' to exercise political authority in ways that the market reform agenda prevented it from doing so. Crucially, this process was intensely political, showcasing the struggle for power between state elites, bureaucratic authorities, and SOE managers.

The following section draws out four key comparative insights taken from the case studies of Petrobras and Codelco which are useful to extend further: (1) the relationship between national elites and bureaucrats within governments and SOEs (or what I refer to as 'state–state (SOE) relations'); (2) the *political* role of SOEs in buffering demands from foreign and domestic capital as well as organized workers; (3) the redefinition of the *industrial* role of SOEs in national development; and (4) the significance of internal corporate governance reforms as a response to global competitiveness.

State–State (SOE) Relations

A core element of transformative institutional change in Brazil and Chile took place when the so-called state–state (SOE) relations were reformulated as SOEs became subject to the logic of market liberalization (Nem Singh and Chen 2018). In Chile, Codelco managers embraced the decision of political elites and state bureaucrats to compete directly with the private sector through a hybrid governance model. On the one hand, Codelco was managed through technocratic governance and its presence secured the rights of the state over the subsoil and government control in production through direct participation in the mining industry. Codelco also played a fiscal role, whereby taxes and profits were secured on behalf of the state. On the other hand, the success of Codelco in performing its economic role relies on its capacity to formulate a competitive commercial strategy, reinforcing the need for Codelco to perform on par with international mining companies. Therefore, Codelco state managers faced a double bind—they had to manage the state company through technocratic governance making the SOE competitive, but they do not occupy the economic space that private agents do. For national elites, the implications of this contradictory state–state (SOE) relation are clear: the political establishment recognized that Codelco *should not* be privatized, either partially or in full, because politically and economically its strategic role was too great. For the military, Codelco served as a 'milking cow' to secure the budgetary spending needs of the armed forces, and up until September 2019, a law served to protect the rent-seeking interests of the military by automatically transferring 10% of Codelco's profits to them (Sherwood 2019).[2] Without wider political reform, this political relationship between the security forces of the state and Codelco will remain intact.

In Brazil, the logic of state–state (SOE) relations is more firmly rooted in the developmentalist tradition pervasive among the political classes. From the 1990s, Petrobras managers and state bureaucrats shared a developmentalist vision crafted by the military government in the 1970s: the O&G sector was viewed not simply as a commodity export but as key to industrial development. Even with Cardoso's liberalization agenda, Petrobras's privatization was limited and severely undermined by workers' protests in 1995. And, because the demand for reindustrialization requires energy self-sufficiency, Petrobras would retain much of its market power in the O&G supply chain. Of course, it helped a lot that Petrobras was not exporting oil. Compared to Venezuela, rentier politics was not as restrictive to the capacity of Petrobras to pursue commercial objectives. In the absence of substantial oil reserves until 2007, Brazilian elites accepted the role of Petrobras as an internationally

---

[2] *Ley Numero 21.174* was passed in Congress in September 2019 entitled 'A Law Establishing a New Mechanism for Financing the Strategic Capabilities of National Defence'. This replaces *Ley Orgánica 18.948* and *Ley Numero 1.263 de 1975*, which together outline the constitutional right to acquire 10% of Codelco sales for the armed forces as well as the administrative rules on the funds of the armed forces.

competitive national champion. In other words, industrial policy principles remained intact in the face of global competition. Scholarly accounts allude to this 'open economy' industrial strategy as a globalization strategy (Kasahara and Botelho 2019; Schrank and Kurtz 2005). Thus, Cardoso opted for a corporatization strategy: the break-up, asset selling, and reorganization of the Petrobras system in order to strip out uncompetitive and underperforming business segments of the company while expanding its competencies and technological advancement in parts of the business with the most potential for profit and commercialization (Brooks and Kurtz 2016; Priest 2016). Unlike Codelco, Petrobras officials and their political counterparts shared a vision of reforming the NOC to promote an SOE-centred growth model, not eliminate the NOC altogether from the post-liberalization period.

To conclude, SOE reforms have not been insulated from power struggles; rather, political choices over the specifics of the SOE reform agenda were reflective of the embedded nature of SOEs in domestic politics. The pace and scope of reforms are highly distinct in both Chile and Brazil in so far as they reflect the policy preferences and power configurations in the domestic arena. Put differently, the relative power of SOE managers in relation to state bureaucrats and politicians reflected the tendency to give more (or less) autonomy to the state company. The extent to which SOEs can assert corporate autonomy is a relevant causal factor explaining the institutional arrangements among natural resource producers globally. In China, where a centralized power structure guided the process of SOE reforms, state elites had a stronger hand and directed the reforms in ways that reflected the desire of the centralized state (Z. Chen and Chen 2019; L. Chen and Chulu 2022; Eaton 2016). In addition, the CCP's decision to support the expansion of SOEs and domestic companies overseas through state-backed finance and centralized banking is by itself a by-product of the institutional evolution of the Chinese political system (see Chapter 10). By contrast, the Norwegian model demonstrates the long-standing tradition of their political system, separating political powers between political bodies and regulatory agencies, as well as the general preference to manage the NOC Statoil as a private company (Thurber and Istad 2012).

Finally, through the comparative approach of the book, Brazil and Chile demonstrate the politics of balancing power relations between SOE managers who aspire for greater corporate autonomy and insulation from societal pressures on the one hand, and, on the other hand, politicians and civil society forces—especially organized labour—who seek to restrain the tendency of SOE managers to pursue unfettered growth and commercial objectives at the expense of societal objectives or public goods provision. Put differently, SOE reforms are not only about a battle of ideas about how to turn domestic companies into national champions. Instead, the SOE reform process represents the contestation of material interests among contending agents within institutionalized contexts. While a typology or roadmap on how to reform state–state (SOE) relations is beyond the scope of this book, the comparative case study approach emphasizes the need to study the diverse institutional arrangements aimed at reforming SOEs and managing them as a function of power struggles and historical conflicts.

The Political Role of SOEs in Buffering Competing Demands

One of the major findings of the empirical case studies of this book counters the assumption of the literature on the inevitability of SOE privatization. Because the scholarship on public enterprises often takes a negative view of the economic role of SOEs, the literature often reads SOEs as excessively political, thereby requiring a radical depoliticization of SOE management and its relationship with the national state. Firstly, SOEs are assumed as a conduit of rent-seeking and distributive politics, as the case of Venezuela's PDVSA under Chávez illustrates. Secondly, SOEs are considered highly interwoven in the national state, and therefore they can neither be devoid of politics nor assert corporate autonomy vis-à-vis politicians. The *Lava Jato* scandal is often interpreted in this way. However, what is missing in these interpretations is the fact that SOEs—especially NOCs—have always been historically politicized entities, and yet, some of them have become highly successful international companies that delivered windfall profits to national governments, developed technological innovation as solutions to the specific geological problems associated with the country's natural resource reserves, and served as agents of structural transformation by playing a vital role in building vertically integrated supply chains and linking the mining industry to the productive economy. The question, then, is to identify the underlying conditions upon which the national government can maximize the potential of SOEs to contribute to national industrial transformation.

To answer this complex question demands recognizing the *political roles* that SOEs performed between 1980s and 2010s to buffer competing demands from a range of societal and economic actors. In Brazil, Petrobras successfully guided a coherent oil policy during the post-war years and built a domestic supply chain of equipment, engineering, and services in the O&G

sector. Through this feat in the past, its tradition of maintaining an arms-length relationship with the Brazilian federal government proved very useful to retain its corporate autonomy amidst the complex reforms aimed at dismantling Petrobras's monopoly in the oil industry. More importantly, the SOE-driven strategy in the sector enabled the national government under the PT to pursue an ambitious linkage-based industrial policy as a globalization strategy (Kasahara and Botelho 2019; Massi and Nem Singh 2018; 2020). Given the strong statist tradition, a developmentalist strategy in the O&G sector was easier to implement, and even under the Right, discussions on Petrobras reforms were confined under the logic of global competition—not simply the selling of Petrobras assets for the sake of economic ideology. As Chapter 8 demonstrates, Petrobras has successfully returned to its commercially profitable state, albeit under stringent rules as a result of the *Lava Jato* investigation. For these reasons, Petrobras maintains its role as a buffer against foreign oil interests. Thanks to its ultra-deep-sea engineering technology, Petrobras maintains strategic control over the oilfields being auctioned via joint ventures and production sharing contracts.

In Chile, however, maintaining a strong state enterprise was at odds with the neoliberal strategy and widespread privatization of the Chilean economy. In this way, Codelco reflects the old developmentalism lingering in the fringes of policymaking as the country was locked into the neoliberal tripod, with professional networks and technocrats strongly adhering to neoclassical economics (Bril-Mascarenhas and Madariaga 2019; Madariaga 2020). Compared to Petrobras, Codelco has often served as a buffer against the excessive marketization policies of the Centre-Left government and the Right-led coalition under Sebastian Piñera. Despite the neoliberal hegemony pervasive in the Chilean political system, an apparent consensus exists on the need to retain Codelco as a fully state-owned entity. Codelco played a buffer role between state and private capital. As a 100% state-owned company capable of competing against private mining companies, the Chilean state could guarantee a stable contribution on fiscal resources. Importantly, Codelco owns high-grade copper reserves, and, thus, such arrangement also secures the future benefits of Chilean citizens from their mineral wealth. In other words, Chile has avoided the resource curse because of how it has successfully maintained the competitiveness of Codelco as a national champion, not just through public policies related to managing the mineral wealth.

With copper becoming an even more important commodity in the clean energy transition, current President Gabriel Boric has recognized the success of the SOE-driven resource governance model and has publicly proclaimed the need to protect Codelco from privatization and to ensure windfall profits are returned to the company in the form of investments (Presidential Press 2022). While strengthening the SOE, Boric has also sought to instil a sense of public responsibility in Codelco, pushing it to play a more active role in avoiding the perpetuation of 'sacrifice zones' in the name of national economic development. For sustainability in a mining economy to work, the state through the SOE needs to address deep-seated inequalities, which includes mitigating the uneven impacts of mineral extraction between the capital and the communities at the extractive frontiers (Nem Singh 2021). As the lithium debate discussed in Chapter 6 illustrates, the model of full state ownership in strategic sectors is likely to continue as Chile plays a major geopolitical role as the primary source of lithium-ion batteries needed for the renewable energy transition.

Finally, SOEs play a role in shaping the relationship between host states and multinational capital. The strategic nature of mineral and O&G extraction implies that Latin American governments are reluctant to allow foreign companies to operate freely within the extractive sector. While Brazil and Chile follow the FDI imperative—meaning the embrace of regulatory frameworks to promote FDI—their SOEs tend to mitigate the uncertainty, high sunk costs, and general risks preventing the private sector from making important investments in the mining industry. Through the development of technocratic expertise and geological knowledge to solve specific problems associated with their mineral reserves, Petrobras and Codelco serve as agents of industrial development with political support from significant segments of their societies. In creating productivity-focussed SOEs rather than being mechanisms of distributive politics, their national developmental strategy based on a more dominant market role for SOEs has enabled wider legitimacy for elites towards their claims of resource sovereignty and of the acceptability of state-led growth models. In this way, Latin American governments—certainly Brazil and Chile—are likely to maintain their SOEs as a political buffer against foreign acquisition. One lesson worth reflecting on, particularly in the context of African politics, is how to build a constructive relationship between financial elites and SOEs. If managed well, SOEs can tame the excesses of Western companies or Chinese capital dominating mining, infrastructure, and connectivity projects in Africa (Ambe-Uva 2017; Cai 2018; Lee 2017; Ohashi 2018; Taylor and Zajontz 2020). This point is particularly salient for other Latin American countries as well, given that most states now face an increasingly uneven relationship with China. Regional governments pursue industrial and trade strategies that can complement China's economic growth agenda, while also placating Latin America countries' discontentment over their historical relationship with the

246 Business of the State

US (Bernal-Meza and Xing 2020; Cui and García 2016; Fornes and Mendez 2018; Mendez and Turzi 2020).

Redefining the Role of SOEs in Industrial Development

Historically, SOEs were conceived as strategic geopolitical agents embedded in the logic of national security imperatives, which meant that their efficiency and productive capabilities were secondary priorities. However, some SOEs—especially NOCs—were tasked with a developmental function for producing and managing natural resource wealth (Marcel and Mitchell 2006; Nem Singh and Chen 2018; Thurber and Istad 2012). During the 1970s, the oil bonanza was a critical juncture for oil exporters—an opportunity for developing countries to catch up with the West through oil-financed industrial policies. This, in turn, meant a substantial change in how SOEs were viewed. Not only were SOEs perceived as the political extension of the national state, but also these entities acquired economic functions, and after the second commodity boom in the 2000s, SOEs are back on the development agenda. This time, SOEs bear a dual role connected to a country's industrial development: (1) to generate profit by operating like a private entity, and (2) to guarantee national income for the state that can be reinvested to build economic linkages. As the book shows, SOEs can play a wider developmental role by maximizing windfall profits directly as a producer rather than collecting fiscal resources via taxation. When SOEs develop their technological niche in oligopolistic natural resource markets, they can also develop solutions to highly specific geological problems or become agents of industrial development through the formation of sectoral linkages and vertical integration within supply chains. By recognizing a wider range of developmental functions in the period of economic globalization, SOEs can be conceived as market players in their own right, not simply an extension of the national state and its geopolitical interests.

In Brazil, there was no question that SOEs—Petrobras most notably—became a key pillar of the country's industrialization in the 20th century (Priest 2016; Randall 1993; Trebat 1983). As Chapter 8 illustrates, there is continuity in the role of Petrobras in building sectoral linkages, developing a domestic chain of competent suppliers of goods and services, and securing windfall profits in the most lucrative exploration and production segment of the O&G value chain. Despite the corruption scandal, Petrobras remains an important actor to assert market dominance in a highly prized sector. In Chile, the economic role of Codelco is clearly articulated among political elites and bureaucrats. Its presence seeks to maintain strategic control over the country's richest copper reserves, as an SOE that explores, produces, and processes minerals to provide the national government with security in relying on the mineral sector for long-term economic development. While Codelco did not play a wider role in promoting national industrialization, its fiscal role has enabled the *Concertación* coalition and their succeeding governments to finance poverty reduction strategies alongside gradual reinvestments in capital and labour beyond the mining sector. Additionally, Codelco functions like Petrobras in creating linkages between the natural resource and productive sectors of the national economy. Given the recent debates surrounding development of the lithium industry in Latin America, the idea of strengthening strategic SOEs appears to be viewed as common sense among Chilean policymakers. Thus, the book challenges the typical image of Chile as a neoliberal poster child; if anything, Codelco is the clearest exemplar of a successful model of resource nationalism for developing countries. Despite waves of liberalization and privatization, natural resources were—and remain—a state-sanctioned affair not to be easily given to foreign control. But to succeed in defending resource sovereignty, regulatory reforms in favour of state ownership must come together with policies supporting the creation and retention of highly competitive SOEs which can challenge the technological superiority of private capital and promote structural transformation.

As the empirical chapters demonstrate, the role of SOEs in industrial development has diverged since the post-liberalization period. In Chile, the strength of private sector legitimacy as the motor of economic development makes a stronger interventionist role for Codelco politically difficult to argue, despite overwhelming evidence of its role in proffering fiscal stability and generating sectoral linkages around the mining industry. Thus, it is a political choice to limit Codelco's function and to rely on a hybrid development strategy that continues to elevate the legitimacy of private capitalists in generating innovation and competitiveness. However, under current President Gabriel Boric, there exist some important changes in the ideological orientation of the state—and the public more widely—in viewing the role of public enterprises in strategic industries. In Brazil, Petrobras had to wrestle with frequent politicization of its management due to the tradition of developmentalism. The state company was given wide policy latitude to determine oil policy and the ways it can finance and expand the oil industry in the absence of large reserves to produce for global markets. To this extent, Petrobras's role in industrialization has evolved over time: while the NOC began as a nationalist impulse against foreign interest in oil, the company made its objective to

248　Business of the State

create a vertically integrated oil supply chain—this meant finding profitability in other segments of the value chain such as in refining and transport (mid-stream) and producing oil derivatives (downstream). Thus, its overall role was to facilitate and support the broader industrialization agenda, not to become a mere exporter of crude oil. And it had done so by clearly defining its measures of success, such as ensuring oil independence and developing sectoral linkages without significant oil reserves.

For Petrobras, the challenge is not to elicit support for its existence, but to maintain its independence from political actors. As the *Lava Jato* scandal painfully shows, it has not been enough for Petrobras to put in place internal management reforms and corporate restructuring to prevent political interference in its decision-making. As highlighted in the analysis of the corruption scheme in Chapter 8, Petrobras operates in a political system highly conducive for rent-seeking and corruption. Thus, to conclude, defining how SOEs play a role in industrial development is not an easy task mainly because their roles are often intertwined with the political context. States often have a clear vision of the role of the SOE in the country's wider developmental strategy. Under such conditions, institutional arrangements around SOE corporate governance can be implemented with clearly delineated rules set to constrain the abuse of public enterprises, thus avoiding turning SOEs into vehicles of private accumulation of wealth. It must be noted, however, that using SOEs for sectoral and rent-seeking interests not only limits the potential of SOEs to take a wider industrialization function, but also delegitimizes state ownership as a developmental strategy.

Restructuring Corporate Governance in SOEs

The comparative approach of the book emphasizes a new empirical phenomenon: unlike SOEs in the 1960s–1970s, public enterprises today have been restructured in response to the globalization imperative. Unlike their earlier organizational forms, in the 1990s SOEs across industrializing countries were subjected to corporate governance reforms with three objectives in mind: (1) to change their ownership structure by introducing private investors; (2) to enhance their internal accountability mechanisms, thereby reducing traditional instruments of rent-seeking and political interference; and (3) to reorient the goals of the company from simply following the dictates of the state towards a dual responsibility so as to improve its commercial performance to ensure its profitability and to deliver social and economic goods by way of retaining some form of state controls in how companies operate and compete with private capital.

In Brazil, the reform strategy was focussed on resolving the principal-agency problem[3] through the separation of SOE ownership and SOE, to place profitability as a core business objective of the company. Petrobras was listed on the NYSE in 2000, with foreign and institutional shareholders allowed to acquire non-voting capital shares. Politically, this move was perceived as a compromise or a means of reducing excessive state intervention in the company, as per other SOEs in Brazil that were also listed on the NYSE, to open access to capital in overseas financial markets for their operational and business expansion.

In Chile, corporate governance reforms focussed on the professionalization of Codelco by introducing more technocratically minded members to its Board of Directors and reducing the seat allocation for ministers within the decision-making body. This was intended to enhance the 'expertise' within the company, thereby depoliticizing its day-to-day management. The ownership structure of Codelco is ultimately unreformed, which means that the overall direction of the company hinges on the discretion of the national government. Consistent with general trends in Chile, organized labour also holds a specific veto power in the corporate structure of public enterprises by way of maintaining a seat on the Board of Directors. In other words, the aristocratic status of mining unions has been preserved even during the liberalization period. Although neoliberalism has diminished the overall power of workers in collective bargaining across the Chilean economy, the strategic position of copper workers within the institutional arrangement of corporate governance enables the state to retain social peace in the mines. While the state has indeed deployed mechanisms of co-optation, organized workers indirectly shape the mining policy in Chile. The capacity to bargain and to negotiate painful reforms in Codelco and Enami is a major feature of the Chilean resource governance model, which is an enviable feat other Latin American resource producers have failed to replicate.

Overall, state activism is exercised in both cases differently, based on their idiosyncratic national contexts, and in response to the constraints imposed by history, institutional dynamics, and existing power arrangements between states and foreign capital. The outcomes of corporate restructuring in Brazil and Chile are clear: SOEs have become high-functioning economic agents that can deliver windfall profits, bargain with the national state, and, importantly, make hard decisions on business planning and investments. These day-to-day management decisions would sometimes require labour

---

[3] As discussed in Chapters 2 and 6, when there are no private shareholders in an SOE and the state is the principal agent, if problems of accountability arise it is very difficult to penalize mistakes, and citizens suffer when SOEs underperform but no one is held to account.

compliance, adoption of foreign technology, or even retrenchment, especially during price downturns. Corporate autonomy thus serves as a proxy for successful restructuring and stable institutional arrangements between contending economic and political forces. Finally, and most importantly, the capacity to adopt corporate reforms means that the most painful decision—the privatization of SOEs—can be averted. In so doing, the costs of market reforms can be shared among key stakeholders in resource-producing societies.

Extending the Argument in Latin America

The dynamics of institutional continuity and change explored in this book are not exclusively unique to Brazil and Chile. Policymaking in resource-rich countries shares some important similarities, notably the importance of natural resource sovereignty in shaping the direction of trade and industrial policy, especially in the post-2008 political economy. To start with, the changing international context, namely the rise of China, the delegitimization of the Washington Consensus, and soaring commodity prices were important factors that pushed Latin America to a 'Left' or 'post-neoliberal' turn. However, as the following sections highlight, most studies simply argue that Latin America has moved towards a neo-extractivist model. This policy shift, however, did not come without costs: the formidable challenge of export diversification and industrial transformation remain as a constraint despite resource nationalism. This chapter aims to highlight the limits of the resource nationalism argument as a general blueprint for natural resource producers, showing, instead, through a further analysis of the cases of Peru and Venezuela, the conditions for success for SOEs.

Resource Nationalism in Latin America

The return of resource nationalism in Latin America did not come as a surprise. According to Wilson (2015), resource nationalism refers to policy changes in the ownership structure of the industry, the property rights and operations of private capital vis-à-vis public enterprises, and the capacity of the state to capture natural resource rents. The demand for nationalizing resources comes from a multitude of pressures—internally, through domestic societal mobilization in defence of resource ownership, especially from labour and civil society; externally, as an elite response to changing international contexts, such as high commodity prices and apparent longevity in Chinese demand for natural resources; or from an ideological perspective, a reflection of growing discontentment against the failure of market-led governance models and privatization (Nem Singh 2019, 544). From 2003 onwards, Latin America witnessed the rise of resource nationalism under Leftist governments. However, as noted by Haslam and Heidrich (2016), there are many forms of resource nationalism, depending on the degree of policy change in ownership structures and level of private sector participation.

In Latin America, governments implemented taxation and fiscal measures to increase the revenue intake of the state while also experimenting with how to finance social and industrial policy through natural resources. Different types of fiscal measures, including income and corporate taxes, royalties, and other forms of special fees, were charged to companies extracting minerals and oil. Latin American states converted the commodity boom either through direct public receipt of revenues by way of taxation or via SOEs and majority shareholding in companies. The most successful in maximizing the windfall profits are those that managed to strike a balance between capturing rents and guaranteeing tax stability in the sector. In other words, countries like Brazil and Chile have retained their approach of undertaking moderate tax reforms such that companies have remained profitable despite raising taxes and royalties. However, in nearly all cases, Latin American governments have failed to create an institutional environment where state enterprises could thrive as a competitor against private capital. As the section below details, Venezuela is an extreme case where a successful SOE has lost its productive capacity due to excessive state interference.

Venezuela: A Petro-State Without Corporate Autonomy

To understand the failure of Venezuela, we must return to the origins of PDVSA and the institutional context upon which oil nationalization was forged. Although oil nationalization in Venezuela was conflict-averse and consensually forged among political elites in a democratic setting, as discussed in Chapter 3, the role of PDVSA was widely contested. PDVSA was established in 1976 and pursued an 'internationalisation strategy' to distribute its crude oil in world markets (Baena 1999, 8). The NOC became responsible for the modernization and expansion of the oil industry in Venezuela, including buying up the refinery segment of the value chain (Di John 2014, 337). Its ownership structure diverged from traditional NOCs

252   Business of the State

in the 20th century as the architects of nationalization policy feared the 'Pemexization' of the oil industry (Philip 1982; Yergin 1992).[4] A two-prong solution was crafted: to divest and regulate the terms of oil concessions—as opposed to the outright monopoly found in Brazil and Mexico—and to impose a severe fiscal regime on oil companies to maximize rent capture during an export boom. Thus, PDVSA combined the legal status of an SOE and the embodiments of a large private holding company (Baena 1999, 18–19; Brewer-Carías 2021, 193–205). Yet, the state became dependent on oil rents, and thus PDVSA was a target of excessive political interference. For example, it was routinely subject to executive and legislative controls, including from the Ministry of Energy that set out the country's oil policy. Congress also had the power to approve agreements for technical cooperation and commercialization with ex-concessionaires (Baena 1999, 48–49). At the same time, PDVSA developed a highly technocratic workforce and had very close ties with the President, thereby enabling PDVSA to influence key decisions in the oil industry and neutralizing political actors. Through its special status, PDVSA retained many features of a private company, including the freedom of action on commercial decisions. Thus, while the state sometimes meddled with its budgetary independence, PDVSA's administrative and financial autonomy equipped its managers to undertake very difficult decisions on how to best develop the oilfields.

PDVSA was undoubtedly a success story of an NOC borne with wide policy latitude, giving the company the capacity to pursue an internationalization strategy. Firstly, PDSVA adopted a vertically integrated model of organization to rationalize the industry structure (Brewer-Carías 2021, 205–234). Inspired by the multinational corporation (MNC) model, PDVSA state managers encouraged competition among affiliates, leading to client-based negotiations between subsidiaries and the elimination of overlapping functions among subsidiaries. By 1976 the number of oil companies operating in Venezuela was reduced from 35 to 14, including PDVSA. Secondly, PDVSA transformed itself into an international oil player by increasing investments, improving its refining capabilities, and establishing technological cooperation agreements with multinational oil enterprises (Baena 1999, 68–74; Hults

---

[4] Following the nationalist ideas of the Revolutionary government and after an uncomfortable history of mutual mistrust between the Mexican government and IOCs, Mexico nationalized its oil assets in 1938. However, due to growing politicization of NOC management and labour conflicts, one of the key objectives of Pemex after nationalisation was the fulfilment of the domestic market through the production of cheap oil. This, in turn, led to chronic capital shortages for reinvestment in the sector and signiificant loss in share of international oil market (Baena 1999: 34, 211). Deeply penetrating oil reforms in Venezuela were often justified by avoiding the 'Pemexization' of the industry, conjuring images of deep financial crisis of the Mexican oil company due to excessive fiscal payments and massive indebtedness.

2012, 426–429). Over time, the company successfully established new ties with non-traditional oil companies and gradually reduced dependence on ex-concessionaires. Finally, PDVSA hired engineers and technocrats as opposed to 'commissars' in government agencies, thereby outmanoeuvring the Ministry of Energy in setting oil policies. Oil technocrats from the private sector valued meritocracy and cost maximization. Fearing politicization, they often clashed with ministers concerned with rent capture and interfering in company decisions (Baena 1999, 66–67). PDVSA pursued corporate governance policies in pursuit of freedom of action, which included acquiring technological know-how and access to capital through joint ventures with IOCs. Nevertheless, the company was unable to deflect government demands based on political considerations as opposed to criteria for market competitiveness (Baena 1999; Rosales 2018).

However, after the oil boom in the 1970s, PDVSA's pursuit of autonomy did not sit well with the deteriorating political and economic conditions from 1983 onwards. During the oil price collapse in 1986 and heightened competition in world oil markets, PDVSA insulated itself by depositing foreign earnings in US banks and fought to buy refineries abroad amidst looming crisis at home (Baena 1999, 196–200; Rosales 2018, 446–447). The 1980s crisis provoked a more aggressive internationalization strategy from PDVSA by focussing on enlarging market share and minimizing market uncertainties. Critics accused PDVSA of behaving like a 'state within the state', whereby decisions over investments, production, and internationalization were made in defiance of congressional interference (Mommer 2003; Rosales and Sánchez 2021, 647).

By the time Hugo Chávez assumed the presidency in 1999, PDVSA was operating as if it was an IOC.[5] However, Venezuela's economic performance was mediocre, with rising poverty rates, rapid deterioration of productivity in non-oil sectors, and an export collapse in the post-crisis years (Di John 2009; Hausmann and Rodríguez 2014). These conditions shaped the new interactions between the state and PDVSA, which would create a new cycle of contention from 2000 onwards as economic liberalization and its pro-investment model were blamed for the problems of the country, even if the state's dependence on the oil industry was largely responsible amidst low oil prices, uncompetitive non-oil sectors, and high debt (Hults 2012, 431).

---

[5] There is a substantial literature on *Chavismo*—(1) the sociopolitical roots of Chávez's rise to power and consolidation of his popular movement (Andrews-Lee 2021; Corrales 2014; Monaldi and Penfold 2014); (2) the technologies of governance, strategies of domination, and discursive power of Chavismo (Corrales and Penfold 2011; Hawkins 2010); and (3) the consequences of Chavista policies, especially on managing mineral wealth (Hults 2012; Rosales and Sánchez 2021).

254 Business of the State

Chávez took full advantage of the commodity boom to establish himself in power. This was most astutely observed when he disenfranchised PDVSA of its fiscal independence and corporate autonomy. Chávez's reform of PDVSA included the appointment of General Guaicaipuro Lameda as PDVSA president in October 2000, which broke the tradition of naming oil industry technocrats or businessmen for the position. Chávez announced the passage of the *Decreto con Fuerza de Ley Organica de Hidrocarburos* (Hydrocarbons Law) in November 2001, which increased royalty rates by 30% and lowered income tax rates to 50% (Hults 2012, 432). He also reversed the policy of allowing foreign oil companies to hold majority interests in strategic partnerships with PDVSA. In response, Fedecámaras, the largest business association in Venezuela, launched a national strike. In January 2002, Lameda along with other industry managers publicly criticized the oil legislation. Chávez removed him from his post. In response to Chávez's choice of Gastón Parra Luzardo, an economist and banker, as Lameda's replacement, his lack of managerial experience in the oil industry provoked widespread protest against the growing politicization of the NOC and for the need to 'return to meritocracy' (Rosales 2018, 454–456). A national strike ensued that almost removed Chávez from power had it not been for popular mobilization on the streets in support of the government and the reassertion of the military's backing for Chávez. Once back in control, Chávez fired 18,000 of the 33,000 PDVSA employees, with the result that the company lost 30–40% of its technocratic staff (Hults 2012, 434). Thus, PDVSA was transformed from an internationally oriented NOC to a subservient public enterprise at the disposal of the Venezuelan state.

PDVSA became an instrument of state discretion, firstly through the elimination of the traditional checks and balance typically deployed to counter unfettered government intervention in the past (Corrales and Penfold 2011); and secondly, PDVSA's social responsibilities expanded in line with the broader ideological warfare of the Chávez government. The company was compelled to perform social goals, notably by directly financing and managing social programmes known as *Misiones Bolivarianas* (Bolivarian Missions). Since 2008, PDVSA's subsidiary, *Producción y Distribución Venezolana de Alimentos* (PDVAL) has run a price-controlled food distribution network. The government also siphoned off other PDVSA revenues to finance Chávez's overseas initiatives in Latin America. PDVSA's spending for these non-core obligations rose from US$14 million in 2002 to nearly US$14 billion by 2007 (Hults 2012, 434).

The Venezuelan state steadily eroded its institutional capabilities—first, due to the negative effects of oil dependence on institutional development, and second, as a result of Chávez's reforms to concentrate decision-making towards executive power—and subsequently, it became highly incapable of responding effectively once the oil boom ended in 2014. Under President Maduro, Venezuela's dwindling oil revenues have been worsened by the persistent underperformance of PDVSA in producing and refining heavy crude oil (Rosales and Sánchez 2021). With the benefit of hindsight, three key factors account for Venezuela's economic performance since the 1970s: declining oil production, waning total factor productivity in non-oil export industries, and the incapacity of the Venezuelan economy to move resources into alternative industries in response to the precipitous decline of oil rents from the 1970s onwards (Hausmann and Rodríguez 2014, 17). Accordingly, oil dependence leads to an inability to develop new exports. The Venezuelan economy is left vulnerable to the volatility of international oil markets. Yet, unlike in the 1970s, the state has very little influence as the power of the oil cartel weakened. With the country's sparce product space, companies struggle to develop capabilities to build alternative export industries, rendering its response to export collapse a complete failure (Hausmann and Rodríguez 2014, 33, 43). In the next section, I discuss the absence of state ownership in Peru as a problem for mineral producers.

Peru: Neoliberalism Without State Ownership

The other extreme response to economic globalization in Latin America was to promote neoliberalism without any kind of state ownership, as the Peruvian example shows. To start with, neoliberalism in Peru took place under a period of economic crisis and instability. Alberto Fujimori (1990–1995) turned towards a neoliberal authoritarian policy regime through the militarization of politics or *autogolpe* (self-coup) (Crabtree 1998; Vergara and Watanabe 2019). By 1990, SOEs were operating with annual losses of US$2.5 billion, which meant that privatizing state assets would simultaneously ease fiscal outflows and alleviate the dire finances of the state. The privatization of about 150 companies yielded a revenue of US$9.2 billion; it also shrunk the public sector share of the GDP back to its 1950 levels (Crabtree and Durand 2017, 80–81). The majority of former SOEs were bought by transnational companies or through joint ventures—indicative of the weakness of domestic capital that has been a feature of the economy from the guano republic until the contemporary era of economic globalization. This stands in contrast with Chile, where domestic capitalists have enjoyed both protection and market power under the Pinochet dictatorship. And crucially, in Chile

256 Business of the State

the privatization of strategic assets like ports, highways, and cemeteries came together with continued state ownership and the expansion of hydrocarbons and mining concessions.

The Peruvian Constitution, enacted in 1993 under Fujimori, guarantees a stable and attractive legal framework to promote private investment, with an emphasis on non-discrimination between domestic and foreign players.[6] By 2012, the Peruvian government had awarded 23 million hectares (about 17% of the country's total land surface) in concessions to mining companies (Crabtree and Durand 2017, 82). Thus, private investment was touted as the engine of growth and the state with limited economic role in industrial development. Most legal and tax stability agreements served as guarantees for private companies so that investment conditions would remain unchanged for 10 years. These agreements cover a wide range of clauses, including the statutes of companies' income taxes, remittances, export promotion regimes (such as drawbacks, or refunds of duties), administrative procedures, and labour hiring regimes in effect at the time of the investment contract (US Department of State 2021).

Apart from privatization, state institutions were overhauled to concentrate decision-making powers in the Ministry of Finance (MEF). Fujimori placed an internationally trained cadre of technocrats in key positions of government whose principal background was working in the private sector and international financial institutions (Crabtree and Durand 2017, 88–90; Wise 2003). But unlike the bureaucratic autonomy of Brazilian technocrats pursuing statist policies, the MEF enjoyed high levels of autonomy, exercising this power to abolish the statist legacy of the Velasco government. Their purpose was to build a new system that was attractive to private companies through taxation policies. They also honoured previous loan obligations to reestablish Peru's reputation as a responsible creditor and a magnet of FDI. Following the Chilean pathway of neoliberalism, Peru also emphasized the significance of trade policy by reducing tariffs, updating commercial procedures for incoming investors, and signing free trade agreements (FTAs). By the time the commodity boom arrived in 2003, Peru was already on its way to strengthen its relationship with the US, culminating in the US–Peru FTA (PTPA), signed into force on 1 February 2009.[7] Between 2010 and 2016, the

---

[6] In addition, three legislations were put in place to consolidate the regulatory framework. These legislative decrees include: 1a) Legislative Decree 662 approves foreign investment legal stability regulations (1993), (2) Legislative Decree 757 approves the private investment growth framework law (1993), and (3) Supreme Decree 162-92-EF (1993) approves private investment guarantee mechanism regulations (US Department of State 2021).

[7] According to the US Department of State, 'The PTPA protects all forms of investment. U.S. investors enjoy the right to establish, acquire, and operate investments in Peru on an equal footing with local investors in almost all circumstances' (US Department of State 2021).

country also signed 13 more FTAs with countries including Chile, China, India, and the EU (Crabtree and Durand 2017b, 92–93).

At the heart of Peru's trade liberalization was the pursuit of rents from natural resource extraction during the commodity boom (2003–2014). While a move to renationalize and reorganize market power in favour of national states took place in many parts of the Southern Cone, Peru instead—like its situation in the 1930s—opted for a commodity export-based growth model embedded in an investment-friendly policy regime. As Figure 9.2 shows, as the share of manufacturing contribution to GDP precipitously declined from 1986 onwards, the share of extractives gradually rose. However, the significance of the waning contribution of manufacturing should not be exaggerated during this time, given that the emphasis on industrialization only occurred under Velasco's military government from 1968 to 1975. The post-Velasco governments, especially under Fujimori, were a return to the extractivist model. Natural resources remain the driver of investments and productive activities in the economy. By 2003, Peruvian development strategy was locked in the natural resource sector.

Peru's commitment to an extractivist, private sector-driven model is most exemplified in the problems faced by the country's biggest SOE, *Petroperú*, in the O&G sector. President Ollanta Humala (2011–2016) appointed Humberto Campodónico as president of NOC Petroperú between August 2011

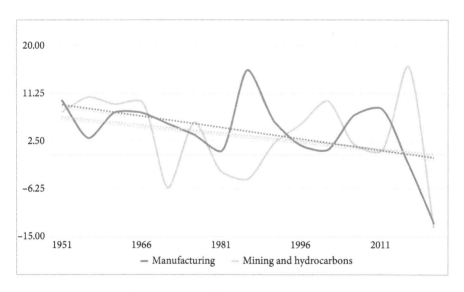

Figure 9.2 Evolution of Peruvian manufacturing and extractive industries—sectoral contribution to GDP as a percentage.

Source: Banco Central de Reserva del Perú (n.d.) (adapted).

and January 2013, with the objective of moving into the lucrative upstream segment of the value chain instead of being relegated to the refineries and downstream sector (Kozak 2011). Campodónico and his Petroperú Board wanted to modernize the Talara refinery by increasing its refining capacity from 65,000 to 95,000 b/d. He also sought to corporatize the company to improve its credit rating and gain access to financial markets. His vision was to transform Petroperú following the SOE model of Colombia's Ecopetrol or Brazil's Petrobras, whereby a mix of public and private incentives guides the company's business strategy (Schipani 2013). However, Campodónico resigned in 2015 after only two years at Petroperú, citing conflicts with government over energy policy as the contract for the most lucrative oil block no. 192 was about to expire. President Humala faced congressional opposition when he controversially sought for an amendment in the law to clarify that Petroperú could only operate after the concessionaire Pacific Exploration and Production had finished its contract in 2017. Instead, Congress passed the bill without changes, citing Petroperú's role in refining, transport, and commercialization of the oil block (Reuters 2015). Humala interpreted this as a bad signal for investment.

These political conflicts surrounding the model of natural resource extraction in Peru reflect the difficulty of challenging the neoliberal extractivist model embedded since the Fujimori era. Campodónico's most important project—the modernization of the Talara refinery to increase the NOC's strategic role for Peru—spanned three presidential governments and was intensively politicized in Congress and among ministries. While the modernization plans were proposed as early as 2007 under President Alan García (2006–2011), it was not until President Humala came to power in 2011 that a legislative project was approved in December 2013, and finally modified in August 2015, to restructure Petroperú and facilitate the refinery project by providing guarantees on its potential loans. However, it likewise barred the company from undertaking any other major investment until the Talara modernization was completed. President Pedro Pablo Kuczynski (2016–2018) made a firm commitment to the significance of the project, and by raising the issue of restructuring the NOC once again (Economist Intelligence Unit 2017), the promotion of the modernization of the Talara refinery throughout the 2010s became the most significant effort to improve SOE participation in the extractive sector. To date, its modernization has been largely financed by a mixture of bonds, external capital, and its own capital (Petroperú 2021).

The core problems of the Peruvian model remain the same—a cycle of political decisions weakening state capacity, which in turn exacerbate redistributive politics, especially when subnational institutions are incapable of managing mineral wealth (Arce 2014; Arellano-Yanguas 2012; Gustafsson and Scurrah 2019; Orihuela 2013). In contrast to Chile's hybrid development strategy, Peru failed to develop a feedback loop in which state ownership could channel some of the mineral wealth revenues back into the mining sector, and to utilize SOEs as a means of building sectoral linkages. Mineral states captured by a dominant private sector cannot break the cycle of institutional weakness and disincentives for high-risk decision-making. Thus, political elites have difficulties in creating mechanisms for structural transformation.

Conclusions

This chapter has examined the significance of state ownership from a comparative perspective. By drawing out the similarities and differences between Brazil and Chile, the book makes an innovative argument in relation to state ownership. Firstly, contrary to previous literature, SOEs did not simply become private entities, and, instead, national states built regulatory frameworks embracing pro-FDI policies and defending SOEs in their strategic sectors. The scholarship arguing SOEs as bad for economic development is subject to empirical debate, and the book thoroughly rejects this argument. Secondly, through a comparison of very different SOEs in Brazil and Chile, the book reclaims the importance of studying historical conditions as a causal variable influencing divergent institutional pathways in achieving neoliberal reforms. While the claim that neoliberalism leads to variegated trajectories of reforms is not entirely new, the emphasis on the process of consolidating power and retaining key features of the old developmental state model in Latin America is novel. To put it differently, states charted their owned pathways of market liberalization based on the idiosyncratic political conditions. Pragmatic states with strong SOEs rejected conformity with the Washington Consensus. After three decades of neoliberal reforms, Brazil and Chile illustrate a hybrid model that considers the delicate balance between market competition and SOE dominance. Thus, neoliberalism may have been a critical juncture for the Southern Cone, but the political agency of states enabled the construction of market-conforming governance models that retain significant elements of the developmental statism.

A second objective of this chapter has been to extend the argument to the regional context of other Latin American states. Unlike arguments on resource nationalism, the success of resource-producing states in maximizing the developmental benefits of their strategic natural resource sectors lies in the capacity of these states to sustain their productivity-enhancing economic agents, namely their SOEs. In Venezuela, despite two oil booms and an export bonanza, the state failed at export diversification. The big-push, oil-financed industrialization model suffered from multiple economic problems and institutional weakness. Under Chávez's socialist strategy, PDVSA experienced chronic government intervention, especially when trying to balance commercial and government interests. By contrast, the lack of any form of state ownership in Peru closed any possibilities for the national state to assert centralized political authority within the mining industry, thereby impacting negatively on its capacity for export diversification. Chapter 10 will close the book by examining the return of the developmental state—its prospects and challenges—outside of Latin America and the future of mineral producers based on the changing geopolitical contexts in the 21st century.

10
The Future of Latin America's Natural Resource States in the 21st Century

If Chile was the cradle of neoliberalism, it will also be its grave.

Gabriel Boric, President-Elect[1]

We want fairer international trade. We want to resume our partnerships with the United States and the European Union on new terms. We are not interested in trade agreements that condemn our country to the eternal role of exporter of commodities and raw materials. Let us re-industrialize Brazil, let us invest in the green and digital technology.

Lula da Silva, President-Elect[2]

While the return of several Leftist political parties in parts of Latin America has led to recollections of the perceived historic success of their rule in the commodity boom years in the 2000s, the challenge of structural transformation for natural-resource-producing states has remained the same. For Gabriel Boric and Lula da Silva, natural resources are recognizably the backbone of their future governance model. Their formidable task is not just to end the creation of sacrifice zones in the extractive frontiers, but more broadly to govern in ways that promote an inclusive, democratically sensitive, and environmentally sustainable governance model. These two leaders came, or in Lula's case returned, to power at distinctive critical junctures in their respective countries. In December 2021 amidst a global COVID-19 pandemic, the Chilean electorate voted Gabriel Boric and his Left-wing coalition *Apruebo Dignidad* as President and ruling coalition. The 35-year-old former student movement leader turned politician beat the Right-wing candidate José Antonio Kast, gaining 55.87% of the electoral vote in the

---

[1] Cambero 2021.
[2] Brasilwire (2022); Maciel (2022).

Business of the State. Jewellord T. Nem Singh, Oxford University Press. © Jewellord T. Nem Singh (2024).
DOI: 10.1093/oso/9780198892212.003.0010

second round. Boric had collaborated in the *Acuerdo por la Paz Social y la Nueva Constitución*, which foreclosed the protests branded as *estallido social*. The movement was the culmination of societal critiques against the Chilean model of neoliberalism. His electoral campaign recognized the demand for a 'common horizon of economic prosperity and the assurance of social rights, [that] there has been a rich and constructive debate on the pace of the reforms'.[3] Boric's economic proposals aimed to address the concentration of wealth and evasion of royalties by large mining companies in Chile, specifically proposing to implement a flexible taxation regime corresponding to price fluctuations, to increase the royalty contribution up to 1% of GDP, and to utilize mineral revenues for Chile's green transition.[4] Crucially, Boric placed local industrial development at the heart of his policy by seeking to promote copper refining and processing in the mining regions of Chile.

On the other side of the continent, Lula was reelected in a very tight election against Jair Bolsonaro, winning only 50.9% of the vote in the second run. Amidst the political divisions plaguing the country, Lula proposes to reclaim an assertive state that not only promotes a new industrial policy under the programme *Nova Industria Brasil*, including the possibility of a new royalty tax on high-value minerals, but also, and crucially, seeks to undo Bolsonaro's legacy of expanding mineral extraction in the Amazon rainforest at the expense of indigenous peoples' land rights (C. Silva 2023). Lula's mining and environmental advisors seek to rationalize investments for energy transition, zero deforestation, and zero carbon emissions (Brasilwire 2022; Venditti 2022). His challenge is not confined to domestic politics, as Brazil faces a new geopolitical context as the country recovers from a decade-long political crisis. China is now Brazil's largest trade partner since 2009, while its Western allies seek new sources of critical minerals for the clean energy transition, and the Latin American continent is looking for new leadership in the face of renewed efforts from Asian and Western powers to reposition the region as a raw material producer in the 21st century.

In this context, this chapter reflects on the lessons from the empirical analysis in the book, in terms of both the theoretical implications of studying state ownership as a development strategy and the practical consequences of the case studies, which emphasize hybrid developmental strategies as a response to the changing external contexts in the world economy. The chapter begins with a critical examination of the advantages of using a theoretical framework which combines historical institutionalism (HI) and state ownership to

---

[3] https://www.servel.cl/wp-content/uploads/2021/06/5_PROGRAMA_GABRIEL_BORIC.pdf.
[4] https://www.servel.cl/wp-content/uploads/2021/06/5_PROGRAMA_GABRIEL_BORIC.pdf.

The Future of Latin America's Natural Resource States in the 21st Century   **263**

analyse the commodity boom during the 2000s. In particular, it draws out the lessons from the most successful developmental state to date: China. Following this discussion, it maps out the importance of state ownership in natural resource governance, particularly in promoting innovation and export diversification. Finally, the book closes by identifying important trends in the 21st century: (1) the consolidation of China as an economic powerhouse and its consequences for mineral exporters; (2) the challenge faced by Latin American states to overcome their historically constituted position in the international economy as suppliers of raw materials to industrialized countries; and (3) the prospects and challenges for mineral states as the clean energy transition increasingly becomes dependent on increasing mineral extraction from the Global South.

Theoretical Contributions

Since the commodity boom of the 2000s (2003–2013), most natural-resource-intensive states in Latin America's Southern Cone have embraced resource nationalism as a globalization strategy, although varying degrees of state ownership were also implemented in the rest of the developing world (Gudynas 2016; Haslam and Heidrich 2016; Jepson 2020; Kaup and Gellert 2017). In Latin American scholarship, 'neoextractivism' was shorthand to the regional response that included an export bonanza alongside a governance model that was principally concerned with the intensive and extensive exploitation of natural resources with some form of redistributive politics to placate societal resistance (Burchardt and Dietz 2014; Gudynas 2016; 2020). To their credit, Left-Centre governments managed the commodity boom well, fuelling a golden age of social welfare in some Latin American countries (Grugel and Riggirozzi 2012; 2018; Petras and Veltmeyer 2009; Philip and Panizza 2011). But like previous cycles of natural resource extraction, rentier politics conditioned both political elites and citizens to become dependent on mineral wealth for the expansion of social and poverty alleviation policies. Myopic decision-making stalled difficult economic reforms from being implemented—mostly done after the price crash that signalled the end of the commodity boom, leading to more concessions for private companies and less developmental space for public agencies. These policies ranged from counter-cyclical measures to cushion the negative effects of price fluctuations, investments in new sectors to create alternative export sectors, and managing resource wealth in a sustainable manner. Even Brazil, historically the regional leader for industrialization, failed to escape resource

264 Business of the State

dependency. By the time the political Right had secured power amidst the crisis, Brazil had embraced its role as producer and provider of soya, iron, and basic commodities to a resource-hungry and rapidly industrializing China—a bilateral relationship that accelerated the capacities of Brazilian companies to salvage their dwindling manufacturing sector (Santoro 2022, Chapters 2 and 3). To briefly conclude, the regional response to the commodity boom was lacklustre in so far as promoting industrialization efforts is concerned.

As discussed in Chapter 2 and demonstrated in the case studies included in this book, HI offers some advantages in analysing the export bonanza and its implications for the political economy of development in Latin America, beyond traditional scholarship that excessively focussed on the rise and fall of the Left and recent emphasis on electoral and parliamentary politics. Both approaches have failed to account for the role of institutional legacies and political conflicts in the state–state (SOE) relationship.

Firstly, the HI perspective provides a powerful analytical lens emphasizing gradual and incremental routes of institutional stability and change as a way of explaining why some things appear to stay the same despite significant waves of political changes across the region. As Brazil and Chile demonstrate, neoliberalism and neodevelopmentalism should not be treated as binary opposites; rather, these governance models are better understood as phases of capitalist modernization across a continuum. Policy innovations are applied by national elites through simultaneous adaptations of market incentives and state regulation to manage natural resource sectors. Returning to Figure 1.5 in the book—which offers an analytical strategy for examining developmental states through the interface of how big the developmental role of the state should be and the extent to which states can seek new industrial strategies away from traditional manufacturing to forge new sectorial bases for development—neoextractivist governance models can be situated within the question of whether development strategies would be based on traditional comparative advantages—natural resources in the case of Latin America—or whether states would be more willing to undertake more risks to find new niches in the technological race in the 21st century.

Secondly, the HI perspective provides answers as to why similar policies lead to divergent outcomes. By identifying institutional continuity and change, the book offers a new understanding in what ways political decisions are constrained by institutional structures and political legacies, thereby leading to radically different pathways. For example, Brazil and Venezuela both embraced an assertive role for the state in promoting a big-push industrial policy based on natural resource revenues. Yet Brazil's SOE policy was far more successful than Venezuela's in guaranteeing freedom of action (SOE

The Future of Latin America's Natural Resource States in the 21st Century   **265**

autonomy) and internationalization. This is partly due to the legacies of the Varguista state in Brazil, in terms of establishing stronger institutional capacity and effective coordination to direct industrial policy. But this is also partially due to the response of the Venezuelan state to rentier politics as the overflow of natural resource wealth constrained political leaders who failed to channel revenues into industrialization in a coherent manner. While both states deployed broadly similar strategies, the specific strategies of Petrobras and PDVSA in developing the oil industry explain the different outcomes. Venezuela's structural conditions, namely high dependence on oil revenues, and the tendency of elites to treat PDVSA as an infinite source of income prevented the SOE from building an autonomous relationship that could support a coherent industrial strategy. With rent-seeking groups competing for access to oil revenues, PDVSA also had to wrestle with various political actors influencing the policy direction in the oil industry. By contrast, Brazil's lack of significant oil reserves meant that multinational oil capital was less interested in the country, which gave Petrobras wider policy latitude to promote energy self-sufficiency and vertical integration of supply chains (Massi and Nem Singh 2020).

Thirdly, the book speaks to debates on neoliberal convergence (Bell 2005; Taylor 2010) and the so-called varieties of capitalism debate (Bruff and Horn 2012; Ebenau 2012; Schmidt 2009),[5] as the sectoral analysis demonstrates the uneven implementation of neoliberal reforms in Latin America. Given the strategic importance of oil and copper for Brazil and Chile, respectively, there were limited efforts to dismantle SOEs and to rely on foreign capital for sectoral development. By contrast, the failure to establish SOEs in Peruvian mining and to promote a developmental role for PDVSA amidst the introduction of market reforms demonstrates the limited institutional capability of Peru and Venezuela. Unsurprisingly, in both countries, neoliberal reforms provoked political contestation and a radical shift away from a developmental role for the state.[6] At its broadest, Left-leaning governments in the region reaffirmed the extractivist model with varying models of political citizenship to socialize natural resource rents and public ownership of the subsoil in a new redistributive political agenda based on the repoliticization of natural

---

[5] Some have extended the varieties of capitalism (VoC) framework and argued that Latin America posits a hierarchical market economy (HME) model, where the relations between companies and other actors are primarily based on orders and directives from those with more economic power, whilst market relations and coordination are less influential mechanisms (Sánchez-Ancochea 2009; Schneider and Soskice 2009).
[6] In Brazil, scholars characterize economic reforms as changing the continuities of a developmentalist state with national industrialization as its core strategy (Bielchowsky 1988; Nunes 1997). By contrast, Taylor (2006) describes neoliberalism in Chile as one marked by power asymmetries and persistent conflicts between states, organized businesses, and labour unions.

266 Business of the State

resource governance and a compensatory state (Gudynas 2020; Jepson 2020; Riofrancos 2020).

Finally, HI offers a political perspective on natural resource dependence that moves away from the deterministic accounts of institutional deterioration and policy failures (discussed in Chapter 2) based on resource curse arguments. Thus far, no systematic discussion exists to explain the corruption uncovered in the *Lava Jato* investigation despite the early successes of institution building in Brazil. Resource curse arguments likewise fail at its most obvious case: why did Venezuela experience sustained democratic regimes and successful economic performance between 1920 and 1970, only to be reversed from the 1980s onwards (Di John 2014; Dunning 2008; Hausmann and Rodríguez 2014)? The HI framework with its attention to institutional dynamics accounts for the temporality of institutional development and the interactions between political choices and structural conditions. While resource endowments undoubtedly shape political choices towards opening ownership structures towards foreign capital or in establishing state enterprises, the political economy scholarship must embrace political science explanations regarding how elites in primary exporting countries choose to take divergent pathways of neoliberal reforms. And, most importantly, the HI framework has the analytical purchase of examining the fit between institutions and industrial strategy, which is important to explain why the pursuit of similar policies ends up with radically opposite developmental outcomes. While natural-resource-producing states seek to industrialize through their natural resource industries, the effectiveness of industrial policy varies depending on the timing of reforms and the overall fit between economic policies and institutional development (Di John 2009; 2014). In other words, political conflicts interact with historical legacies to produce quite distinctive growth strategies and divergent developmental outcomes.

Why State Ownership Matters in the 21st Century

Why did states embrace resource nationalism and state intervention as a globalization strategy during the commodity boom of the 2000s, despite the failures of Latin American developmentalism in the 1970s? The political economy scholarship provides two interesting answers to this question, which point to broader trends in the 21st century. Firstly, within Latin American political economy, the return of the state has been understood in terms of neostructuralism and neodevelopmentalism arguments—both literatures consider how declining political support for the Washington Consensus has

The Future of Latin America's Natural Resource States in the 21st Century 267

produced variegated forms of state–market relations. The commodity boom enabled natural-resource-producing states to gain new fiscal resources to finance new initiatives aimed at structural transformation. Alongside external demands for resource extraction, political consensus over free market orthodoxy began to wane. Thus, societal mobilization against neoliberalism produced varying experiments of state-led growth models aimed at remaking state–market relations and forging a new social contract towards a more inclusive citizenship regime (Kapiszewski et al. 2021; E. Silva and Rossi 2018). Far from converging towards free market orthodoxy, the dynamics of institutional change and stability shaped the responses of the state towards external and internal political economy dynamics. The case studies of Chile and Brazil demonstrate alternative hybrid growth strategies which combine pro-FDI regulatory frameworks and corporate governance reforms within the SOE sector.

Examining the broader contours of the global political economy, scholars have pointed to the 2008 financial crisis in the West as the critical juncture for state capitalism and developmental states (Alami et al. 2022; Nem Singh 2023; Nem Singh and Ovadia 2018). These studies are prefaced by a wider scholarship that probes the rise of China's unique developmental state model and its industrial strategy, which have served as inspiration for the renewal of state activism as a strategy towards globalization and low carbon adaptation (Z. Chen and Chen 2019; L. Chen and Chulu 2022; Jackson et al. 2021; Zhang and Gallagher 2016). Therefore, in an attempt to map out the broader changes in the global political economy, the following section focuses on China as the emerging model of the developmental state in the 21st century. In seeking to understand the Chinese globalization strategy based on 'advance of the state and retreat of the market', the book sets out the next task for political economy scholars—that is, to map out the diversity of developmental states as a response to the challenges in the 21st century.

China: The Developmental State of the 21st Century?

Chinese reforms followed the general principle of efficiency-improving and pursuing institutional change compatible with interests embedded in the political system. While these two principles are widely accepted, deemed simple, and conform with core principles of markets, the specific forms and mechanisms of transitional institutions are far from standard. For Yingqi Qian (2017, 28–31), Chinese reforms followed a dual track approach, whereby on one track economic agents are assigned rights to and obligations

268 Business of the State

for fixed planned prices based on pre-existing plans, and on the other track market prices are introduced so economic agents can participate in new markets. In so doing, economic reform is an explicitly political strategy to implement a reform without losers—maintaining prices under plan track creates compensation for losers from market liberalization while market prices guarantee the creation of rents to be used for innovation and profit-making. Put simply, the dual track strategy is meant to take advantage of existing institutions while facilitating further institutional change.

By the 2020s, it had become clear that the Chinese growth model is centred on large enterprises capable of operating overseas through the Belt and Road Initiative (BRI) project. While there are huge, non-state enterprises in China, especially in technology-intensive sectors, the conspicuous presence of state-backed financing and restructuring of state enterprises adheres to the SOE-based development strategy discussed in this book. If one identifies a critical juncture, it was the 2008 financial crisis that led Chinese policymakers to believe that the Western liberal economic model was not as infallible as one imagined. Importantly, the post-2008 crisis context gave Chinese leadership the confidence to pursue state-directed economic development as an alternative to the Washington Consensus.

Prior to the 2008 financial crisis, China had already pursued a process of state-induced industrial restructuring and sectoral reforms to consolidate state power in strategic sectors. China began to push its central SOEs to undertake a series of high-profile acquisitions of private companies. In the space of about a decade, a new doctrine emerged: 'the advance of the state, retreat of the private sector' (*guojin mintiu*). As documented by various scholars, the advance of state activism in China is more conspicuous in some sectors than others, notably in energy and basic industries—O&G, mining, and technology, to name a few—and this process itself was preceded by the recentralization of state institutions through the formation of the State-Owned Assets Supervision and Administration Commission (SASAC) (Z. Chen and Chen 2019; Eaton 2016).[7] As Hsueh (2011) notes, during the 2000s selective reregulation occurred, whereby the strategic importance of a sector determined whether central SOEs would play a leading role in its restructuring. This, in turn, created the space for private entrepreneurs to flourish in so-called non-priority sectors, in which (Chinese) non-state enterprises are expected to become the dominant force. The precise definition of 'lifeline

---

[7] While SASAC assumed responsibility for several of the largest SOEs under the oversight of the centralized government, there remain significant portions of the state-owned economy managed by regional or local government offices. Beyond finance, the SASAC system excludes the powerful railway and tobacco SOEs (Eaton 2016, 16).

industries' and 'key areas' was open to interpretation. In December 2006, the Chinese State Council released a list of lifeline industries in the press which included the following sectors: defence, power grid, petroleum and petrochemicals, telecommunications, coal, civil aviation, and shipping. In these sectors, central SOEs would have a 'commanding presence' and high administrative barriers to entry would be set up, while national security and strategic economic interests determined the degree to which competition with international companies is allowed (Eaton 2016, 5–6). While mainstream political economists interpreted Chinese market reforms as having conformed with market liberalization, today China's selective liberalization appears to be a deliberate strategy to find its competitive advantage in a world order built around the rules of hegemonic Western powers.

While it is tempting to interpret the advance of the state in China as a smooth and historically determined process, there was far more contingency and uncertainty prior to the consolidation of state activism in 2013. Across different sectors, the centralized state had to contend with pressures from below to induce competition among regions despite creating monopoly sectors, and economic policies were also created in response to the changing external conditions, especially in the context of China's entry into the World Trade Organization (Z. Chen and Chen 2019; Eaton 2016).

The party leadership had exercised immense flexibility to adapt to the rapid changes brought forth by globalization. As Pei (2006, 31) aptly puts it, following the logic of political survival, gradualism—as opposed to a big bang approach—was deemed the most successful strategy to enact market reforms. Through incremental changes, the Chinese state could protect rents in vital sectors, while centralized decision-making provided the party with an upper hand in aligning rent acquisition from booming sectors with the overall state objective of pursuing state-controlled liberalization. While 'low-rent' non-priority sectors like agriculture were liberalized quickly, 'high-rent' or lifeline sectors such as energy and telecommunications were left squarely in the hands of the state. To maintain control, financial reforms were enacted to align with the personal interests of politicized technocrats. These reforms produced centralized banking, absorption of the enormous debts of the state-owned banks, and higher barriers for private actors to enter the financial sector (Shih 2007). To put it simply, regulatory frameworks were gradually aligned with the desire for large, centralized SOEs that would enable Chinese political authority to maintain a very tight control over the process of state transformation. In other words, coalition building and economic reforms complemented the institutional changes conceived by the centralized state (L. Chen and Chulu 2022).

270   Business of the State

What does the centralized system of SOEs in strategic sectors look like in post-2008 China? Hu Angang, an influential scholar based at Tsinghua University, identifies four major characteristics of Chinese SOEs: (1) steady access to China's abundant state capital (*xionghou*) has provided SOEs with leverage to rapidly expand, and this has powered their ascent to the ranks of Fortune 500; (2) contrary to assumptions that non-economic goals are antithetical to development, in China the role of SOEs in supporting the state means that they have served as indispensable tools for stability. This includes embracing their role in national poverty reduction as sources of employment and business opportunities in China's peripheral regions, thereby serving as a mechanism of redistribution to temper excessive inequalities in capital accumulation; (3) SOEs enjoy a political advantage—they are better run than private companies (where decision-making is typically split between managers and owners) because the SOE Party Committee, representing the one-party state, makes vital decisions for these huge companies with one voice; and (4) SOEs have an organizational advantage, which is reflected in more harmonious industrial relations due to the close working relationship between management and labour (cited in Eaton 2016, 112–113).

Additionally, there are two important realities that can help explain the political choice to pursue an SOE-based development strategy. Firstly, the Chinese Communist Party (CCP)'s overarching concern for political survival and necessity for legitimacy, especially after the Tiananmen Square massacre in 1989, led to more pragmatic reforms after 1990. With the collapse of the Soviet Union, Chinese policymakers were acutely aware of the need for gradualism and careful state-crafting as the country slowly established a three-tier system of managed competition. Pearson (2005; 2011) sums up this Chinese growth model neatly: the state maintains an arms-length relationship with less-competitive sectors and gives way for non-state enterprises to become the main players; industrial policy is often employed in the middle layer of the economy consisting of 'pillar industries' such as the automobile sector, which brings both state and non-state actors together while restructuring the sector to bolster the comparative advantages of domestic companies; and the top-level strategic tier of the economy is carefully managed through oligopolistic competition among centralized SOEs. However, under President Xi Jinping (2013–present) this balance between market and state power is gradually shifting in favour of the latter, with uncertainty looming large as regards the future of private enterprise in China. The centralized state under Xi is more concerned with political and security issues, with economic restructuring increasingly shaped by China's BRI project which aims to extend

Chinese influence across the world economy through massive infrastructure, connectivity, and energy sector investments linking both maritime and land-based trade and investment.

China's industrial policy based on centralized SOEs is a clear example of how industrializing economies have adopted and reconfigured the developmental state model to suit their specific political contexts and economic needs. While some of the elements have been retained, notably the presence of SASAC as a coordinating agency and the deployment of state-led finance to mobilize domestic resources for Chinese companies, the role of SOEs in China's growth strategy is more encompassing than the earlier East Asian developmental states. Most importantly, state pragmatism serves as the key principle in economic policymaking.

As part of a state-induced restructuring of strategic sectors to consolidate its market power in the aftermath of the 2008 financial crisis, China's development strategy has been to pursue industrial upgrading—defined as 'the process by which economic actors move from relatively low-value to relatively high-value activities in global production networks' (Gereffi 2005, 171)—through the deployment of strong state control mechanisms in carefully identified strategic industries, and a movement away from primary products towards high-technology manufacturing. Therefore Chinese manufactured exports are more important than natural-resource-based products, and in terms of manufacturing, high- and medium-technology exports have slowly displaced low-technology goods (Gereffi 2018, 212–219).

In the metal mining industry, Chinese market power became apparent through its emphasis on supply chain integration. As part of its upgrading strategy, China made significant investments in the supply chain of processed minerals and value-added commodities through in-country processing activities. Such industrial strategy defies conventional theories on the resource curse and offers evidence on the success of 'linkages' policy between mineral extraction and manufacturing. Let us take the case of iron ore—a traditional export of Brazil (see Figure 10.1). As China increased iron ore imports from 70 million metric tons (or 14.4% of global imports) in 2000 to 932 million metric tons in 2015 (or 68.4% of global imports) (ECLAC 2016, 81), the country also became the biggest producer of processed iron ore, surpassing its main sources of raw iron—Brazil and Australia. In aluminium manufacturing, China's exports increased its market share from 5.4% in 2004 to 13.4% in 2014, overtaking Germany as the key exporter of processed aluminium, with the industrialized Asian countries as its principal destination (49.2%), followed by the EU (14.3%) and US (12.7%). Such pattern of growing control over the supply chain of minerals beyond the upstream segment is replicated

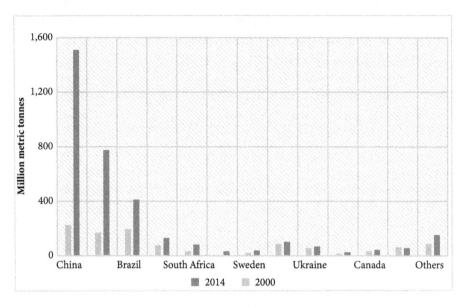

Figure 10.1 Key iron ore producers in the world, 2000 and 2014.
Source: ECLAC (2016, 85) in Nem Singh (2019).

across many commodities, notably copper, bauxite, and, recently, lithium, cobalt, and REEs.

In the context of the clean energy transition, Chinese overseas acquisitions of critical minerals like lithium, cobalt, and nickel, alongside control over processing technology have produced geopolitical anxiety among Western countries—a result of not only unprecedented strategic control over resource markets but also growing distrust of China's commitment to economic globalization. Tightening natural resource markets combined with global decarbonization efforts has yielded soaring demands for critical metals worldwide. At the same time, the pace of China's assertive industrial policy has meant a growing concentration of market power towards the downstream segment of the supply chain of clean energy technologies. While Chinese market power is deemed a threat to national security and raises uncertainty over the clean energy transition, China's strategic grip on essential commodities needed to produce electric vehicles, wind turbines, and solar panels also demonstrates the possibilities for mineral states to take advantage of the new commodity boom (Nem Singh 2021).

Overall, the outcome of China's developmental state model—sometimes referred to as *state capitalism*—is undeniable: China has become the second most economically dynamic country in the world. Through strategic industrial policy, China has returned to the world as a global political and economic powerhouse (Naughton 2021; Nolan 2001; Tsai and Naughton 2015). Between 1980 and 2015, China's real GDP grew by an average of 9.6% annually and its GDP per capita soared from US$200 to US$8,000 (Huang 2016, 315). As a result, China's return in the world stage has invariably produced new patterns of global and regional trade, finance, and investment. Yet the muscular power of the Chinese state, apart from demonstrating new possibilities for state-led development, has also shown its dark side. Given the high levels of resource dependency of Latin American states for mineral revenues, China's policy towards establishing resource control through vertical integration of supply chains may be constraining the developmental space for the region.

Implications of China's Developmental State for Latin America

China's growing economic power has consequences for the trade relationship between China and Latin America—a relationship increasingly premised on Chinese continuous economic growth, rather than on mutual interdependence. China's investment and finance in the region are principally concentrated in mining and energy resources. In 2017, China purchased about 1/5 of all extractive exports from the region, with natural resource exports constituting more than 50% of Latin America and the Caribbean (LAC) exports to China (Ray and Gallagher 2017, 1). Although the China boom cooled off at the end of the commodities super-cycle in 2013, Latin America has retained its relationship with the new economic superpower across trade, investment, and finance.

That Chinese demand for primary materials is consequential for Latin American developmental strategy is now indisputable, and given the concentration of Chinese trade and investments in the energy and mining sectors, export diversification in Latin America will remain a formidable challenge. Since the end of the commodity cycle in 2013, Latin American countries have already begun to suffer from deindustrialization due to their commodity specialization, and those states considered as regional manufacturing powerhouses—Argentina, Brazil, and Mexico—have not displayed resilience amidst Chinese competition. At the other extreme, traditional mineral states of the 19th and 20th centuries—Bolivia, Ecuador, Chile, and Venezuela—have further embedded their economies and development strategies in natural resource extraction (Bernal-Meza and Xing 2020; Jenkins 2018). Alongside voluntarily embracing primary export strategies, the commodity boom has driven Latin America to abandon grand strategies of industrialization premised on the revitalization of their manufacturing and agricultural capabilities. And, as the price boom eclipsed in 2013, except for Chile, Latin American economies experienced sharp declines in fiscal income, and even multiple political crises (Castillo and Martins 2016; Jenkins 2015).

Conclusion: Latin America in the Era of Strategic Competition

Without any clear prospects for reindustrialization, the future of Latin American development in the 21st century clearly rests on how effectively governments manage their natural resources, for both export diversification and reinvestment in potentially dynamic sectors. The first step in crafting a new development strategy, however, requires deep reflections on the failure of the Latin American strategies of the past. As a starting point, it is no coincidence that as East Asia became the most dynamic region in the world economy by the end of the 20th century, Latin America suffered from unsustainable debt, erratic growth rates, and incoherent industrial planning. This book has shown that the initial conditions in Latin America—its dependency on natural resources—are an important historical constraint that democratic and authoritarian governments failed to overcome. By contrast, East Asia's export-oriented industrialization (EOI) was premised on economic growth as the primary source of legitimacy for governance, and its various routes towards labour-intensive manufacturing were crafted in response to systemic vulnerability (Doner et al. 2021; 2005).

This book aims to push this argument further. As Gereffi (2018, 45–47) points out, development strategies during the 20th century were particular responses to the problems faced by developing countries as they moved from notions of national autonomous development towards global market integration as the overarching logic of state action. He identifies two commodity chains that come together with a corresponding strategy: (1) *producer-driven commodity chains*, which refer to industries in which transnational corporations and large, integrated industrial enterprises control the production system—including backward, forward, and fiscal linkages—and are therefore characterized as capital- and technology-intensive sectors like automobiles, computers, aircraft, mining, O&G, and electric machinery; and (2) *buyer-driven commodity chains*, which refer to industries in which large retailers, brand-named merchandisers, and trading

The Future of Latin America's Natural Resource States in the 21st Century   **275**

companies play a central role in establishing decentralized production networks in several developing countries. Trade-led industrialization became common in labour-intensive, consumer-goods-oriented industries covering garments, footwear, consumer electronics, toys, houseware goods, and a variety of hand-crafted items. Drawing from Gereffi's approaches towards supply chain governance, peripheral states, according to their domestic markets and industrial organizational structures, responded to opportunities and constraints. The first group of countries include large resource-rich economies in Latin America—Argentina, Brazil, and Mexico—alongside South Asia (e.g. India and Bangladesh), and Eastern Europe, which pursued some form of ISI in order to develop their own industrial production facilities, taking advantage of their huge domestic markets. The second group of countries include resource-poor regions of East Asia, which switched from ISI towards EOI to stimulate the rapid growth of export markets (Gereffi 2018, 47–49; Gereffi and Wyman 1990). Taking these two strategies as historical evidence of successful industrialization, the Latin American approach was clearly inferior compared to the East Asian EOI model.

As empirical analysis in this book demonstrates, natural resource dependency was not the only reason for such failure. But, if Latin America's developmental malaise is somewhat connected to its natural resource sector, then Latin American policymakers cannot simply ignore the dual challenge of resource governance and industrialization. This is particularly salient for Brazil, which is now positioning itself as a global energy player by maximizing the potential of pre-salt production in the context of a world retreating from fossil fuel dependency and pushing for decarbonization. As Petrobras Director of Exploration and Production Joelson Falção Mendes argues, 'there is no contradiction between retaining fossil fuels as part of national energy policy and pursuing alternative cleaner energy sources ... given that oil will still occupy an important place in Brazilian energy matrix alongside renewables' (Pooler 2023).

To this extent, the book has offered a valuable answer in the effective crafting of regulatory frameworks and corporate governance reforms in favour of state ownership in strategic industries. China's strategy of increasing state assertiveness already demonstrates one possibility for undertaking complex economic transition in response to economic globalization. While there exists no blueprint for successful industrialization, comparative and historical evidence already show the need for policymakers to rethink their policy design choices to respond to supply chain dominance and the ensuing technological race especially among industrialized countries. We are, in other words, entering an era of new strategic competition. Latin American states, and developing countries more widely, must begin to recalibrate their developmental strategies to align with these new political realities.

In the new context of clean energy transition, the pathway of China in the critical minerals sector is worth returning to as an example of structural transformation based on natural resources. For almost three decades, China made concerted efforts to develop new separation and refining technologies, thereby increasing its control over the processing of mineral ores (Kalantzakos 2018; Klinger 2017). Today, metal ores like lithium, iron, and REEs are transported all over the world back to China in order to be processed and then used as inputs for technology-intensive end products. Through state ownership, there appears to be an opportunity for sectoral linkages-based policies between mining and the productive economy to generate high-value-added activities, alleviating some of the negative consequences of the resource curse effects. While it is now widely acknowledged that the extractivist model cannot deliver inclusive growth for Latin America, future research needs to pay attention to the question of promoting sectoral linkages and building new technological niches. The modest contributions of this book are to show how Petrobras and Codelco managed to facilitate effective resource governance and, in the future, what types of public policy efforts are needed to promote export diversification and inclusive development.

By offering a historically sensitive account of state activism in Latin America, this book has showcased important lessons for natural-resource-producing states outside the region. Through an examination of industrial strategies in strategic sectors in Chile (mining) and Brazil (O&G) in the 20th and 21st centuries, the book also makes a vital contribution to challenge the general prejudice against state ownership as part of national globalization strategies. Moving forward, this book has shown that state ownership is likely to remain: national elites will seek to reform SOEs and not privatize their assets, for natural resource sovereignty runs deep in the hearts of Latin American citizens. The challenge in the 21st century is how to make natural resource governance models more effective, inclusive, and, to a limited extent, more democratic when the challenge is greater than domestic politics. The rise of China is a critical juncture, not only in terms of showing the relevance of developmental states as a governance model today, but also because China's state power likewise presents new constraints for Latin America and the developing world. This book invites younger scholars to rethink the value of natural resources in development, but perhaps more importantly, it sets out a new pathway for scholarship to consider the exercise of state agency as a vital response to economic globalization amidst new challenges in the second quarter of the 21st century.

References

ABENAV. 2016. 'Dados do Setor. Brasilia'. Rio de Janeiro: Associação Brasileira das Empresas de Construção Naval e Offshore (ABENAV) (Brazilian Association of Shipbuilding and Offshore Companies).

Afonso, José Roberto, and Bernardo Guelber Fajardo. 2015. 'Evolução da Taxa de Investimentos e a Indução Pelo Setor Público'. Proceedings of Conference, Nota Técnica IBRE/FGV, Rio de Janeiro, 1 April.

Aiginger, Karl, and Dani Rodrik. 2020. 'Rebirth of Industrial Policy and an Agenda for the Twenty-First Century'. *Journal of Industry, Competition and Trade* 20 (2): 189–207.

Alami, Ilias, Milan Babic, Adam D. Dixon, and Imogen T. Liu. 2022. 'Special Issue Introduction: What Is the New State Capitalism?' *Contemporary Politics* 28 (3): 245–263.

Almeida, Maria Hermínia Tavares de. 1996. *Crise Econômica e Interesses Organizados*. São Paulo: Edusp/Fapesp.

Almeida, Maria Hermínia Tavares de, and Maurício Moya. 1997. 'A Reforma Negociada: O Congresso e a Política de Privatização'. *Revista Brasileira de Ciências Sociais* 12 (34): 119–132.

Altson, Lee J., Marcus Andres Melo, Bernado Mueller, and Carlos Pereira. 2016. *Brazil in Transition: Beliefs, Leadership and Institutional Change*. Princeton Economic History of the Western World series. Princeton: Princeton University Press.

Amann, Edmund, and Werner Baer. 2009. 'The Macroeconomic Record of the Lula Administration, the Roots of Brazil's Inequality, and Attempts to Overcome Them'. In *Brazil Under Lula: Economy, Politics and Society Under the Worker-President*, edited by Joseph Love and Werner Baer, 27–43. Basingstoke: Palgrave Macmillan.

Amatori, Franco, Robert Millward, and Pier Angelo Toninelli, eds. 2018. *Reappraising State-Owned Enterprise a Comparison of the UK and Italy*. London: Routledge.

Ambe-Uva, Terhemba. 2017. 'Whither the State? Mining Codes and Mineral Resource Governance in Africa'. *Canadian Journal of African Studies/Revue Canadienne Des Études Africaines* 51 (1): 81–101.

Amengual, Matthew. 2016. *Politicized Enforcement in Argentina: Labor and Environmental Regulation*. Cambridge: Cambridge University Press.

Ames, Barry. 1995. 'Electoral Rules, Constituency Pressures, and Pork Barrel: Bases of Voting in the Brazilian Congress'. *Journal of Politics* 57 (2): 324–343.

Ames, Barry. 2001. *The Deadlock of Democracy in Brazil*. Ann Arbor: University of Michigan Press.

Amsden, Alice. 1992. *Asia's Next Giant: South Korea and Late Industrialization*. New York: Oxford University Press.

Amsden, Alice. 2001. *The Rise of 'The Rest': Challenges to the West from Late-Industrializing Economies*. New York: Oxford University Press.

Amsden, Alice. 2007. *Escape from Empire: The Developing World's Journey Through Heaven and Hell*. Cambridge, MA: MIT Press.

Andreucci, Diego. 2016. 'Governing Extraction: Regulation, the State and Social Struggles Over Minerals and Hydrocarbons in Bolivia'. PhD dissertation. Barcelona: Autonomous University of Barcelona.

278   References

Andrews-Lee, Caitlin. 2021. *The Emergence and Revival of Charismatic Movements: Argentine Peronism and Venezuelan Chavismo*. Cambridge: Cambridge University Press.

Ang, Yuen Yuen. 2020. *China's Gilded Age: The Paradox of Economic Boom and Vast Corruption*. Cambridge: Cambridge University Press.

ANP. 2010. *Anuário Estatístico Brasileiro Do Petróleo, Gás Natural e Biocombustíveis: 2010*. Rio de Janeiro: Agencia Nacional do Petróleo, Gás Natural e Biocombustíveis.

ANP. 2011. *Anuário Estatístico Brasileiro Do Petróleo, Gás Natural e Biocombustíveis: 2011*. Rio de Janeiro: Agencia Nacional do Petróleo, Gás Natural e Biocombustíveis.

ANP. 2018. *Anuário Estatístico Brasileiro Do Petróleo, Gás Natural e Biocombustíveis: 2018*. Rio de Janeiro: Agencia Nacional do Petróleo, Gás Natural e Biocombustíveis.

ANP. 2019. *Anuário Estatístico Brasileiro Do Petróleo, Gás Natural e Biocombustíveis: 2019*. Rio de Janeiro: Agencia Nacional do Petróleo, Gás Natural e Biocombustíveis.

ANP. 2022 *Mapa de Exploração e Produção de Petróleo e Gás Bacia de Campos e Santos Pologono de Pré-sal*. Rio de Janeiro: Agencia Nacional do Petróleo, Gás Natural e Biocombustíveis.

Antunes, Ricardo, Marco Aurelio Santana, and Luci Praun. 2019. 'Chronicle of a Defeat Foretold: The PT Administrations from Compromise to the Coup'. Translated by Daniela Issa. *Latin American Perspectives* 224 (46): 85–104.

Araujo, Fernando, Paulo Roberto Dalcol, and Waldimir Pirró e Longo. 2011. 'A Diagnosis of Brazilian Shipbuilding Industry on the Basis of Methodology for an Analysis of Sectorial Systems of Innovation'. *Journal of Technology Management & Innovation* 6 (4): 151–171.

Arce, Moisés. 2014. *Resource Extraction and Protest in Peru*. Pittsburgh: University of Pittsburgh Press.

Arellano-Yanguas, Javier. 2012. 'Mining and Conflict in Peru: Sowing the Minerals, Reaping a Hail of Stones'. In *Social Conflict, Economic Development and Extractive Industry: Evidence from South America*, edited by Anthony Bebbington, 89–111. London: Routledge.

Armijo, Leslie Elliott, and Sybil D. Rhodes. 2017. 'Explaining Infrastructure Underperformance in Brazil: Cash, Political Institutions, Corruption, and Policy Gestalts'. *Policy Studies* 38 (3): 231–247.

Arsel, Murat, Barbara Hogenboom, and Lorenzo Pellegrino. 2016. 'The Extractive Imperative in Latin America'. *The Extractive Industries and Society* 3 (4): 880–886.

Artestis, Philip, and Alfredo Saad-Filho, eds. 2007. *Political Economy of Brazil: Recent Economic Performance*. London: Palgrave Macmillan.

Arthur, W. Brian. 1989. 'Competing Technologies, Increasing Returns, and Lock-In by Historical Events'. *The Economic Journal* 99 (394): 116–131.

Atienza, Miguel, Marcelo Lufin, and Juan Soto. 2018. 'Mining Linkages in the Chilean Copper Supply Network and Regional Economic Development'. Resources Policy 70 (101154), March.

Atkinson, Anthony B., and Joseph E. Stiglitz. 2015. *Lectures on Public Economics: Updated Edition*. Princeton: Princeton University Press.

Auty, Richard M. 1993. *Sustaining Development in Mineral Economies: The Resource Curse Thesis*. London: Routledge.

Auty, Richard M., ed. 2001. *Resource Abundance and Economic Development*. Oxford: Oxford University Press.

Auty, Richard M., and Alan G. Gelb. 2001. 'Political Economy of Resource Abundant States'. In *Resource Abundance and Economic Development*, edited by Richard M. Auty, 126–144. Oxford: Oxford University Press.

Azmeh, Shamel, and Khalid Nadvi. 2014. 'Asian Firms and the Restructuring of Global Value Chains'. *International Business Review* 23 (4): 708–717.

References 279

Baena, Cesar E. 1999. *The Policy Process in a Petro-State: An Analysis of PDVSA's (Petróleos de Venezuela SA's) Internationalisation Strategy*. London: Routledge.

Baer, Werner. 2008. *Brazilian Economy: Growth and Development*. 7th ed. Boulder: Lynne Rienner Publishers.

Bajpai, Rajni, and Bernard Myers. 2020. *Enhancing Government Effectiveness and Transparency: The Fight Against Corruption*. Washington, DC: World Bank.

Ballinger, Benjamin, Diego Schmeda-Lopez, Benjamin Kefford, Brett Parkinson, Martin Stringer, Chris Greig, and Simon Smart. 2020. 'The Vulnerability of Electric-Vehicle and Wind-Turbine Supply Chains to the Supply of Rare-Earth Elements in a 2-Degree Scenario'. *Sustainable Production and Consumption* 22 (April): 68–76.

Ban, Cornel. 2013. 'Brazil's Liberal Neo-Developmentalism: New Paradigm or Edited Orthodoxy?' *Review of International Political Economy* 20 (2): 298–331.

Banco Central de Reserva de Perú. n.d. *PBI Minería Metálica e Hidrocarburos*. Lima: Banco Central de Reserva de Peru.

Bande, Jorge. 2011. 'CODELCO's New Corporate Governance: 18 Months After'. Presentation to the 2011 Meeting of the Latin American Network of Corporate Governance of State-Owned Enterprises, Bogotá, Colombia, 8–9 September.

Baptista, Asdrúbal, and Bernard Mommer. 1987. *El Petróleo en el Pensamiento Económico Venezolano: Un Ensayo*. Caracas: Ediciones IESA.

Barandiarán, Javiera. 2019. 'Lithium and Development Imaginaries in Chile, Argentina and Bolivia'. *World Development* 113 (January): 381–391.

Barbier, Edward B. 2012. 'Scarcity, Frontiers and Development'. *The Geographical Journal* 178 (2): 110–122.

Barham, Bradford, Stephen Bunker, and Denis O'Hearn, eds. 1994. *States, Firms and Raw Materials: The World Economy and Ecology of Aluminum*. Wisconsin: University of Wisconsin Press.

Barma, Naazneen, Kai Kaiser, Tuan Minh Le, and Lorena Viñuela. 2011. *Rents to Riches?* Washington, DC: World Bank.

Barómetros Cerc. 2011. 'Mayo–Junio. Barómetro de la Politica'.

Barrera, Manuel. 1981. *Worker Participation in Company Management in Chile: A Historical Experience*. Geneva: UNRISD Publications.

Barton, Jonathan R. 2002. 'State "Continuismo" and "Pinochetismo:" The Keys to the Chilean Transition'. *Bulletin of Latin American Research* 21 (3): 358–374.

Barzel, Yoram. 1997. *Economic Analysis of Property Rights (Political Economy of Institutions and Decisions)*. 2nd ed. Cambridge: Cambridge University Press.

Bebbington, Anthony, and Jeffrey Bury. 2013. *Subterranean Struggles: New Dynamics of Mining, Oil, and Gas in Latin America*. Austin: University of Texas Press.

Bebbington, Anthony, Leonith Hinojosa, Denise Humphreys Bebbington, Maria Luisa Burneo, and Ximena Warnaars. 2008. 'Contention and Ambiguity: Mining and the Possibilities of Development'. *Development and Change* 39 (6): 887–914.

Bebbington, Anthony, Abdul-Gafaru Abdulai, Denise Humphreys Bebbington, Marja Hinfelaar, and Cynthia Sanborn. 2018. *Governing Extractive Industries: Politics, Histories, Ideas*. Oxford: Oxford University Press.

Beblawi, Hazem. 1990. 'The Rentier State in the Arab World'. In *The Arab State*, edited by Giocamo Luciani, 85–98. London: Routledge.

Beblawi, Hazem, and Giacomo Luciani, eds. 1987. *The Rentier State*. London: Routledge.

Behuria, Pritesh. 2019. 'Twenty-First Century Industrial Policy in a Small Developing Country: The Challenges of Reviving Manufacturing in Rwanda'. *Development and Change* 50 (4), 1033–1062.

280 References

Behuria, Pritesh. 2020. 'The Domestic Political Economy of Upgrading in Global Value Chains: How Politics Shapes Pathways for Upgrading in Rwanda's Coffee Sector'. *Review of International Political Economy* 27 (2): 348–376.

Bell, Stephen. 2005. 'How Tight Are the Policy Constraints? The Policy Convergence Thesis, Institutionally Situated Actors and Expansionary Monetary Policy in Australia'. *New Political Economy* 10 (1): 65–89.

Bergquit, Charles. 1986. *Labour in Latin America: Comparative Essays on Chile, Argentina, Venezuela and Colombia*. Stanford: Stanford University Press.

Bernal-Meza, Raúl, and Li Xing. 2020. *China–Latin America Relations in the 21st Century: The Dual Complexities of Opportunities and Challenges*. International Political Economy Series. Cham: Springer Nature.

Berrios, Ruben, Andrae Marak, and Scott Morgenstern. 2011. 'Explaining Hydrocarbon Nationalization in Latin America: Economics and Political Ideology'. *Review of International Political Economy* 18 (5): 673–697. https://doi.org/10.1080/09692290.2010.493733

Bian, Morris L. 2005. *The Making of the State Enterprise System in Modern China: The Dynamics of Institutional Change*. Cambridge, MA: Harvard University Press.

Bielchowsky, Ricardo. 1988. *Pensamento Econômico Brasileiro. O Ciclo Ideológico do Desenvolvimentismo*. Rio de Janeiro: IPEA/INPES.

Bloch, Harry, and David Sapsford. 1997. 'Some Estimates of Prebisch and Singer Effects on the Terms of Trade Between Primary Producers and Manufacturers'. *World Development* 25 (11): 1873–1884.

BNDES. 2012. *Perspectivas de Investimento na Indústria: 2012–2015. 100. Visão do Desenvolvimento*. Brasília: Brazilian Development Bank (BNDES).

Brasilwire. 2022. 'Lula's Victory Speech, 30/10/2022'. *Brasilwire* 1 November.

Braun-Llona, Juan, Matías Braun-Llona, Ignacio Briones, José Díaz, Rolf Lüders, and Gert Wagner. 2000 'Economía Chilena 1880–1995. Estadísticas Históricas'. Documento de Trabajo 187. Santiago: Instituto de Economía Pontifica Universidad Católica de Chile.

Bräutigam, D. 2002. 'Building Leviathan: Revenue, State Capacity, and Governance'. *IDS Bulletin* 33: 1–17.

Bräutigam, Deborah, Odd-Helge Fjeldstad, and Mick Moore. 2008. *Taxation and State-Building in Developing Countries: Capacity and Consent*. Cambridge: Cambridge University Press. https://doi.org/10.1017/CBO9780511490897

Bresser-Perreira, Luiz Carlos. 2006. 'O Novo Desenvolvimentismo e a Ortodoxia Convencional'. *São Paulo em Perspectiva* 20 (3): 5–24.

Brewer-Carías, Allan R. 2021. *Estudios Sobre Petróleos de Venezuela S.A. (PDVSA) y la Industria Petrolera Nacionalizada. 1974–2021*. Caracas: Editorial Jurídica Venezolana.

Breznitz, Dan. 2007. *Innovation and the State: Political Choice and Strategies for Growth in Israel, Taiwan and Ireland*. New Haven: Yale University Press.

Bridgman, Benjamin, Victor Gomes, and Arilton Teixeira. 2008. 'The Threat of Competition Enhances Productivity'. Meeting Papers 302. Society for Economic Dynamics, http://www.economicdynamics.org/meetpapers/2008/paper_302.pdf.

Bril-Mascarenhas, Tomás, and Aldo Madariaga. 2019. 'Business Power and the Minimal State: The Defeat of Industrial Policy in Chile'. *Journal of Development Studies* 55 (6): 1047–1066.

Bril-Mascarenhas, Tomás, and Antoine Maillet. 2019. 'How to Build and Wield Business Power: The Political Economy of Pension Regulation in Chile, 1990–2018'. *Latin American Politics and Society* 61 (1): 101–125.

Brinks, Daniel M., Steven Levitsky, and Maria Victoria Murillo. 2020. *The Politics of Institutional Weakness in Latin America*. New York: Cambridge University Press.

Brooks, Sarah M. 2004. 'Explaining Capital Account Liberalization in Latin America: A Transitional Cost Approach'. *World Politics* 56 (3): 389–430.

Brooks, Sarah M. 2015. 'Social Protection for the Poorest: The Adoption of Antipoverty Cash Transfer Programs in the Global South'. *Politics & Society* 43 (4): 551–582.

Brooks, Sarah M., and Marcus J. Kurtz. 2007. 'Capital, Trade, and the Political Economies of Reform'. *American Journal of Political Science* 51 (4): 703–720.

Brooks, Sarah M., and Marcus J. Kurtz. 2012. 'Paths to Financial Policy Diffusion: Statist Legacies in Latin America's Globalization'. *International Organization* 66 (1): 95–128.

Brooks, Sarah M., and Marcus J. Kurtz. 2016. 'Oil and Democracy: Endogenous Natural Resources and the Political "Resource Curse"'. *International Organization* 70 (2): 279–311.

Brooks, Sarah M., and Marcus J. Kurtz 2016. 'Natural Resources and Economic Development in Brazil'. In *New Order and Progress: Development and Democracy in Brazil*, edited by Ben Ross Schneider. Oxford Academic.

Brownlee, Jason. 2007. *Authoritarianism in an Age of Democratisation*. Cambridge: Cambridge University Press.

Bruff, Ian, and Laura Horn. 2012. 'Varieties of Capitalism in Crisis?' *Competition and Change* 16 (3): 161–168.

Bruton, Garry D., Igor Filatotchev, Steven Si, and Mike Wright. 2013. 'Entrepreneurship and Strategy in Emerging Economies'. *Strategic Entrepreneurship Journal* 7 (3): 169–180.

Bruton, Garry D., Mike W. Peng, David Ahlstrom, Ciprian Stan, and Kehan Xu. 2014. 'State-Owned Enterprises Around the World as Hybrid Organizations'. *Academy of Management Perspectives* 29 (1): 92–114.

Buchanan, James M. 1980. 'Rent Seeking and Profit Seeking'. In *Toward a Theory of the Rent-Seeking Society*, edited by James M. Buchanan, Robert D. Tollison, and Gordon Tullock, 3–15. College Station: Texas A&M University Press.

Bulfone, Fabio. 2022. 'Industrial Policy and Comparative Political Economy: A Literature Review and Research Agenda'. *Competition & Change* 27 (1): 22–43.

Bulmer-Thomas, Victor. 2014. The Economic History of Latin America Since Independence. 3rd ed. Cambridge Latin American Studies. Cambridge: Cambridge University Press.

Bunker, Stephen, and Paul Ciccantell. 2003. 'Generative Sectors and the New Historical Materialism: Economic Ascent and the Cumulatively Sequential Restructuring of the World Economy'. *Studies in Comparative International Development* 37 (4): 3–30.

Bunker, Stephen G. 1984. 'Modes of Extraction, Unequal Exchange, and the Progressive Underdevelopment of an Extreme Periphery: The Brazilian Amazon, 1600–1980'. American Journal of Sociology 89 (5 March). https://doi.org/10.1086/227983

Bunker, Stephen G. 1988. *Underdeveloping the Amazon: Extraction, Unequal Exchange, and the Failure of the Modern State*. Chicago: The University of Chicago Press.

Bunker, Stephen G. 1996. 'Raw Material and the Global Economy: Oversights and Distortions in Industrial Ecology'. *Society & Natural Resources* 9 (4): 419–429. https://doi.org/10.1080/08941929609380984

Bunker, Stephen, and Paul Ciccantell. 2005. *Globalization and the Race for Resources*. Baltimore: see Johns Hopkins University Press.

Burchardt, Hans-Jürgen, and Kristina Dietz. 2014. '(Neo-)Extractivism—A New Challenge for Development Theory from Latin America'. *Third World Quarterly* 35 (3): 468–486.

Cai, Kevin G. 2018. 'The One Belt One Road and the Asian Infrastructure Investment Bank: Beijing's New Strategy of Geoeconomics and Geopolitics'. *Journal of Contemporary China* 27 (114): 831–847.

Cambero, Fabian. 2021. 'Former Protest Leader Boric Seeks to Bury Chile's "Neoliberal" Past'. *Reuters* 17 November.

Campbell, Bonnie. 2009. *Mining in Africa: Regulation and Development*. London: Pluto Press.

282 References

Campbell, John L. 2001. 'Institutional Analysis and the Role of Ideas in Political Economy'. In *The Rise of Neoliberalism and Institutional Analysis*, edited by John L. Campbell and Ove K. Pedersen, 159–190. Princeton: Princeton University Press.

Capoccia, Giovanni, and R. Daniel Kelemen. 2007. 'The Study of Critical Junctures: Theory, Narrative, and Counterfactuals in Historical Institutionalism'. *World Politics* 59 (3): 341–369.

Cardoso, Fernando Henrique, and Enzo Faletto. 1979. *Dependency and Development in Latin America*. Berkeley: University of California Press.

Carvalho, José Murilo. 1996. *Teatro de Sombras—A Política Imperial*. Rio de Janeiro: Editora UFRJ/Relume Dumará.

Carvalho, Laura and Rugitsky, Fernando. 2015. 'Growth and distribution in Brazil in the 21st century: revisiting the wage-led versus profit-led debate'. Department of Economics FEA/USP Working Paper Series, n. 2015-2025.

Cashin, Paul, C. John McDermott, and Alasdair Scott. 2002. 'Booms and Slumps in World Commodity Prices'. *Journal of Development Economics* 69 (1): 277–296.

Castillo, Mario, and Antonio Martins Neto. 2016. *Premature Deindustrialization in Latin America*. Production Development Series. Santiago: Economic Commission for Latin America and the Caribbean (ECLAC).

Castro, Armando, and Shaz Ansari. 2017. 'Contextual "Readiness" for Institutional Work. A Study of the Fight Against Corruption in Brazil'. *Journal of Management Inquiry* 26 (4): 351–365.

Cavarozzi, Marcelo 1992. 'Patterns of Elite Negotiation and Confrontation in Argentina and Chile'. In *Elites and Democratic Consolidation in Latin America and Southern Europe*, edited by John Higley and Richard Gunther, 208–236. New York: Cambridge University Press.

Chaudhry, Kiren Aziz. 1997. *The Price of Wealth: Economies and Institutions in the Middle East*. Cornell Studies in Political Economy. Ithaca: Cornell University Press.

Chen, Ling, and Buhe Chulu. 2022. 'Complementary Institutions of Industrial Policy: A Quasi-Market Role of Government Inspired by the Evolutionary China Model'. *Third World Quarterly* 44 (9): 1981–1996.

Chen, Zhiting, and Geoffrey C. Chen. 2019. 'The Changing Political Economy of Central State-Owned Oil Companies in China'. *The Pacific Review* 34 (3): 379–404.

Cherif, Reda, and Fuad Hasanov. 2019. 'The Return of the Policy That Shall Not Be Named: Principles of Industrial Policy'. WP/19/74. IMF Working Paper. Washington, DC: International Monetary Fund.

Chimhowu, Admos O., David Hulme, and Lauchlan T. Munro. 2019. 'The "New" National Development Planning and Global Development Goals: Processes and Partnerships'. *World Development* 120 (August): 76–89.

Clapham, Christopher. 2018. 'The Ethiopian Developmental State'. *Third World Quarterly* 39 (6): 1151–1165.

Cochilco. 2009. *Cochilco Anuario 2009*. Santiago: Comisión Chilena del Cobre.

Cochilco. 2010. *Cochilco Anuario 2010*. Santiago: Comisión Chilena del Cobre.

Cochilco. 2019. *Cochilco Anuario 2019*. Santiago: Comisión Chilena del Cobre.

Codelco. 1998. *Codelco Annual Report 1998*. Santiago: Corporación Nacional del Cobre.

Codelco. 1999. *Codelco Annual Report 1999*. Santiago: Corporación Nacional del Cobre.

Codelco. 2001. *Codelco Annual Report 2001*. Santiago: Corporación Nacional del Cobre.

Codelco. 2004. *Codelco Annual Report 2004*. Santiago: Corporación Nacional del Cobre.

Codelco. 2007. *Codelco Annual Report 2007*. Santiago: Corporación Nacional del Cobre.

Codelco. 2009. *Codelco Annual Report 2009*. Santiago: Corporación Nacional del Cobre.

Codelco. 2010. *Codelco Annual Report 2010*. Santiago: Corporación Nacional del Cobre.

Codelco. 2013. *Codelco Annual Report 2013*. Santiago: Corporación Nacional del Cobre.

Codelco. 2015. *Codelco Annual Report 2015*. Santiago: Corporación Nacional del Cobre.

Codelco. 2018. *Codelco Annual Report 2018*. Santiago: Corporación Nacional del Cobre.

Codelco. 2019. *Codelco Annual Report 2019*. Santiago: Corporación Nacional del Cobre.

Collier, Simon. 1993. 'From Independence to the War of the Pacific'. In *Chile Since Independence*, edited by Leslie Bethell, 1–32. Cambridge: Cambridge University Press.

Collier, Ruth Berins and David Collier. 1991. *Shaping the Political Arena: Critical Junctures, the Labor Movement, and Regime Dynamics in Latin America*. Princeton, NJ: Princeton University Press.

Collier, Ruth Berins, and David Collier. 2002. *Shaping the Political Arena. Critical Junctures, the Labour Movement, and Regime Dynamics in Latin America*. Notre Dame: University of Notre Dame Press.

Collier, Paul, and Anke Hoeffler. 2004. 'Greed and Grievance in Civil War'. *Oxford Economic Papers* 56 (4): 563–595.

Collier, Simon, and Willliam F. Slater. 2004. *A History of Chile, 1808–2002*. 2nd ed. Cambridge: Cambridge University Press.

Comisión Minería y Desarollo de Chile. 2014. *Una Plataforma de Futuro para Chile*. Santiago: Comisión Minería y Desarollo de Chile.

Comisión Chilena del Cobre (COCHILCO). 2020. *COCHILCO Annual Statistics 2019*. Santiago de Chile: CODELCO.

Cook, Maria Lorena. 2007. *The Politics of Labour Reform in Latin America: Between Flexibility and Rights*. University Park: Pennsylvania State University Press.

Coronil, Fernando. 1997. *The Magical State: Nature, Money, and Modernity in Venezuela*. Chicago: University of Chicago Press.

Corrales, Javier. 2014. 'Explaining Chavismo: The Unexpected Alliance of Radical Leftists and the Military in Venezuela Under Hugo Chávez'. In *Venezuela Before Chávez: Anatomy of an Economic Collapse*, edited by Ricardo Hausmann and Francisco Rodríguez, 371–406. University Park: Pennsylvania State University Press.

Corrales, Javier, and Michael Penfold. 2011. Dragon in the Tropics: Hugo Chavez and the Political Economy of Revolution in Venezuela. Brookings Latin America Initiative Book. Washington, DC: Brookings Institution Press.

Cox, Robert W. 1981. 'Social Forces, States and World Orders: Beyond International Relations Theory'. *Millennium* 10 (2): 126–155.

Crabtree, John. 1998. 'Neo-Populism and the Fujimoro Phenomenon'. In *Fujimoro's Peru: The Political Economy*, edited by John Crabtree and Jim Thomas, 7–23. London: Institute of Latin American Studies.

Crabtree, John, and Francisco Durand. 2017. *Peru: Elite Power and Political Capture*. London: Zed Books.

Crocco, Francisca Gutiérrez. 2017. 'Coping with Neoliberalism Through Legal Mobilization: The Chilean Labour Movement's New Tactics and Allies'. In *Social Movements in Chile: Organization, Trajectories and Political Consequences*, edited by Sofia Donoso and Marisa von Bülow, 191–217. London: Palgrave Macmillan.

Cruzat A., Ximena. 1981. *El Movimiento Mancomunal en el Norte Salitrero: 1901–1907*. Santiago: CLACSO (Mimeo).

Cui, Shoujun, and Manuel Pérez García. 2016. *China and Latin America in Transition: Policy Dynamics, Economic Commitments, and Social Impacts*. London: Palgrave Macmillan.

Dabrowski, Janusz M., Michal Federowicz, and Anthony Levitas. 1991. 'Polish State Enterprises and the Properties of Performance: Stabilization, Marketization, Privatization'. *Politics & Society* 19 (4): 403–437.

Damasceno, Eduardo 1995 'Reservas Minerais e as Privatizações', Folha de Sao Paulo. http://www1.folha.uol.com.br/fsp/1995/12/23/dinheiro/5.html (accessed 18 June 2012).

284 References

Dantas, Eva. 2006. 'The Development of Knowledge Networks in Latecomer Innovation Systems: The Case of PETROBRAS in the Brazilian Offshore Oil Industry'. DPhil thesis. Brighton: SPRU, University of Sussex.

Dantas, Eva, and Martin Bell. 2009. 'Latecomer Firms and the Emergence and Development of Knowledge Networks: The Case of Petrobras in Brazil'. *Research Policy* 38 (5): 829–844.

Campos Neto, Carlos Alvares da Silva, and Fabiano Mezadre Pompermayer, eds. 2014. 'Investimentos e Financiamentos Na Indústria Naval Brasileira 2000–2013'. In *Ressurgimento da Indústria Naval no Brasil (2000–2013)*, edited by Carlos Alvares da Silva Campos Neto, and Fabiano Mezadre Pompermayer. Brasília: IPEA.

David, Paul A. 1985. 'Clio and the Economics of QWERTY'. *The American Economic Review* 75 (2): 332–337.

De Oliveira, Adilson. 2012. 'Brazil's Petrobras: Strategy and Performance'. In *Oil and Governance: State-Owned Enterprises and the World Energy Supply*, edited by David G. Victor, David R. Hults, and Mark C. Thurber, 515–556. Cambridge: Cambridge University Press.

De Oliveira, Marco Guedes, and Deywisson Ronaldo de Souza. 2016. 'Brazil's "White Coup"'. *World Affairs: The Journal of International Issues* 20 (2): 142–151.

De Paula, Luiz Fernando, André de Melo Modenesi, and Manoel Carlos C. Pires. 2015. 'The Tale of the Contagion of Two Crises and Policy Responses in Brazil: A Case of (Keynesian) Policy Coordination?' *Journal of Post Keynesian Economics* 37 (3): 408–435.

Del Prete, Davide, Giorgia Giovannetti, and Enrico Marvasi. 2018. 'Global Value Chains: New Evidence for North Africa'. *SI: Global Value Chains* 153 (May): 42–54.

Di John, Jonathan. 2009. *From Windfall to Curse? Oil and Industrialization in Venezuela, 1920 to the Present*. University Park: Pennsylvania State University Press.

Di John, Jonathan. 2011. 'Is There Really a Resource Curse? A Critical Survey of Theory and Evidence'. *Global Governance* 17 (2): 167–184.

Di John, Jonathan. 2014. 'The Political Economy of Industrial Policy in Venezuela'. In *Venezuela Before Chávez: Anatomy of an Economic Collapse*, edited by Ricardo Hausmann and Francisco Rodríguez, 321–370. University Park: Pennsylvania State University Press.

Diniz, Eli. 1978. *Empresário, Estado, e Capitalismo no Brasil: 1930–1945*. Rio de Janeiro: Editora Paze Terra.

Doner, Richard F., Bryan K. Ritchie, and Dan Slater. 2005. 'Systemic Vulnerability and the Origins of Developmental States: Northeast and Southeast Asia in Comparative Perspective'. *International Organization* 59 (2): 327–361.

Doner, Richard F., Gregory W. Noble, and John Ravenhill. 2021. *The Political Economy of Automotive Industrialization in East Asia*. New York: Oxford University Press.

Donoso, Sofia. 2017. '"We Are the Engine of the Enterprise, and Yet, We Are Like Its Illegitmate Children": The Contract Workers' Movement in Chile and Its Claims for Equal Labour Rights'. In *Demanding Justice in the Global South: Claiming Rights*, edited by Jean Bernadette Grugel, Jewellord Nem Singh, Lorenza B. Fontana, and Anders Uhlin, 99–127. Basingstoke: Palgrave Macmillan.

Donoso, Sofia, and Marisa von Bülow. 2017. *Social Movements in Chile: Organization, Trajectories, and Political Consequences*. Basingstoke: Palgrave Macmillan. 10.1057/978-1-137-60013-4.

Döring, Heike, Rodrigo Salles Pereira dos Santos, and Eva Pocher. 2017. 'New Developmentalism in Brazil? The Need for Sectoral Analysis'. Review of International Political Economy 24 (2): 332–362. https://doi.org/10.1080/09692290.2016.1273841

Drake, Paul. 1993. 'Chile, 1930–1958'. In *Chile Since Independence*, edited by Leslie Bethell, 87–128. Cambridge: Cambridge University Press.

References 285

Dunning, Thad. 2008. *Crude Democracy: Natural Resource Wealth and Political Regimes.* Cambridge Studies in Comparative Politics. Cambridge: Cambridge University Press.

Duran-Palma, Fernando, and Diego López. 2009. 'Contract Labour Mobilisation in Chile's Copper Mining and Forestry Sectors'. *Employee Relations* 31 (April): 245–263.

Eaton, Sarah. 2016. *The Advance of the State in Contemporary China: State–Market Relations in the Reform Era.* Cambridge: Cambridge University Press.

Ebenau, Matthias. 2012. 'Varieties of Capitalism or Dependency? A Critique of the VoC Approach for Latin America'. *Competition and Change* 16 (3): 206–223.

Economic Commission for Latin America and the Caribbean (ECLAC). 2013. *Economic Survey of Latin America and the Caribbean: Three Decades of Uneven and Unstable Growth.* Santiago: United Nations.

Economic Commission for Latin America and the Caribbean (ECLAC). 2016. *Foreign Direct Investment in Latin America and the Caribbean.* Santiago: United Nations.

Economist Intelligence Unit. 2017. 'Peru Aiming to Get Refinery Project on Track'. *The Economist* 23 March.

El Mostrador. 2010. 'La Tragedia de los 33 Mineros Vista por las Organizaciones Sindicales Chilenas'. *El Mostrador* 9 August.

El Mostrador. 2011a. 'Trabajadores de CODELCO Inician Paro de 24 Horas en Protesta a Eventual Privatización de la Minera'. *El Mostrador* 11 July.

El Mostrador. 2011b. 'Sindicatos de CODELCO Dicen que la Paralización es Total'. *El Mostrador*

El Mostrador. 2011c. 'No Hay Ninguna Intención de Privatizar Codelco'. *El Mostrador* 11 July.

El Mostrador. 2011d. 'Barómetro de la Política Agosto–Septiembre 2011'. *El Mostrador.*

Erten, B., and J.A. Ocampo. 2013. 'Super Cycles of Commodity Prices since the Mid-Nineteenth Century'. *World Development* 44: 14–30. https://doi.org/10.1016/j.worlddev.2012.11.013.

Etchemendy, Sebastián. 2011. *Models of Economic Liberalization: Business, Workers, and Compensation in Latin America, Spain, and Portugal.* Cambridge: Cambridge University Press.

European Commission. 2020a. *Critical Materials for Strategic Technologies and Sectors in the EU—A Foresight Study.* Luxembourg: Publications Office of the European Union.

European Commission. 2020b. *Study on the EU's List of Critical Raw Materials—Final Report.* Luxembourg: Publications Office of the European Union.

Evans, Peter. 1979. *Dependent Development: The Alliance of Multinational, State, and Local Capital in Brazil.* Princeton: Princeton University Press.

Evans, Peter. 1995. *Embedded Autonomy: States and Industrial Transformation.* Princeton: Princeton University Press.

Fails, Matthew D., and Marc C. DuBuis. 2015. 'Resources, Rent Diversification, and the Collapse of Autocratic Regimes'. *Political Research Quarterly* 68 (4): 703–715.

Faoro, Raymundo. 2012. *Os Donos do Poder: Formação do Patronato Político Brasileiro.* 5th ed. São Paolo: Editora Globo.

Federação Única dos Petroleiros (FUP). 2011. 'Greve de 1995'. 1 December. Accessed 10 April 2012, http://www.fup.org.br/2012/greve/greve-1995.

Fermandois, Joaquín, Jimena Bustos, and María José Schneuer. 2009. *Historia Política Del Cobre, 1945–2008.* Santiago: Centro de Estudios Bicentenario.

Centeno, Miguel A., and Agustin E. Ferraro, eds. 2013. *State and Nation Making in Latin America and Spain: Republics of the Possible.* Vol. 2. Cambridge: Cambridge University Press.

286 References

Ferraro, Agustin E., and Miguel A. Centeno, eds. 2018. *State and Nation Making in Latin America and Spain: The Rise and Fall of the Developmental State.* Cambridge: Cambridge University Press.

Folha de São Paulo. 1995. 'Operação Foi Determinada por FHC na Segunda'. *Folha de São Paulo* 25 May. Accessed 14 July 2012, http://www.abcdeluta.org.br/materia.asp?id_CON=788.

Folha de São Paulo. 2003. 'Outro Lado: Maioria Contesta Dados da Lista', Folha de São Paulo. http://www1.folha.uol.com.br/fsp/brasil/fc1505200323.htm (accessed 18 June 2012).

Fonseca, Pedro Cézar Dutra. 1989. *Vargas: o Capitalismo em Construção: 1906–1954.* Rio de Janeiro: Brasiliense.

Fonseca Monteiro, Cristiano. 2011. 'Political Dynamics and Liberalization in the Brazilian Air Transport Industry: 1990–2002'. *Brazilian Political Science Review* 5 (1). https://doi.org/10.1590/1981-3880201100010002

Fornes, Gaston, and Alvaro Mendez. 2018. *The China–Latin America Axis: Emerging Markets and Their Role in an Increasingly Globalised World.* 2nd ed. Cham: Palgrave Macmillan.

Forum on Royalty, Cluster, and Innovation. 2005. '6 Preguntas Claves Del 6 Preguntas Claves Del Impuesto Especifico a Impuesto Especifico a la Minería'. Presentation delivered at *Foro Royalty, Cluster e Innovación. Una Oportunidad para el Desarrollo Regional*, Calama, Chile, 26 April.

Frank, Volker. 2002. 'The Labour Movement in Democratic Chile, 1990–2000'. Working Paper 298. Notre Dame: Helen Kellogg Institute of International Studies, University of Notre Dame.

Frank, Volker. 2004. 'Politics Without Policy: The Failure of Social Concertation in Democratic Chile, 1990–2000'. In *Victims of the Chilean Miracle: Workers and Neoliberalism in the Pinochet Era, 1973–2002*, edited by Peter Winn, 125–163. Durham: Duke University Press.

Federación de los Trabajadores del Cobre (FTC). 2006. *Propuesta Nacional II. Los Trabajadores del Cobre para El Futuro del CODELCO – Chile.* Santiago de Chile: FTC.

Fundación Chile. 2014. *Proveedores de la Minería Chilena: Estudio de Caracterización.* Santiago: Fundación Chile.

Fundación Chile. 2019. *Caracterización de Proveedores de la Minería Chilena.* Santiago: Fundación Chile.

Furtado, Celso. 1970. *Economic Development of Latin America: A Survey from Colonial Times to the Cuban Revolution.* Cambridge: Cambridge University Press.

Furtado, Celso. 1995. *Formação Econômica do Brasil.* 23rd ed. São Paulo: Editora Nacional.

Gallagher, Kevin. 2016. *The China Triangle: Latin America's China Boom and the Fate of the Washington Consensus.* Oxford: Oxford University Press.

Gallagher, Kevin, and Roberto Porzekanski. 2010. *The Dragon in the Room: China and the Future of Latin American Industrialization.* Stanford: Stanford University Press.

Gallo, Carmenza. 2008. 'Tax Bargaining and Nitrate Exports: Chile, 1880–1930'. In *Taxation and State-Building in Developing Countries: Capacity and Consent*, edited by Deborah Brautigam, Odd-Helge Fjelstad, and Mick Moore, 160–182. Cambridge: Cambridge University Press.

Garretón, Manuel Antonio. 2003. *Incomplete Democracy: Political Democratisation in Chile and Latin America.* Chapel Hill: University of North Carolina Press.

Geddes, Barbara. 1996. *Politician's Dilemma: Building State Capacity in Latin America.* First Edition. Berkeley: University of California Press.

Geddes, Barbara, and Artur Ribeiro Neto. 1992. 'Institutional Sources of Corruption in Brazil'. *Third World Quarterly* 13 (4): 641–661.

Gellert, Paul K. 2010. 'Extractive Regimes: Toward a Better Understanding of Indonesian Development'. *Rural Sociology* 75 (1): 28–57.

Gellert, Paul K. 2012. 'Extraction and the World-System'. In Routledge Handbook of World-Systems Analysis. 1st Edition. London: Routledge.

Gereffi, Gary. 2005. 'The Global Economy: Organization, Governance, and Development'. In *The Handbook of Economic Sociology*, edited by Neil Joseph Smelser and Richard Swedberg, 2nd ed., 160–182. Princeton: Princeton University Press.

Gereffi, Gary. 2014. 'Global Value Chains in a Post-Washington Consensus World'. *Review of International Political Economy* 21 (1): 9–37.

Gereffi, Gary. 2018. *Global Value Chains and Development: Redefining the Contours of 21st Century Capitalism*. Cambridge: Cambridge University Press.

Gereffi, Gary, and Donald L. Wyman, eds. 1990. *Manufacturing Miracles: Paths of Industrialization in Latin America and East Asia*. Princeton: Princeton University Press.

Gerschenkron, Alexander. 1962. *Economic Backwardness in Historical Perspective*. Cambridge, MA: Belknap Press of Harvard University Press.

Gerschewski, Johannes. 2020. 'Explanations of Institutional Change: Reflecting on a "Missing Diagonal"'. *American Political Science Review* 115 (1): 218–233.

Goldstein, Andrea. 1999. 'Brazilian Privatisation in International Perspective: The Rocky Path from State Capitalism to Regulatory Capitalism'. *Industrial and Corporate Change* 8 (4): 673–711.

Goldstein, A. 2002. 'Embraer: From National Champion to Global Player'. *Cepal Review* 77: 97–115.

Gong, Huiwen, Robert Hassink, and Cassandra C. Wang. 2022. 'Strategic Coupling and Institutional Innovation in Times of Upheavals: The Industrial Chain Chief Model in Zhejiang, China'. *Cambridge Journal of Regions, Economy and Society* 15 (2): 279–303.

González, Francisco E. 2008. *Dual Transitions from Authoritarian Rule: Institutionalized Regimes in Chile and Mexico, 1970–2000*. Baltimore: Johns Hopkins University Press.

Gonzalez, Ricardo, and Carmen Le Foulon Morán. 2020. 'The 2019–2020 Chilean Protests: A First Look at Their Causes and Participants'. *International Journal of Sociology* 50 (3): 227–235.

González Miranda, Sergio. 2002. *Hombres y Mujeres de la Pampa: Tarapacá en el Ciclo de Expansión del Salitre*. 2nd edn. Santiago: LOM Editorial.

Grugel, Jean, and J.T. Nem Singh. 2013 'Citizenship, Democratization and Resource Politics'. In *Resource Governance and Developmental States in the Global South: Critical International Political Economy Perspectives*, edited by Jewellord Nem Singh and France Bourgouin, 61–83. Basingstoke: Palgrave Macmillan.

Grugel, Jean, and Jewellord Nem Singh. 2015. 'Protest, Citizenship and Democratic Renewal: The Student Movement in Chile'. *Citizenship Studies* 19 (3–4): 353–366.

Grugel, Jean, and Pía Riggirozzi. 2012. 'Post-Neoliberalism in Latin America: Rebuilding and Reclaiming the State After Crisis'. *Development and Change* 43 (1): 1–21.

Grugel, Jean, and Pía Riggirozzi. 2018. 'Neoliberal Disruption and Neoliberalism's Afterlife in Latin America: What Is Left of Post-Neoliberalism?' *Critical Social Policy* 38 (3): 547–566.

Guaíra. 2016. 'Sérgio Moro—o Queridinho do Brasil'. *Guaíra* 19 March.

Guajardo, Juan Carlos B. 2008. *Mineral Rents and Social Development in Chile*. Geneva: UNRISD Publications.

Guajardo, Juan Carlos B. 2012. 'Mineral Rents and Social Development in Chile'. In *Mineral Rents and the Financing of Social Policy: Opportunities and Challenges*, edited by Katja Hujor. New York: Palgrave Macmillan and UNRISD, pp. 185–222.

Gudynas, Eduardo. 2016. 'Natural Resource Nationalisms and the Compensatory State in Progressive South America'. In *The Political Economy of Resources and Development:*

From Neoliberalism to Resource Nationalism, edited by Paul Alexander Haslam and Pablo Heidrich, 103–117. London: Routledge.

Gudynas, Eduardo. 2020. *Extractivisms: Politics, Economy and Ecology.* Nova Scotia: Fernwood Publishing.

Guimarães, Alexandre Quieroz. 2003. 'Institutions, State Capacity and Economic Development—The Political Economy of Import Substitution Industrialisation in Brazil'. PhD dissertation. Sheffield: University of Sheffield.

Gustafson, Bret. 2020. *Bolivia in the Age of Gas.* Durham: Duke University Press.

Gustafsson, Maria-Therese, and Martin Scurrah. 2019. 'Strengthening Subnational Institutions for Sustainable Development in Resource-Rich States: Decentralized Land-Use Planning in Peru'. *World Development* 119 (July): 133–144.

Gylfason, Thorvaldur. 2001. 'Natural Resources, Education, and Economic Development'. *15th Annual Congress of the European Economic Association* 45 (4): 847–859.

Haarstad, Håvard. 2009. 'Globalization and the New Spaces for Social Movement Politics: The Marginalization of Labor Unions in Bolivian Gas Nationalization'. *Globalizations* 6 (2): 169–185.

Haarstad, Håvard. 2012. 'Extracting Justice? Critical Themes and Challenges in Latin American Natural Resource Governance'. In *New Political Spaces in Latin American Natural Resource Governance,* edited by Håvard Haarstad, 1–16. New York: Palgrave Macmillan.

Haggard, Stephan. 2015. 'The Developmental State Is Dead: Long Live the Developmental State!' In *Advances in Comparative-Historical Analysis,* edited by James Mahoney and Kathleen Thelen, 39–66. Strategies for Social Inquiry. Cambridge: Cambridge University Press.

Haggard, Stephan, and Robert Kaufman. 1996. *The Political Economy of Democratic Transitions.* Princeton: Princeton University Press.

Hagopian, Frances. 1996. *Traditional Politics and Regime Change in Brazil.* Cambridge: Cambridge University Press.

Hall, Peter. 1986. *Governing the Economy: The Politics of State Intervention in Britain and France.* New York: Oxford University Press.

Hall, Peter. 1989. *The Political Power of Economic Ideas: Keynesianism Across Nations.* Princeton: Princeton University Press.

Hall, Peter. 1993. 'Policy Paradigms, Social Learning and the State'. *Comparative Politics* 25 (3): 275–296.

Hall, Peter, and David Soskice, eds. 2001. *Varieties of Capitalism: The Institutional Foundations of Comparative Advantage.* Oxford: Oxford University Press.

Hamilton-Hart, Natasha, and Yeung, Henry Wai-chung. 2021. 'Institutions under pressure: East Asian states, global markets and national firms'. *Review of International Political Economy* 28 (1): 11–35. https://doi.org/10.1080/09692290.2019.1702571.

Hammond, John L. 2011. 'The Resource Curse and Oil Revenues in Angola and Venezuela'. *Science & Society* 75 (3): 348–378.

Hancké, Bob, Martin Rhodes, and Mark Thatcher, eds. 2007. *Beyond Varieties of Capitalism: Conflict, Contradictions, and Complementarities in the European Economy.* Oxford: Oxford University Press.

Harvey, David, Neil M. Kellars, Jakob B. Madsen, and Mark E. Whoar. 2010. 'The Prebisch–Singer Hypothesis: Four Centuries of Evidence'. *The Review of Economics and Statistics* 92 (2): 367–377.

Haslam, Paul, and Pablo Heidrich, eds. 2016. *The Political Economy of Natural Resources and Development.* London: Routledge.

Hauge, Jostein. 2019. 'Should the African Lion Learn from the Asian Tigers? A Comparative-Historical Study of FDI-Oriented Industrial Policy in Ethiopia, South Korea and Taiwan'. *Third World Quarterly* 40 (11): 2071–2091.

Hausmann, Ricardo, and Francisco Rodríguez. 2014. 'Why Did Venezuelan Growth Collapse?' In *Venezuela Before Chávez: Anatomy of an Economic Collapse*, edited by Ricardo Hausmann and Francisco Rodríguez, 15–50. University Park: Pennsylvania State University Press.

Hawkins, Kirk A. 2010. *Venezuela's Chavismo and Populism in Comparative Perspective.* Cambridge: Cambridge University Press.

Hay, Colin. 2001. 'The "Crisis" of Keynesianism and the Rise of Neoliberalism in Britain: An Ideational Institutionalist Approach'. In *The Rise of Neoliberalism and Institutional Analysis*, edited by John L. Campbell and Ove K. Pedersen, 193–218. Princeton: Princeton University Press.

Hay, Colin. 2011. 'Ideas and the Constructions of Interests'. In *Ideas and Politics in Social Science Research*, edited by Daniel Béland and Robert Henry Cox, 65–82. Oxford: Oxford University Press.

Heiss, Claudia, and Patricio Navia. 2007. 'You Win Some, You Lose Some: Constitutional Reforms in Chile's Transition to Democracy'. *Latin American Politics and Society* 49 (3): 163–190.

Henley, D.E.F. 2012. 'Agrarian Roots of Industrial Growth: Rural Development in Southeast Asia and Sub-Saharan Africa'. *Development Policy Review* 30 (s1): 25–47.

Henley, D.E.F. 2015. *Asia-Africa Development Divergence: A Question of Intent.* London: Zed Books.

Herb, Michael. 1999. *All in the Family: Absolutism, Revolution and Democracy in the Middle Eastern Monarchies.* Albany: State University of New York Press.

Herb, Michael. 2003. 'Taxation and Representation'. *Studies in Comparative International Development* 38 (3): 3–31.

Herb, Michael. 2005. 'No Representation without Taxation? Rents, Development, and Democracy'. *Comparative Politics* 37 (3): 297–316.

Herb, Michael. 2014. *The Wages of Oil: Parliaments and Economic Development in Kuwait and the UAE.* Ithaca: Cornell University Press.

Hertog, Steffen. 2010a. 'Defying the Resource Curse. Explaining Successful State-Owned Enterprises in Rentier States'. *World Politics* 62 (2): 261–301.

Hertog, Steffen. 2010b. *Princes, Brokers, and Bureaucrats. Oil and the State in Saudi Arabia.* Ithaca: Cornell University Press.

Hirschman, Albert. 1981. *Essays in Trespassing: Economics to Politics and Beyond.* New York: Cambridge University Press.

Hirschman, Albert. 2013. *The Essential Hirschman.* Princeton: Princeton University Press.

Hochstetler, Kathryn, and Alfred P. Montero. 2013. 'The Renewed Developmental State: The National Development Bank and the Brazil Model'. *Journal of Development Studies* 49 (11): 1484–1499.

Holodny, Elena. 2015. 'The 13 Fastest-Growing Economies in the World'. World Economic Forum, 16 June. Accessed March 2022.

Hsueh, Roselyn. 2011. *China's Regulatory State.* Ithaca: Cornell University Press.

Huang, Yiping. 2016. 'Understanding China's Belt & Road Initiative: Motivation, Framework and Assessment'. *China Economic Review* 40 (September): 314–321.

Hults, David R. 2012. 'Petróleos de Venezuela, S.A. (PDVSA): From Independence to Subservience'. In *Oil and Governance: State-Owned Enterprises and the World Energy Supply*, edited by David G. Victor, David R. Hults, and Mark Thurber, 418–477. Cambridge: Cambridge University Press.

Humphreys, Macartan, Geoffery D. Sachs, and Joseph E. Stiglitz. 2007. *Escaping the Resource Curse.* New York: Columbia University Press.

Hunter, Wendy. 1997. *Eroding Military Influence in Brazil: Politicians against Soldiers.* Chapel Hill: University of North Carolina Press.

290 References

Hunter, Wendy. 2010. *The Transformation of the Workers' Party in Brazil, 1989–2009*. Cambridge: Cambridge University Press.

Ibáñez Santa María, Adolfo. 2003. *Herido en el Ala: Estado, Oligarquías y Subdesarrollo, Chile 1924–1960*. Santiago: Editorial Biblioteca Americana.

Immergut, Ellen M. 1998. 'The Theoretical Core of the New Institutionalism'. *Politics & Society* 26 (1): 5–34. https://doi.org/10.1177/0032329298026001002

Instituto de Pesquisa Econômica Aplicada (IPEA). 2020. *Brazilian Economic Outlook Carta de Conjuntura*. Paris: IPEA.

International Energy Agency. 2021. 'The Role of Critical Minerals in Clean Energy Transitions'. World Energy Outlook Special Report. Paris: IEA.

Jackson, Margaret M., Joanna I. Lewis, and Xiliang Zhang. 2021. 'A Green Expansion: China's Role in the Global Deployment and Transfer of Solar Photovoltaic Technology'. *Energy for Sustainable Development* 60 (February): 90–101.

Jenkins, Rhys. 2015. 'Is Chinese Competition Causing Deindustrialization in Brazil?' *Latin American Perspectives* 42 (6): 42–63.

Jenkins, Rhys. 2018. *How China Is Reshaping the Global Economy: Development Impacts in Africa and Latin America*. Oxford: Oxford University Press.

Jepson, Nicholas. 2020. *In China's Wake: How the Commodity Boom Transformed Development Strategies in the Global South*. New York: Columbia University Press.

Jepson, Nicholas. 2021. 'Hidden in Plain Sight: Chinese Development Finance in Central and Eastern Europe'. *Development and Change* 52 (5): 1222–1250.

Jerez, Bárbara, Ingrid Garcés, and Robinson Torres. 2021. 'Lithium Extractivism and Water Injustices in the Salar de Atacama, Chile: The Colonial Shadow of Green Electromobility'. *Political Geography* 87 (May): 102382.

Jones, Pauline, and Erika Weinthal. 2010. *Oil Is Not a Curse: Ownership Structure and Institutions in Soviet Successor States*. Cambridge Studies in Comparative Politics. Cambridge: Cambridge University Press.

Kalantzakos, Sophia. 2018. *China and the Geopolitics of Rare Earths*. New York: Oxford University Press.

Kang, David C. 2002a. 'Bad Loans to Good Friends: Money Politics and the Developmental State in South Korea'. *International Organization* 56 (1): 177–207.

Kang, David C. 2002b. *Crony Capitalism: Corruption and Development in South Korea and the Philippines*. New York: Cambridge University Press.

Kang, Nahee. 2014. 'Towards Middle-Range Theory Building in Development Research: Comparative (Historical) Institutional Analysis of Institutional Transplantation'. *Progress in Development Studies* 14 (3): 221–235. https://doi.org/10.1177/1464993414521338

Kang, Nahee, and Jo Kahee. 2021. 'State–Business Relations in Flux: Capturing the Structural Power of Business in South Korea's Green Industrial Policy'. *Journal of Contemporary Asia* 51 (5): 713–736.

Kapiszewski, Diana, Steven Levitsky, and Deborah J. Yashar. 2021. 'Inequality, Democracy, and the Inclusionary Turn in Latin America'. In *The Inclusionary Turn in Latin American Democracies*, edited by Deborah J. Yashar, Diana Kapiszewski, and Steven Levitsky, 1–56. Cambridge: Cambridge University Press.

Karl, Terry Lynn. 1990. 'Dilemmas of Democratization in Latin America'. *Comparative Politics* 23 (1): 1–21.

Karl, Terry Lynn. 1997. *The Paradox of Plenty: Oil Booms and Petro-States*. Studies in International Political Economy. Oakland: University of California Press.

Kasahara, Yuri, and Antonio José Junquiera Botelho. 2019. 'Ideas and Leadership in the Crafting of Alternative Industrial Policies: Local Content Requirements for the Brazilian Oil and Gas Sector'. *Comparative Politics* 51 (3): 385–405.

Katz, Andrea Scoseria. 2018. 'Making Brazil Work? Brazilian Coalitional Presidentialism at 30 and its Post-Lava Jato Prospects'. *Revista de Investigações Constitucionais* 5 (3): 77–102.

Kaup, Brent Z. 2010. 'A Neoliberal Nationalization? The Constraints on Natural-Gas-Led Development in Bolivia'. *Latin American Perspectives* 37 (3): 123–138.

Kaup, Brent Z., and Paul K. Gellert. 2017. 'Cycles of Resource Nationalism: Hegemonic Struggle and the Incorporation of Bolivia and Indonesia'. *International Journal of Comparative Sociology* 58 (4): 275–303.

Kikeri, Sunita, and Aishetu Fatima Kolo. 2005. 'Privatization: Trends and Recent Developments'. 3765. World Bank Policy Research Working Paper. Washington, DC: World Bank.

Kikeri, Sunita, John Nellis, and Mary Shirley. 1994. 'Privatization: Lessons from Market Economies'. *The World Bank Research Observer* 9 (2): 241–272.

Kim, Kyunghoon. 2019. 'Using Partially State-Owned Enterprises for Development in Indonesia'. *Asia Pacific Business Review* 25 (3): 317–337.

Kingstone, Peter. 1999. *Crafting Coalitions for Reform: Business Preferences, Political Institutions and Neoliberalism in Brazil*. Philadelphia: Pennsylvania University Press.

Kirby, Peadar. 2009. 'Neo-Structuralism and Reforming the Latin American State: Lessons from the Irish Case'. *Economy and Society* 38 (1): 132–153.

Kirby, Peadar. 2010. 'Globalisation and State–Civil Society Relations: Lessons from Latin America'. Paper presented at the ECPR workshop, 'Towards Strong Publics? Civil Society and the State in Latin America', Munster, 23–25 March.

Klinger, Julie Michelle. 2017. *Rare Earth Frontiers: From Terrestrial Subsoils to Lunar Landscapes*. Ithaca: Cornell University Press.

Klinger, Julie Michelle, and Joshua S.S. Muldavin. 2019. 'New Geographies of Development: Grounding China's Global Integration'. *Territory, Politics, Governance* 7 (1): 1–21.

Kohli, Atul. 2004. *State-Directed Development: Political Power and Industrialisation in the Global Periphery*. Cambridge: Cambridge University Press.

Koning, Edward Anthony. 2016. 'The Three Institutionalisms and Institutional Dynamics: Understanding Endogenous and Exogenous Change'. *Journal of Public Policy* 36 (4): 639–664.

Korinek, Jane. 2013. 'Mineral Resource Trade in Chile: Contribution to Development and Policy Implications'. 145. OECD Trade Policy Papers. Paris: OECD Publishing.

Kornai, János. 1979. 'Resource-Constrained Versus Demand-Constrained Systems'. *Econometrica* 47 (4): 801–819.

Kornai, János. 1986. 'The Soft Budget Constraint'. *Kyklos* 39 (1): 1–30.

Kornai, János. 1992. *The Socialist System: The Political Economy of Communism*. Oxford: Oxford University Press.

Kornai, János, Eric Maskin, and Gérard Roland. 2003. 'Understanding the Soft Budget Constraint'. *Journal of Economic Literature* 41 (4): 1095–1136.

Kozak, Robert. 2011. 'PetroPeru Plans to Resume Oil Output, Sell Shares'. *Marketwatch* 15 November.

Krueger, Anne O. 1974. 'The Political Economy of the Rent-Seeking Society'. *The American Economic Review* 64 (3): 291–303.

Krueger, Anne O. 2002. *Why Crony Capitalism Is Bad for Economic Growth*. Washington, DC: Hoover Press.

Kumar, Yogesh, Jordan Ringenberg, Soma Shekara Depuru, Vijay K. Devabhaktuni, Jin Woo Lee, Efstratios Nikolaidis, Brett Andersen, and Abdollah Afjeh. 2016. 'Wind Energy: Trends and Enabling Technologies'. *Renewable and Sustainable Energy Reviews* 53 (January): 209–224.

292 References

Kurtz, Marcus J. 2001. 'State Developmentalism Without a Developmental State: The Public Foundations of the "Free Market Miracle" in Chile'. *Latin American Politics and Society* 43 (2): 1–25.

Kurtz, Marcus J. 2009. 'Social Foundations of Institutional Order: Reconsidering War and "Resource Curse" in Third World State-Building'. *Politics and Society* 37 (4): 479–520.

Kurtz, Marcus J. 2013. *Latin American State Building in Comparative Perspective: Social Foundations of Institutional Order*. Cambridge: Cambridge University Press.

Kurtz, Marcus J., and Sarah M. Brooks. 2008. 'Embedded Neoliberal Reform in Latin America'. *World Politics* 60 (2): 231–280.

Kurtz, Marcus J., and Sarah M. Brooks. 2011. 'Conditioning the "Resource Curse": Globalization, Human Capital, and Growth in Oil-Rich Nations'. *Comparative Political Studies* 44 (6): 747–770.

Kwiatkowski, Grzegorz, and Paweł Augustynowicz. 2016. 'State-Owned Enterprises in the Global Economy–Analysis Based on Fortune Global 500 List'. Paper presented at Managing Intellectual Capital andInnovation for Sustainable and Inclusive Society, Bari, Italy.

La Nación. 2011. 'Acogen querella de mineros de la San José contra el Estado', La Nación. http://www.nacion.cl/noticias/site/artic/20110805/pags/20110805135222.html# (accessed 12 September 2011).

La Porta, Rafael, Florencio Lopez-De-Silanes, and Andrei Shleifer. 2002. 'Government Ownership of Banks'. *Journal of Finance* 57 (1): 265–301.

Landau, Elena. 1995. 'O Ritmo das Privatizações no Brasil', Folha de Sao Paulo. http://www1.folha.uol.com.br/fsp/1995/9/03/dinheiro/4.html (accessed 18 June 2012).

Lange, Matthew. 2003a. 'Embedding the Colonial State: A Comparative-Historical Analysis of State Building and Broad-Based Development in Mauritius'. *Social Science History* 27 (3): 397–423.

Leahy, Joe. 2017. 'Brazil's State-Controlled Companies Pursue Reinvention'. *Financial Times*. Accessed 8 June 2017.

Leão, Luciana de Souza. 2018. 'A Double-Edged Sword: The Institutional Foundations of the Brazilian Developmental State, 1930–1985'. In *State and Nation Making in Latin America and Spain: The Rise and Fall of the Developmental State*, edited by Agustin E. Ferraro and Miguel A. Centeno, 157–176. Cambridge: Cambridge University Press.

Lebdioui, Amir. 2019. 'Chile's Export Diversification Since 1960: A Free Market Miracle or Mirage?' *Development and Change* 50 (6): 1624–1663.

Lebdioui, Amir. 2020. 'Local Content in Extractive Industries: Evidence and Lessons from Chile's Copper Sector and Malaysia's Petroleum Sector'. *The Extractive Industries and Society* 7 (2): 341–352.

Lederman, Daniel, William Maloney, Thad Dunning, and Cameron A. Shelton. 2008. 'In Search of the Missing Resource Curse [with Comments]'. *Economía* 9 (1): 1–57.

Lee, Ching-Kwan. 2017. *The Specter of Global China: Politics, Labour and Foreign Investment in China*. Chicago: University of Chicago Press.

Leite, Carlos, and Jens Weidmann. 1999. 'Does Mother Nature Corrupt? Natural Resources, Corruption, and Economic Growth'. Washington, DC: International Monetary Fund.

Leiva, Fernando. 2008. *Latin American Neostructuralism: The Contradictions of Post-Neoliberal Development*. Minneapolis: University of Minnesota Press.

Leiva, Fernando. 2019. 'Economic Elites and New Strategies for Extractivism in Chile'. European Review of Latin American and Caribbean Studies / Revista Europea de Estudios Latinoamericanos y del Caribe (108): 131–152. https://www.jstor.org/stable/26878966

Leiva Gómez, Sandra. 2009. 'La Subcontratación en la Minería en Chile: Elementos Teóricos Para el Análisis'. *Polis: Revista Latinoamericana* 8 (24): 111–131. http://polis.revues.org/1540.

References   293

Levi, Margaret, 1988. *Of Rule and Revenue*. Berkeley: University of California Press.

Levitsky, Steven, and Kenneth M. Roberts, eds. 2011. *The Resurgence of the Latin American Left*. Baltimore: Johns Hopkins University Press.

Lewis, Joanna I. 2013. *Green Innovation in China: China's Wind Power Industry and the Global Transition to a Low-Carbon Economy*. New York: Columbia University Press.

Libertad y Desarrollo. 2005. 'El Primer Costo del Royalty', Temas Públicas, No. 713, March 18 issue. http://www.lyd.com.

Libertad y Desarrollo. 2004. 'Royalty a la Minería: Aserruchando la Viga Maestra', Temas Públicas, No. 671, April 23 issue. http://www.lyd.com.

Libertad y Desarrollo. 2002. 'Propuestas de Impuesto a la Minería: ¿Debate Razonable? Temas Públicas, No. 589, August 2 issue. http://www.lyd.com.

Lima, Paulo César. 2009a. *O Pré-Sal e o Novo Marco Legal*. Brasilia: Library of Câmara dos Diputados, August, http://www.aslegis.org.br/images/stories/artigospessoais/Publicacoes-Artigos-pessoais-Politica-Energetica-II/O_Pre-Sal_e_o_novo_marco_legal_Agosto_2009.pdf.

Lima, Paulo César. 2009b. *Modelo Institucional do Setor Petrolífero Nacional e Possíveis Alterações*. Brasilia: Library of Câmara dos Diputados, July, http://bd.camara.gov.br/bd/bitstream/handle/bdcamara/4845/modelo_institucional_lima.pdf?sequence=1.

Lima-de-Oliveira, Renato. 2019. 'Resource-Led Industrial Development in the Oil and Gas Global Value Chain'. In *Innovation in Brazil: Advancing Development in the 21st Century*, edited by Elisabeth B. Reynolds, Ben Ross Schneider, and Ezequiel Zylberberg, 282–302. London: Routledge.

Limoeiro, Danilo, and Ben Ross Schneider. 2019. 'Institutions, Politics and State-Led Innovation'. In *Innovation in Brazil: Advancing Development in the 21st Century*, edited by Elizabeth B. Reynolds, Ben Ross Schneider, and Ezequiel Zylberberg. London: Routledge.

Londoño, Ernesto. 2017. 'A Judge's Bid to Clean Up Brazil From the Bench'. *The New York Times* 25 August.

Loveman, Brian. 1976. *Struggle in the Countryside: Politics and Rural Labour in Chile, 1919–1973*. Bloomington: Indiana University Press.

Machado, Iran F., and Silvia F. de M. Figueirôa. 2001. '500 Years of Mining in Brazil: A Brief Review'. *Resources Policy* 27 (1): 9–24.

Maciel, Camila. 2022. 'In His First Speech, Lula Says That Fighting Poverty Is His Mission'. *Agência Brasil* 31 October.

Maciel, Vladimir Fernandes, and Paulo Roberto Arvate. 2010. 'Tamanho do Governo Brasileiro: Conceitos e Medidas'. *Revista de Administração Contemporânea* 14 (1): 1–19.

Madariaga, Aldo. 2020. 'The Three Pillars of Neoliberalism: Chile's Economic Policy Trajectory in Comparative Perspective'. *Contemporary Politics* 26 (3): 308–329.

Mahoney, James. 2003. 'Strategies of Causal Assessment in Comparative Historical Analysis'. In *Comparative Historical Analysis in the Social Sciences*, edited by James Mahoney and Dietrich Rueschemeyer, 337–372. Cambridge: Cambridge University Press.

Mahoney, James, and Kathleen Thelan. 2009. 'A Theory of Gradual Institutional Change'. In *Explaining Institutional Change: Ambiguity, Agency, and Power*, edited by James Mahoney and Kathleen Thelan, 1–37. Cambridge: Cambridge University Press.

Malkin, Anton. 2022. 'The Made in China Challenge to US Structural Power: Industrial Policy, Intellectual Property and Multinational Corporations'. *Review of International Political Economy* 29 (2): 538–570.

Manky, Omar. 2018. 'Resource Mobilisation and Precarious Workers' Organisations: An Analysis of the Chilean Subcontracted Mineworkers' Unions'. *Work, Employment and Society* 32 (3): 581–598.

294 References

Marcel, Valérie, and John V. Mitchell. 2006. *Oil Titans: National Oil Companies in the Middle East*. London: Brookings Institution Press.

Massi, Eliza. 2014. 'The Political Economy of Development Finance: The BNDES and Brazilian Industrialisation'. PhD dissertation. London: School for Oriental and African Studies, University of London.

Massi, Eliza, and Jewellord Nem Singh. 2016. 'Resource Nationalism and Brazil's Post-Neoliberal Strategy'. In *The Political Economy of Natural Resources and Development: From Neoliberalism to Resource Nationalism*, edited by Paul Alexander Haslam and Pablo Heidrich, 158–186. London: Routledge.

Massi, Eliza, and Jewellord Nem Singh. 2018. 'Industrial Policy and State-Making: Brazil's Attempt at Oil-Based Industrial Development'. *Third World Quarterly* 39 (6): 1133–1150.

Massi, Eliza, and Jewellord Nem Singh. 2020. 'The Energy Politics of Brazil'. In *The Oxford Handbook of Energy Politics*, edited by Kathleen J. Hancock and Juliann Emmons Allison, 617–643. Oxford: Oxford University Press.

Maxwell, Philip, and Mauricio Mora. 2020. 'Lithium and Chile: Looking Back and Looking Forward'. *Mineral Economics* 33 (1): 57–71.

Mazzucato, Mariana. 2013. *The Entrepreneurial State: Debunking Public Versus Private Sector Myths*. London: Anthem Press.

Mazzucato, Mariana. 2016. 'Innovation, the State and Patient Capital'. In *Rethinking Capitalism: Economics and Policy for Sustainable and Inclusive Growth*, edited by Michael Jacobs and Mariana Mazzucato, 98–118. Chichester: Wiley-Blackwell.

Mazzucato, Mariana, and Caetano C.R. Penna. 2015. *Mission-Oriented Finance for Innovation*. London: Rowman & Littlefield International.

McMahon, Gary, and Susana Moreira. 2014. *The Contribution of the Mining Sector to Socioeconomic and Human Development*. Extractive Industries for Development series no. 30. Washington, DC: World Bank.

Mehlum, Halvor, Karl Moene, and Ragnar Torvik. 2006. 'Institutions and the Resource Curse'. *The Economic Journal* 116 (508): 1–20.

Meller, Patricio, and Pablo Parodi. 2017. *Del Programa de Proveedores a la Innovación Abierta en la Minería*. Santiago: CIEPLAN.

Mello, Eduardo, and Matias Spektor. 2016. 'How to Fix Brazil: Breaking an Addiction to Bad Government'. *Foreign Affairs* 95 (5): 102–110.

Mello, Eduardo, and Matias Spektor. 2018. 'Brazil: The Costs of Multiparty Presidentialism'. *Journal of Democracy* 29 (2): 113–127.

Mendez, Alvaro, and Mariano Turzi. 2020. *The Political Economy of China–Latin America Relations: The AIIB Membership*. Cham: Palgrave Pivot.

Millward, Robert. 2007. *Private and Public Enterprise in Europe: Energy, Telecommunications and Transport, 1830–1990*. Cambridge Studies in Economic History. Cambridge: Cambridge University Press.

Ministerio del Trabajo. 2006. *Agenda Laboral*. 28 December. Santiago: Ministerio del Trabajo.

Mommer, Bernard. 1986. *La Cuestión Petrolera*. Caracas: Fondo Editorial Tropykos.

Mommer, Bernard. 2003. 'Subversive Oil'. In *Venezuelan Politics in the Chavez Era: Class, Polarization, and Conflict*, edited by Steve Ellner and Daniel Hellinger, 131–146. Boulder: Lynne Rienner Publishers.

Monaldi, Francisco, and Michael Penfold. 2014. 'Institutional Collapse: The Rise and Decline of Democratic Governance in Venezuela'. In *Venezuela Before Chávez: Anatomy of an Economic Collapse*, edited by Ricardo Hausmann and Francisco Rodríguez, 285–320. University Park: Pennsylvania State University Press.

Montenegro, Ricardo Sá. 2003. 'O Setor Petroquimico'. In *BNDES Histórias Setoriais*. Rio de Janeiro: BNDES.

Montero, Alfred P. 1998. 'State Interests and the New Industrial Policy in Brazil: The Privatisation of Steel, 1990–1994'. *Journal of Interamerican Studies and World Affairs* 40: 27–62.

Moran, Theodore. 1977. *Multinational Corporations and the Politics of Dependence: Copper in Chile.* Princeton: Princeton University Press.

Moreno, María Antonia, and Cameron A. Shelton. 2014. 'Sleeping in the Bed One Makes: The Venezuelan Fiscal Policy Response to the Oil Boom'. In *Venezuela before Chávez: Anatomy of an Economic Collapse*, edited by Ricardo Hausmann and Francisco Rodríguez, 259–284. University Park: Pennsylvania State University Press.

Morgenstern, Scott, and Nacif Benito, eds. 2002. *Legislative Politics in Latin America.* New York: Cambridge University Press.

Morris, Mike, Raphael Kaplinsky, and David Kaplan. 2012. '"One Thing Leads to Another"— Commodities, Linkages and Industrial Development'. *Resources Policy* 37 (4): 408–416.

Mosley, Paul. 2012. *The Politics of Poverty Reduction.* Oxford: Oxford University Press.

Mueller, Bernardo, and Carlos Pereira. 2002. 'Credibility and the Design of Regulatory Agencies in Brazil'. *Brazilian Journal of Political Economy* 22 (3): 449–472.

Murillo, Maria Victoria. 2001. *Labour Unions, Partisan Coalitions, and Market Reforms in Latin America.* New York: Cambridge University Press.

Murillo, Maria Victoria. 2009. *Political Competition, Partisanship, and Policy Making in Latin American Public Utilities.* Cambridge Studies in Comparative Politics. Cambridge: Cambridge University Press.

Murshed, Syed Mansoob, and Leandro Antonio Serino. 2011. 'The Pattern of Specialization and Economic Growth: The Resource Curse Hypothesis Revisited'. *Structural Change and Economic Dynamics* 22 (2): 151–161.

Musacchio, Aldo, and Sergio Lazzarini. 2014. *Reinventing State Capitalism: Leviathan in Business, Brazil and Beyond.* Cambridge, MA: Harvard University Press.

Musacchio, Aldo, and Sergio Lazzarini. 2016. 'The Reinvention of State Capitalism in Brazil, 1970–2012'. In *New Order and Progress: Development and Democracy in Brazil.* New York: Oxford University Press.

Musacchio, Aldo, and Emilio I. Pineda Ayerbe. 2019. 'The State of SOEs in Latin America and the Caribbean'. In *Fixing State-Owned Enterprises: New Policy Solutions to Old Problems*, edited by Aldo Musacchio and Emilio I. Pineda Ayerbe, 33–80. Washington, DC: Inter-American Development Bank.

Musacchio, Aldo, Emilio I. Pineda Ayerabe, and Gustavo García. 2015. 'State-Owned Enterprise Reform in Latin America Issues and Possible Solutions'. *Inter-American Development Bank* 1 January.

Naughton, Barry. 2021. *The Rise of China's Industrial Policy, 1978–2020.* Boulder: Lynne Rienner Publishers.

Navarro, Lucas. 2018. 'The World Class Supplier Program for Mining in Chile: Assessment and Perspectives'. *Special Issue on Mining Value Chains, Innovation and Learning* 58 (October): 49–61.

Nem Singh, Jewellord. 2010. 'Reconstituting the Neostructuralist State: The Political Economy of Continuity and Change in Chilean Mining Policy'. *Third World Quarterly* 31 (8): 1413–1433.

Nem Singh, Jewellord. 2012a. 'Chile's Mining Unions and the "New Left", 1990–2010'. In *Civil Society and the State in Left-Led Latin America: Challenges and Limitations to Democratization*, edited by Barry Cannon and Peader Kirby, 141–157. London: Zed Books.

Nem Singh, Jewellord. 2012b. 'Who Owns the Minerals? Repoliticizing Neoliberal Governance in Brazil and Chile'. *Journal of Developing Societies* 28 (2): 229–256.

296 References

Nem Singh, Jewellord. 2014. 'Towards Post-Neoliberal Resource Politics? The International Political Economy (IPE) of Oil and Copper in Brazil and Chile'. *New Political Economy* 19 (3): 329–358.

Nem Singh, Jewellord. 2018. 'Governing Natural Resources'. In *Handbook of Latin American Governance*, edited by Pía Riggirozzi and Christopher Wylde, 355–370. London: Routledge.

Nem Singh, Jewellord. 2019. 'Natural Resources'. In *Handbook of Contemporary International Political Economy*, edited by Timothy Shaw, Laura Mahrenbach, Craig Murphy, Renu Modi, and Xu Yi-Chong, 539–557. London: Palgrave Macmillan.

Nem Singh, Jewellord. 2021. 'Mining Our Way out of the Climate Change Conundrum? The Power of a Social Justice Perspective'. Latin America's Environmental Policies in Global Perspective. Washington, DC: The Wilson Center.

Nem Singh, Jewellord. 2022. 'The Renaissance of the Developmental State in the Age of Post-Neoliberalism'. In *Handbook of Governance and Development*, edited by Wil Hout and Jane Hutchison, 97–114. Cheltenham: Edward Elgar Publishing.

Nem Singh, Jewellord. 2023. 'The Advance of the State and the Renewal of Industrial Policy in the Age of Strategic Competition'. *Third World Quarterly* 44 (9): 1919–1937. https://doi.org/10.1080/01436597.2023.2217766.

Nem Singh, Jewellord, and Geoffrey C. Chen. 2018. 'State-Owned Enterprises and the Political Economy of State–State Relations in the Developing World'. *Third World Quarterly* 39 (6): 1077–1097.

Nem Singh, Jewellord, and Jesse Salah Ovadia. 2018. 'The Theory and Practice of Building Developmental States in the Global South'. *Third World Quarterly* 39 (6): 1033–1055.

Nem Singh, Jewellord, and France Bourgouin, eds. 2013. *Resource Governance and Developmental States in the Global South: Critical International Political Economy Perspectives*. International Political Economy. Basingstoke: Palgrave Macmillan.

Nishijima, Marislei, Flavia Mori Sarti, and Regina Célia Cati. 2019. 'The Underlying Causes of Brazilian Corruption'. In *Corruption in Latin America: How Politicians and Corporations Steal from Their Citizens*, edited by Robert Rotberg, 29–56. London: Springer.

Nolan, Peter. 2001. *China and the Global Economy: National Champions, Industrial Policy and the Big Business Revolution*. Basingstoke: Palgrave Macmillan.

North, Douglas C. 1990. *Institutions, Institutional Change and Economic Performance. Political Economy of Institutions and Decisions*. Cambridge: Cambridge University Press.

Nunes, Edson, A. 1997. A Gramática Política do Brasil—Clientelismo e Insulamento Burocrático. Rio de Janeiro: Jorge Zahar Editor.

O'Brien, Rosalba. 2014. 'Chile Passes Landmark Tax Reform into Law'. *Reuters* 11 September.

Ocampo, José Antonio. 2017. 'Commodity-led Development in Latin America'. In *Alternative Pathways to Sustainable Development: Lessons from Latin America*, edited by Gilles Carbonnier, Humberto Campodónico, and Sergio Tezanos Vásquez, 51–76. Geneva: Graduate Institute of International and Development Studies.

OECD. 2011. *State-Owned Enterprise Governance Reform An Inventory of Recent Change*. Paris: Organisation for Economic Co-Operation and Development (OECD).

Offner, Amy C. 2019. *Sorting Out the Mixed Economy: The Rise and Fall of Welfare and Developmental States in the Americas*. Princeton: Princeton University Press.

O Globo. 1957. 'Suspeitas de corrupção na Petrobras'. *O Globo* 8 October, Frontpage.

Ohashi, Hideo. 2018. 'The Belt and Road Initiative (BRI) in the Context of China's Opening-up Policy'. *Journal of Contemporary East Asia Studies* 7 (2): 85–103.

Orihuela, José Carlos. 2013. 'How Do "Mineral-States" Learn? Path-Dependence, Networks, and Policy Change in the Development of Economic Institutions'. *World Development* 43 (March): 138–148.

Orihuela, José Carlos. 2018. 'Institutions and Place: Bringing Context Back into the Study of the Resource Curse'. *Journal of Institutional Economics* 14 (1): 157–180.

Orihuela, José Carlos, and Rosemary Thorp. 2012. 'The Political Economy of Managing Extractives in Bolivia, Ecuador and Peru'. In *Social Conflict, Economic Development and Extractive Industry: Evidence from South America*, edited by Anthony Bebbington, 27–45. London: Routledge.

Oseland, Stina Ellevseth, Håvard Haarstad, and Arnt Fløysand. 2012. 'Labor Agency and the Importance of the National Scale: Emergent Aquaculture Unionism in Chile'. *Political Geography* 31 (2): 94–103.

Ovadia, Jesse Salah. 2016. *The Petro-Developmental State in Africa: Making Oil Work in Angola, Nigeria and the Gulf of Guinea*. London: Hurst.

Ovadia, Jesse Salah, and Christina Wolf. 2018. 'Studying the developmental state: theory and method in research on industrial policy and state-led development in Africa' *Third World Quarterly* 39 (6): 1056–1076.

Oxhorn, Philip. 1998. 'Is the Century of Corporatism Over? Neoliberalism and the Rise of Neopluralism'. In *What Kind of Democracy? What Kind of Market? Latin America in the Age of Neoliberalism*, edited by Philip Oxhorn and Graciela Ducatenzeiler, 195–217. University Park: Pennsylvania State University Press.

Oxhorn, Philip, and Graciela Ducatenzeiler, eds. 1998. *What Kind of Democracy? What Kind of Market? Latin America in the Age of Neoliberalism*. University Park: Pennsylvania State University Press.

Pache, Anne-Claire, and Filipe Santos. 2010. 'When Worlds Collide: The Internal Dynamics of Organizational Responses to Conflicting Institutional Demands'. *The Academy of Management Review* 35 (3): 455–476.

Pache, Anne-Claire, and Filipe Santos. 2013. 'Inside the Hybrid Organization: Selective Coupling as a Response to Competing Institutional Logics'. *Academy of Management Journal* 56 (4): 972–1001.

Pananond, Pavida. 2013. 'Where Do We Go from Here? Globalizing Subsidiaries Moving Up the Value Chain'. *Emerging Market Firm Competitiveness: Internationalization, Innovation and Institutions (3Is)* 19 (3): 207–219.

Pardelli, Guilliana. 2010. 'Appendix 1: The Growth Acceleration Programme (PAC)'. In *Brazil Infrastructure: Paving the Way*. Morgan Stanley Blue Paper, 5 May. Accessed 15 July 2012, http://www.morganstanley.com/views/perspectives/pavingtheway.pdf.

Parra, Francisco. 2004. *Oil Politics—A Modern History of Petroleum*. London: I.B. Tauris & Bloomsbury Publishing.

Pearson, Margaret M. 2005. 'The Business of Governing Business in China: Institutions and Norms of the Emerging Regulatory State'. *World Politics* 57 (2): 296–322.

Pearson, Margaret M. 2011. 'Variety Within and Variety Without: The Political Economy of Chinese Regulation'. In *Beyond the Middle Kingdom: Comparative Perspectives on China's Capitalist Transformation*, edited by Scott Kennedy, 25–43. Stanford: Stanford University Press.

Pei, Minxin. 2006. *China's Trapped Transition: The Limits of Developmental Autocracy*. Cambridge, MA: Harvard University Press.

Pei, Minxin. 2016. *China's Crony Capitalism: The Dynamics of Regime Decay*. Cambridge, MA: Harvard University Press.

Pentland, William. 2013. 'World's Five Largest Offshore Oil Field'. *Forbes* 7 September.

298 References

Petras, James, and Henry Veltmeyer. 2009. *What's Left in Latin America? Regime Change in New Times*. Farnham: Ashgate.

Petras, James. 1972. 'Chile: Nacionalización, Transformaciones Socioeconómicas, y Participación Popular'. *Cuadernos de la Realidad Nacional* 11: 3–24.

Petrobras. 2007. 'Petrobras Annual Report 2007'. Rio de Janeiro: Petrobras.

Petrobras. 2010. 'Petrobras Annual Report 2010'. Rio de Janeiro: Petrobras.

Petrobras. 2013. 'Petrobras Annual Report 2013'. Rio de Janeiro: Petrobras.

Petrobras. 2015a. 'Petrobras Annual Report 2015'. Rio de Janeiro: Petrobras.

Petrobras. 2015b. 'Petrobras Management Report 2015'. Rio de Janeiro: Petrobras.

Petrobras. 2018. 'Petrobras Annual Report 2018'. Rio de Janeiro: Petrobras.

Petrobras. 2019. 'Petrobras Management Report 2019'. Rio de Janeiro: Petrobras.

Petrobras. 2020. 'Petrobras Investor Relations 2020'. Rio de Janeiro: Petrobras.

Petroperù. 2021. 'Petroperú SA—Fichas de Proyectos de Inversión Modernización Refinería Talara'. Formato Numero 17, October. Lima: Petroperù.

Philip, George. 1982. *Oil and Politics in Latin America: Nationalist Movements and State Companies*. Cambridge: Cambridge University Press.

Philip, George, and Francisco Panizza. 2011. *The Triumph of Politics: The Return of the Left in Venezuela, Bolivia and Ecuador*. Cambridge: Polity Press.

Pickup, Megan. 2018. 'The Political Economy of the New Left'. *Latin American Perspectives* 46 (1): 23–45.

Pinheiro, Armando Castelar, Regis Bonelli, and Ben Ross Schneider. 2004. *Pragmatic Policy in Brazil: The Political Economy of Incomplete Market Reform*. Texto Para Discussão Numero 1035. Rio de Janeiro: IPEA.

Pollack, Mark A. 1996. 'The New Institutionalism and EC Governance: The Promise and Limits of Institutional Analysis'. *Governance* 9 (4): 429–458. https://doi.org/10.1111/j.1468-0491.1996.tb00251.x

Pomfret, Richard, and Patricia Sourdin. 2018. 'Value Chains in Europe and Asia: Which Countries Participate?' *SI: Global Value Chains* 153 (May): 34–41.

Pooler, Michael. 2023. 'Petrobras Aims to Transform Brazil into Global Energy Power: South American Nation Set to Join World's Top Crude Producers by End of Decade'. *Financial Times* 19 November.

Posner, Richard A. 1975. 'The Social Costs of Monopoly and Regulation'. *Journal of Political Economy* 83 (4): 807–827.

Postali, Fernando Antonio. 2009. 'Petroleum Royalties and Regional Development in Brazil: The Economic Growth of Recipient Towns'. *Resources Policy* 34 (4): 205–213.

Prates, Daniela Magalhães, Barbara Fritz, and Luiz Fernando de Paula. 2017. 'Brazil at Crossroads: A Critical Assessment of Developmentalist Policies'. In *The Brazilian Economy Since the Great Financial Crisis of 2007/2008*, edited by Philip Arestis, Carolina Troncoso Baltar, and Daniela Magalhães Prates, 9–39. Cham: Springer Nature.

Prebisch, Raul. 1950. The Economic Development of Latin America and Its Principal Problems, United Nations Department of Economic Affairs, Economic Commission for Latin America (ECLA), New York. http://archivo.cepal.org/pdfs/cdPrebisch/002.pdf.

Presidential Press. 2022. 'Presidente de la República Gabriel Boric Font Anuncia Inicio del Proceso de Cierre de Fundición Ventanas: "No Queremos Más Zonas de Sacrificio"'. Government of Chile, 17 June.

Priest, Tyler. 2016. 'Petrobras in the History of Offshore Oil'. In *New Order and Progress: Development and Democracy in Brazil*, edited by Ben Ross Schneider, 53–77. Oxford: Oxford University Press.

Punto Minero. 2005. 'Royalty II en la Cámara'. April. Santiago de Chile: Ministerio de Minería en Chile.

PWC. 2014. 'A Indústria Brasileira de Petróleo e Gás'. São Paulo: PricewaterhouseCoopers Brasil (PWC).

Qian, Yingyi. 2017. *How Reform Worked in China: The Transition from Plan to Market.* Cambridge, MA: MIT Press.

Radon, Jenkins. 2005. 'The ABCs of Petroleum Contracts: License-Concession Agreements, Joint Ventures and Production-Sharing Agreements'. In *Covering Oil: A Reporter's Guide to Energy and Development*, edited by Svetalana Tsalik and Anya Schiffrin, 61–86. New York: Open Society Institute.

Ramamurti, Ravi, and Raymond Vernon, eds. 1991. *Privatization and Control of State-Owned Enterprises.* Washington, DC: World Bank.

Randall, Laura. 1993. *The Political Economy of Brazilian Oil.* New York: Praeger.

Ray, Rebecca, and Kevin P. Gallagher. 2017. *China–Latin America Economic Bulletin. 2017 Edition.* Discussion Paper 2017-1. Boston: Boston University.

Resende, Paulo. 2009. 'Chapter 2.1. Infrastructure: Will PAC Really Accelerate Growth?'. In *Brazil Competitiveness Report 2009*, edited by Irene Mia, Emilio Lozoya Austin, Carlos Arruda, Marina Silva Araújo, 31–39. Geneva: World Economic Forum.

Reuters. 2014. 'Factbox: Chile Tax Reform Set to Be Approved'. *Reuters* 10 September.

Reuters. 2015. 'Peru Congress Overrides President, Boosts State Energy Firm'. *Reuters* 23 October.

Riesco, Manuel, Gustavo Lagos Matus, and Marcos Lima. 2005. 'The "Pay Your Taxes" Debate: Perspectives on Corporate Taxation and Social Responsibility in the Chilean Mining Industry'. Geneva: United Nations Research Institute for Social Development. http://www.unrisd.org/80256B3C005BCCF9/httpNetITFramePDF?ReadForm&parentunid=D0911BEE223DF74EC12570AC0032E4E2&parentdoctype=paper&netitpath=80256B3C005BCCF9/(httpAuxPages)/D0911BEE223DF74EC12570AC0032E4E2/$file/riesco-pp.pdf.

Riofrancos, Thea. 2020. *Resource Radicals: From Petro-Nationalism to Post-Extractivism in Ecuador.* Radical Américas series. Durham: Duke University Press.

Rixen, Thomas, and Lora Anne Viola. 2014. 'Putting Path Dependence in Its Place: Toward a Taxonomy of Institutional Change'. *Journal of Theoretical Politics* 27 (2): 301–323.

Roberts, Kenneth M. 2003. 'Party System Collapse amid Market Restructuring in Venezuela'. In *Post-Stabilization Politics in Latin America: Competition, Transition, Collapse*, edited by Carol Wise and Riordan Roett, 249–288. Washington, DC: Brookings Institution Press.

Roberts, Kenneth M. 2016. '(Re)Politicizing Inequalities: Movements, Parties, and Social Citizenship in Chile'. *Journal of Politics in Latin America* 8 (3): 125–154.

Roll, Michael. 2014. *The Politics of Public Sector Performance: Pockets of Effectiveness in Developing.* London: Routledge.

Rosales, Antulio. 2018. 'Pursuing Foreign Investment for Nationalist Goals: Venezuela's Hybrid Resource Nationalism'. *Business and Politics* 20 (3): 438–464.

Rosales, Antulio, and Miriam Sánchez. 2021. 'The Energy Politics of Venezuela'. In *The Oxford Handbook of Energy Politics*, edited by Kathleen J. Hancock and Juliann Emmons Allison, 645–662. New York: Oxford University Press.

Ross, Michael L. 1999. 'The Political Economy of the Resource Curse'. *World Politics* 51 (2): 297–322.

Ross, Michael L. 2001a. 'Does Oil Hinder Democracy?' *World Politics* 53 (3): 325–361.

Ross, Michael L. 2001b. *Timber Booms and Institutional Breakdown in Southeast Asia.* Cambridge: Cambridge University Press.

Ross, Michael L. 2006. 'A Closer Look at Oil, Diamonds, and Civil War'. *Annual Review of Political Science* 9: 265–300. https://doi.org/10.1146/annurev.polisci.9.081304.161338

300 References

Ross, Michael L. 2012. *The Oil Curse: How Petroleum Wealth Shapes the Development of Nations*. Princeton: Princeton University Press.

Ross, Michael L. 2015. 'What Have We Learned about the Resource Curse?'. *Annual Review of Political Science* 18: 239–259. https://doi.org/10.1146/annurev-polisci-052213-040359

Rossi, Federico M. 2017. *The Poor's Struggle for Popular Incorporation: The Piquetero Movement in Argentina*. Cambridge: Cambridge University Press.

Rudra, Nita, and Nathan M. Jensen. 2011. 'Globalization and the Politics of Natural Resources'. *Comparative Political Studies* 44(6): 639–661.

Saad-Filho, Alfredo, and Lecio Morais. 2018. *Brazil: Neoliberalism Versus Democracy*. London: Pluto Press.

Sachs, Jeffrey D. 1992. 'Privatization in Russia: Some Lessons from Eastern Europe'. *The American Economic Review* 82 (2): 43–48.

Sachs, Jeffrey, and Andrew Warner. 1995. 'Economic Reform and the Process of Global Integration'. *Brookings Papers on Economic Activity* 1995 (1): 1–118.

Sachs, Jeffrey and Andrew Warner. 1995. Revised 1997, 1999. Natural resource abundance and economic growth. National Bureau of Economic Research. Working Paper No.5398, Cambridge, MA.

Sachs, Jeffrey, and Andrew Warner. 1999. 'The Big Push, Natural Resource Booms and Growth'. *Journal of Development Economics*, 59 (1): 43–76.

Sánchez-Ancochea, Diego. 2009. 'State, Firms and the Process of Industrial Upgrading: Latin America's Variety of Capitalism and the Costa Rican Experience'. *Economy and Society* 38 (1): 62–86.

Sanderson, Henry. 2022. *Volt Rush: The Winners and Losers in the Race to Go Green*. London: Oneworld.

Santoro, Maurício. 2022. *Brazil–China Relations in the 21st Century: The Making of a Strategic Partnership*. Cham: Springer Nature.

Santos, Fabiano, and Fernando Guarnieri. 2016. 'From Protest to Parliamentary Coup: An Overview of Brazil's Recent History'. *Journal of Latin American Cultural Studies* 25 (4): 485–494.

Santos, Rodrigo S.P., and Bruno Milanez. 2015. 'Topsy-Turvy Neo-Developmentalism: An Analysis of the Current Brazilian Model of Development'. *Revista de Estudios Sociales* 53: 12–28.

Sawyer, Suzana, and Edmund Terence Gomez, eds. 2012. *The Politics of Resource Extraction: Indigenous Peoples, Multinational Capital, and the State*. Basingstoke: Palgrave Macmillan.

Saylor, Ryan. 2014. *State-Building in Boom Times: Commodities and Coalitions in Latin America and Africa*. Oxford: Oxford University Press.

Schamis, Hector E. 2002. *Re-Forming the State: The Politics of Privatization in Latin America and Europe*. Interests, Identities, and Institutions in Comparative Politics. Ann Arbor: University of Michigan Press.

Schipani, Andres. 2013. 'PetroPeru Hopes to Follow in Steps of Ecopetrol'. *Financial Times* 9 December.

Schmidt, Vivien. 2009. 'Putting the Political Back Into Political Economy by Bringing the State Back in Yet Again'. *World Politics* 61 (3): 516–546.

Schmitter, Philippe. 1971. *Interest Conflict and Political Change in Brazil*. Stanford: Stanford University Press.

Schmitter, Philippe. 1972. *Interest Conflict and Political Change in Brazil*. Stanford: Stanford University Press.

Schmitter, Philippe. 1974. 'Still the Century of Corporatism?' *The Review of Politics* 36 (1): 85–131.

Schneider, Ben Ross. 1991. *Politics Within the State: Elite Bureaucrats and Industrial Policy in Authoritarian Brazil*. Pitt Latin American series. Pittsburgh: University of Pittsburgh Press.

Schneider, Ben Ross. 2004a. *Business Politics and the State in Twentieth-Century Latin America*. Cambridge: Cambridge University Press.

Schneider, Ben Ross. 2004b. 'Organizing Interests and Coalitions in the Politics of Market Reform in Latin America'. World Politics 56 (3): 456–479.

Schneider, Ben Ross. 2009a. 'A Comparative Political Economy of Diversified Business Groups, or How States Organize Big Business'. *Review of International Political Economy* 16 (2): 178–201.

Schneider, Ben Ross. 2009b. 'Hierarchical Market Economies and Varieties of Capitalism in Latin America'. *Journal of Latin American Studies* 41 (3): 553–575.

Schneider, Ben Ross. 2013. *Hierarchical Capitalism in Latin America: Business, Labor, and the Challenges of Equitable Development*. Cambridge Studies in Comparative Politics. Cambridge: Cambridge University Press.

Schneider, Ben Ross, and David Soskice. 2009. 'Inequality in Developed Countries and Latin America: Coordinated, Liberal, and Hierarchical Systems'. *Economy and Society* 38 (1): 17–52.

Schrank, Andrew, and Marcus J. Kurtz. 2005. 'Credit Where Credit Is Due: Open Economy Industrial Policy and Export Diversification in Latin America and the Caribbean'. *Politics & Society* 33 (4): 671–702.

Secretariat for Social Communication of the Presidency of Brazil (SECOM). 2010. 'Brazil Announces Phase 2 of the Growth Acceleration Programme', March 30. Accessed 15 July 2012, http://blogs.worldbank.org/growth/brazil-announces-phase-twogrowth-acceleration-program#secom.

Securities and Exchange Commission (SEC). 2002. *Annual Report 2002: Petróleo Brasileiro S.A.—Petrobras*. Washington, DC: SEC.

Sehnbruch, Kirsten. 2006. *The Chilean Labour Market: A Key to Understanding Latin American Labour Markets*. New York: Palgrave Macmillan.

Sehnbruch, Kirsten, and Sofia Donoso. 2020. 'Social Protests in Chile: Inequalities and Other Inconvenient Truths about Latin America's Poster Child'. *Global Labour Journal* 11 (1): 52–58.

Senate Press. 2004. 'Empresarios Mineros: "No es el Momento de Hablar de Royalty"'. Accessed 28 May 2012, http://www.senado.cl/prontus_galeria_noticias/site/artic/20080204/pags/20080204153811.html.

Senate Press. 2005. *Modificación Impuesto Específico a la Minería Ley 20.469 del 16 de Junio 2005*. Santiago: Senate Press.

Servicio Nacional de Geologia y Minería (SERNAGEOMIN). 2010. Annual Statistics. Santiago: SERNAGEOMIN. http://www.sernageomin.cl/.

Shafer, D. Michael. 1994. *Winners and Losers: How Sectors Shape the Developmental Prospects of States*. Cornell Studies in Political Economy. Ithaca: Cornell University Press.

Sherwood, Dave. 2019. 'Chilean Lawmakers Abolish Law Requiring Codelco to Finance Military'. *Reuters* 24 July.

Shever, Elana. 2012. *Resources for Reform: Oil and Neoliberalism in Argentina*. Stanford: Stanford University Press.

Shih, Victor. 2007. *Factions and Finance in China: Elite Conflict and Inflation*. Cambridge: Cambridge University Press.

Shih, Victor. 2021. 'Constructing a Chinese AI Global Supply Chain in the Shadow of "Great Power Competition"'. In *Geopolitics, Supply Chains, and International Relations in East Asia*, edited by Etel Solingen, 60–76. Cambridge: Cambridge University Press.

302 References

Shirley, Mary M. 1999. 'Bureaucrats in Business: The Roles of Privatization Versus Corporatization in State-Owned Enterprise Reform'. *World Development* 27 (1): 115–136.

Shleifer, Andrei. 1998. 'State Versus Private Ownership'. *Journal of Economic Perspectives* 12 (4): 133–150.

Sicsú, João, Luiz Fernando de Paula, and Renaut Michel. 2007. 'Por que Novo- Desenvolvimentismo?' *Revista de Economia Política* 27 (4): 507–524.

Sikkink, Kathryn. 1991. *Ideas and Institutions: Developmentalism in Brazil and Argentina.* Ithaca: Cornell University Press.

Silva, Cedê. 2023. 'Lula Moves Against Bill Allowing Mining on Indigenous Land'. The Brazilian Report 31 March.

Silva, Eduardo. 2009. *Challenging Neoliberalism in Latin America.* Cambridge: Cambridge University Press.

Silva, Patricio. 2008. *In the Name of Reason: Technocrats and Politics in Chile.* University Park: Pennsylvania State University Press.

Silva, Patricio. 2018. 'The Chilean Developmental State: Political Balance, Economic Accommodation, and Technocratic Insulation, 1924–1973'. In *State and Nation Making in Latin America and Spain: The Rise and Fall of the Developmental State*, edited by Ferraro A. E and Centeno M. A, 284–314. New York: Cambridge University Press.

Silva, Eduardo, and Federico M. Rossi, eds. 2018. *Reshaping the Political Arena in Latin America: From Resisting Neoliberalism to the Second Incorporation.* Pittsburgh: University of Pittsburgh Press.

SINAVAL. 2012. *Brazil: Offshore and Shipbuilding Industries Overview.* Rio de Janeiro: Sindicato Nacional da Indústria da Construção e Reparação Naval e Offshore (SINAVAL). http://sinaval.org.br/wp-content/uploads/SINAVAL-BrazilianShipyardsOverview-Jan2012.pdf.

Singer, Hans. 1950. 'The Distribution of Gains Between Investing and Borrowing Countries', American Economic Review, Papers and Proceedings 40: 473–485.

Smith, Benjamin. 2007. *Hard Times in the Lands of Plenty: Oil Politics in Iran and Indonesia.* Ithaca: Cornell University Press.

Smith, Peter S. 1969. 'Petroleum in Brazil: A Study in Economic Nationalism'. PhD dissertation. New Mexico: The University of New Mexico.

Smith, Peter S. 1976. *Oil and Politics in Modern Brazil.* Toronto: Macmillan Canada.

Soifer, Hillel David. 2009. 'The Sources of Infrastructural Power: Evidence from Nineteenth-Century Chilean Education' *Latin American Research Review* 44 (2): 158–180.

Soifer, Hillel David. 2015. *State Building in Latin America.* Cambridge: Cambridge University Press.

Sola, Lourdes. 1998. *Ideias Econômicas, Decisões Políticas.* São Paulo: Edusp.

Solingen, Etel. 2021. 'Introduction: Geopolitics and Global Supply Chains'. In *Geopolitics, Supply Chains, and International Relations in East Asia*, edited by Etel Solingen, 1–22. Cambridge: Cambridge University Press.

Stepan, Alfred. 1971. *The Military in Politics. Changing Patterns in Brazil.* Princeton: Princeton University Press.

Stepan, Alfred, ed. 1973. *Authoritarian Brazil: Origins, Policies, Future.* New Haven: Yale University Press.

Stevens, Paul. 2012. 'Saudi Aramco: The Jewel in the Crown'. In *Oil and Governance: State-Owned Enterprises and the World Energy Supply*, edited by David G. Victor, David R. Hults, and Mark Thurber, 173–233. Cambridge: Cambridge University Press.

Stiglitz, Joseph E. 1993. 'The Role of the State in Financial Markets'. *The World Bank Economic Review* 7 (suppl_1): 19–52.

Stiglitz, Joseph E. 2002. *Globalization and its Discontents.* New York: W.W. Norton.

Stubrin, Lilia. 2017. 'Innovation, Learning and Competence Building in the Mining Industry. The Case of Knowledge Intensive Mining Suppliers (KIMS) in Chile'. *Resources Policy* 54 (December): 167–175.

Svampa, Maristella, and Enrique Viale. 2015. *Maldesarrollo: La Argentina del Extractivismo y el Despojo*. Buenos Aires: Katz Editors.

Sztutman, Andre Medeiros, and Dante Mendes Aldrighi. 2019. 'Political Connections and Access to Brazilian Development Bank's Loans'. São Paulo: University of São Paulo (FEA-USP).

Takagi, Yusuke, Veerayooth Kanchoochat, and Sonome Tetsushi. 2019. *Developmental State Building: The Politics of Emerging Economies*. Cham: Springer.

Tandeter, Enrique. 2006. 'The Mining Industry'. In *The Cambridge Economic History of Latin America, Volume 1: The Colonial Era and the Short Nineteenth Century*, edited by Victor Bulmer-Thomas, John H. Coatsworth, and Roberto Cortes-Conde, 357–394. Cambridge: Cambridge University Press.

Taylor, Ian, and Tim Zajontz. 2020. 'In a Fix: Africa's Place in the Belt and Road Initiative and the Reproduction of Dependency'. *South African Journal of International Affairs* 27 (3): 277–295.

Taylor, Marcus. 2006. *From Pinochet to the 'Third Way': Neoliberalism and Social Transformation in Chile*. Chicago: Pluto Press.

Taylor, Marcus. 2010. 'Evolution of the Competition State in Latin America: Power, Contestation, and Neo-liberal Populism'. *Policy Studies* 31 (1): 39–56.

Taylor, Mark Zachary. 2016. *The Politics of Innovation: Why Some Countries Are Better than Others at Science and Technology*. Oxford: Oxford University Press.

Taylor, Matthew. 2020. *Decadent Developmentalism: The Political Economy of Democratic Brazil*. Cambridge: Cambridge University Press.

Teichman, Judith A. 2003. *The Politics of Freeing Markets in Latin America: Chile, Argentina, and Mexico*. Chapel Hill: University of North Carolina Press.

Thee, Kian Wie. 2012. *Indonesia's Economy Since Independence*. Pasir Panjang: ISEAS–Yusof Ishak Institute.

Thelen, Kathleen. 1999. 'Historical Institutionalism in Comparative Politics'. *Annual Review of Political Science* 2: 382.

Thorp, Rosemary, Stefania Battistelli, Yvan Guichaoua, José Carlos Orihuela, and Maritza Paredes. 2012. *The Developmental Challenges of Mining and Oil: Lessons from Africa and Latin America*. Basingstoke: Palgrave Macmillan.

Thurber, Mark, and Benedicte Tangen Istad. 2012. 'Norway's Evolving Champion: Statoil and the Politics of State Enterprise'. In *Oil and Governance: State-Owned Enterprises and the World Energy Supply*, edited by David G. Victor, David R. Hults, and Mark Thurber, 599–654. Cambridge: Cambridge University Press.

Thurbon, Elizabeth. 2016. *Developmental Mindset*. Ithaca: Cornell University Press.

Tilly, Charles. 1992. *Coercion, Capital and European States, AD 990–1992*. Cambridge, MA: Blackwell Publishers.

Toninelli, Pier Angelo, ed. 2000. *The Rise and Fall of State-Owned Enterprise in the Western World*. Comparative Perspectives in Business History. Cambridge: Cambridge University Press.

Tõnurist, Piret. 2015. 'Framework for Analysing the Role of State-Owned Enterprises in Innovation Policy Management: The Case of Energy Technologies and Eesti Energia'. *Technovation* 38 (April): 1–14.

Topik, Steven, and Mario Samper. 2006. 'The Latin American Coffee Commodity Chain: Brazil and Costa Rica'. In *From Silver to Cocaine: Latin American Commodity Chains and the Building of the World Economy, 1500–2000*, edited by Steven Topik, Carlos Marichal, and Zephyr Frank, 118–146. Durham: Duke University Press.

Tordo, Silvana, Osmel E. Manzano, and Yahya Anouti. 2013. *Local Content in the Oil and Gas Sector*. Washington, DC: World Bank.

Trebat, Thomas J. 1983. *Brazil's State-Owned Enterprises: A Case Study of the State as Entrepreneur*. Cambridge Latin American Studies. Cambridge: Cambridge University Press.

304 References

Triner, Gail D. 2011. *Mining and the State in Brazilian Development*. Perspectives in Economic and Social History. London: Pickering & Chatto.

Tsai, Kellee S., and Barry Naughton. 2015. 'Introduction'. In *State Capitalism, Institutional Adaptation, and the Chinese Miracle*, edited by Barry Naughton and Kellee S. Tsai, 1–24. Comparative Perspectives in Business History. Cambridge: Cambridge University Press.

Tugwell, Franklin. 1975. *The Politics of Oil in Venezuela*. Stanford: Stanford University Press.

Ugarte Cataldo, José Luis. 2006. 'Sobre Relaciones Laborales Triangulares: La Subcontratación y el Suministro de Trabajadores'. *Ius et Praxis* 12 (1): 11–29.

Ulfelder, Jay. 2007. 'Natural-Resource Wealth and the Survival of Autocracy'. *Comparative Political Studies* 40 (8): 995–1018.

United States of America vs. Braskem SA 2016a. Plea Agreement CR No. 16-644, United States District Court Eastern District of New York.

United States of America vs. Odebrecht SA. 2016b. Plea Agreement CR No. 16-643, United States District Court Eastern District of New York.

US Department of State. 2021. '2021 Investment Climate Statements: Peru'. Lima: US Embassy in Peru.

Valenzuela, Arturo. 1978. *The Breakdown of Democratic Regimes: Chile*. Baltimore: Johns Hopkins University Press.

Van Donge, J. K., Henley, D., Lewis, P. 2012. 'Tracking Development in South-East Asia and sub-Saharan Africa: The Primacy of Policy'. *Development and Policy Review* 30 (1). https://doi.org/10.1111/j.1467-7679.2012.00563.x.

Venditti, Bruno. 2022. 'Brazil's President-Elect Lula Vows Greener Mining'. *Mining.com* 30 October.

Vergara, Alberto, and Aaron Watanabe. 2019. 'Presidents Without Roots: Understanding the Peruvian Paradox'. *Latin American Perspectives* 46 (5): 25–43.

Vergara, Angela. 2008. *Copper Workers, International Business, and Domestic Politics in Cold War Chile*. University Park: Pennsylvania State University Press.

Vickers, John Stuart, and George Yarrow. 1988. *Privatization: An Economic Analysis*. Cambridge, MA: MIT Press.

Victor, David G., David R. Hults, and Mark Thurber. 2012. 'Introduction and Overview'. In *Oil and Governance: State-Owned Enterprises and the World Energy Supply*, edited by David G. Victor, David R. Hults, and Mark Thurber, 3–31. Cambridge: Cambridge University Press.

Villarzú, Juan R. 2005. 'CODELCO y el Modelo de Alianza Estratégica'. Powerpoint presentation by the executive president of Codelco, Santiago, 21 October.

Vu, Tuong. 2010a. *Paths to Development in Asia: South Korea, Vietnam, China and Indonesia*. Cambridge: Cambridge University Press.

Vu, Tuong. 2010b. 'Studying the State Through State Formation'. *World Politics* 62 (1): 148–175.

Wade, Robert Hunter. 1990. *Governing the Market: Economic Theory and the Role of Government in East Asian Industrialization*. Princeton: Princeton University Press.

Waldner, David. 1999. *State Building and Late Development*. Ithaca: Cornell University Press.

Waterbury, John. 1994. 'Democracy Without Democrats? The Potential for Political Liberalization in the Middle East'. In *Democracy Without Democrats? The Renewal of Politcs in the Muslim World*, edited by Salamé Ghassan, 23–47. London: I.B. Taurus.

Waterbury, John. 1997. 'Fortuitous By-Products'. *Comparative Politics, Transitions to Democracy: A Special Issue in Memory of Dankwart Rustow* 29 (3): 383–402.

Wedeman, Andrew. 2012. *Double Paradox: Rapid Growth and Rising Corruption in China*. Ithaca: Cornell University Press.

Weinthal, Erika, and Pauline Jones Luong. 2006. 'Combating the Resource Curse: An Alternative Solution to Managing Mineral Wealth'. *Perspectives on Politics* 4 (1): 35–53.

Weiss, Linda. 1998. *The Myth of the Powerless State: Governing the Economy in the Global Era*. Cambridge: Polity Press.

Weiss, Linda, and John Hobson. 1995. *States and Economic Development: A Comparative Historical Analysis*. Cambridge: Polity Press.

Weiss, Linda and Elizabeth Thurbon. 2020. Developmental State or Economic Statecraft? Where, Why and How the Difference Matters, New Political Economy. https://doi.org/10.1080/13563467.2020.1766431.

Weyland, Kurt. 2002. 'Limitations of Rational-Choice Institutionalism for the Study of Latin American Politics'. *Studies in Comparative International Development* 37 (1): 57–85.

Weyland, Kurt, Raúl L. Madrid, and Wendy Hunter, eds. 2010. *Leftist Governments in Latin America: Successes and Shortcomings*. Cambridge: Cambridge University Press.

Wiens, David, Paul Poast, and William Roberts Clark. 2014. 'The Political Resource Curse: An Empirical Re-Evaluation'. *Political Research Quarterly* 67 (4): 783–794.

Wilson Center. 2016. 'Judge Sérgio Moro on "Handling Political Corruption Cases in Brazil"'. 14 July. Rule of Law Lecture series.

Wilson, Jeffrey D. 2015. 'Understanding Resource Nationalism: Economic Dynamics and Political Institutions'. *Contemporary Politics* 21 (4): 399–416.

Winn, Peter, ed. 2004. *Victims of the Chilean Miracle: Workers and Neoliberalism in the Pinochet Era, 1973–2002*. Durham: Duke University Press.

Wirth, John D. 1970. *The Politics of Brazilian Development, 1930–1954*. Stanford: Stanford University Press.

Wise, Carol. 2003. *Reinventing the State: Economic Strategy and Institutional Change in Peru*. Michigan: University of Michigan Press.

World Bank. n.d. 'GDP Growth (Annual %)—Mongolia'. Washington, DC: World Bank.

World Bank. 2015. *Global Economic Prospects, January 2015: Having Fiscal Space and Using It*. Washington, DC: World Bank.

World Investment Report. 2013. *Global Value Chains: Investment and Trade for Development*. New York: UNCTAD.

Wright, Gavin, and Jesse Czelusta. 2004. 'The Myth of the Resource Curse'. *Challenge* 47 (2): 6–38.

Xavier Junior, Carlos Eduardo Ramos. 2012. 'Políticas de Conteúdo Local no Setor Petrolífero'. Discussion Paper 1775. Brasília: Instituto de Pesquisa Econômica Aplicada (IPEA).

Yashar, Deborah J. 2005. *Contesting Citizenship in Latin America: The Rise of the Indigenous Movements and Postliberal Challenges*. Cambridge: Cambridge University Press.

Yergin, Daniel. 1992. *The Prize: The Epic Quest for Oil, Money, and Power*. New York: Simon and Schuster.

Yeung, Godfrey. 2019. '"Made in China 2025": The Development of a New Energy Vehicle Industry in China'. *Area Development and Policy* 4 (1): 39–59.

Yeung, Henry Wai-chung. 2016. *Strategic Coupling: East Asian Industrial Transformation in the New Global Economy*. Ithaca: Cornell University Press.

Yeung, Henry Wai-chung. 2017. 'State-Led Development Reconsidered: The Political Economy of State Transformation in East Asia since the 1990s'. *Cambridge Journal of Regions, Economy and Society* 10 (1): 83–98.

Yoder, Richard A., Philip L. Borkholder, and Brian D. Friesen. 1991. 'Privatization and Development: The Empirical Evidence'. *Journal of Developing Areas* 25 (3): 425–434.

Zapata, Francisco. 1975 . *Los Mineros de Chuquicamata ¿Productores o Proletarios?* Mexico City: Centro de Estudios Sociológicos, Colegio de México.

Zhang, Fang, and Kelly Sims Gallagher. 2016. 'Innovation and Technology Transfer Through Global Value Chains: Evidence from China's PV Industry'. *Energy Policy* 94 (July): 191–203.

Index

For the benefit of digital users, indexed terms that span two pages (e.g., 52–53) may, on occasion, appear on only one of those pages.

Tables and figures are indicated by an italic *t* and *f* following the page numbers.

A

Africa, 245–246
  supply chains, 7–9, 9*f*
agency, *see* state agency
Aguirre Cerda, Pedro, 84–85
Alessandri, Jorge, 88–89
Allende, Salvador, 90–92, 125
Altamirano, Luis (General), 83–84
Andrade, Ovaldo, 121–122
Ang, Yuen Yuen, 224
Argentina, 273–274
  delimiting foreign-owned enterprises in
    O&G industries, 68–69
  as extractive regime, 39
  industrialization, 66
  national autonomous development, 49
  state-led development, 79–80
Australia, 128–129, 131, 271–272
  as lithium producer, 158–160
  REEs, 4–5
authoritarianism
  Brazil's military government, 94–95,
    101–102, 104, 105
  Fujimori and neoliberal
    authoritarianism, 255–256
  Pinochet and neoliberal
    authoritarianism, 91–94, 109,
    135–137, 236
  rentier state and, 30–31, 35–36
Aylwin, Patricio, 142

B

Bachelet, Michelle, 116–117, 132
  2006 FTC National Proposal, 156
  on lithium, 160–161
  on subcontracting, 121–122, 126–127
Barbosa, Nelson, 209
Betancourt, Romulo, 71–72
Biden, Joe, 3–4

BNDE (*Banco Nacional de Desenvolvimento Econômico*/Brazilian Economic Development Bank), 99
BNDES (*Banco Nacional de Desenvolvimento Econômico e Social*/Brazilian National Economic and Social Development Bank), 57–58, 189, 208, 214–215, 223
  assets, 217–219
  BNDESPAR (subsidiary), 167–168
  institutional reorientation of, 188
  lending, 216–217, 217*t*, 217–219, 218*t*, 222–223
  Petrobras: *Lava Jato* scandal, 214–219
  Petrobras system, restructuring of, 168–169
  PT government and, 188
  restructuring of petrochemical sector, 167–168
Bolivia, 66–67, 81–82, 120–121, 148, 149, 273–274
Bolsonaro, Jair, 223–224, 262
  mineral extraction in the Amazon rainforest, 262
  Petrobras and, 165–166, 236–237
Boric, Gabriel, 244–245, 261–262
Brazil
  1889–1930 First Republic, 94–95
  1922, 1924 attempted coup d'états, 94–95
  1929 global financial crisis, 95
  1930–1964 developmental state, 94–101
  1934 Constitution, 95–96
  1945–1964 democratic period, 97–98
  1959 Cuban Revolution and, 99–101
  1964–1985 military period, 100–105, 166–167, 186–187
  1985–1996 neoliberalism as (partial) post-crisis strategy, 166–170
  1986 Cruzado Plan, 106

308 Index

Brazil (*Continued*)
  1987 Bresser Plan, 106
  2008 crisis, 208
  anti-statism, 222–224
  bureaucracy, 97–98
  China and, 262–264, 273–274
  centralized state, 94–97
  clean energy transition, 262, 275
  coffee, 64, 95, 96–97
  conservative governments, 165–166, 190, 196, 221, 223–224
  corruption, 209–211, 221, 224
  crisis of governance and legitimacy (today), 221, 223–224
  democracy, 94–95, 106
  dependent development, 69
  desenvolvimentismo (developmentalism), 19–21, 26–27, 50, 79–80, 94–95, 166–168, 223–224, 231, 232, 237–238
  desenvolvimentismos: distinction between old and new, 184–187
  developmental state, decline of, 221–225
  development strategies: strong resource extractive component, 18–19
  development strategies and political corruption, 216
  as *dirigiste-corporatist* state, 77
  elites, 19–21, 94–96, 166, 223–224, 232, 233–235
  Estado Novo/New State, 94–97
  export economy, 94–95, 231
  as extractive regime, 39
  hybrid development model, 14–15, 26–27, 43–44, 46–49, 48*f*, 50, 59–60, 177–178, 230, 232, 259, 266–267
  industrialization/industrial policy, 19–21, 66, 96–97, 166, 221–223, 232, 261–264
  institutional development, 50, 196
  labour movements/conflicts, 95–98
  lost decade, 106–108
  market reforms, 22, 43–45, 222–223
  Middle East and, 103–104, 203–204
  military, the, 97–99
  national autonomous development, 49
  nationalization of natural resources, 95–97

  national security and natural resources, 95–96, 99, 102–103, 237–238
  natural-resource-based development, 40, 261–262
  neoliberalism, 22, 26–27, 166–170, 233–237
  novo desenvolvimentismo/new developmentalism, 166, 184–186
  poverty reduction, 209–210, 215
  private sector, 95–96
  privatization, 168
  resource curse, 14–15
  resource dependency, 263–264
  Rousseff's developmentalist strategy, 208–209
  shipbuilding industry, 190–192
  state activism, 233–235, 249–250
  state-building, 24–25, 80, 94–95
  state capitalism, 184, 188–189
  state intervention, 14–15, 19–21, 50, 94–95, 98, 177–178
  taxation, 95–96, 209, 251, 262
  technocracy, 50, 98–101, 167–168
  trade balance, 182–184, 183*f*
  Venezuela/Brazil comparison, 264–265
  World War II, 96–97
  see also Brazil/Chile comparison; Cardoso, Fernando Henrique; Lula da Silva, Luiz Inácio; Rousseff, Dilma; Vargas, Getúlio
Brazil: O&G sector, 13–14
  1996–2018 continuity and change in, 169–170, 170*t*
  1997–2002 'Norwegian model', 173–178
  1997 Petroleum Law (Lei 9.478), 173–179, 190–192, 203–204, 236–237
  age of oil in Brazil, 182–187
  age of pre-salt: institutional change, 187–188
  ANP (*Agência Nacional do Petróleo*/National Petroleum Agency), 175–181, 189–190, 192–193
  BNDES and, 167–168, 188, 189
  CNPE (*Conselho Nacional de Política Energética*/National Council for Energy Policy), 177
  competition, 165–166, 175–178, 190–193

Index 309

concessions regime, 97–98, 175, 181–182, 187–188, 190–192
as 'contestable market', 195–196
desenvolvimentismo: institutional continuity under Cardoso, 178–181, 189–190, 192–193
'developmentalist' orientation, 19–21, 237–238
distribution downstream segment, 193, 195*t*
DL 2.004, 98–99, 102–103
ecological costs of hydrocarbon extraction, 179
environment protection, 179
fiscal regimes, 173–175, 174*t*, 178–179, 179*t*, 181–182
foreign participation in, 68–69, 97–98, 166–167, 173–175, 177–178, 181, 192–193, 238–239
industrialization and, 95–98, 165–166, 178–179, 181, 186–187, 196, 199
industrialization under PT, 188–193
intersectoral linkages, 18–19, 184, 188–192, 233–235, 246–247
IOCs, 47–49, 108, 166–167, 175–176, 190–192
LCRs (local content requirements), 178–182, 182*f*, 188–190, 191*t*, 192–193, 222–223, 232
Lula/Cardoso comparison regarding O&G sector, 181–182, 188–189
market opening reforms, 166–167, 173–175, 177–178, 236–237
nationalist restrictions on foreign exploration activities, 95–96, 98–99
oil exploration, 98–99, 192–193, 194*t*
oil governance model, 192–196
oil nationalization, 95–99, 166–167
'oil question', 97–99
payments attached to taxes, 178, 179*t*
Petróleo é Nosso campaign, 97–99
pre-salt reserves, 184, 185*f*, 186–188, 190–193
privatization, 167–168, 168*t*, 168–170, 177–178
production-sharing regime, 181–182, 187–188
PT in power, 181–182
rent-seeking, 165–166
SOEs and, 168

state developmentalism: institutional continuity, 166
state ownership, 165–167, 192–193, 195–196
technological innovation, 188–189
see also Petrobras
Brazil: SOEs, 17–19, 95–98, 223–224
Brazil/Chile comparison, 27–28, 80, 233–235
Cardoso, Fernando Henrique and, 168, 177–178
CSN (*Companhia Siderúrgica Nacional*), 96–97
CVRD/Vale (*Companhia Vale do Rio Doce*), 96–97, 169–170, 184–186, 236–237
O&G sector, 168
PPSA/Petró-Sal (Pré-Sal Petróleo S.A., Brazil), 187–188
privatization, 168, 177–178
SOEs as central pillar of development strategy, 19–21
see also Petrobras
Brazil/Chile comparison, 24–26, 230–239, 259
developmentalism, 24–25
divergent models of natural resource governance, 231–232
hybrid development models, 19–21, 50, 231–235, 234*f*, 237–238
institutional stability and change, 232–233
natural-resource-based development, 25–26
neoliberalism, 235, 237–239
policy instruments of resource control, 238–239
SOEs, 27–28, 80, 233–235
state activism, 249–250
state capacity, 25
state dominance, 41–42
successful state-building, 24–25
timing, sequencing, and pace of market reforms, 236–237
see also Petrobras/Codelco comparison
Brooks, Sarah M., 41–42
Bruton, Garry D., 58–59
Bulmer-Thomas, Victor, 64, 79–80
Bunker, Stephen, 37

310 Index

bureaucracy
  Brazil, 97–98
  bureaucratic corruption, 224
  Chile, 83–84, 87
  East Asian states, 13
  extractive bureaucracy, 34–35
  Latin America, 79–80
  meritocratic bureaucracy, 37–38
  Petrobras, 176–177, 205–206, 236–237
  petro-states, 34
  professional bureaucracy, 50
  SOEs, 51, 233
  state capacity and, 13
  Venezuela, 70, 75–77

C

Campodónico, Humberto, 257–258
capitalism
  emerging supply chains in renewable
    energy capitalism, 7–12
  varieties of capitalism debate, 265–266
  see also state capitalism
carbon emission reduction, 158–159, 267
  Brazil, 262
  UN Paris Agreement, 4–5, 7–9
  see also decarbonization
Cardoso, Fernando Henrique, 167–168
  1994 Real Plan, 168
  desenvolvimentismo: institutional
    continuity under Cardoso, 178–181
  fiscal regime, 173–175
  Lula/Cardoso comparison regarding
    O&G sector, 181–182, 188–189
  market opening reforms, 173–175,
    177–178, 236–237
  neoliberalism, 166
  O&G sector governance, 170*t*
  oil governance model: *institutional*
    layering, 165–166
  patronage system, 215
  Petrobras and, 168–175, 241–242
  poverty reduction: Family Health
    Strategy, 215
  SOEs privatization, 168, 177–178
Castello Branco, Humberto de Alencar
  (General), 101–102
CATL (Contemporary Amperex Technology
  Co. Limited, China), 10–12

CDI (*Comissão de Desenvolvimento
  Industrial*/Commission of Industrial
  Development, Brazil), 99
centre/periphery dynamics, 37, 39–40
Cepalistas, 32–33, 71–72, 109–110, 116–117
Chávez, Hugo, 77–78, 243, 253–255,
  259–260
Chen, Geoffrey C., 14, 55, 58–59
Chile, 136–137
  1925–1973 developmental state, 81–91
  1929 global financial crisis, 83–84
  1973 military coup d'état, 81–82, 90–91
  1978 Labour Code, 121–123, 126–127,
    157–158
  1980 Constitution, 111–112
  1982 economic crisis, 92–93
  1990–1999 neoliberal continuity with
    changes, 111–115
  1990–2016 total factor productivity,
    131, 131*f*
  2000–2010 incremental
    changes, 115–127
  2010–2020 growth model amidst
    turbulent times, 127–134
  2019 October *estallido social*, 128,
    135–136, 162–163, 261–262
  bureaucracy, 83–84, 87
  capital–labour relations, 162
  centralized state, 81–82, 90, 109
  'Chicago Boys', 91–92, 231–232
  China and, 116, 129
  clean energy transition, 261–262
  clientelism, 81–82
  Concertación governments: changes
    introduced by, 116–121
  Concertación governments: neoliberal
    governance, 93–94, 109–115, 127–129,
    135–137, 153, 231–232, 236
  democracy, 81–82, 90–94, 135–136, 236
  developmentalism, 26–27, 79–80,
    91–92, 231
  elites, 19–21, 81–82, 111–112, 157–158,
    231–235
  Estado de Compromiso/State of
    Compromise, 85–86, 135–136
  export-oriented model, 81–84, 90,
    110–111, 134–135, 231
  extractivism, 18–19, 273–274
  hybrid development model, 14–15,
    26–27, 43–44, 46–49, 43*f*, 50, 59–60,

109–110, 134–135, 137, 147, 163, 230–232, 259, 266–267
hybrid development model: contradictions, 139–140
industrialization, 66, 84–87, 110–111
institutional development, 50, 109–111, 120–121
ISI, 84–85, 87, 231
LCRs, 161
market reforms, 22, 43–45
myth of neoliberal Chile, 140–143
natural-resource-based development, 27, 40, 136, 148–149, 249, 261–262
neoliberalism, 22, 26–27, 47–49, 90–94, 109, 135–137, 163, 231–236, 246–247, 261–262
neostructuralism, 109–110, 134–137
political system, 81–82
poverty reduction, 120–122, 126–128, 136–137, 139, 148–149, 246–247
private sector, 93–94, 135, 139–140, 231–232, 247–248
'private sector-driven growth', 109–111, 136–137
public–private partnerships, 134–135, 139–140
resource curse, 14–15, 244
state: subsidiary role in the economy, 109–111, 135
state activism, 232–235, 249–250
state-building, 24–25, 80, 82–85
state intervention, 14–15, 19–21, 50, 83–84, 163
state ownership, 50, 139–140, 231–232
state protectionism, 83, 91–92
taxation, 81–82, 87–88, 251, 261–262
technocracy, 50, 85–86, 93–94, 110–113, 137, 139, 163, 231–232
US–Chile relations, 84–92, 147–148, 155
War of the Pacific, 81–83
see also Brazil/Chile comparison; Pinochet, Augusto
Chile: lithium mining, 158–161, 163, 244–245
Albemarle SCL (Sociedad Chilena de Litio, US), 159–161
Codelco subsidiary: Salar de Maricunga SpA, 161
copper/lithium comparison, 159–160
first-stage lithium production, 160*t*

FMC (US), 159–160
National Lithium Commission, 160–161
National Lithium Strategy, 161
private sector, 159–160
SQM (Sociedad Química y Minera de Chile, Chile), 159–161
Tianqi Lithium Corporation (China), 159–160
see also Chile: mining sector
Chile: mining sector
1951 Washington Agreement, 147–148, 155
1983 Mining Code, 92, 111–112, 118, 236
1990–2009 public and private (foreign) mining investment, 114–115, 115*f*
2002 *Expomin* meeting, 117–118
2004 *Expomin* meeting, 118
2005 new Royalty Law, 111, 113, 116–121, 128
2007 Subcontracting Law, 121–128, 157–158
2010 Copiapó mining accident, 162–163
Chileanización del Cobre/Chileanization of Copper, 87, 89–90, 147–148
copper, 82*f*, 83–84, 86–87, 124–125
copper production, 129, 129*t*, 130*f*
depoliticization of copper governance, 112–113, 145
'developmentalist' orientation, 18–21
DL 600 (Foreign Investment Statute), 92, 111, 114–115, 117–118, 160, 236
DL 11.828, 87
DL 16.425, 89–90
DL 18.097, 111–112
FDI, 111, 114, 127–128, 144*f*, 231–232
fiscal contribution of, 119–120, 120*f*, 121*t*
hybrid mining model, 111–112, 127–129, 139–140, 147–148, 158–159
hybrid mining model: continuity and change, 109–111, 114–115, 120–121, 136, 236
labour flexibility, 114, 121–127, 139–140, 149–150, 153, 154, 156, 157–158, 163, 231–232
labour movements/conflicts, 87–93, 116, 123–126, 145–146, 162–163
'labour question', 114, 121–125, 149–156
mining industries, 13–14
nationalization, 82–84, 87, 88–92, 143, 147–148

312 Index

Chile: mining sector (*Continued*)
National Service Customs Resolution No. 2757, 113–114
neocorporatism, 155–156
neoliberal mining regime, 236
nitrate, 82–83, 82*f*, 83
Nuevo Trato/New Treaty, 87–88
outsourcing, 131
ownership of Chilean nitrate economy, 82–83, 83*t*, 83
prices of key exports, 82*f*
private mining labour conflicts, 157–158
private sector, 109–110, 113–114, 126, 139–140
radicalization of copper mines, 87–88, 90–91
state ownership, 90, 109–110
Statute of Copper Workers, 87–88
taxation, 82–84, 87, 111–113, 117–120, 120*f*, 121*t*, 160–161
technology and innovation, 118, 129, 131–134
trade unions, 87–88, 150–153, 151*t*, 152*f*, 155–158, 236, 249
US ownership of Chilean cooper mines, 88–89
vertical *disintegration*, 131
World Class Supplier Programme (PPCM/*Programa de Proveedores de Clase Mundial*), 131–134, 133*t*
see also Chile: lithium mining; Codelco
Chile: SOEs, 85
Banco Estado, 146–147
Brazil/Chile comparison, 27–28, 80, 233–235
CAP (*Compañia de Acero del Pacífico*/Pacific Steel Company), 85
corporate governance reforms, 139
depoliticization of, 139
ENAMI (*Empresa Nacional de Minería*/National Mining Enterprise), 90–93, 114–115, 146–148, 249
ENAP (*Empresa Nacional de Petróleo*/National Petroleum Enterprise), 85, 146–147
ENDESA (*Empresa Nacional de Electricidad*/National Electricity Enterprise), 85

intersectoral linkages, 18–19, 233–235, 247–248
neoliberalism and privatization of SOEs, 91–92, 147
SEAM (Mechanized Agriculture Equipment Service), 85
SEP (Public Enterprise System), 147
SOEs as central pillar of development strategy, 19–21
SOEs as instruments for maximizing fiscal capture on behalf of the state, 139
state's strategic control over SOEs, 146–147
state–state (SOE) relations, 146–147
see also Codelco
China
2008 financial crisis, 268
Brazil and, 262–264, 273–274
BRI (Belt and Road Initiative), 16, 268, 270–271
CCP (Chinese Communist Party), 9–10, 242, 269–271
Chile and, 116, 129
China-induced commodity boom, 49, 272, 273
Chinese growth model, 268, 270–271
clean energy, 10–12
clean energy technologies: supply chains, 9–12, 272
clean energy transition, 3–4, 272, 276
climate targets and dependency on China, 4–5
consolidation as economic powerhouse and consequences for mineral exporters, 262–263
copper production, 129, 129*t*, 130*f*
corruption and economic growth, 224
CRMs, 9–12, 272, 276
as developmental state, 28, 240, 267–274, 276
economic globalization and, 272, 275–276
export-led manufacturing strategy, 9–10
EU's dependency on China for CRMs supply, 5–7, 8*f*
as global political and economic powerhouse, 272–273
Latin America and, 245–246, 273–274, 276
market economy, 16, 240

Index **313**

market reforms, 22, 43–44, 269
national security, 268–269, 272
natural resource chain and, 130
REEs, 4–7, 271–272, 276
reforms, 267–271
renewable energy, 3–4
SASAC (State-owned Assets Supervision
and Administration
Commission), 57–58, 268–269, 271
state activism, 268–269, 275–276
state capitalism, 9–10, 272–273
state ownership, 13–14, 276
US/China relations, 5–7
China: industrial policy, 9–12, 267,
270–273
'advance of the state, retreat of
the private sector' (*guojin mintiu*),
268–269
EVs, 10–12
industrial upgrading, 271–272
iron ore, 271–272, 272*f*
NEVs, 10–12
outward-looking policy of securing
Global South's
minerals/hydrocarbons, 10–12
private sector, 268–271
SOEs, 9–10, 268–271
supply chains, 9*f*, 9–12, 129–130
supply chains: vertical integration
in, 10–12, 271–273
China: SOEs, 17–18, 233–235, 240, 270
industrial policy and SOEs, 9–10,
268–271
reforms, 206–207, 242
SOE-based development
strategy, 270–271
clean energy
China, 10–12
EU, 5–7
US, 3–7
clean energy technologies
China: supply chains, 9–12, 272
CRMs and, 4–5, 5*f*, 5–7, 272
division of labour and technological gaps
between developed/developing
countries, 7–9
emerging supply chains in renewable
energy capitalism, 7–12
REEs and, 4–5, 7–9
supply chains, 11*f*

clean energy transition, 7–9
Brazil, 262, 275
Chile, 261–262
China, 3–4, 272, 276
metals required to construct green
infrastructure, 158–159
prospects and challenges for mineral
states, 262–263
structuralism: reinforcing the unequal,
hierarchical world order, 9–10
clientelism
Chile, 81–82
Petrobras: *Lava Jato* scandal, 36–37
Venezuela, 70, 77
climate change
2021 COP26 (Conference on Climate
Change, Glasgow), 158–159
climate emergency, 3–4
climate targets and dependency on
China, 4–5
CNP (*Conselho Nacional do
Petróleo*/National Petroleum Council,
Brazil), 95–96, 98–99
Cochilco (*Comisión Chilena del
Cobre*/Chilean Copper
Commission), 109, 112–113
Codelco (Chile), 19
100% state ownership, 55–57, 140–142,
156, 231–232, 244
1973–1989 consolidation of neoliberalism
in Chile, 91–94
1982 Mining Code, 92
autonomy, 139–140, 142, 149–150
Board of Directors, 140–143,
145–146, 249
as buffer between the public and
private, 139–140, 148–149, 154
CEO, 145
Chilean government/Codelco
relations, 59–60, 137, 139–140, 143,
145, 148–150, 240–241
commodity price volatility, 49–50
competitiveness, 22, 142, 143, 145,
149–150, 153–156, 240–241, 244
Concertación governments' hybrid
mining strategy, 114–115, 142–143,
148–149, 154, 155
continuity/changes between natural
resource developmentalism and
neoliberalism, 26–27, 47–49

314 Index

Codelco (Chile) (*Continued*)
  corporate governance reforms, 19, 22,
    92–93, 139–140, 141*t*, 145–146,
    149–150, 154, 163, 230, 249
  creation of, 90–92
  depoliticization of, 145, 155–156, 249
  developmental role, 233–235, 244
  DL 600 (Foreign Investment Statute),
    92, 111
  DL 1.349, 92
  DL 1.350, 92
  DL 1.530 (*Ley Reservada del
    Cobre*), 231–232
  DL 19.137 (Codelco Law), 142, 145
  economic globalization and, 163
  effective resource governance, 276
  elites, 19, 22, 147–148
  FDI and, 92–93, 143, 144*f*, 244–245
  fiscal contribution/role, 119–120, 120*f*,
    121*t*, 147–148, 148*f*, 240–241, 244,
    246–247
  hybrid governance model, 240–241,
    244–245, 247–248
  lithium subsidiary: Salar de Maricunga
    SpA, 161
  managers of, 142–143, 145, 149–150, 154,
    157, 240–241
  military regime and, 92, 141–142,
    231–232, 240–241
  modernization of, 153–155, 162
  neoliberalism, 27, 49–50, 139–140, 163,
    230, 244
  ownership/management separation, 22
  performance, 25–26, 139, 240–241,
    244–245
  Pinochet and, 91–93, 143, 149–150,
    159–160, 231–232
  politics and, 139, 142–143, 148–150, 163,
    233–235
  principal-agency dilemma, 145
  private sector/Codelco
    comparison, 114–115, 143, 144*f*
  private sector standards for Codelco
    efficiency performance, 139–140
  privatization, refusal to, 22, 24, 45,
    47–49, 92, 140–142, 147–148, 162, 163,
    230, 240–241, 244–245
  profitability of, 19–21
  public/private (foreign) mining
    investment under Pinochet, 92–93, 93*f*

  rent-seeking, 141–142, 148–149,
    231–232, 240–241
  resource nationalism, 246–247
  revenues, 53–54, 147–148
  role in 21st-century Chile, 147–150
  state intervention, 27, 50
  state ownership, 91–94, 140–142
  state ownership: consequences, 143–147
  success, 240–241, 244–245
  taxation, 148–149, 240–241
  technocracy, 142, 154, 155–156, 163,
    240–241, 244–245
  technological innovation, 230, 244–245
  World Class Supplier
    Programme, 133–134
  see also Chile: mining sector;
    Petrobras/Codelco comparison
Codelco and labour force, 139, 157–158
  Alianza Estratégica/StrategicAlliance,
    153–156, 155*t*
  contractual workers, 125–126, 145–146,
    150–154, 156
  corporatist framework for permanent
    workers, 145–146, 153, 154, 156, 157
  FTC (*Federación de los Trabajadores del
    Cobre*/Copper Workers'
    Federation), 127, 145–146,
    153–154, 156
  labour flexibility, 124–127, 139–140,
    149–150, 153, 154, 156
  'labour question', 125, 149–156
  strikes, 125, 162
  subcontracting, 123–125, 124*t*, 125–127,
    145–146, 150–151, 156
  tensions between the state, Codelco, and
    labour unions, 27, 123, 124–127,
    145–146, 149–150, 154–155, 163
  unsustainable growth strategy, 162
Collor de Mello, Fernando, 107–108,
    167–168, 210–211
Colombia, 66, 79–80
colonialism, 37, 39–40
commodities
  buyer-driven commodity
    chains, 274–275
  'commodity lottery', 64
  Latin America, 64
  producer-driven commodity
    chains, 274–275

Index 315

systemic approaches to primary
commodity production, 37–40
commodity boom, 15–16, 35–36, 40, 246
Brazil, 47–49, 178–179, 182–184,
186–187, 189, 196, 233–235
Chile, 47–49, 154, 233–235
China-induced commodity boom, 49,
272, 273
Latin America, 46–47, 49–50, 251,
261–264, 266–267, 273–274
Peru, 256–257
Venezuela, 254
Compete, Brasil, 179–181
competition/competitiveness
Brazil: O&G sector, 165–166, 175–178,
190–193
Codelco, 22, 142, 143, 145, 149–150,
153–156, 240–241, 244
Latin America in era of strategic
competition, 274–276
Petrobras, 22, 47–49, 181–182, 190–195,
203–208, 241–244
*Confederación de la Producción y el
Commercio* (Chile), 84–85
Consejo Minero (Mining Council,
Chile), 113–114
CORFO (*Corporación de Fomento*,
Chile), 84–87, 131, 134–135, 161
'embedded autonomy', 85–86
ISI, 84–85
technocracy, 85–86
Coronil, Fernando, 77
corporate governance reforms, 275–276
elites and, 17–19
see also SOEs: corporate governance
reforms
corruption
Brazil, 209–211, 221, 224
bureaucratic corruption, 224
China, 224
collusive corruption, 209, 211, 219, 221
'degenerative' corruption, 209–210
'developmental' corruption, 209–210,
214–216
East Asia, 209–211, 214–215, 224
elites, 33
exchange-based corruption, 224
political corruption, 22–23, 198,
206–207, 216
rentier state, 33

resource curse, 36–37
structural corruption, 210–211, 214–215
Venezuela, 70–71, 76–78
see also Petrobras: corruption; Petrobras:
Lava Jato scandal
Costa, Paulo Roberto, 219–220
COVID-19 pandemic, 5–7
Cox, Robert, 136–137
CRMs (critical raw materials)
China, 5–7, 8*f*, 9–12, 272, 276
clean energy technologies and, 4–5, 5*f*,
5–7, 272
critical minerals as 'hot commodities', 4
EU, 5–7, 8*f*
as 'hot commodities', 4
increased demand for, 4–7, 272
Latin America, 7–9
supply chains, 4, 9–12
see also REEs
CTC (*Confederación de Trabajadores del
Cobre*/Copper Workers Confederation,
Chile), 87–90, 125, 126–127
Cuevas, Cristian, 125
CUT (*Central Única de Trabajadores de
Chile*), 89–90, 127
CUT (*Central Única dos Trabalhadores,
Brazil*), 169–170

D
decarbonization, 9–10, 275
global decarbonization, 3–4, 9–10, 272
technology and, 3–4, 9–10
see also carbon emission reduction; clean
energy technologies; critical raw
materials, critical minerals; UN Paris
Agreement
development
20th century development
strategies, 274–275
dependent development, 3–4, 69, 274
extractivism–development debate, 30–31
Latin America: natural resources as
building blocks of development
model, 64–67
market forces and, 29

316 Index

development (*Continued*)
  resource curse, economic growth, and rentier state models, 31–37
  state and, 29–30
developmental state
  Argentina, 79–80
  Brazil/Chile comparison, 24–25
  Chile, 18–21, 26–27, 79–80, 91–92, 231
  China, 28, 240, 267–274, 276
  Codelco: developmental role, 233–235, 244
  Colombia, 79–80
  'developmental' corruption, 209–210, 214–216
  developmentalism as eclipsed by neoliberal reforms in O&G sector, 108
  developmentalist mindset, 78–79
  developmental role of the state, 16, 17f, 17–18
  diversity of developmental states as response to 21st century challenges, 267
  economic globalization and, 12–13, 46–47
  elites and, 12–13, 231
  emerging developmental states, 12–13
  Latin American developmental state, 67–79, 231
  Latin American *vs.* East Asian developmental states, 78–80
  market reforms and death of *old* developmental state, 233
  Mexico, 79–80
  neoliberalism and, 16, 259, 264
  sectoral basis of development strategy, 16, 17f, 18–19
  SOEs: developmental role, 12–21, 53–54, 63–64, 231, 233, 246–248, 259, 270–271
  SOEs: developmental role in economic globalization era, 12, 22, 51–52, 163, 233–235, 240, 246
  SOEs: developmental role and state intervention, 14–15, 21, 229
  state capacity and, 12–13, 231
  state capitalism and, 267
  state intervention as development strategy, 83–84, 229
  state ownership as development strategy, 12–19, 22

  state socialism and developmental strategy, 19–21
  see also Brazil; Chile
development studies, 3–4, 7–9, 23–24
Dias, Felipe, 193–195
Di John, Jonathan, 34–35, 77–78
Donoso, Sofia, 126, 150–151

E
East Asia
  bureaucracy, 13
  corruption, 209–211, 214–215, 224
  decarbonization agenda, 9–10
  developmentalist mindset, 78–79
  export-oriented industrialization, 274–275
  industrial policy, 78–79
  Latin America/East Asia comparison, 72–73, 274–275
  Latin America/East Asia comparison: developmental states, 78–80
  state capacity, 13
  successful industrial experience of, 13
  supply chains, 7–9, 9f
ECLAC/CEPAL (Economic Commission for Latin America and the Caribbean), 32–33
economic globalization
  China, 272, 275–276
  Codelco and, 163
  developmental state and, 12–13, 46–47
  domestic configurations and, 24
  hybrid development strategies and, 26–27, 230, 233–235, 240
  industrial policy and, 177–178, 240
  Latin America, 27–28, 46–47, 255–256
  'logic of globalization', 17–18, 24, 38–39, 42–43, 46–47
  natural resources, neoliberalism, and state intervention in globalization era, 29
  neoliberal globalization, 16, 46–47, 50–51
  'open economy' industrial strategy as globalization strategy, 241–242
  Petrobras and, 177–178, 180–181, 184, 196, 238–239
  resource nationalism as globalization strategy, 263–264, 266–267

SOEs: developmental role in economic globalization era, 12, 22, 51–52, 163, 233–235, 240, 246
  state agency and, 22, 29, 39–40, 276
  state ownership and, 24, 26, 51–52, 233–235
  state ownership as globalization strategy, 50–59, 233, 276
Ecuador, 66–67, 120–121, 148, 149, 273–274
elites (ruling, political, state elites)
  Brazil, 19–21, 94–96, 166, 223–224, 232, 233–235
  Chile, 19–21, 81–82, 111–112, 157–158, 231–235
  Codelco, 19, 22, 147–148
  corporate governance reforms, 17–19
  corruption, 33
  developmental states and, 12–13, 231
  distinction between policy elites and SOE managers, 46
  hybrid development model and, 231–232
  Latin America, 64–66, 79–80
  path-breaking institutional reforms and, 30–31
  Petrobras and, 19, 22, 190–192, 196, 232
  rentier state, 33
  ruling elites/SOE managers relationship, 14
  state intervention and, 17–18
energy, *see* clean energy; renewable energy
environmental issues
  Brazil: O&G sector, 179
  see also climate change
EU (European Union)
  clean energy, 5–7
  CRMs, 5–7, 8*f*
  dependency on China for CRMs supply, 5–7, 8*f*
  EVs, 4–5
  REEs, 5–7
  supply chains, 7–9, 9*f*
Evans, Peter, 46, 69
EVs (electric vehicles)
  Asian countries and race to produce EV cars, 9–10
  batteries, 10–12
  China, 10–12
  EU, 4–5
  lithium-ion batteries, 158–159, 244–245

minerals needed for, 4–5, 158–159
  REEs needed for, 4–5
  US, 4
  see also NEVs
export-oriented economy/development
  Brazil: export economy, 94–95, 231
  Chile: export-oriented model, 81–84, 90, 110–111, 134–135, 231
  China, 9–10
  East Asia: export-oriented industrialization, 274–275
  Latin America, 63–68
  Peru, 66–67, 257
  productivism, 134–135
extractivism
  Argentina, 39
  Brazil, 39
  Chile, 18–19, 273–274
  extractive bureaucracy, 34–35
  extractive regimes: distinguishing features, 37–39
  extractivism/development debate, 30–31
  as growth model/strategy, 14, 49–50
  Indonesia, 37–39
  Latin America, 38–39, 276
  Peru, 27–28, 257–258
  Venezuela, 273–274
  see also neoextractivism

F

Falção Mendes, Joelson, 275
FDI (foreign direct investment)
  Brazil: O&G sector and foreign participation in, 68–69, 97–98, 166–167, 173–175, 177–178, 181, 192–193, 238–239
  Chile: mining sector, 111, 114, 127–128, 144*f*, 231–232
  Codelco, 92–93, 143, 144*f*, 244–245
  hybrid development model and, 43–44, 46–47
  natural-resource-based development: states/foreign capital relationship, 239
Ffrench Davis, Ricardo, 117
FMC (Mining Federation of Chile), 157–158
Franco, Itamar, 168
Frei, Eduardo (Jr.), 117
Frei, Eduardo (Sr.), 88–90

318 Index

Fujimori, Alberto, 255–258
  neoliberal authoritarianism, 255–256
FUP (*Federação Única dos Petroleiros,*
    Brazil), 169–170

G
García, Alan, 258
Garotinho, Anthony, 179–180
Garrastazu Médici, Emílio
    (General), 102–103
Geisel, Ernesto (General), 102–104
Gellert, Paul, 37–38
Gereffi, Gary, 274–275
globalization, *see* economic globalization
Golborne, Laurence, 162
Gómez, Juan Vicente, 70
González von Marees, Jorge, 84
governance
  Brazil: crisis of governance and legitimacy
    (today), 221, 223–224
  good governance as cure to rentier
    state, 34
  see also corporate governance reforms;
    natural resource governance
GVC (global value chain), 7–9, 18–19,
    203–204

H
Hall, Peter, 44–45
Haslam, Paul Alexander, 250–251
Heidrich, Pablo, 250–251
HI (historical institutionalism)
  advantages of, 264–266
  agency and institutional change, 26
  as analytical approach, 19, 24, 26, 30,
    44–50, 81, 116, 163, 166, 229–230, 259,
    262–263
  institutional change and stability, 26,
    45–50, 59–60, 264–265
  institutions: definition of, 44–45
  Latin America: SOEs and economic
    development, 26
Hirschman, Albert, 29, 190–192
Horta Barbosa, Júlio Caetano
    (General), 95–98
Hsueh, Roselyn, 268–269
Hu Angang, 270
Humala, Ollanta, 257–258
hybrid development model, 24, 43*f*, 59–60,
    262–263

Brazil, 14–15, 26–27, 43–44, 46–49, 48*f*,
    50, 59–60, 177–178, 230, 232, 259,
    266–267
Brazil/Chile comparison, 19–21, 50,
    231–235, 234*f*, 237–238
Chile, 14–15, 26–27, 43–44, 46–49, 43*f*,
    50, 59–60, 109–110, 134–135, 137,
    139–140, 147, 163, 230, 231–232, 259,
    266–267
Chile: hybrid mining model, 111–112,
    127–129, 139–140, 147–148, 158–159
Chile: hybrid mining model, continuity
    and change, 109–111, 114–115,
    120–121, 136, 236
Codelco: hybrid governance
    model, 240–241, 244–245, 247–248
economic globalization and, 26–27, 230,
    233–235, 240
elites and, 231–232
FDI and, 43–44, 46–47
as historically constituted outcome, 231,
    237–238
hybrid institutional arrangements, 47–49
SOEs and, 14, 50, 229, 231, 233–235, 239
states: shift from state intervention
    towards hybrid developmental
    role, 239
  see also developmental state;
    neoliberalism

I
Ibañez, Carlos, 83–84, 87–88
IFIs (international financial
    institutions), 16, 41–42, 68, 239
IMF (International Monetary Fund), 77
India, 17–18, 256–257
Indonesia
  as extractive regime, 37–39
  SOEs, 17–18, 206–207
  state ownership, 13–14
  taxation, 35
industry/industrial policy/industrialization
  Argentina, 66
  Brazil, 19–21, 66, 96–97, 166, 221–223,
    232, 261–264
  Brazil: O&G sector and
    industrialization, 95–98, 165–166,
    178–179, 181, 186–193, 196, 199
  Brazil: shipbuilding industry, 190–192

buyer-/producer-driven commodity
chains, 274–275
Chile, 66, 84–87, 110–111
Colombia, 66
as defensive globalization strategy, 16
de-industrialization, 31–32, 273–274
development strategy: natural resource
extraction/national industrialization
nexus, 25
East Asia: export-oriented
industrialization, 274–275
economic globalization and industrial
policy, 177–178, 240
industrial development, definition, 23–24
industrial upgrading, 18–19, 271–272
Latin America, 65–68, 78–79, 251,
263–264
market reforms and industrial policy, 233
Mexico, 66
'mission-oriented' policies, 19–21
natural resource-based
development/industrialization
interaction, 24, 42, 69, 266
natural-resource-based
industrialization, 12, 15, 18–19
natural resources and
industrialization, 3–4, 15, 67–68
'open economy' industrial strategy as
globalization strategy, 241–242
Petrobras/Codelco comparison:
industrial development, 244–248
Petrobras and industrialization, 181, 184,
192, 202–203, 232, 241–247, 264–265
sectoral basis of development strategy
and, 18–19
SOEs and industrialization, 25–26,
79–80, 229–230, 243, 246–248, 271
state and industrial development, 240
successful industrialization, 275–276
Third World states and
industrialization, 39–40
trade-led industrialization, 274–275
Uruguay, 66
Venezuela, 27–28, 70–78, 259–260
see also China: industrial policy; ISI
institutional development
Brazil, 50, 196
Chile, 50, 109–111, 120–121
corporate governance reforms and
institutional development of SOEs, 59

HI framework, 46–50, 266
natural resource governance: pattern of
institutional stability and change, 43*f*
natural resource-intensive
regimes, 33–36
natural resource-intensive regimes:
institutional change in, 40–44, 43*f*
Peru, 66–67
petro-states and, 34
'political resource curse', 33
rentier state, 34–35
resource curse and, 37
state and, 30, 40–41
theory of institutional stability and
change, 26, 45–50, 59–60, 264–265
Venezuela, 69, 254–255
see also HI
Inter-American Development Bank, 68–69
International Energy Agency, 7–9
IOCs (international oil companies)
Brazil: O&G sector, 47–49, 108, 166–167,
175–176, 190–192
Petrobras and, 102–105, 108, 175
Venezuela, 70–71
ISI (import substitution
industrialization), 231
Chile, 84–85, 87, 231
failure of ISI model, 108
Latin America, 25, 65–68
Petrobras and, 100, 103–104

K
Karl, Terry Lynn, 34, 71–72, 77
Kubitshek, Juscelino, 100–101
Kuczynski, Pedro Pablo, 258
Kurtz, Marcus J., 35, 41–42
Kuwait, 35–36

L
labour-related issues
Chile: mining sector and labour
flexibility, 114, 121–127, 139–140,
149–150, 153, 154, 156, 157–158, 163,
231–232
Chile: mining sector and labour
movements/conflicts, 87–93, 116,
123–126, 145–146, 162–163
Chile: mining sector and 'labour
question', 114, 121–125, 149–156

320 Index

labour-related issues (*Continued*)
  Chile: mining sector and trade
    unions, 87–88, 150–153, 151*t*, 152*f*,
    155–158, 236, 249
  labour conflicts, 90–91
  Latin America: decline of labour
    politics, 158
  Latin America: labour movement, 63,
    79–80
  Petrobras/Codelco comparison:
    employment policy, 205–206
  Petrobras and labour
    management/employment
    policy, 205–206, 205*f*
  Petrobras and labour
    movements/conflicts and
    strikes, 100–101, 169–170
  see also Codelco and labour force
Lagos, Ricardo, 115–119, 121–122
Lameda, Guaicaipuro (General), 254
Latin America
  1929 global financial crisis, 65–67
  1930s Great Depression, 64–66, 83
  bureaucracy, 79–80
  challenge to overcome historically
    constituted position as suppliers of raw
    materials, 262–263
  China and, 245–246, 273–274, 276
  commodities, 64
  commodity boom, 46–47, 49–50, 251,
    261–264, 266–267, 273–274
  CRMs, 7–9
  deindustrialization, 273–274
  dependent development, 69, 274
  developmental state, 67–79, 231
  developmental states in Latin America *vs.*
    East Asia, 78–80
  domestic market expansion/*crecimiento
    hacia adentro*, 65
  East Asia/Latin America
    comparison, 72–73, 274–275
  economic globalization, 27–28, 46–47,
    255–256
  elites, 64–66, 79–80
  in era of strategic competition, 274–276
  export-oriented growth, 63–68
  extractivist model, 38–39, 276
  industrialization, 65–68, 263–264
  industrial policy, 78–79, 251
  ISI, 25, 65–68

labour movement, 63
labour politics, decline of, 158
'Left'/'post-neoliberal' turn, 250,
  261–262, 265–266
Left: rise and fall of, 49–50
liberalization period: retention of SOEs
  and regulatory reforms, 42
natural-resource-based
  development, 30–31, 35–36
natural resource governance, 42, 43*f*,
  43–47
natural resources as building blocks of
  development model, 64–67
neodevelopmentalism, 14, 266–267
neoextractivism, 14–15, 250, 263–264
neoliberalism, 21–22, 46–47, 63–64, 259,
  265–266
neostructuralism, 266–267
oil nationalization, 73–75, 237–238,
  251–252
political economy, 49–50, 266–267
rentier politics, 263–264
resource curse, 67–68
resource nationalism, 14, 63, 79–80, 229,
  250–251, 263–264, 266–267
return of the state, 266–267
shift towards neoliberalism without SOEs
  privatization, 42, 43*f*, 46–47
state activism, 63–64, 235, 276
state intervention, 79–80
supply chains, 7–9, 9*f*
taxation, 251
trade unions, 79–80
US investment in, 68–69, 69*t*
World War II, 65–66
see also Brazil; Chile; Peru; SOEs: Latin
  America; Venezuela
Lazzarini, Sergio, 176–177, 184–186
LCRs (local content requirements)
  Brazil: O&G sector, 178–182, 182*f*,
    188–190, 191*t*, 192–193, 222–223, 232
  Chile, 161
Leiva, Fernando, 135
liberalization
  economic liberalization, 34, 41–42
  Latin America in liberalization period:
    retention of SOEs and regulatory
    reforms, 42
  political liberalization, 35–36
  trade liberalization, 34

see also market reforms; neoliberalism

Lima, Marcos, 139, 145

lithium
  Australia as lithium producer, 158–160
  lithium-ion batteries, 158–159, 244–245
  lithium world production, 158–159, 159*t*
  see also Chile: lithium mining

Lula da Silva, Luiz Inácio, 181, 208, 261–262
  development strategy, 216–217
  Lula/Cardoso comparison regarding O&G sector, 181–182, 188–189
  Nova Industria Brasil programme, 262
  O&G sector governance, 170*t*
  patronage system, 215
  Petrobras and, 165–166, 184, 187
  poverty reduction: *Bolsa Familia*, 215

M

Madariaga, Aldo, 136, 236

Maduro, Nicolás, 254–255

Majluf, Nicolas, 145

Malaysia, 4–5, 35, 39, 179

Mantega, Guido, 208–209

Marin, Pedro, 141–142, 157–158

market reforms
  Brazil, 22, 43–45, 222–223
  Brazil: O&G sector and market opening reforms, 166–167, 173–175, 177–178, 236–237
  Brazil/Chile comparison, 236–237
  Chile, 22, 43–45
  China, 22, 43–44, 269
  death of *old* developmental state and, 233
  as exogenous/endogenous factor, 43–44
  free markets, 24, 41–42
  industrial policy and, 233
  privatization, 24
  SOEs and, 43–45

Mazzucato, Mariana, 14

MENA (Middle East and North Africa), 35–36, 102–103
  see also Middle East

methodology, *see* research: methodology and theoretical contributions

Mexico, 273–274
  delimiting foreign-owned enterprises in O&G industries, 68–69
  industrialization, 66

Pemex (*Petróleos Mexicanos*), 53–54, 98–99
  state-led development, 79–80

Middle East
  Brazil/Petrobras and, 103–104, 203–204
  rentier state and, 30–31, 35–36
  see also MENA

middle-income countries, 13
  growth strategies of selected middle-income countries, 18–19, 20*f*
  industrial policies, 18–19
  SOEs, 17–19

Minera Escondida (BHP Billiton mining company), 92–93, 113, 126, 131–134, 158
  strikes, 154, 162

minerals
  critical minerals as 'hot commodities', 4
  EVs, minerals needed for, 4–5, 158–159
  iron ore producers, 271–272, 272*f*
  see also Chile: mining sector; CRMs; REEs

Mongolia, 4–5, 15–16, 128–129

Moro, Sergio (Judge), 221

Mozambique, 15–16

Musacchio, Aldo, 52, 176–177, 184–186

Myanmar, 15–16

N

nationalization of resources, *see* resource nationalism

national security, 41–42, 202–203
  Brazil: national security and natural resources, 95–96, 99, 102–103, 237–238
  China, 268–269, 272
  SOEs and, 246, 268–269

natural resources
  industrialization and, 3–4, 15, 67–68
  natural resource politics, 14–15
  see also minerals; REEs

natural-resource-based development, 24, 29, 30
  Brazil, 40, 261–262
  Brazil/Chile comparison, 25–26
  challenges, 18–19
  Chile, 27, 40, 136, 148–149, 249, 261–262
  globalization and, 31
  historical institutionalist account of, 31, 44–50

322 Index

natural-resource-based development (*Continued*)
  Latin America, 30–31, 35–36
  literature on, 30–31
  natural resource-based development/industrialization interaction, 24, 42, 69, 266
  natural-resource-based industrialization, 12, 15, 18–19
  natural resource dependence, 266, 275
  Prebisch–Singer hypothesis, 32–33
  rentierism and natural resources, 12, 30–31
  resource curse, economic growth, and rentier state models, 31–37
  state intervention in, 29–30, 33
  states/foreign capital relationship, 239
  systemic approaches to primary commodity production, 37–40
  underdevelopment and natural resources, 12, 30–33
  see also SOEs; state ownership
natural resource governance, 12, 41–42
  21st century challenge, 276
  divergent models of, 231–232, 239
  governance models based on political choices between manufacturing and nature resources, 18–19, 20*f*
  Latin America, 42, 43*f*, 43–47
  mineral governance, 3–4
  natural resource-intensive regimes, 33–36
  natural resource-intensive regimes: institutional change in, 40–44, 43*f*
  natural resources/neoliberalism/state intervention interactions, 29, 41–42
  natural resources/neoliberalism/state ownership interactions, 41–42
  neoextractivist governance model, 264
  pattern of institutional stability and change, 43*f*
  SOEs and, 27–28
  state ownership and, 26–27, 262–263
natural resource sovereignty, 41–42, 45, 250
  Chile, 92
  SOEs and, 245–247, 276
  Venezuela, 70
Navarro, Lucas, 133–134

NCIC (National Council of Competitiveness and Innovation, Chile), 132, 134–135
NCMD (National Commission for Mining and Development, Chile), 132
Nem Singh, Jewellord, 14, 24, 46–47, 55, 58–59
neoclassical economics, 53–54
neodevelopmentalism
  Brazil: *novo desenvolvimentismo*, 166, 184–186
  Latin America, 14, 266–267
neoextractivism, 12, 264
  Latin America, 14–15, 250, 263–264
  see also extractivism
neoinstitutionalism, 43–46
neoliberalism
  Brazil, 22, 26–27, 166–170, 233–237
  Brazil/Chile comparison, 235, 237–239
  Codelco, 27, 49–50, 91–94, 139–140, 163, 230, 244
  developmentalism as eclipsed by neoliberal reforms in O&G sector, 108
  developmental state and, 16, 259, 264
  embedded neoliberalism, 41–42, 231–232
  as endogenous, self-perpetuating force driving market liberalization, 233
  Fujimori and neoliberal authoritarianism, 255–256
  Latin America, 21–22, 46–47, 63–64, 259, 265–266
  Latin America: shift towards neoliberalism in natural resource governance without SOEs privatization, 42, 43*f*, 46–47
  natural resources/neoliberalism/state intervention interactions, 29, 41–42
  natural resources/neoliberalism/state ownership interactions, 41–42
  neoliberal convergence, 265–266
  neoliberal globalization, 16, 46–47, 50–51
  path-shaping influence of, 42–44, 46–47
  Peru, 27–28, 67, 255–260, 265–266
  Petrobras, 49–50, 108, 168–170, 196, 230, 232
  Pinochet and neoliberal authoritarianism, 91–94, 109, 135–137, 236

pragmatic neoliberalism, 147
  SOEs and, 22, 233
  SOEs: Latin America, 24, 26–27, 42, 46–47, 63–64, 80
  state ownership/neoliberalism interactions, 17–18, 27–28, 42–43, 233
  Venezuela, 77, 265–266
  see also Chile
neostructuralism, 266–267
NEVs (new energy vehicles), 10–12
  see also EVs
NGOs (non-governmental organizations), 3–4
NOCs (national oil companies)
  developmental role, 246
  Norway, 13–14, 207–208
  politics and, 243
  Saudi Arabia, 13–14, 207–208
  see also O&G sector; PDVSA; Petrobras; SOEs
North, Douglass, 44–45
Norway, 165–166, 179, 242
  NOCs, 13–14, 207–208
  NPD (Norwegian Petroleum Directorate), 176–177
Nunes, Janari (Colonel), 100–101, 198–199

O
ODEPLAN (National Planning Office, Chile), 88–89, 91–92
OECD (Organisation for Economic Co-operation and Development), 55, 127–128
Offner, Amy C., 233
O&G sector (oil and gas), 14
  developmentalism as eclipsed by neoliberal reforms in O&G sector, 108
  see also Brazil: O&G sector; NOCs; Petrobras
ONIP (*Organização Nacional da Indústria do Petróleo*/National Organization of Petroleum Industry, Brazil), 180–181
OPEC (Organization of the Petroleum Exporting Countries), 76

P
Parente, Pedro, 22–23, 197–198, 221–222
Parra Luzardo, Gastón, 254
path dependency, 26, 223–225

elites and path-breaking institutional reforms, 30–31
SOEs, 24
state ownership and, 30
PDSB (Brazilian Social Democratic Party), 165–166, 181, 219–220
PDVSA (Petróleos de Venezuela, S.A.), 73–75
  Chávez, Hugo and, 243, 254–255, 259–260
  efficiency and productive capability, 76–77
  failure of, 251, 259–260, 264–266
  internationalization strategy, 251–253
  Maduro, Nicolás, 254–255
  oil nationalization, 73–75, 251–252
  origins of, 251–252
  political interference/politicization, 251–254
  rent-seeking and distributive politics, 243
  spending in non-core obligations, 254
  state interference, 251, 254, 259–260, 264–265
  state objectives, 73–77, 98–99, 251–252
  state/PDVSA relationship, 253–254
  success of, 252–253
  as subservient public enterprise, 254
  technocracy, 251–254
  see also Venezuela
Pei, Minxin, 211, 269
Pérez, Carlos Andrés, 72–75, 77
Pérez Jiménez, Marcos, 70–71
Peru
  1950 Mining Code, 66–67
  1993 Constitution, 256
  2009 US–Peru FTA (PTPA), 256–257
  commodity boom, 256–257
  contentious politics, 148
  copper production, 129
  'empresarios dialogantes', 67
  evolution of manufacturing and extractive industries, 257f
  excessive marketization, 27–28
  export-oriented growth, 66–67, 257
  extractivist model, 27–28, 257–258
  FTAs (free trade agreements), 256–257
  institution building, 66–67
  limited institutional capability, 265–266
  neoliberalism, 27–28, 67, 265–266

324 Index

Peru (*Continued*)
  neoliberalism without state
    ownership, 255–260
  Petroperú, 257–258
  private sector-driven model, 257–258
  SOEs, 255–256, 258–259, 265–266
  SOEs: privatization, 255–256
  state capacity, 258–259
Petrobras (Brazil), 19
  1960 Link Report, 100, 103–104
  1964–1985 military period, 101–105,
    166–167
  1997 Constitutional Amendment No.
    5, 173–175
  1997 Petroleum Law (Law
    9.478), 173–177
  2010 Pre-Salt Law (Law 12.350), 187
  autonomy, 22–23, 27, 99–103, 165–166,
    187–188, 196, 221–222, 236–237,
    243–244, 248
  BNDES and, 168–169
  Brazilian government/Petrobras
    relationship, 59–60, 104–105,
    181–182, 195–196, 204, 223, 236–237,
    241–242
  bureaucracy, 176–177, 205–206, 236–237
  CENAP/CENPES (Centre of Oil Upgrade
    and Studies), 101–102, 105
  commodity price volatility, 49–50
  competitiveness, 22, 47–49, 181–182,
    190–195, 203–208, 241–244
  concessions regime, 175, 181
  continuity/changes between natural
    resource developmentalism and
    neoliberalism, 26–27, 47–49, 108,
    178–182, 241–242
  corporate governance reforms, 19, 22, 27,
    104–105, 168–170, 196, 206, 223–224,
    230, 232, 236–237, 241–242, 249
  creation of, 98–99, 166–167
  debt accumulation, 198–200, 200f, 220,
    224, 232
  deepwater/ultra deepwater
    production, 105–108, 166–167,
    169–170, 188–189, 192–193, 198–204,
    232, 243–244
  developmental role, 233–235
  distribution downstream segment, 193,
    195t

  economic globalization and, 177–178,
    180–181, 184, 196, 238–239
  effective resource governance, 276
  elites and, 19, 22, 190–192, 196, 232
  Executive Board, 205–206
  financing of, 98–100, 102–105
  industrialization and, 181, 184, 192,
    202–203, 232, 241–247, 264–265
  IOCs and, 102–105, 108, 175
  ISI model, 100, 103–104
  labour management/employment
    policy, 205–206, 205f
  labour movements/conflicts and
    strikes, 100–101, 169–170
  market-conforming behaviour, 166
  market value and net equity, 199–200,
    201f
  as mixed public–private company, 98–99,
    187–188, 206
  modernization of, 192
  neoliberalism, 49–50, 108, 168–170, 196,
    230, 232
  net income and losses, 199–200, 201f
  new developmentalism, 166
  offshore development, 98, 100, 101–102,
    104–105, 175, 179–180, 199, 202–204,
    207–208
  oil exploration, 98–107, 107f, 108,
    165–167, 173–175, 187, 188–189,
    192–193, 200–202, 202f, 219
  oil monopoly, 99, 102–103, 106–108,
    166–167, 169–170, 193, 202–204, 232
  oil monopoly: end of, 108, 165–166,
    173–176, 236–237, 243–244
  oil production, 106–107, 107f, 108,
    165–166, 173–175, 187, 188–189,
    192–193, 203t, 219
  'oil question', 184
  ownership/management separation, 22
  performance, 25–26, 103–104, 198–202
  politics/politicization, 99–101, 107–108,
    187, 196, 198–199, 233–235, 237,
    243–244, 247–248
  pre-salt reserves, 184, 185f, 186–188,
    190–193, 200–203, 236–237
  privatization, refusal to, 22, 24, 47–49,
    107–108, 169–170, 196, 223–224, 230,
    236–237, 241–242
  PROCAP (R&D programme), 105

profitability, 99–100, 100*t*, 102–104,
181–182, 247–249
public–private partnerships, 102–103
R&D contribution to Brazil's O&G
sector, 203–204, 204*f*, 207–208, 232
refining sector, 102–104, 106*f*, 193,
219–220
shareholding structure, 55–57, 98–99,
206, 207*f*
size, 53–54, 190, 198, 208–209
state developmentalism/neoliberalism
interaction, 27, 206
state intervention, 22–23, 50, 99–100,
196, 198
state objectives, 98–100, 103–104,
166–167, 238–239, 243–244, 249
state ownership, 107–108, 169–170, 196,
206
success, 106–107, 198–203, 202*f*, 203*t*,
207–208, 243–244, 247–248
technocracy, 244–245
technological advancement/
innovation, 105–107, 166, 198–204,
230, 244–245
vertical integration of O&G
industry, 101–103, 232, 247–248,
264–265
see also Brazil
Petrobras: corruption, 198–199
DIP ('Internal Document of the Petrobras
System'), 219–220
PCPP (Corruption Prevention
Programme), 220
see also Petrobras: *Lava Jato* scandal
Petrobras: *Lava Jato* scandal (Operation Car
Wash), 59, 211–214, 212*f*, 243
before *Lava Jato*, 198–208
BNDES, 214–219
bribery, 197–198, 211, 213–214
cartel of construction
companies, 197–198, 209–215,
217–220
collusive corruption, 209, 211, 219–221
contract bid rigging, 197–198, 211–213
corruption, 22–23, 27, 36–37, 196,
197–198, 210–211, 216–217, 224,
248, 266
corruption and economic growth, 215
illicit money laundering, 209–210,
213–214

embezzlement, 197–198
impacts of, 192, 196, 207–208, 219–220,
243–244
imprisonment of people involved in, 198,
221
Janus face of corruption, 209–214
lack of internal audit
mechanism, 197–198
Lava Jato corruption scheme, 211–214,
212*f*
Lava Jato investigation, 198–200,
208–209, 211, 213–221, 224, 243–244
Odrebrecht Group, 213–214, 217–219
patronage and clientelism, 36–37
Petrobras executives, 197–198, 211, 213,
219–220
Petrobras's business strategy
mistakes, 200, 224
PMDB (Brazilian Democratic Movement
Party), 213–214
political aftermath of the *Lava Jato*
scandal, 221–223
political basis of industrial
policymaking, 198, 216, 224
political parties, 213–215, 219–221
political system and corruption, 196,
206–207, 213–219, 224
PT and, 209–210, 213–216
rent-seeking, 27, 36–37, 165–166,
197–198, 216–217, 248
state intervention, 196, 206–207, 237
Petrobras: subsidiaries, 101–103, 216
BNDES restructuring of Petrobras
system, 168–169
Braspetro, 103–104, 107–108
elimination of, 168–169
FAFEN (*Fábrica de Fertilizantes
Nitrogenados*), 169–170
Interbras, 104, 107–108, 168–169
Petrofertil, 107–108
Petromisa, 104, 107–108, 168–169
Petroquisa, 101–102, 107–108, 168–169
privatization of, 107–108, 168–169
RENAVE (*Empresa Brasileira de Reparos
Navais*), 107–108
Petrobras/Codelco comparison, 239–250
autonomy, 149–150
corporate governance reforms, 242–243,
248–250
employment policy, 205–206

Petrobras/Codelco comparison (*Continued*)
industrial development, 244–248
innovation, 147–148
political role in buffering competing
demands, 243–246
state activism, 249–250
state–state (SOE) relations, 240–243
see also Brazil/Chile comparison
petro-states
bureaucracy, 34
financing growth strategies through oil
revenues, 72–73
taxation, 34
Venezuela, 26–27, 69, 70–72, 251–255,
259–260
Philip, George, 97–98
Pineda Ayerbe, Emilio I., 52
Piñera, Sebastian, 127–128, 162–163, 244
Pinochet, Augusto (General), 90–91,
93–94, 135
1978 Labour Code, 121–123, 126–127,
157–158
1979 *Plan Laboral*, 114
Codelco and, 91–93, 143, 149–150,
159–160, 231–232
Leyes Organicas/Organic Laws, 111–112
neoliberal authoritarianism, 91–94, 109,
135–137, 236
Right's political privileges created
by, 111–112
see also Chile
political economy, 37, 43–44
2008 financial crisis, 267
Brazil, 64
developmental states and neoliberal
globalization, 16
East Asian states: successful industrial
experience of, 13
Latin America, 49–50, 266–267
'logic of globalization', 24
resource curse, 14, 266
state ownership, 17–18, 30, 42–43,
229–230
politics
Chile: political system, 81–82
Codelco and politics, 139, 142–143,
148–150, 163, 233–235
as contingent factor that shape
incremental institutional changes, 19

Petrobras: politics/politicization, 99–101,
107–108, 187, 196, 198–199, 233–235,
237, 243–244, 247–248
SOEs: depoliticization of, 239, 243
SOEs: political role of, 51, 229, 233–235,
243
see also Petrobras: *Lava Jato* scandal
Prebisch, Raul: Prebisch–Singer
hypothesis, 32–33
private sector
Brazil, 95–96
Chile, 93–94, 135, 139–140, 231–232,
247–248
Chile: lithium mining, 159–160
Chile: mining sector, 109–110, 113–114,
126, 139–140, 157–158
Chile: 'private sector-driven
growth', 109–111, 136–137
China: 'advance of the state, retreat of the
private sector' (*guojin
mintiu*), 268–269
China: industrial policy and private
sector, 268–271
Codelco: private sector standards for
efficiency performance, 139–140
Codelco/private sector
comparison, 114–115, 143, 144*f*
Peru: private sector-driven
model, 257–258
private companies/SOEs
comparison, 17–18, 52–53, 239
see also Chile: lithium mining, SQM for
lithium; *Minera Escondida* (BHP
Billiton for mining)
privatization
Brazil, 167–168, 168*t*, 169–170, 177–178
market reforms and, 24
see also SOEs: privatization
productivism, 134–135
logic of productivism, 134–135, 143, 148
PT government (*Partido dos Trabalhadores*,
Brazil), 165–166, 181
BNDES and, 188
corruption, 209–210
industrial strategy, 188–192
novo desenvolvimentismo/new
developmentalism, 166, 184, 186–187,
223–224
O&G sector governance, 170*t*

Petrobras: *Lava Jato* scandal
  and, 209–210, 213–216
Petrobras's debt accumulation, 198–200
political/economic power fusion, 23–24
pre-salt reserves and, 184, 186–188
rent-seeking, 36–37, 209
see also Lula da Silva, Luiz Inácio;
  Petrobras: *Lava Jato* scandal; Rousseff,
  Dilma

R
rational choice institutionalism, 45
redistribution
  redistributive policies, 38,
    179, 182–184, 209
  redistributive politics, 148–149, 178–179,
    263–266
REEs (rare earth elements)
  Australia, 4–5
  China, 4–7, 271–272, 276
  clean energy technologies and, 4–5, 7–9
  EU, 5–7
  EVs and, 4–5
  industrial applications and products, 5, 6t
  supply diversification strategies, 5
  see also CRMs
renewable energy
  China, 3–4
  emerging supply chains in renewable
    energy capitalism, 7–12
  lithium extraction, 158–159
  solar power, 3–4
  wind power, 3–4, 158–159
rentier state, 15, 30–31
  authoritarianism and, 30–31, 35–36
  Brazil: O&G sector and
    rent-seeking, 165–166
  Codelco: rent-seeking, 141–142,
    148–149, 231–232, 240–241
  corruption, 33
  critique of theory of, 34–36, 59–60
  elites, 33
  good governance and strong political
    institutions as cure to rentier state, 34
  institutional development and, 34–35
  Latin America: rentier politics, 263–264
  MENA, 35–36
  Middle East, 30–31, 35–36
  natural resources and rentierism, 12,
    30–31

Petrobras: *Lava Jato* scandal and
  rent-seeking, 27, 36–37, 165–166,
  197–198, 216–217, 248
'political resource curse', 33
PT government: rent-seeking, 36–37, 209
rent distribution, 31
rent-seeking, 33
resource curse, economic growth, and
  rentier state models, 31–37
SOEs, 243, 248
state intervention, 33
taxation, 34–35
Venezuela, 70, 73–75, 77–78, 251–252,
  264–265
Republic of Congo, 15–16
research: methodology and theoretical
  contributions
  arguments, 12–14, 19–24, 42–43, 43f,
    44–49, 230–239, 259–260
  case studies, 22, 25, 26–27, 81
  comparative approach:
    Brazil/Chile, 24–26
  empirical evidence from Latin
    America, 12–14, 19
  industrial development: criteria
    for, 23–24
  research questions, 12
  theoretical contributions, 27, 239,
    262–266, 276
  see also HI
resource curse
  Brazil, 14–15
  Chile, 14–15, 244
  corruption, 36–37
  critique of theory of, 34–37, 59–60, 266,
    271–272
  de-industrialization, 31–32
  Dutch disease, 31–32
  inevitability of, 14
  institutional development and, 37
  Latin America, 67–68
  limitations to export diversification and
    industrial expansion, 16
  natural resources and anti-developmental
    effects for producing states, 12
  political economy, 14, 266
  'political resource curse', 33
  production aspect of mineral
    extraction, 31–32

328 Index

resource curse (*Continued*)
  resource curse, economic growth, and
    rentier state models, 31–37
  Venezuela, 34–35, 266
resource nationalism, 229, 250–251
  Brazil: nationalization of natural
    resources, 95–99, 166–167
  Chile: mining sector and
    nationalization, 82–84, 87, 88–92, 143,
    147–148
  Codelco as successful model of, 246–247
  expropriation of assets, 79–80, 238–239
  as globalization strategy, 263–264,
    266–267
  Latin America, 14, 63, 79–80, 229,
    250–251, 263–264, 266–267
  Latin America: oil
    nationalization, 73–75, 237–238,
    251–252
  limits of resource nationalism
    argument, 250, 259–260
  oil as 'black gold', 238–239
  Venezuela, 70–71, 73–75, 251–252
Roberts, Kenneth M., 77–78
Rousseff, Dilma
  2016 impeachment, 209, 221
  developmentalist strategy, 208–209
  Lula/Rousseff comparison, 208–209
  'New Macroeconomic Matrix', 208–209
  O&G sector governance, 170*t*
  Petrobras and, 165–166, 219–220
  Petrobras: *Lava Jato* scandal and, 213,
    221
  Petrobras's debt accumulation, 198
Russia, 5–7

S
Sarney de Araújo Costa, José, 106
Saudi Arabia, 165–166
  NOCs, 13–14, 207–208
Sauer, Ildo, 193–195
Schamis, Hector E., 240
Sikkink, Kathryn, 79–80
Silva, Patricio, 85–86
Singapore, 13–14, 206–207
  SOHC (Temasak Holding Company in
    Singapore), 57–58
Singer, Hans: Prebisch–Singer
  hypothesis, 32–33
SOEs (state-owned enterprises)

bureaucracy, 51, 233
as *change agents*, 44–45
conflicting roles as bureaucratic arm and
  quasi-independent commercial
  company, 14–15, 21, 221–222, 246
depoliticization of, 239, 243
developmental role, 12–21, 53–54,
  63–64, 231, 233, 246–248, 259, 270–271
developmental role in economic
  globalization era, 12, 22, 51–52, 163,
  233–235, 240, 246
economic efficiency: challenges, 52–53
as embodiment of national
  sovereignty, 79–80
emergence of, 50
hybrid development model and, 14, 50,
  229, 231, 233–235, 239
as hybrid organizations, 54–55, 240
ideological warfare and delegitimization
  of SOEs as engines of economic
  development, 108
industrialization and, 25–26, 79–80,
  229–230, 243, 246–248, 271
market reforms and, 43–45
middle-income countries, 17–19
national security and, 246, 268–269
natural resource governance and, 27–28
natural resource sovereignty
  and, 245–247, 276
neoliberalism and, 22, 233
path dependence, 24
political role of, 51, 229, 233–235, 243
private companies/SOEs
  comparison, 17–18, 239
rent-seeking, 243, 248
shares of SOEs on Fortune Global 500
  list, 53*f*
SOE output to GDP in selected emerging
  markets, 54*f*
state-building and, 80
success of, 14, 243
variety in forms and sizes, 53–54
see also China: SOEs; NOCs
SOEs: autonomy, 21, 229–230, 242
  Codelco, 139–140, 142, 149–150
  conditions for autonomy, 27–28
  Latin America, 63–64
  Petrobras, 22–23, 27, 99–103, 165–166,
    187–188, 196, 221–222, 236–237,
    243–244, 248

Petrobras/Codelco comparison, 149–150
staff hiring: merit *vs* political appointments, 21–23
technological advantage and political autonomy from national governments, 15
SOEs: corporate governance reforms, 12–14, 19, 54–59, 229, 233
centralized state control with majority ownership, 58–59
centralized state control with minority ownership, 58–59
Chile: SOEs, 139
Codelco, 19, 22, 92–93, 139–140, 141*t*, 145–146, 149–150, 154, 163, 230, 249
decentralized state control with majority ownership, 58–59
decentralized state control with minority ownership, 58–59
gradual liberalization and selective SOE reforms, 206–207
incentives for productivity, 59
inducing a private company mindset in a public entity, 59
institutional development of SOEs, 59
objectives, 248
partial privatization/corporatization, 55–57, 206
SOEs's performance and, 59
Petrobras, 19, 22, 27, 104–105, 168–170, 196, 206, 223–224, 230, 232, 236–237, 241–242, 249
Petrobras/Codelco comparison, 242–243, 248–250
typology of SOE reforms, 55–59, 56*t*
see also SOEs: privatization
SOEs: Latin America
Andean region, 149, 233–235
autonomy of SOEs, 63–64
developing indigenous industrial capacity and human capital stocks, 26–27
developmentalism, 63–64
national autonomy idea, 63–64
neoliberalism and SOEs, 24, 26–27, 42, 46–47, 63–64, 80
Peru, 255–256, 258–259, 265–266
privatization, 21–22, 42, 43*f*, 45–47, 50
role in developing indigenous industrial capacity and human capital stocks, 63

role in facilitating national industrialization, 79–80
SOE-led growth model in natural resource sectors, 63–64, 259–260
state activism, 63–64
Venezuela, 73–77
see also Brazil: SOEs; Chile: SOEs; Codelco; Petrobras
SOES: performance, 59
autonomy from states and, 22–23
Codelco, 25–26, 139, 240–241, 244–245
corporate governance reforms and, 59
industrial development: criteria for, 23–24
innovation and productive capacity, 22
Petrobras, 25–26, 103–104, 198–202
policy objectives, achivement of, 22
private enterprises/SOEs comparison, 52–53
SOEs: privatization, 19–22, 42, 54–55, 240, 243
Brazil, 168, 177–178
Chile: neoliberalism and privatization of SOEs, 91–92, 147
Codelco: refusal to privatization, 22, 24, 45, 47–49, 92, 140–142, 147–148, 162, 163, 230, 240–241, 244–245
historical antecedents as precondition for states to thwart SOEs' privatization, 19–22
Latin America, 21–22, 45, 50, 235
Latin America: shift towards neoliberalism in natural resource governance without SOEs privatization, 42, 43*f*, 46–47
partial privatization/corporatization, 55–57, 206
Peru, 255–256
Petrobras: refusal to privatization, 22, 24, 47–49, 107–108, 169–170, 196, 223–224, 230, 236–237, 241–242
resistance to privatization, 19, 54–55, 59, 240
SOE managers and, 21, 54–55
state socialism and developmental state strategy, 19–21
technical expertise as obstacle to privatization, 50
trade unions and, 54–55

330 Index

SOEs managers, 52–54
  Codelco, 142–143, 145, 149–150, 154, 157, 240–241
  decentralized control-monitoring scheme and, 58–59
  distinction between policy elites and, 46
  ruling elites/SOE managers relationship, 14
  SOEs privatization and, 21, 54–55
  state–state (SOE) relations and, 50–51, 242–243
SOHC (state-owned holding company), 57–58
SONAMI (*Sociedad Nacional de Minería*/National Mining Association, Chile), 113–114, 118–119, 146–147
South Korea, 77
state
  'compensatory state', 38
  development and, 29–30
  entrepreneurial state, 14
  industrial development and, 240
  institutional development and, 30, 40–41
  Latin America: return of the state, 266–267
  see also developmental state
state activism, 24, 229–230, 240, 267
  Brazil, 233–235, 249–250
  Chile, 232–235, 249–250
  China, 268–269, 275–276
  HI approach and, 46
  Latin America, 63–64, 235, 276
  Petrobras/Codelco comparison, 249–250
  see also state agency
state agency, 12–13, 24, 40, 276
  economic globalization and, 22, 29, 39–40, 276
  institutional changes and, 19
  see also state activism
state-building, 29
  Brazil, 24–25, 80, 94–95
  Chile, 24–25, 80, 82–85
  SOEs and, 80
state capacity
  Brazil/Chile comparison, 25
  bureaucracy and, 13
  developmental state and, 12–13, 231
  East Asian states, 13
  SOEs and, 21
state capitalism, 17–18, 53–54, 267

  Brazil, 184, 188–189
  China, 9–10, 272–273
  developmental state and, 267
  shares of SOEs on Fortune Global 500 list, 53*f*
  SOE output to GDP in selected emerging markets, 54*f*
  state capitalism/economic development relation, 27–28, 53–54, 229–230
state intervention, 16
  Brazil, 14–15, 19–21, 50, 94–95, 98, 177–178
  Chile, 14–15, 19–21, 50, 83–84, 163
  Codelco, 27, 50
  control over strategic sectors (O&G and mining), 41–42, 229
  as development strategy, 83–84, 229
  elites and, 17–18
  Latin America, 79–80
  natural-resource-based development and, 29–30, 33
  natural resources/neoliberalism/state intervention interactions, 29, 41–42
  Petrobras, 22–23, 50, 99–100, 196, 198
  Petrobras: *Lava Jato* scandal and, 196, 206–207, 237
  rentier state and, 33
  SOEs's developmental role and, 14–15, 21, 229
  state: shift from state intervention towards hybrid developmental role, 239
state ownership, 262–263, 266–267, 275–276
  Brazil: O&G sector, 165–167, 192–193, 195–196
  Chile, 50, 139–140, 231–232
  Chile: mining sector, 90, 109–110
  China, 13–14, 276
  Codelco, 91–94, 140–147
  Codelco: 100% state ownership, 55–57, 140–142, 156, 231–232, 244
  as development strategy, 12–19, 22
  development view, 51–52
  economic globalization and, 24, 26, 51–52, 233–235
  as globalization strategy, 50–59, 233, 276
  Indonesia, 13–14
  natural resource governance and, 26–27, 262–263

natural resources/neoliberalism/state ownership interactions, 41–42
path dependency and, 30
Petrobras, 107–108, 169–170, 196, 206
political economy, 17–18, 30, 42–43, 229–230
political view, 51–52
role in institutional capacity-building and industrial policy expansion, 27–28
social view, 51–52
state ownership/neoliberalism interactions, 17–18, 27–28, 42–43, 233
state ownership through SOEs, 12
state–state (SOE) relations, 26–28, 43–45, 52–53, 264
  Brazilian government/Petrobras relationship, 59–60, 104–105, 181–182, 195–196, 204, 223, 236–237, 241–242
  centralized/decentralized institutional control over SOE operations, 55, 57–59
  Chile, 146–147
  Chilean government/Codelco relations, 59–60, 137, 139–140, 143, 145, 148–150, 240–241
  as conceptual leverage to explain state transformation, 50–51
  new relationships among state actors, 46
  Petrobras/Codelco comparison, 240–243
  principal-agency dilemma, 55, 145, 249
  SOE: majority *vs.* minority shareholder ownership, 55–57
  SOE managers and, 50–51, 242–243
  Venezuelan state/PDVSA relationship, 253–254
structuralism, 9–10
subsoil rights, 21–22
  Brazil, 96–97, 187
  Chile, 111–112
  Venezuela, 70
supply chains
  Africa, 7–9, 9f
  China, 9f, 129–130
  China: supply chains vertical integration, 10–12, 271–273
  clean energy technologies, 11f
  COVID-19 pandemic and breakdown of vital supply chains, 5–7
  CRMs, 4, 9–12

East Asia, 7–9, 9f
EU, 7–9, 9f
fragmentation in global supply chains, 18–19
Latin America, 7–9, 9f
Petrobras: vertical integration of O&G industry, 101–103, 232, 247–248, 264–265
regional shares in key technologies across sector supply chains, 7–9, 9f
SOEs and vertical integration, 246
US, 7–9, 9f
see also clean energy technologies: supply chains; GVC

T
Taiwan, 13–14, 72–73, 202–203, 214–215
Távora, Juarez (General), 97–98
taxation
  Brazil, 95–96, 209, 251, 262
  Brazil: O&G sector and payments attached to taxes, 178, 179t
  Chile, 81–82, 87–88, 251, 261–262
  Chile: mining sector, 82–84, 87, 111–113, 117–120, 120f, 121t, 160–161
  Codelco, 148–149, 240–241
  corporate taxes, 76
  Indonesia, 35
  Latin America, 251
  petro-states and, 34
  rentier state, 34–35
  tax avoidance, 117–118
  tax evasion, 117
  Venezuela, 76
technocracy
  Brazil, 50, 98–101, 167–168
  Chile, 50, 85–86, 93–94, 110–113, 137, 139, 163, 231–232
  Codelco, 142, 154, 155–156, 163, 240–241, 244–245
  PDVSA, 251–254
  Petrobras, 244–245
technology and innovation
  Brazil: O&G sector and technological innovation, 188–189
  Chile: mining sector, 118, 129, 131–134
  Codelco, 230, 244–245
  decarbonization and, 3–4, 9–10

332 Index

technology and innovation (*Continued*)
 Petrobras, 105–107, 166, 198–204, 230, 244–245
 Petrobras/Codelco comparison: innovation, 147–148
 SOEs: technical expertise as obstacle to privatization, 50
 SOEs: technological advantage and political autonomy from national governments, 15
 technology transfer towards poorer developing countries, 18–19
 see also clean energy technologies
Temer, Michel, 222–223
 O&G sector governance, 170*t*
 Petrobras and, 165–166, 221–223, 236–237
 Petrobras: *Lava Jato* scandal and, 213, 221
Torres, Gumersindo, 70
Trebat, Thomas J., 184–186
Trump, Donald J., 5–7
Turkey, 17–18, 39, 53–54

U

UAE (United Arab Emirates), 35–36
UN Paris Agreement (2015 United Nations Paris Agreement on Climate Change), 4–5, 7–9
Uruguay, 66
US (United States)
 Chile/US relations, 84–92, 147–148, 155
 China/US relations, 5–7
 clean energy, 3–7
 EVs, 4
 supply chains, 7–9, 9*f*
 US investment in Latin America, 68–69, 69*t*

V

Vargas, Getúlio, 94–99, 232, 264–265
 1951 re-election, 98
 Estado Novo/New State, 94–95, 166–167
Velasco, Juan, 67, 256–257
Velosa da Fonseca, Venina, 219–220
Venezuela
 1943 Hydrocarbons Act, 70–71
 1958 *Punto Fijo* pact, 71–72
 Brazil/Venezuela comparison, 264–265
 bureaucracy, 70, 75–77

central government expenditures, 73–75, 74*f*, 75–77
central government investment and public debt, 73–75, 75*f*
clientelism, 70, 77
commodity boom, 254
corruption, 70–71, 76–78
CVP (*Corporación Venezolano del Petróleo*), 70–71
delimiting foreign-owned enterprises in O&G industries, 68–69
democracy, 70–72, 77
economic reforms, 76–78
erratic growth performance, 70
extractivism, 273–274
fiscal revenues of Venezuelan governments, 72*t*, 72–73
foreign borrowing, 73–76
industrialization, 27–28, 70–78, 259–260
institutionalization of oil wealth management, 71–72
limited institutional capability, 265–266
nationalization, 70–71, 73–75, 251–252
neoliberalism, 77, 265–266
oil dependence, 254–255, 264–265
as petro-state, 26–27, 69, 70–72
as petro-state without corporate autonomy, 251–255, 259–260
regime decay, 77, 120–121, 254–255
rentier state/rent-seeking, 70, 73–75, 77–78, 251–252, 264–265
resource curse, 34–35, 266
SOEs, 73–77
'sowing the oil' (*sembrar el petróleo*), 70–72
taxation, 76
VIF (Venezuelan Investment Fund), 73
 see also PDVSA
Vergara, Angela, 90
Villarzú, Juan, 153–154
Vu, Tuong, 19–21

W

Washington Consensus, 16, 250, 259, 266–268
Wedeman, Andrew, 213
Wilson, Jeffrey D., 250–251
World Bank, 68–69, 240

world historical approaches, 37–40
limitations, 40
World War II, 65–66, 96–97
WTO (World Trade
Organization), 179–180, 269

X
Xi Jinping, 3–4, 270–271

Z
Zylberstajn, David, 175–176, 179–180